Elea... o... Aquitaine

About the Author

Sara Cockerill studied Law at the University of Oxford. Between 1990 and 2017 she was a barrister and later a QC specialising in commercial law. She has had a lifelong interest in English history, which led her to write *Eleanor of Castile: The Shadow Queen*, the first full-length biography of Edward I's beloved queen. She is married with one cat, and divides her time between London and the seaside.

Eleanor of Aquitaine

Queen of France and England, Mother of Empires

Sara Cockerill

AMBERLEY

For Nigel (of course)

First published 2019
This edition published 2022

Amberley Publishing
The Hill, Stroud
Gloucestershire, GL5 4EP

www.amberley-books.com

British Library Cataloguing in Publication Data.
A catalogue record for this book is available from the British Library.

ISBN 978 1 3981 1239 1 (paperback)
ISBN 978 1 4456 4618 3 (ebook)

Typesetting by Aura Technology and Software Services, India.
Printed in India.

Contents

The immediate family

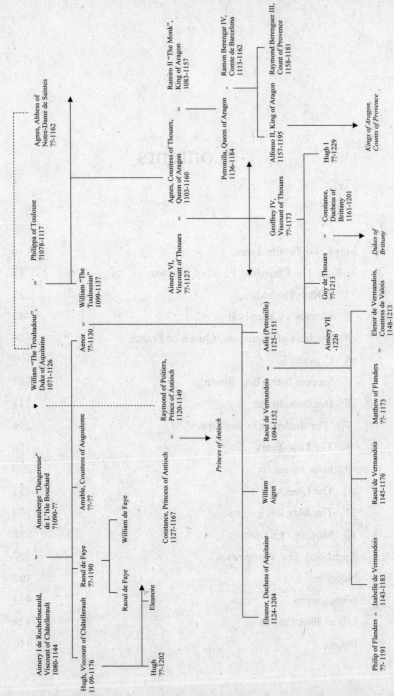

The benefits of consanguinity

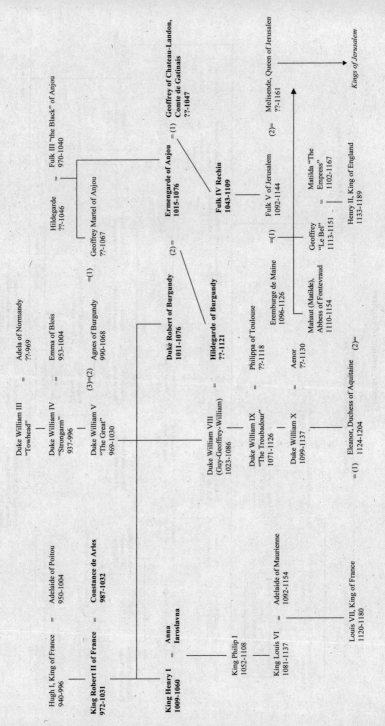

Eleanor, mother of empires

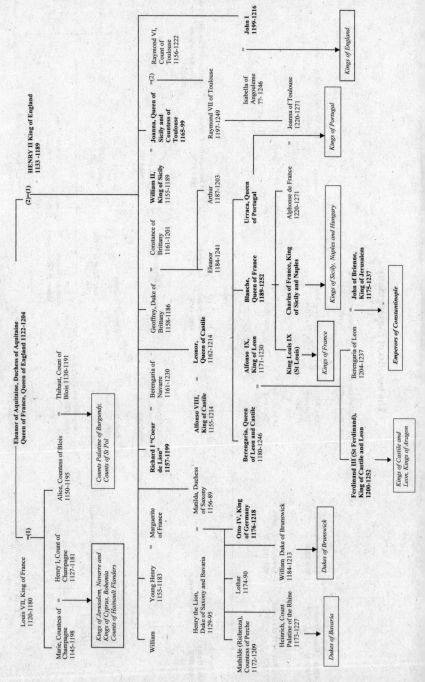

The forgotten family

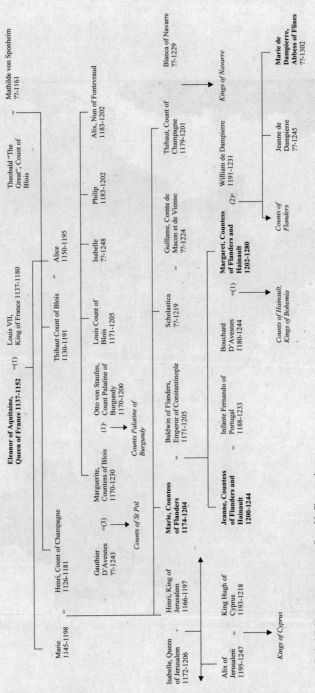

Entries in **bold** represent apparent custodians of the Eleanor psalter

The geopolitical landscape: Eleanor, the Angevins and their neighbours, 1154.

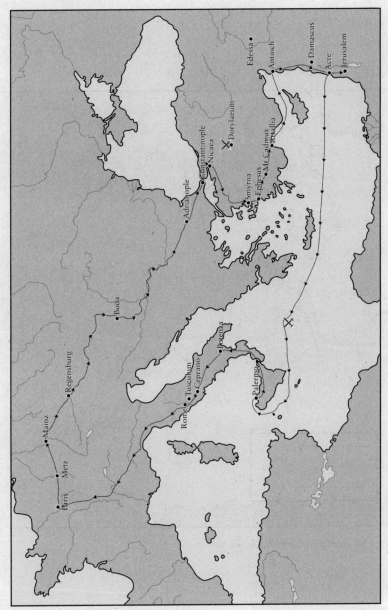

The route which Eleanor and Louis followed on the Second Crusade.

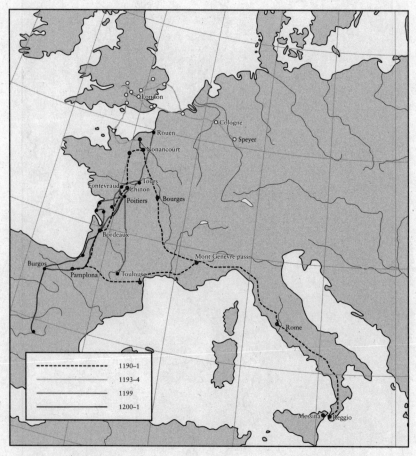

Eleanor's movements during her 'retirement'.

The Changing Faces of Eleanor

Do we know what we think we know about Eleanor?
RaGena DeAragon

The Eleanor of history has been overshadowed by an Eleanor of
wishful thinking and make-believe.
Professor Nicholas Vincent

Writing about Eleanor of Aquitaine has been a very different
experience to writing about Eleanor of Castile. With the latter,
my almost universal experience was that people had no idea at
all who she was. Indeed, if they claimed they had any idea, they
were probably confusing her with Eleanor of Aquitaine. With the
senior Eleanor, however, the experience has been in this respect
wildly different – nearly everyone has some idea of who Eleanor of
Aquitaine was. Indeed, some rather implausible people – including
a number of senior members of the English judiciary – have outed
themselves as Eleanor of Aquitaine fans. The problem this time
around has been more that I have found myself disappointing
people by telling them that what they think they know about
Eleanor probably isn't true. I am now quite used to a look which
mixes disappointment with a measure of disbelief when I deliver
this news.

This is a key point for which my readers should be prepared
before they go any further into this book. What you think you
know about Eleanor may not be true. Indeed, this book will
suggest that many so-called 'facts' about Eleanor and her life are

false, or at best unsupported by evidence. I know that there are a lot of Eleanor fans out there with very clear views of who she was, what she did and just how exceptional a woman she was. I know this not least because I started writing this book as one of them. I have read and enjoyed just about every biography of Eleanor – and also many of the excellent historical novels which take her as their heroine. I was very fond of the picture which they gave me. I did not start writing this book with any great thoughts of debunking accepted views. In truth, Eleanor had long been my idea of a dream subject because, love them as I did, I did not find any of the existing biographies entirely satisfactory – and because the kind people at Amberley offered me my choice of subject. With that offer there, I simply wanted to see if I could do any better.

When writing about Eleanor of Castile, I began with a vague idea of what I might find – and what I found was that and much, much more. She was a woman who was not billed as in any way exceptional, but proved to be so – to the extent that I still think of her as a rather terrifying role model. With Eleanor of Aquitaine, the experience has been rather more disconcerting; I started with a clear idea of what I might find, and while some of this was confirmed I also found some things which I never expected. I also found that some long-cherished beliefs had to be given up. Most shockingly, I found that some of the supposedly established facts espoused in a number of biographies were actually groundless speculation; I also found instances where biographers had accepted as fact stories which fall apart under the slightest critical scrutiny.

Part of this is down to a central problem inherent in writing about Eleanor. She was born nearly nine hundred years ago into a world which ceased to exist even before the Renaissance. To some extent, therefore, any search for a truthful image of her is almost impossible – this is guaranteed by the scarcity of material and our inability, with our modern prejudices, to properly comprehend what we do have. The history of biographical study of Eleanor has illustrated amply the temptation of reading current trends across to the examination of her life. It is this which has led to the mantra of Eleanor as the hyper-exceptional woman, which the facts do not sustain. But the fact that capturing something like a true image is very difficult is no reason not to try.

The picture of Eleanor that has emerged from my study shows her to be somewhat less exceptional, somewhat less of a rebellious feminist icon – and considerably less of a player in the genesis of troubadour poetry and chivalric ideals than most existing biographies would suggest. This may not come as a big surprise to some readers – recent years have seen much revisionist scholarship on the subject of Eleanor's life. The articles in 'Eleanor of Aquitaine Lord and Lady' (ed. Wheeler and Parsons) and 'Plantagenets et Capetiens' (ed. Aurell) are key to this reassessment, as is the brilliant 'Inventing Eleanor' by Michael Evans. Two sets of articles deserve special mention. The first is Labande's 1952 work *'Pour une image véridique d'Aliénor d'Aquitaine'*, which was at the forefront of scholarly reassessment of Eleanor. The second is Jane Martindale's magisterial collection of articles on Eleanor and Eleanor's later life. I, among others, had hoped that Martindale would release a full definitive biography of Eleanor. Had she done so, I strongly suspect that this book would not have been written.

I have gratefully absorbed the thoughts of the academics who have so carefully re-evaluated aspects of Eleanor's life. The place where I have landed in my assessment of Eleanor has been much influenced by their reasoning. As I have said, that place is to see Eleanor as a much less exceptional figure than she has often been portrayed as being – particularly in her early years, but also to an extent in her famed later flowering. Having said that, I do nonetheless find her very inspiring, particularly in two respects. The first is in her resolution in dealing with unbelievably difficult circumstances repeatedly and throughout her life – so much so that I now regard her as something of a poster girl for resilience. The second, perhaps apt to someone of my age, is her willingness to embrace considerable change and responsibility at a time in life when it is tempting, now as then, to think that the game is played out and that starting afresh is impossible. One other thing that very much surprised me: I find her a much warmer and nicer person than I had anticipated, which has been a great pleasure. She comes across as a much better mother than her reputation would suggest. If I had a personal problem and I had a choice of the two Eleanors to take it to, I'd pick Eleanor of Aquitaine every time.

I appreciate that some of what I have to say on these subjects will be as unwelcome to my readers as it initially was to me, and

I have thought long and hard about how best to help non-academic readers understand why, having looked closely at the evidence and tried to understand its value, I have differed from previous writers – and to what extent points are debatable. In the end, it has seemed to me that there is no choice but to be much more 'up front' with readers than any previous biography has been about the sources from which the facts are taken and what issues there are with treating those sources as reliable.

However, this does not mean that the book is full of references to obscure chronicles; the sources for Eleanor's life are very often identifiable and interesting people about whom we know quite a lot. Perhaps because I am a lawyer by training, I have concluded that these people should be regarded as our witnesses to Eleanor's life. A reference to a chronicle often suggests unquestionable fact, but from life, stage, and television we all know quite a lot about witnesses. Put in these terms, we can all understand that these are simply people whose paths have crossed with Eleanor's at key points (or sometimes who have heard stories from the people who actually met Eleanor). We can understand that witnesses are fallible, and may have agendas that can affect their evidence. And we can see Eleanor not just as a queen, impossibly remote from day-to-day humanity, but as the woman who inhabited a busy court full of clever civil servants and clerics and who interacted with them on a day-to-day business.

So, in the appendix you will find a list of the main witnesses. This is designed to give a brief pen portrait of each of them, providing some idea of how they interacted with Eleanor and the kind of life they led. Where I make controversial points, these descriptions will make my assessments of their evidence easier to follow and evaluate; very useful, as it may well be that readers will disagree with me on some of the issues.

Those who find this warning unwelcome should perhaps pause to consider just how much Eleanor's reputation has changed over the years; the reinterpretation I will be offering is far from radical compared to some of the extremes occupied by other representations of Eleanor. For example, the earliest 'post-Eleanor' representations, in the thirteenth century and reaching on into the fourteenth, were relentlessly negative. Indeed, this period is known by Eleanor scholars as the time of the 'Black Myth' or

'Black Legend'. Its origins are perhaps best seen in the relentlessly anti-Angevin campaign waged – with great success – by King Philip Augustus of France. Under his aegis, 'historians' and chroniclers produced stories which portrayed Henry II's family in a bad light, exploiting negative press to create fully formed tales of infamy.

Eleanor's past – divorced Queen of France, rebellious Queen of England, about whose conduct on Crusade rumours had swirled for years – was the motherlode for such work, and it is no surprise to find such slim pickings as the contemporary chroniclers left expanded upon with considerable talent by these sources. So, by mid-way through the thirteenth century we have fully formed tales of Eleanor's supposed incest with her uncle Raymond, and with Henry II's father, Geoffrey le Bel. We also have salacious tales of her disrobing before her lords, of her descent from a diabolical ancestor, of her attempted seduction of her local bishop at a papal congress and also (anachronistically, since he was a child when she was in the Holy Land) Saladin. To this period too we owe the oft-repeated story that Eleanor and the troubadour Bernard de Ventadorn were lovers.[1]

Such tales, seen perhaps at their best in the work of the avowedly pro-Capetian Ménestral de Reims, then seep across the Channel and feed into political concerns there (not least the dubious status of pro-active foreign queens in England at that point), resulting in a decidedly confused portrayal of Eleanor by the gossipy but fairly reliable Matthew Paris, in which some genuine praise of Eleanor is mixed with apparent acceptance of the Crusade stories, including adultery with an unnamed infidel prince. With such negativity associated with her, Eleanor then came to assume a literally diabolical aspect; conflating the stories of the Angevins' diabolical ancestry with Eleanor's then-accepted wickedness, the Middle English poem *Richard Coeur de Lion* actually says that Richard's mother was of demonic origin, although this rather oddly provides Richard with the necessary powers to withstand Saladin's black magic.[2]

The English sources, who continued to respond negatively to foreign queens, are the source for the next development in the Black Myth: Eleanor's murder of Fair Rosamund. Interestingly, this began not as a twist on Eleanor's reputation but as part of the continued hostility to Henry III's queen, Eleanor of Provence.

In the earliest surviving versions of the tale, the queen who murders Rosamund is Eleanor of Provence (born about 1220) and not Eleanor of Aquitaine. The hostility which gives rise to the story belongs to another, but in due course the tale (by now very popular) becomes attributed to the Eleanor who actually did exist at the same time as the historical Rosamund, further eroding Eleanor's reputation, so that as the sixteenth century dawns most people would have had an unremittingly negative view of Eleanor of Aquitaine.

This is evidenced by the writings of the time, which go on to portray Eleanor as not just wicked but lecherous too. While Shakespeare sees her only as a 'canker'd grandam' and mother of strife, Andrew Munday has her attempting to blackmail Robin Hood into a sexual encounter. Another story has her committing adultery with William Marshal, whose name was indeed linked with that of a queen (Young Henry's queen, Marguerite of France), but again the wrong queen is identified in later writings. A similar effect was produced by the delightful 'Lamentable Fall of Queen Elenor ...', a seventeenth-century work ostensibly about Eleanor's great-great-granddaughter Eleanor of Castile but which introduces a number of elements of Eleanor of Aquitaine's Black Myth, as well as that of Eleanor of Provence.[3]

Even historians who sought to rescue Eleanor's reputation, as critical evaluation of historical sources became once again fashionable, did not help. The early historians of Poitou and Aquitaine, Besly and Bouchet, still accepted rather more of the myth than the sources would justify, and Eleanor's first biographer, de Larrey, is the source for the story of Eleanor the Amazon Queen, a tenacious myth that has fed into the maintenance of the other Crusade stories.[4]

Thus was the ground muddied in preparation for the politically inspired historical writings of the nineteenth century, which have proved influential until the fairly recent past. In France there was the work of Michelet, whose hostility to Eleanor appears to stem in part from her bad press and in part from how well that fitted into his own anti-establishment agenda. In England, the Stricklands, in their *Lives of the Queens of England*, took a moral approach to the analysis of their subjects. While Eleanor did not fit as neatly as some into their 'good queen/bad queen' dichotomy, their compromise approach, which was to portray her as feckless in youth but a pleasing echo of the Victorian *status quo* in old age, served to reprise a number of the wilder stories about Eleanor. Furthermore, the huge circulation they achieved, and their reputation as researchers at the time, did much to give those stories credence. Meanwhile, English male historians, ignoring the later stories, also did their level best to consign Eleanor to footnote status.[5]

It was in reaction to these dual injustices that feminist historians of the twentieth century came to create what Evans has called 'the Golden Myth'; Amy Kelly, Marion Meade and Regine Pernoud bent over backwards to bring to the fore every possible act or influence which could be credited to Eleanor. Kelly brought to the fore the myth of Eleanor and the Courts of Love, Meade celebrated her as a feminist before her time, and Pernoud argued for her influence in bringing troubadour culture to the barbarous north. Each is clear in her ambition to write a serious biography of Eleanor and derides fictionalisation of her life. Each, however, does fall prey to the pernicious fictionalising tendency; and each fails to pick up certain aspects of the pre-existing myth, again contributing to the establishment of these myths as perceived facts. Finally, in each case subsequent work has shown the main thrust of the biography to be either misconceived (as in the Courts of Love) or resting on very insubstantial foundations.

This, I hope, demonstrates that Eleanor's story as told to date is open to the re-evaluation which I have attempted in this book; and indeed that this re-evaluation is part of a process which has already moved a long way. I leave my readers to decide for themselves how much or how little of my vision they accept.

The other thing that readers will find is that this book does not try to give any complete account of Henry II's reign, the Becket dispute, the internecine strife which took place between Henry and his sons, or the achievements of Richard 'the Lion-Heart'. I have been determined to make this a relentlessly Eleanor-centric biography. So, when Eleanor is in prison and her sources of information are poor, Henry and the family drop out of focus. Similarly, when Richard is in the Holy Land, when news of him would take months to reach Eleanor, I leave him out of the picture.

Where I have given much more information than previous biographers, apart from as regards the witnesses, is when talking about the Church. One of the things which has struck me when researching this book is how our current distance from all things religious has manifested in the biographies. That, I am convinced, is an anachronistic approach – and my view on this is supported by interesting survivals in the contemporaneous documents, by recent painstaking scholarship (notably that of Nicholas Vincent) and even by a hugely exciting discovery made in the Netherlands during the course of my writing – of which more later.

The bottom line is this: Eleanor lived in a world where religion was far more present in daily life, and the actual surviving evidence points clearly to an Eleanor who was very much engaged both with matters of religion and with churchmen. In order to bring this out I have therefore had to set out rather more information than might be expected about a few of the personalities of the twelfth-century Church, and the theological debates which were a part of common debate at the time.

Another point to note is that I have taken some liberties with names. Anyone who has read any work of history or fiction covering this period will be aware that it is an era afflicted with distressingly few Christian names. Eleanor's son Young Henry once gave a banquet only for those within his household called William – and filled a hall. Eleanor's family is also replete with Eleanors, Matildas and Alices. I have therefore tried to give at least each major female character a unique version of their name to minimise confusion. With the male characters, better known to history, and less prone to be referred to by a variety of spellings in the chronicles, this has not been entirely possible without causing annoyance and confusion to those who know these characters by well-established names. I have endeavoured to clarify who is who in the index, but a printable 'Disambiguation List' can also be found on my website, and may come in useful.

Finally a few thanks: to Michael Prestwich, Elizabeth Chadwick and Michael Evans, who assisted with comments on the draft (including picking up a number of howlers and prompting me to crucial further thought about the Radegonde mural); to Nicholas Vincent for so kindly allowing me sight of both his invaluable summary of the charter materials and his and Judith Everard's reworked Itinerary (which appear as VC and

Itinerary 2 in the Notes); to Colette Bowie for sight of her forthcoming Spanish biography of Leonor; and to June Morgan for turning my footnote-heavy chapters into acceptable text for submission. Thanks also to all those who have kept comments and encouragement coming over Facebook, and followed Eleanor's adventures there ... and of course to Nigel, for never saying he was bored when I wittered on about Eleanor!

Sara Cockerill
London, July 2019

1

A Rich Heritage

Homo alienigena et apud exteras gentes nutritus et institutus
speciles Aquitanorum consuetudines at inaudita iura non
sufficiat edocere.
[A foreigner brought up and educated among other peoples
cannot sufficiently expound the peculiar customs and strange
laws of the Aquitanians.]
John of Salisbury, Letter 177

'At the time when the countess Agnes was at the head of the
county of Poitou with her sons William and Geoffrey and
administered the Duchy vigorously, as it was in her power.
Charter in the cartulary of the Abbey of Saint-Maixent

If we want to reach a truthful image of Eleanor of Aquitaine, we
should to try to see her not in our own context but in hers. Only
in this way can some of her actions be made to make sense and her
preoccupations and motivations understood.

This chapter therefore has three aims. The first is to try to create
some sense of the rich portfolio of lands to which Eleanor was
heiress, and some of the issues rooted in the history of those lands,
which flared into life during her reign as duchess and proved key to
her story. The second aim is to outline some of the family history
which would have been intimately familiar to Eleanor, forming the
background to her childhood. The heroes of her lands would have
been held up to her as exemplars, just as she has been held up to
others as an exemplar ever since her death, and some aspects of her
family history cast long shadows over the events of her life. Finally,

this chapter will set the stage for Eleanor's own birth with the story of her remarkable grandfather William 'the Troubadour', a man long credited with a huge influence on her life.

The story of Aquitaine is ferociously tangled, but there are important strands which can be extracted from it.

The first, which has other effects alluded to below, is that significant amounts of Eleanor's lands fell within the area in which Roman forces were concentrated under the Roman Empire. Aquitaine was indeed reflected in the province 'Gallia Aquitainia'. This had effects in itself, but also in drawing the southern portion of Eleanor's lands closer to the other areas with powerful Roman influences: Gallia Narbonensis and Gallia Cisalpina. Such influences had remained in place throughout the centuries in which the Roman Empire fell, and brought new influences to bear.

In 507, the Belgic/German Kingdom of the Franks brought Aquitaine under nominal control. But a powerful dukedom of Vasconia-Aquitaine was ruled essentially independently of the northern Frankish kingdom until the era when the conflict between the European powers and the seemingly unstoppable Islamic invaders – who had recently swept into Iberia and up through the Pyrenees – reached Aquitaine. As a result, self-government in Aquitaine came to an end for a time, but ethnically the region remained distinct from France, with a Gallo-Roman-Basque ethnicity which continued to mark its people out from the northern Frankish territories; unsurprisingly, northern rule was not welcomed.

It was Charlemagne who elevated Aquitaine to the status of a kingdom for his son Louis the Pious, appointing a number of lords to conduct its administration. One of these was Eleanor's earliest distinguished ancestor: William of Orange, Count of Toulouse, also known as St William of Gellone. A grandson of Charlemagne, he led the forces of Aquitaine in a gallant defeat against a further Islamic incursion into the region of Orange (in Provence) and was later one of the victorious campaigners who won Barcelona back from the invaders. His career as a campaigner was to become a popular subject for the epic poems known as *chansons de geste*. That fame was assisted by his canonisation in 1066, but perhaps even more so by the romance of his story, for William had taken as his second wife a Saracen lady called Orable, the widow of the Wali of Orange.[1] Interestingly, the fact that William had two wives living at the time of his death seems not to have been regarded as a hindrance to his canonisation.

In the years of strife which followed Charlemagne's death, the Frankish kingdom in the north rapidly disintegrated. The internal pressures led to a major fracture – the split of France from the remainder of Charlemagne's empire. By the Treaty of Verdun in 843, two of Louis the Pious' sons took the German, Italian and Low Countries elements, together with Alsace, Lorraine, Provence and Burgundy, while the third took the remainder of France. However, Aquitaine was not part of this division; the descendants of a deceased son, Pepin, remained kings of Aquitaine for a time.

In the redesigned empire, internal pressures remained and were exacerbated by the fact that France came to face a new massive threat in the form of the Vikings, or Northmen, who sacked Paris itself in 845 and were subsequently held at bay through the expedient of huge bribes. Ultimately, the price of this weakness was the grant to the Northmen – or Normans, as they were to become known – of substantial territories in the north of the country: Normandy.

By the start of the eleventh century, the King of France's own landholdings were confined to a small island of territory based around Paris – the 'Ile de France' – and some pockets of Crown lands edging eastwards towards Champagne and across the Loire to Bourges and Orleans.[2] These were dwarfed by the size of the surrounding counties, and even by the landholdings of the Church. With such weakness evident, pressure from the individual counties and duchies became hard to withstand. Consequently, their perceived influence in the lands over which they were notionally feudal lords was also much diminished – it can be no coincidence that in this period counts or viscounts frequently presaged their charters not by a reference to the holding of their lands 'by the King's grace' but simply by a reference to God's grace.

For the former Kingdom of Aquitaine, the problems were far less drastic but had nonetheless resulted in a division. By 854, the northernmost parts had become the portion of the counts of Poitou, descendants of the Frankish monarchy. The remainder was divided into two duchies: Aquitaine and Gascony. Gascony, seen by the Gascons as a kingdom, notionally remained an independent duchy until 1052, but the power of the titular duke was chipped away throughout this period by the cession of major territories to the counts of Bearn, Bigorre, Armagnac, Astarac and Comminges, as well as the nobles of the most prosperous town, Bordeaux. As for Poitou and Aquitaine, they were quickly reunited under the Frankish line but on the whole the rulers tended to style themselves as just Count of Poitou, because this represented the reality of their power; they did control very substantial and prosperous lands in Poitou, but in Angoulême, La Marche and Périgord substantial landholdings were held by powerful local nobles, who were also tied to each other by strong bonds of kinship.

These divisions within Aquitaine reflect divisions in the people and culture of the area arising out of the Roman occupation. The first division is linguistic. It is often said that the *langue d'oc* was Eleanor's native language. That is almost certainly wrong. In the first place, it is an anachronism: before the fourteenth century, the language of the south appears to have been referred to as the *lengua romana* or simply 'roman', as opposed to the *langue du roi* or 'frances'. In the second place, it reflects a misconception about its use. The *lengua romana* was not a language peculiar to Aquitaine but was in fact used right across the Pyrenees to Languedoc and Provence and on into the Alps – the locations of the former Roman provinces. This accounts for the fact that there is a very close correlation between the *langue d'oc* (now called Occitan) and Catalan; each language is easily comprehensible to speakers of the other. By contrast, speakers of the *lengua romana* and *langue du roi* would struggle to understand each other. Furthermore, that linguistic north/south divide did not follow modern territorial divisions but those of the former provinces.

There was also a division in the approach to legal matters, with the approach of the Romans and their successors gaining greater traction in the southern former provinces than it was to do in the north; at the very least, the system of vassalage was far more nuanced and varied in the south than it was in the north. Another key respect in which there appears to have been a considerable distinction was the question of women's rights. The evidence is necessarily fragmentary and inspires passionate arguments, but the balance of scholarship favours the view that in two important respects the position of women in the southern regions of France was far more favourable than it was in the Frankish/Norman north.

The first area was inheritance. At least between the ninth and eleventh centuries, the rules of inheritance operating in the 'Roman' regions favoured equal inheritance between men and women – and in some regions the position of women was even better than that of men. In Provence, for example, a widow would become legally the head of the household on her husband's death. However, in the northern parts of Aquitaine and in Poitou, inheritance rights were prejudicial to women. The position in the true south was similar to that in the Iberian Peninsula, where in 1099 the throne of León and Castile was inherited by Urraca, also known as 'Empress of all the Spains and Empress of Galicia'. Urraca, the cousin of Eleanor's grandfather, and her father's sole legitimate heir, was freely accepted as queen regnant by her subjects and ruled in her own right until her death in 1126. To give some flavour of her independence one need only cite the fact that her death in childbirth arose from a pregnancy to her latest lover, having long since discarded her uncongenial husband.

In the tenth century, then, several key southern fiefs were in the hands of women, and rates of female inheritance to substantial lands ran at roughly double the percentage which pertained in the north. Almost every dynasty in the area 'could name the matriarchs of their near or distant past'.[3] The position of women in this regard was weakening considerably by the time of Eleanor's birth – and she would feel the effects of the fact that her life coincides with a period of negative change for the visibility and power of noble women – but it was still the case that in Eleanor's lifetime there would be greater evidence of female power in the south than in the north.

To give two examples, roughly contemporary to Eleanor are her neighbour Ermengarde, Viscountess of Narbonne, and Petronilla, Queen of Aragon. The former was heir to a territory in the heart of the former Roman south, and was to rule her fiefdom in her own right, being upheld by the King of France as entitled to judge men. The latter, Eleanor's slightly younger cousin, was to inherit and co-rule the kingdom of Aragon between 1157 and 1174.

The second influence favouring women in the south was the survival of the Visigothic dower system, which obliged the husband's family to make a payment or other provision on marriage to the bride, instead of the Roman *dos* or dowry system, which concentrated on payments by the bride's family to the husband. In *Girart de Roussillon*, an Occitan romance of the twelfth century, brides are offered immensely rich dowers – lands, castles, ports, jewels and bullion – and this reflects the reality of the era in at least some cases. This dower system continued in place in Iberia until well into the thirteenth century, but already it was becoming less marked, or was accompanied by a dowry paid by the bride's family, even in the Occitan territories in the twelfth century. Thus when Eleanor's daughter married Alfonso VIII of Castile she was provided with a very rich dower by him; but she brought a dowry also, and a rather significant one at that.

In the northern French regions, meanwhile, emphasis on dowry was much greater, and any dower which a woman received would, as the years passed, increasingly tend to become effective only on widowhood. This is why the examples of formidable ladies in northern France in this period, though far from uncommon, are more often widows, who gained much greater freedom of action and financial resources once no longer subject to a husband's authority.

Tensions of this sort meant that in the lands further south, in true Aquitaine and towards Gascony, the exercise of power for a Frankish lord remained extremely difficult. By the time of Eleanor's birth and for some generations before, the emphasis on the Poitevin portion of the honour is very evident; and this is reflected in the fact that until Eleanor's marriages any documents within Poitou-Aquitaine would be written with the ruler's comital number being placed before the ducal one. So, the first of the line of dukes from which Eleanor was to descend was known as William I of Poitou, III of Aquitaine. As a child, Eleanor probably thought of herself as 'Eleanor of Poitou'.

One can see this political reality in the earlier count-dukes' stories. William I/III, or William 'the Towhead', was born and died in Poitiers and was the founder of a library there, but seems to have had little contact with the wider duchy. Similarly, William III/V 'the Great', whose reign bridged the tenth and eleventh centuries, was not so named for his exercise of power over his duchy but for his promotion of religion and peace – again largely in the region around Poitiers. Poitiers gained its own cathedral school under his rule, and having been raised by a mother who was familiar with the northern French intellectual rebirth he promoted similar learning and culture in his own court at Poitiers.[4] But his patronage and his religious foundations remained very much at the Poitevin end of the duchy.

Another theme which can be seen among the dukes of Aquitaine in the years from the tenth to early twelfth centuries is the high incidence of formidable wives. William I/III's wife Adela, a daughter of the first Duke of Normandy, was reputed to wear the trousers in their household. Their son William II/IV, though called 'Strong Arm', suffered the repeated banishment of his paramours by his strong-minded wife Emma of Blois. Indeed, she went further, not only deserting him for years at a time for his misdeeds but even organising the punitive gang-rape of one of his mistresses. Not satisfied with such mild discipline, she finally 'encouraged' her husband to retire to a monastery in 993, and with him gone she took the duchy into her own capable hands, guiding young William III/V 'the Great' right up until her own death in 1004.

Emma certainly appears to have been honoured and remembered in Eleanor's family, for the historian of the Abbey of Maillezais, Pierre de Maillezais, embedded a highly sympathetic biography of her in his history of the abbey, which was written for one of her descendants, Eleanor's great-grandfather William VI/VIII. He repeatedly stresses Emma's status and her power – for example in the foundation of the monastery right on a disputed border between her natal family and the county of Poitou. He also portrays her anger at her husband's infidelities as entirely righteous, and, interestingly, while he emphasises and approves her repeated forgiveness of her husband, he shows tacit approval for her assumption of her husband's lands and powers as the consequence of a rightful vengeance against him. This approach may be not entirely unrelated to the fact that it was Emma who founded the Abbey of Maillezais – again in the northern parts of her husband's lands, between Poitiers and the sea.[5]

But perhaps most prominent of the militant ladies of Poitou/ Aquitaine was Agnes of Burgundy, the third wife of William 'the Great'. This lady, though remarried to Count Geoffrey of Anjou, returned to Poitiers on the accession of her eldest son as William V/VII, and acted as effective regent not just throughout his reign but also for ten years of the reign of her second son, Guy-Geoffrey-William (William VI/VIII).[*] Indeed, charters from the era record that particular grants were given 'at the time when the Countess Agnes was at the head of the county of Poitou with her sons William and Geoffrey and administered the Duchy vigorously, as it was in her power'.[6]

Nor was this the full extent of Agnes' influence. She mentored her daughter Agnes, the wife of the German Emperor Henry III,

---

[*] The young man was christened Guy, but adopted the name Geoffrey at his mother's urging to improve his chances of being named heir to Anjou by her new husband. He then adopted the name William on accession as count-duke in Poitou-Aquitaine

and collaborated with Emma of Normandy, the mother of Edward the Confessor, in a number of pious projects. She was also a notable religious foundress. With Geoffrey of Anjou she founded the abbey at Vendôme, but she was herself the foundress of the famous Abbaye aux Dames, a convent for daughters of the nobility, at Saintes, to which she retired in 1068,[7] and which remained a favoured refuge or career choice for the women of Eleanor's family. She also paid for the construction of the church of St Hilaire-le-Grand in Poitiers, in honour of the city's patron saint.

Perhaps even more significantly, Agnes was the *eminence grise* behind the reunificiation of the duchies of Aquitaine and Gascony. William the Great's second wife had been Sanchia of Gascony, and following the death of her father, Sancho VI, in 1032, Sanchia's son by William, Odo, claimed the title of Duke of Gascony. Agnes and her son Guy-Geoffrey, however, opposed him; according to some accounts this was on the grounds that Guy-Geoffrey was married to the daughter of Sancho VI, whose claim took precedence over the claim of her sister, while others suggest the objection was based on lands gained by a marriage to a wife with holdings in Périgord and Bordeaux. Guy-Geoffrey's recorded position as Comte d'Agen and Bordeaux in 1044 makes the latter account more credible. Matters hung in the balance until Odo, by now Duke of Aquitaine, died in 1039, in battle against his stepmother and either her husband or his half-brother. In either event, it is plain that Agnes' involvement was key. Despite his claim to Gascony, Odo too was buried in the family foundation of Maillezais in the north. The Count of Armagnac then pursued his claim to Gascony against Agnes and Guy-Geoffrey, but was finally defeated in 1062, and signed away his claim[8] before retiring to the Abbey of Cluny. Thus Gascony and Aquitaine were at last reunited under the direction of William VI/VIII – but probably would never have been so but for the formidable Agnes.

By the time of William VI/VIII in the early eleventh century, the political landscape of the French landmass could therefore be divided roughly into three parts, which partly echoed the divisions of Roman Gaul. In the south, bordering the Mediterranean and to the Pyrenees, was the heartland of the *lengua romana*, heavily influenced by its Roman/Visigothic heritage and still largely Gallo-Roman-Basque. To the north was the heartland of the *langue du roi*, stretching across northern France to the borders with the German Empire. Frankish influence was strong here, and the legal tradition was far more influenced by the Germanic legal codes than Roman law. Of this, the territory of the kings of France formed a small part.

The third part was Aquitaine, and it was the bridge between the two cultures. Its rulers were, as we have seen, descended from the Frankish royal family rather than the Visigothic or Basque lines of the south, and with very limited exceptions they had maintained their blood links to the north, marrying principally into Anjou, Normandy and Burgundy and focussing patronage near Poitiers. They also focussed political and military effort northwards, with military struggles with the Angevins being quite as common as marriage ties – for example in relation to the territory around Saintes. Poitou/Aquitaine straddled the borders of the two languages near the confluence of the Garonne and the Dordogne in the east, looping upwards to embrace the Limousin and a portion of the county of La Marche.[9] Thus the rulers of the duchy were themselves based in the territory of the *langue du roi* and of Frankish descent; but they had to understand and respect the different culture of the south in the way that northern nobles simply did not.

Also, as is apparent, Aquitaine was not one unified territory. When one of the main chroniclers of Eleanor's era, Ralph of Diss, said that 'Aquitaine overflows with many kinds of riches, excelling other parts of the western world by so much that historians consider it to be one of the most fortunate and flourishing of the provinces of Gaul',[10] he oversimplified – and created an easy trap for later writers and readers to fall into. What was sometimes called the Duchy of Aquitaine was at least three honours – the county of Poitou, the Duchy of Aquitaine and the Duchy of Gascony – each with their own geographical and cultural characteristics, and each with their separate economic and political problems. Each honour acquired new territories over the years as well, introducing further diversity – and often friction.

There were also very real differences in the ways in which the dukes of Aquitaine held power. The problems of vassalage owed to them have been alluded to, but there were also issues as to what obligations were owed to the King of France. Homage might be due from the Count of Poitou, since the county had provably been created and bestowed by the kings of France, but certainly in 1108 and later William IX refused to perform homage for Aquitaine or to acknowledge the French king's right to intervene directly in affairs of the county, probably because of the duchy's origins as an independent kingdom. Nor was it necessarily the case that Aquitaine could be treated as an indivisible entity; problems concerning the mode by which the Auvergne in particular was held led to a formal inquest in 1177. At this distance of time, the exact relations, or even the issues, cannot be identified; but it is nonetheless clear that the question of homage and feudal obligation was not a simple one, and that Eleanor's ancestors emphatically did not see themselves as being vassals of the King of France for all their territories.[11]

In terms of the different feel of the regions, little remains apart from prejudices. We know that when Agnes of Burgundy's daughter was sent to marry the German Emperor, a German abbot complained of the scandalous customs and indecent standards for dress that she introduced to the imperial court. Orderic Vitalis, for his part, described the Aquitanians and Gascons as being naturally fierce and irresponsible on the First Crusade. Best known, perhaps, is the travellers' guide for pilgrims following the Compostela trail in the twelfth century; this described the Poitevins as vigorous and warlike, witty, generous and good hosts, but it castigated the Gascons as 'frivolous in their words, talkative, mockers, drunkards and gluttons'.[12] A similar approach was taken by Abbot Stephen of St Germain-des-Près, who described the Gascons as flighty and the southerners generally as possessing 'cruel and savage habits'.[13] And the southerners were doing their own stereotyping – they, like the pilgrims' guide, highlight the better standard of living which the northern French enjoyed compared to the Gascons, and contrast the generosity and hospitality of the southerners with the surliness and close-handedness of the affluent northern French.

Culturally, the more affluent nature of the northern lands had been reflected in a more rapid development towards scholarship and a written tradition. Thus it was from the northern tradition that the arose the *chansons de geste*, the first real step in the world of chivalric literature. Controversy still surrounds the dates of the *chansons*, but it seems likely that they reflected the development of an oral tradition which prevailed throughout large parts of Europe – the telling of epic poetry by a bard as an evening's entertainment. But as the written tradition developed, such poems, committed to writing and circulated, effectively became political weapons in the hands of the beleaguered Carolingian monarchy, reminding readers of the glory days of Charlemagne, and serving as both a recruiting standard and a manual for the newly emerging warrior class.

Thus, while versions of the *chansons*, particularly those inspired by William of Orange, did circulate in the southern regions, the mindset which they reflect is very largely that of the northern warrior class. In this respect it is worth noting that the attitude to women in the *chansons* reflects the northern tradition of women as inspirers of hearth and home; the more elevated concepts of a woman's role which can be seen operating in practice in the south are not reflected. In the *chansons* one will not find women exercising authority as a ruler or as a judge of men: '*La Belle Aude*' from the *Chanson de Roland* expires dutifully at the news of his death; and while William of Orange's wife Orable/Guiborc is unusually assertive for a woman in a *chanson de geste*, she confines herself to the role of helpmeet and caregiver, tending his masculine pride so that he can venture forth heroically even after the worst of defeats.[14] Similarly, in *Cantar de mio Cid* Dona Jimena and the Cid's daughters are reactive, crying at his departure, enduring insult in his absence, and restored to happiness and eminence only by his military prowess. Nowhere do we see the fictional equivalents of the real-life Emma of Blois or Agnes of Burgundy – or Urraca of Castile.

The south's response to the *chansons de geste* was to lie in the hands of Eleanor's most celebrated relative, Duke William VII/IX, known as William the Troubadour. Of him – and of his own formidable wife – a little needs to be told before his cultural influence is considered.

William IX was to be no stranger to scandal, and it is therefore quite appropriate that he was the offspring of a highly controversial marriage between William VI/VIII and the very much (at least twenty-five years) younger Hildegarde of Bourgogne, the granddaughter both of Robert II ('the Pious') of France and Fulk ('the Black') of Anjou. Since Robert II's mother was none other than Adelaide of Aquitaine, the daughter of William Towhead of Aquitaine, this was a marriage well within the prohibited degrees of consanguinity. What is more, William VI/VIII also had two discarded wives living; his first wife (who had brought him his claim to Bordeaux) had retreated to the Abbaye aux Dames in Saintes, while his second he had simply repudiated. However, by now well into his forties and lacking a male heir, Duke William was not inclined to balk at these trivialities.

What is perhaps more interesting is that the French royal family also remained keen to make the match, despite its obvious vulnerability. One reason for this is the status the family of Poitou-Aquitaine had by now attained. With the conquest of further territories in Gascony, and the acquisition of the overlordship of the Duchy of Gascony, William VI/VIII now ruled a territory which in geographical and financial terms utterly dwarfed that of the kings of France. His lands stretched right from the Pyrenees across the Massif Central and up to Nantes. He portrayed himself as 'Duke of all the monarchy of Aquitaine'. If further evidence of the status which the duchy had now re-attained is required, one need look no further than the marital fates of William VIII's daughters. His eldest daughter, Agnes, by his second marriage, had been married in 1069 to King Alfonso VI of León and Castile. His younger daughter by Hildegarde, also helpfully called Agnes, was to marry King Pedro I of Aragon and Navarre. The family had, therefore, achieved quasi-royal status.[15]

The marriage therefore proceeded, and duly produced the longed-for son, William, in 1071, and a daughter, Agnes, in 1072. Papal acquiescence was therefore imperative, and William accordingly made a visit to Rome to gain it. Pope Gregory VII refused to recognise the marriage, but did legitimate young William, on condition that his father endowed a substantial new monastery, Montierneuf, again at Poitiers, run by the Cluniac order. With the marriage effectively forbidden, Hildegarde is recorded as residing apart from William by 1076, though she lived on until at least 1120.[16]

Young William was to become an epic figure, one of those rare people whose personality survives the passing of many hundreds of years. Given his pedigree as the son of a fabulously rich and powerful father, and a descendant and relative of royalty by marriage, it should be no surprise to find that he bears the hallmarks of having been thoroughly spoilt; nor that he emerged as a man who gave primacy to his own desires and interests, and possessed a decided turn for thumbing his nose at authority.

Having acceded to the title of Duke of Aquitaine in 1086 at the age of fifteen, it is often said that he then rushed into his first marriage – and divorce – with his cousin Ermengarde of Anjou. If so, this would be quite characteristic; however, recent scholarship has tended to cast doubt on this suggestion.[17] What is clear is that in 1094 he contracted a rather more sensible marriage with Philippa, the daughter of William, Count of Toulouse. This marriage seemed particularly promising, given the attitude to female inheritance in the south, and given the fact that the alternative candidate, Raymond of St-Gilles, had no clearly legitimate heir, his first marriage having been terminated for consanguinity.

It is often alleged that Philippa, to add to her charms, was also the widow of the King of Aragon, but this story is apocryphal; William was her first and only husband. It is more likely that, given her father's death alongside that of King Sancho of Aragon at the Battle of Huesca in June 1094, Philippa had been intended by him to marry one of the sons of the King of Aragon; and it is possible that this marriage was actually intended to remove her from the equation in inheritance terms, leaving the way clear for Raymond of St-Gilles. The marriage to William should probably be read as a declaration of intent from Philippa regarding her rights over Toulouse. William's lands were on the doorstep, and he was young, ambitious of martial glory and doubtless keen to extend the dominions of Aquitaine still further.[18]

For the first few years of their marriage, the claim lay in abeyance – Raymond, a mature man with a track record as Count of St-Gilles, Margrave of Provence and Count of Nimes, was recognised by the Pope as Count of Toulouse. But in 1095 Raymond answered the call to Crusade, departing with his new third wife and baby son in 1096, and leaving his lands in the hands of Bertrand, his son by his dubious first marriage. Non-Crusaders were supposed to respect the lands of those who had taken the cross, but William and Philippa did no such thing. In 1098, while Raymond was at the Siege of Antioch, they marched on Toulouse. It would appear that Bertrand was not popular in Toulouse, for the couple were welcomed by the townspeople, and took up residence there. Indeed, it was in Toulouse that the first child of their marriage, Eleanor's father William, was born in 1099.

But the lure of military glory was too much for William IX, and in 1101 he joined the second wave of the First Crusade, which was being organised to capitalise on the success of the 1096–99 mission. The cost of crusading was always high for a lord leading a contingent, and to finance his participation William mortgaged Toulouse back to Bertrand of Toulouse – a ploy which doubtless sat ill with his wife. Nor can she have been persuaded that the outcome was worth the cost, for William's 'crusade' was a complete disaster. His army was ambushed in Anatolia, and the majority of its troops were killed or captured. Orderic Vitalis suggests that William reached Antioch with only six survivors. It may be that such tepid religious interests as William had were weakened further by his experience of crusading, because from here on in his support for the Church is not apparent.[19] Events at home may also have had an impact, however.

For at this time, Philippa, left behind as regent of Poitou, Aquitaine and Gascony, seems to have been coming under the influence of the charismatic religious leader Robert d'Arbrissel. D'Arbrissel was a preacher of immense power and even seductiveness – one chronicler refers to his 'honeyed words', and his powers were officially recognised by Pope Urban II, who created him an 'apostolic preacher'. He attracted large crowds wherever he went, and fanatical devotion – particularly, it would seem, among women of all ranks. His biographer Baudri, Bishop of Dol, paints a vivid picture: 'The noble lady left her chateau, the peasant woman her cottage, the young girl her parents, and even the courtesan abandoned her shameful pleasures to follow this inspired sower of words.'[20]

But the cause of his appeal to women was nothing frivolous; the man was, in one sense at least, a proto-feminist, espousing equality between the sexes and greater power for women in marriage – including the right, thus far withheld, to accept or refuse a marriage proposed for them. His championship of women has been described by scholars as something unheard of in his era, when respectable theologians routinely described women in the most dismissive and negative of terms – as 'a bag of excrement' for example. It is therefore hardly surprising that his influence on women was profound and next door to irresistible. At the same time, however, d'Arbrissel's feminist credentials should not be overstated. His encouragement of an enclosed life for women indicates that, in line with the accepted theological approach following the Gregorian reforms, he considered all sexual desire as sinful and deriving from original sin, a view which would later lead Hugaccio of Pisa to argue that all sex – even within marriage and even for the procreation of children – was sinful.[21]

For Philippa, apparently deprived of her rights by her father, and then left subject to the whims of her husband when it came to control of her inheritance, the appeal of d'Arbrissel's message is obvious. Certainly he was preaching against heresy – probably the dualism which was to crystallise into Catharism – in the region at around the time of Philippa's residence in Toulouse; Philippa and William are recorded as implementing reforms there on his advice.

And crucially, before her husband's departure on Crusade, Philippa persuaded William to grant Robert the land on which he was to found his great abbey of Fontevraud.[22]

Philippa remained in close contact with d'Arbrissel in her husband's absence. She is recorded as making large concessions to the monks of Saint-Sernin at his urging. The planning of Fontevraud will have been ongoing throughout William's absence, and it is hard to imagine that Philippa, as one of the substantial patrons of the new abbey, was not closely involved with Robert in its development – along with others of his noble devotees, such as Petronilla of Chemille and Hersende of Champagne, the beautiful young noblewomen who were to become the first abbesses of the new foundation.

Fontevraud was a revolutionary concept in that it comprised houses for devotees of both sexes living together as equals. But still more revolutionary was the fact that both houses were under the overall direction of a female abbess. In line with the foundation's primary dedication to Mary, the Mother of God – just coming to the fore as an object of devotion in her own right – the abbess was not to be unmarried but a widow. And while women and men were otherwise technically equal, a key tenet in the house's belief system was the emphasis on women as the incarnation of Mary, the Mother of God. Unsurprisingly, the foundation was to become a magnet for a glittering line-up of noblewomen who wished to escape unwelcome or abusive marriages. Among those who were to be ladies in residence were William IX's reputed first wife, Ermengarde of Anjou; her stepmother (and mistress of King Henri of France) Bertrade de Montfort; Bertrade's half-sister Isabelle de Montfort (a lady noted not just for her beauty but also for her having once ridden into battle wearing armour, like a knight); and ultimately Philippa herself.[23]

Some scholars suggest that William's troubadour vocation was a designed challenge to Robert d'Arbrissel's influence over Philippa; that is probably overstretching the point. But it is certainly the case that it is only after his return from Crusade that William developed the reputations for which he was later best known – as a philanderer and a poet of lust and love. William of Malmesbury notably describes him as wallowing in vice on his return from Jerusalem, and amusing his friends with frivolous poetry. What is more, it is apparent that there was considerable friction between William and Robert on a number of fronts and over many years.

In particular, they had crossed swords publicly over the question of the excommunication of the King of France for his attempted marriage to Bertrade de Montfort. In this context, and bearing in mind d'Arbrissel's famous mission to save prostitutes from a life of sin, the story told by William of Malmesbury that William once spoke of establishing a convent of prostitutes at Niort seems both credible and a deliberate thrust at d'Arbrissel.[24]

But when William first returned, the marriage between himself and Philippa seems to have rubbed along well enough; certainly the chroniclers suggest that five daughters – and possibly a son, Raymond* – were born to them. And when Bertrand de St Gilles died in Syria in 1112, William duly retook Toulouse for Philippa. However, there were apparently tensions within the marriage throughout this time. It appears that William, alienated by his wife's enthusiasm for the religious teachings of d'Arbrissel, was deepening his tendency to anti-clericalism, although his relationship with foundations favoured by his family remained good. By 1114 he was excommunicated by the Church for seizing its goods to assist his own cash flow. His response to this was to confront Peter, Bishop of Poitiers – with whom he had apparently already clashed on many occasions – at the cathedral when he was on the point of pronouncing the anathema. William seized Peter by the hair and threatened to cut his throat if he did not absolve him. The bishop asked the duke for a moment of respite, but as soon as he was released Peter pronounced the sentence of excommunication in a ringing voice before offering his throat again to the knife. 'Well,' William responded, 'obviously I do hate you, but I don't hate you enough to give you the satisfaction of going to Paradise.'[25]

It also appears that William was seeking comfort in other women, and commencing his career as a mocking, light-hearted poet glorying in the pleasures of the flesh – the antithesis of Philippa's serious approach. She can hardly have been amused by his poem 'Companions, I shall name a suitable lyric', where the two fine, lively rides he praises are revealed to be wives of his vassals, and he jokes that his overlordship extends to rights over them as well as their husband's lands. Similarly, in 'Companions, I have had such a poor reception' he complains against vassals who try to keep their wives from him, abusing them for breaking the natural 'law of cunt', in that his use of their wives is likely to improve their family stock.[26]

---

* See Chapter 2 for more information.

Perhaps the most famous of his bawdy songs, however, has been interpreted as having a much deeper, anticlerical purpose, doubling as a direct shot at Gregorian Church reforms encouraging monastic life and possibly at Fontevraud too. This is the poem where a pilgrim is waylaid by two noble ladies who are understood by the context to be nuns, and who are given the names of two of William's aunts who had entered convents. He pretends not to speak their language, and they test him by getting their cat to scratch him violently. When he speaks no recognisable word under this provocation, they have their wicked way with him – 188 times, according to the narrator! The message is a protest against the Church's new theology anathematizing desire, a bold assertion that priests, nuns and pilgrims are hypocrites on this subject – as well, of course, as a paean to physical pleasures.[27]

On the regaining of Toulouse, Philippa departed to reside there for some time, founding a sister house of Fontevraud. It appears that it was in her absence that William committed the outrage for which he is most famous: he commenced an affair with the wife of one of his more significant vassals, the Count of Châtellerault. This lady, Amauberge, is more poetically and appropriately known by her nickname: Dangereuse. But he did not confine himself to occasional flings with this lady; instead he 'abducted' her – although the abduction seems to have been rather notional, with Dangereuse being more than willing – and installed her in a beautiful new tower in the palace of Poitiers, known in her honour as the Maubergeonne Tower.

We know very little of Dangereuse, who was to become Eleanor's grandmother, but the facts that her marriage to Aimery of Châtellerault would have been considered a very real mésalliance – she came from an undistinguished family based in the little town of L'Isle Bouchard – and that she then attracted William the Troubadour's avid attention and held it for the rest of his life suggests strongly that she was a very beautiful woman. Indeed, that nickname, 'Dangereuse', hints itself at attractions of rare strength – a woman whose loveliness was likely to cause trouble.

Dangereuse definitely lived up to her name, for the liaison did cause much trouble for William. It drew on his head a renewed threat of excommunication, this time at the hands of the papal legate Girard, Bishop of Angoulême – an associate of William's on Crusade and a man whose talents (intellectual, administrative and on the charm front) made him one of the most formidable, respected and admired churchmen of his day. But William was not to be moved; he simply looked at the bald legate and replied, 'Your hair will grow in ringlets before I separate from the viscountess.'[28]

The timing suggests that his relationship with Dangereuse inspired a change in William's poetical output, for it is likely that much of his literary output was complete before 1120 – he would seldom be at home for the final six years of his life, and his songs speak mostly of his life in Poitou and Aquitaine. Moreover, his reputation as a poet and hedonist had made it all the way to Normandy and England by the early 1120s, for Orderic Vitalis in Normandy and William of Malmesbury in Wiltshire both give highly coloured descriptions of him and also of his poetry. Vitalis says he outdid the wittiest minstrels, and refers to his skilful manipulation of rhythmic verse.[29]

But the key to William's influence was not such technical skill, or the bawdy humour evident in the descriptions of his earlier works. It was in his development of a vision of courtly love which was to become central both to the culture of the troubadours and to the later development of chivalry. William IX was in fact the earliest recorded troubadour, and the first to write poetry that depicted a powerful and unattainable female ideal. Essentially, in his four surviving troubadour-style songs he hymns a state of affairs where women are neither the powerless tenders of hearth and home seen in the *chansons de geste* nor the objectified sexual pawns visible in his most graphic poems. His has been described as 'an entirely new view of women and of love' – and it chimes with his reported determination to bear Dangereuse's image on his shield in battle.[30]

In these poems, women are seen as having the power to determine men's fates. Song 9 Lines 20–30, for example, run thus:

> Every joy should humble itself
> And every richness bow down before
> My Lady; because of her beautiful welcome,
> And her beautiful, pleasant face;
> And a man would wait a hundred years
> If he could seize the joy of her love.
> Through her joy a sick man can recover,
> And through her anger a fit man can die
> And a wise man can become a fool
> And a handsome man lose his looks
> The most courteous man can become boorish
> And the most vulgar may become gallant.

Later, at the heart of the poem (lines 38–48,) is the core of the code of courtly love:

> If my lady wishes to give me her love
> I will take it and will thank her for it
> And I'll hide it or boast of it
> I will say or do what pleases her
> And I will cherish her reputation
> And do what may promote her praise
> I dare not send her a message through another
> Because I'm so afraid that would anger her
> Nor do I dare, on account of my fear of failure
> To make any real demonstration of my love
> She must do with me as she thinks best
> Because she knows that through her I will become better.

What were William's aims in these poems? This is a topic of hot debate, with some seeing it as a blow in a personal war against Robert d'Arbrissel. Far more convincing is the view that William wished in some sense to speak for the benefits and pleasures which were there to be enjoyed by the women of his own noble order in the world, at a time when conventual life was appealing to many – including his wife. In this sense, William's 'romantic' poems can be seen as partners to his 'bawdy' oeuvre. Both are protests against the Church's approach to desire. In one, he mocks the Church's approach with bold assertions of the naturalness of desire between men and women; in the other he promotes sexual desire but hymns it as not simply natural but as tending to encourage the honour of both men and women in a lay setting, and the woman's power.

Although his inspiration may have been entirely personal, in the encounter with a love which would change his life William can thus be seen as beginning the process of creating a lay Marian figure for women to aspire to and men to worship – a model which gave women a status which they may well have felt themselves to lack. Although in his own poetry this image appears only fleetingly and in a fairly undeveloped form, as the planter of that seed of a more developed idea, William, despite his infidelities and his vulgarities, can be seen as quite as much a promoter of women's rights as the more upright Robert d'Arbrissel.

In his last years, however, William's focus appears to have been on finding a way to regularise his position with the Church and possibly also with Dangereuse. For around 1118, at the time when Philippa appears to have died, William sought to be absolved from his excommunication. While there is some debate over the date of Philippa's death, this step indicates that his circumstances had undergone a change which would enable him to enter into dialogue with the Church. It may well be that he hoped, as a widower, to get the Church's sanction for his relationship with Dangereuse. The fact of his absolution and his having shortly afterwards departed to take the Cross and fight in Spain against the Muslim invaders has the strong flavour of a deal he hoped to see struck with the Church – absolution for him, and possibly Church support for persuading the Viscount of Châtellerault to renounce his wife. Certainly William departed reluctantly on this Crusade, and with thoughts of his soul, for in his song 11, 'Since I feel like singing', he grieves over the need to leave his home and family at the mercy of 'those villainous Gascons and Angevins' and says, 'I have been agreeable and gay, but Our Lord doesn't allow it anymore; now I am so close to the end I can't bear the burden anymore.'[31]

William was to return safely from a successful Crusade, featuring honourably at the Battle of Cutanda in June 1120; but he never did obtain his marriage with Dangereuse. His final recorded act is another unsuccessful attempt to take Toulouse as his son's maternal inheritance in 1123.[32]

2

Eleanor's Childhood

*Ego Willelmus Dei gratia dux Aquitanorum, pro redemption
peccatorum meorum, et pro remedio animae patris mei, do
ecclesiae St Hilaire de Poitiers ... de ambergamento de Chanpot.
... Willielmi ducis Aquitanorum, Aeonordis, Commitissae,
Alienordis filae eorum...*
[I William, by the grace of God Duke of Aquitaine, do hereby
give, for the redemption of my sins and the souls of my
ancestors, the place known as Chanpot. [Witnessed] William,
Duke of Aquitaine, Aenor Countess, Eleanor their daughter...]
Charters of St Hilaire, Poitiers, *c.* 1130

Eleanor's father was that William who was born to Philippa
of Toulouse just after she had first gained control of the city in
1099. He was consequently often referred to as William 'the
Toulousian' – a misleading definition since Toulouse was lost well
before he succeeded to the Duchy of Aquitaine. It is not, however,
as misleading an appellation as his other nickname, 'the Saint', the
origins of which may well lie in sarcasm.

The details of William's early life are scarce and conflicting. With
his father absent on Crusade, he will have spent his earliest years
in the atmosphere of intense religiosity which appears to have
surrounded Philippa. He was still young when his father returned
and the clash of styles between his parents became apparent.
The precise nature of his relationship with his parents is unclear.
Although William the Toulousian is often reported to have rebelled
against his father, the report comes from a later chronicler and
the evidence seems sparse at best. The date of his first reported

rebellion was when he was only thirteen years old, and he can certainly be traced touring the duchy's lands, in partnership with his father, shortly before Duke William IX departed on Crusade in 1120. Indeed, it seems highly unlikely that the duke would have taken this step unless he was in sufficient harmony with his son to leave the duchy in his hands for a prolonged period. His Song 11 also hints at no such friction – he simply worries as to whether his son can hold his lands in his absence.[1]

Finally, if there were a serious lack of consensus between father and son it would appear strange that young William agreed to his father's somewhat controversial matrimonial plans for him; for at some point, probably in his early twenties and after his father's return, he married none other than the daughter of Dangereuse, young Aenor of Châtellerault. Given that the family of Châtellerault were vassals of the house of Aquitaine, that Dangereuse herself hailed from a family of still lesser nobility and that previous dukes had married ladies from other leading ducal or comital families, this match was a considerable mésalliance. It seems very likely to have been a favour done for Dangereuse by Duke William, perhaps following an acknowledgement that their own marriage would not be possible. The marriage of their children therefore provided her with the status of mother to the future duchess and the knowledge that her own bloodline would succeed to the duchy.

The date of the marriage is uncertain. Richard, the biographer of the counts of Poitou, gives it as 1121, but only by reference to a speculative birthdate for Eleanor of 1122. As we shall see below, that date has now been fairly comprehensively rejected by scholars, with the date of 1124 being preferred for Eleanor's birth. It also seems more likely, given William's apparent desire to marry Dangereuse, that the match only took place on his return to Aquitaine in around 1123 – at which point it would finally have been clear that no marriage would happen between him and his adored mistress.

A further small factor adds to the case for an 1123 marriage: Aenor's age. Aenor was the third of the five children Dangereuse had borne her husband before abandoning him and them for William IX in around 1115. Since the two eldest children lived until late in the century (1176 and 1190), it is likely that the children of the marriage commenced to be born not long before this – perhaps around the time Dangereuse is first mentioned as the Viscount of Châtellerault's wife in 1109. It therefore seems fairly likely that

Aenor was born in around 1110–11 and that she was just of canonical age for marriage in 1123, with an age gap of around ten years between her and her new husband.

The evidence for the relationship of William and Aenor is very slight indeed, but what there is suggests that the young couple were fond of each other – William was to refer to her in charters as his 'dear wife'. The charter evidence also suggests that, contrary to the suggestions of many biographers, Aenor enjoyed considerable influence over her husband – a number of donations and grants are recorded as being prompted by her or made at her request. Domestic harmony is also indicated by the fact that three children followed in relatively short succession.

The eldest was Eleanor, born (it is now usually accepted) in 1124. Her name was not a common one at the time, and there may be some truth in the tale that she was called 'Ali-Aenor' or 'another Aenor' after her mother – a sign of affection which again negates suggestions of an unhappy marriage. Whether there was also, as William Marshal suggested, a further reference to 'ali' (possibly meaning exalted) and 'or' (gold) cannot be known. As for the date of her birth, this was frequently given as 1120, 1121 or 1122 in the past. The year 1122 was perhaps the preferred date, drawn from a chronicle which Richard says describes Eleanor as eighty-two years old on her death in 1204. However, that chronicle does not give her age at all. Some opt for 1122 by reference to an alleged swearing of fealty when Eleanor was fourteen, but it appears that this refers to the swearing of fealty to Eleanor on her father's death in 1137, which would have no reference to her age. Most scholars now therefore date Eleanor's birth by reference to the earliest record of her age, a thirteenth-century genealogy created shortly after Eleanor's death, which gives her age at the time of her father's death as thirteen, indicating a birth date of 1124.[2]

The location of Eleanor's birth is still disputed. Three locations have been argued for: Nieul-sur-Autise, Vendée; the Château de Belin, south of Bordeaux; or the Palais d'Ombrière, Bordeaux. There is no evidence for any of them, and indeed Eleanor may have been born somewhere entirely different. The other children of the marriage were young William, known as William Aigret, and Aelis, often referred to as Petronille, perhaps because she was born on or around the saint's day of St Petronilla.[3]

Their respective birth orders and years are unknown, but the fact that William Aigret and Eleanor subscribed a charter with their parents shortly before William Aigret's death in 1130 suggests that William was older than Aelis, and probably born shortly after Eleanor.[4] Consequently, for the first conscious years of her life Eleanor will not have seen herself as the heir to Poitou-Aquitaine; that role was her brother's. It was only on his death – which was apparently very close in time to the death of their mother – that Eleanor became the heir apparent to the duchy.

It is often blithely asserted that Duke William IX loomed large over Eleanor's childhood. In fact, he died on 10 February 1126, when Eleanor was probably not even two years old. Furthermore, following his return from the Spanish Crusade he appears to have been fairly active in his lands, travelling to maintain his claims and deal with disputes among his ever-fractious vassals until shortly before his death. It is therefore most unlikely that Eleanor had any personal memories of him. His myth and his poetry of course remained, and presumably influenced Eleanor as they did the entire court of Aquitaine. And despite his many violent quarrels with the Church at large, his donations to his father's Abbey of Montierneuf had been sufficient to accord him a very honoured reception there in death, with a lavish annual memorial service.[5]

Duke William X has received little attention from historians next to the wealth of adulation and infamy piled on his father. He does, however, appear to have been a father likely to inspire devotion in his children. He was said to be immensely tall and strong, with the appetite of eight men. While Richard, the biographer of the Counts of Poitou, somewhat snidely claims that the tenth duke's brain was far from being as well developed as his physique, there is scope for treating this claim carefully. With Poitiers one of the major centres of learning in France, and with his parents both learned, the duke undoubtedly received a good education. Indeed, we know that his tutor was Rainald, the subcantor of the Poitiers chapter. His history indicates that in fact he retained close ties with some of the most intellectually able men of his time throughout his life. He does seem to have inherited his father's taste for troubadour verse – he is reliably recorded as a patron of two of the foremost poets of the day, Cercamon and Marcabru, though the picturesque reports of a Welsh bard, Bleddri, appear to derive from later sources. He was also a considerable patron of other entertainers, which suggests that his court was lively and musical.[6]

His relatively short incumbency as duke was troubled. William IX had not departed with his vassals in perfect order, and many of them, including the troublesome Lusignan family, seem to have been inclined to try the strength of the young new duke from the outset. He nonetheless achieved some early successes in partnership with the more experienced Vulgrin, Count of Angoulême, but within a year or so the two had fallen out. However, at this point in his career Duke William appears not to have been minded to pick too many fights with his vassals. The earlier years of his rule also evidence extensive religious patronage – sometimes explicitly at Aenor's prompting, but sometimes ironically also inspired by his association with the now long-standing papal envoy Girard of Angoulême. Girard may have been one of his father's adversaries on the subject of Dangereuse, but he was also a close family friend and an associate of Robert d'Arbrissel. Via one route or another, he had come to exert huge influence over the younger William. It was also during this period that William first came under the influence of Geoffroi du Loroux, recently identified with Geoffrey Babion, a prominent teacher of religion in the new 'scholastic' approach, who was rising high in the esteem of the Church. William granted him land at Fontenay le Comte and Sablonceaux for two communities of poor brothers which he had founded.[7]

In 1130, however, Aenor's moderating influence ceased. She and William's heir, young William Aigret, both died within a short time of each other, according to one source, of a fever contracted at Belin. In the next few months the duke proceeded to lay waste to his good relations with the Church, following his entry, on the wrong side, into the disputes which followed the death of Pope Honorius, arising out of a disputed election (prompted initially more by politics than principle) whereby two popes claimed the title of pontiff: Innocent II and Anacletus II. Richard sees William's championing of Anacletus as due to the influence of Girard of Angoulême, whom Innocent was later to describe as his most formidable opponent. Whether it was indeed a blind pursuit of his mentor's cause and whether Girard was, as the chronicles suggest, actuated by no motive higher than a desire to maintain his legatal position may be open to doubt. Certainly a close reading of the course of the dispute suggests that William, like other temporal lords including Henry I of England, found the less reformist Anacletus's views more digestible than those of Innocent on the respect to be given to the temporal authorities in matters where jurisdictions overlapped, such as nominations of bishops to sees within that lord's temporal authority. In line with that possibility, the schism was in fact to be marked by appointments of William's own nominees to vacant sees, including that of Girard to the see of Bordeaux.[8]

Into this dispute now stepped a figure who was to loom somewhat large in Eleanor's early life: St Bernard of Clairvaux, one of the towering figures of a heroic age. At only twenty-five he had been selected by the reforming Cistercian Order's hierarchy to found the monastery from which he was to take his name. In his thirties he was key in developing the Rule of the Knights Templar and was widely famed for his success as a preacher. He was therefore the obvious candidate to offer a recommendation to the king and the bishops of France as to the side which they should take in the schism. Fairly predictably, the reforming Bernard ruled for Innocent, the more hard-line of the two candidates. Following French and English royal acknowledgement of Innocent's authority, Bernard was then despatched to win over William of Aquitaine. After days of persuasion, it appeared that Bernard's personal magnetism had prevailed; a celebratory Mass was held, and Bernard departed. But Girard of Angoulême's influence had soon reasserted itself, and William reiterated his support for Anacletus. The result was that William was excommunicated and excluded from all sacraments (including marriage and Mass) until he was reconciled with the Church.[9]

How strictly this interdict was enforced generally we cannot know, but it seems likely that William will have been deprived of the rites of the Church, initially in Poitiers (William's main residence) and Limoges for it was in those dioceses that William and Girard purported to strip the incumbent bishops of their titles and procure the election of candidates favourable to them.[10] A similar situation will have prevailed in Bordeaux after the death of the incumbent in 1131.

Through the latter portion of Eleanor's childhood, therefore, she was intimately familiar with the concept of serious quarrels between a temporal ruler and the Church. She will also, necessarily, have heard much negative commentary on the Church from those who sided with William, because supporting William necessarily meant opposing the Church. Modern sensibilities tend to dispose us to think that William should have been able to get on perfectly well without the Church's approval, but this line of thought ignores the much deeper hold which religion had even on the more cynical souls of the early twelfth century. While a strong-willed ruler might maintain a degree of indifference about exclusion from Mass, there was lurking the ultimate threat – dying excommunicate would mean a certain ticket to hell. Almost no one would have doubted this as a truth.

At just thirty years old, of course, this would probably have seemed a distant prospect to William. Actually, a more serious problem for him was the fact that no one would marry their daughter to an excommunicate. Thus, while his quarrel with the Church subsisted, he could not remarry and replace the male heir he had just lost. But the evidence suggests that, despite the excommunication dragging on for six years, William was not without a desire to be in harmony with the religious. He did not, for example, simply expel bishops and leave dioceses vacant; he actively sought appointees who would admit him to worship. Furthermore, he continued to make considerable donations, sometimes as a mark of penitence, to religious houses, including that of Fontevraud. All of this indicates – as does his close association with Girard – that he had imbibed rather more of his mother's religiosity than his father's scepticism, and that Eleanor's childhood was much more overtly religious than it is often credited with being.[11]

In the same period, William seems to have become embroiled in rather more territorial and political disputes with his neighbours. He at one stage campaigned against the young Geoffrey 'le Bel' (the Handsome) of Anjou, who at sixteen had recently succeeded his father, Fulk, as Count of Anjou when Fulk decided to take up the opportunity to marry Melisende, the heiress to the throne of Jerusalem. William apparently formed part of a band of opportunist neighbours who thought to pick lands off the young man before he came to his full strength. This coalition brought very limited success – Geoffrey was a canny campaigner despite his youth and beauty – and William was later to campaign with Geoffrey instead. It may even be that it was Geoffrey's very early successes prior to his accession which had recommended him to Henry I as a match for his widowed daughter Matilda, known as 'the Empress', courtesy of her first marriage to the German Emperor Henry V, and now herself heir apparent to the throne of England.

William also became embroiled in rows with a number of his vassals, including the lords of Lusignan and those of Chatelaillon. Only one of these disputes rendered William any real gains – he did win the territory of Aunis. His decision to destroy the harbour of Chatelaillon and grant free port status to La Rochelle was to prove one of his very best decisions; the result was to bring huge prosperity to La Rochelle and, through this, significant revenues to Eleanor and her descendants.

In 1135 the papal authorities decided to try once more to bring William back into the fold, and despatched Bernard of Clairvaux south to this purpose. To assist in the process of sweetening William's view of the papacy, Innocent also arranged the marriage of William's widowed sister Agnes to Raimon, King of Aragon, giving tacit papal acknowledgement of Aquitaine's position as a quasi-royal territory.[12]

Meanwhile, Bernard called on Geoffroi du Loroux – like Innocent a reformer, but one who had personally impressed William – to help him. Loroux, inclined to maintain his role as a leader of an ascetic order in peace, had thus far withstood calls from his peers to use his influence, but at last he was persuaded and proved key in bringing William back to the Church.[13] Loroux's influence saw William more or less accept the status of Innocent, who had acquired almost unanimous support in the past few years, although the duke stood firm on the more personal question of the bishops within his territories; he would not accept the reinstatement of the bishops he had expelled.

But one day St Bernard had a brainwave. While at Mass, he caught sight of William following the service from the door of the church – the nearest he as an excommunicate could come (and an interesting indication of his innate religiosity). Advancing on him with the Host raised before him, Bernard spoke urgently to William, saying, 'We have begged you, but you have spurned us. The servants of god have again beseeched you and you have responded with contempt. But here, now, see the Son of God who comes for you, the Head and the Lord of the Church which you persecute! Here is your judge, at whose name every knee bends throughout the world. Your judge – can you disrespect him as you have his servants?'

The emotion involved in this *coup de théâtre* apparently overcame William, and he passed out briefly. When he regained consciousness, he accepted reconciliation with one of the controversial bishops and submitted himself again to the Church. Over the course of the next year, the bishops would return to their places and William would make massive donations to St Bernard's cause. Most significantly, Girard died in the summer of 1136 and Geoffroi de Loroux, relied on by both Church and William, was elevated without complaint to the vacant archbishopric of Bordeaux.[14]

Meanwhile, William returned to his habit of fighting with his neighbours and briefly joined with Geoffrey of Anjou – now the husband of Matilda, 'the Empress' of England, and father to two sons, Henry and Geoffrey – to conduct a punitive mission into Normandy, which the chronicler Orderic Vitalis says left the lands they invaded in smoking ruins. William's involvement in this campaign is interesting – its primary motivation seems to have been to support the Empress's claim to the English throne, which had been seized by her cousin Stephen of Blois the previous year. William was never short of disputes with his neighbours, but no obvious reason for involvement in this one emerges from the records; this tempts one to suppose that the possibility of a match between one of his daughters and one of Geoffrey's sons may have been under discussion. There is no proof that this was so, however, and suggestions that a match between Eleanor and Henry was tentatively fixed go too far; not least because the ages of the girls vis à vis Henry makes Aelis a more likely match.[15]

However, the campaign was to have one significant result. So brutal had it been that it provided the overt rationale for William's decision in 1137 to make a pilgrimage to Compostela. But there was apparently a more important covert reason, for this cleansing of the various stains on William's reputation was done at the insistence of the family of the woman whom William had now decided to marry: Emma of Limoges, the widow of the lord of Cognac, who was the heir apparent to the Viscount of Limoges and had crucially proven her fertility by bearing two sons already.[16] Now clear of the excommunication, William had realised that he needed to set about producing a new male heir, and he was therefore in no position to demur. Whether, in addition, his collapse at the feet of St Bernard betokened any failing of his health for which he wished to seek intercession can only be a matter of speculation.

Whatever the real cause or causes of his decision William set off on his pilgrimage in March of 1137, timing his departure to allow him to arrive at Compostela in time for Easter. Departing from Poitiers, he was accompanied by his daughters until Bordeaux. There he left them in the care of Geoffroi de Loroux, who had succeeded to the pre-eminent post of influence which had previously been Girard's. His plan was to rejoin his family before summer. Yet, though young and obviously campaign fit a short while previously, he fell ill en route, and died just before he reached his goal, on 9 April 1137. His body was buried before the altar of St James at Compostela.

Eleanor was Countess of Poitou and Duchess of Aquitaine. She was no more than thirteen years old.

This state of affairs, as will be apparent, was not what had been anticipated or intended by the ducal family. When turning to consider Eleanor's upbringing, therefore, we can first jettison the oft-repeated idea that she had been raised to be the heiress to her father's lands and educated with that destiny in mind. At least for the early years of her life, Eleanor will have been raised to think of herself as second in the children's pecking order, and as one whose destiny would depend upon marriage. Even after her brother's death, when her father was thirty or thirty-one, it will have been considered likely that a new wife would emerge, and provide an heir to displace her. This assumption is given a measure of confirmation by the slightly odd fact that no marriage had been arranged for Eleanor before her father's death. Had Eleanor been considered the heiress to Aquitaine it is almost certain that her future would have been settled at an earlier age, as most princesses' marriages were. All Eleanor's own daughters, for example, were at least contracted for, if not actually delivered to their husbands, before they turned twelve. Eleanor's ambiguous status, coupled with her father's dispute with the Church, seems to have precluded an early match.

The form of Eleanor's education is unknown to us. Some biographers assert that she was not sent off to a convent for schooling, but we simply do not know if this is correct. One possible venue for some of Eleanor's childhood schooling would be at her grandmother's foundation at Fontevraud, where a Châtellerault aunt was in residence, where Eleanor would send two of her own children for their education, and where she would ultimately retire from the world. Another possibility is that she and a group of companions were educated by tutors in or around the ducal household, as was the case for the junior English royals of a later generation. The surviving records indicate that the employment of tutors in noble households was not uncommon at this time.

Her father, as we know, was educated at the cathedral school of Poitiers; and this may well have played host to Eleanor also. The Poitiers school was one of the most distinguished in France at this time; we know, for example, that in the eleventh century William the Conqueror's biographer William 'of Poitiers' had been sent from Normandy to Poitiers for his schooling. Eleanor's family had long patronised the establishment, encouraging the recruitment of highly learned men to its roster.[17]

One small detail suggests that Eleanor was in fact educated as part of a rather mixed group – perhaps in something reminiscent of a school class. The chronicler Matthew Paris, writing in St Albans Abbey in the thirteenth century, notes and draws a donation of a ring to the abbey by one Richard Animal, that ring having been given to him by Eleanor because 'in their childhood they were fellow students and playmates'. This paradigm of a mixed group of children learning together is not strange; it is reflected in contemporary vernacular romances which depict young ladies pursuing their studies alongside boys, and would have reflected the mode in the cathedral school.[18]

Much debate has occurred over the thoroughness of Eleanor's education. We know nothing of it for a fact, but we do know that her family inclined to a thorough education, that she was later considered well educated, if not outstandingly learned, and that at the last she chose to be depicted on her grave with a book. It is likely that she was educated to read, if not to write, Latin and that as the future manager of a substantial noble household she was taught a certain amount of mathematics and accounts.

On top of this, of course, the cultural bias of the court of Aquitaine would ensure her familiarity with poetry and romance. Theology played a large part in the education of many children of the era, and if Eleanor was educated in the cathedral school or at Fontevraud, this would follow. Such education would perhaps be less likely if her schooling took place at the ducal court. Turner hypothesises that Eleanor's education was overseen to a significant degree by Geoffroi de Loroux, whom he describes as the Archbishop of Bordeaux in her childhood. But as we have seen, this was a position which Loroux did not attain until 1135. Before that, he appears to have taught rather more mature students in the cathedral school of Angers before his retreat into a period of contemplation prior to the founding of his new institutions in the early years of Eleanor's life.[19] Other writers have suggested the earlier incumbent of Bordeaux, Arnaud de Cabanac, for this role; but his death in 1130 makes him an unlikely mentor, as Eleanor was too young during his life to have entered on serious education.

Overall, the evidence suggests most strongly an education at the cathedral school of Poitiers. If this is the case, Eleanor would have received the kind of education designed to fit a young student for further study in one of the great schools before passing on to a distinguished career in the Church; in other words, a top-flight education – and one designed to inculcate both an interest in learning and a profound religious belief.

Nor should Geoffroi de Loroux's influence at a slightly later stage be neglected. He was plainly much with Eleanor's father in the last couple of years of his life – as Eleanor was entering her teens. He was a teacher with a track record at the higher level of education, and was the author of works which the greatest teacher of the younger generation, Pierre Abelard, would admire. For example, he is credited with a commentary on the Gospel of St Matthew, which was the first to be put in a scholastic form, equipped with theological questions. He was also a man of such true religiosity that the great Peter the Venerable, head of the Abbey of Cluny, wrote with admiration of his rejection of terrestrial desires in the search for a greater spirituality.[20] And we indeed know that Eleanor came, in her turn, to form a very close bond with Geoffrey, who was to remain an influence on her until his death. We can therefore expect Eleanor to have been thoroughly schooled in the best teachings of religion and very probably to have entered on some sort of education in the new scholastic approach by her early teens.

Another important point which should be considered in the context of Eleanor's education is the question of her native tongue. Traditionally it has been asserted that Eleanor's native or preferred tongue was the *lengua romana*. As will be apparent in both the context of her family's history and the geographic bases for her childhood and schooling, this seems implausible. Eleanor will certainly have been educated in northern French, and will almost certainly have been equally fluent in the local variant of the language which was spoken around the Poitiers district. Of recent years, Eleanor scholarship has even in some cases sought to turn the accepted position on its head, and argue that Eleanor probably did not even speak the *lengua romana*.[21] This is surely pressing the point too far – it seems unlikely that the ruling family of Gascony did not trouble to ensure that they spoke the language, particularly when William the Troubadour was regarded as one of the pre-eminent poets of that language and Eleanor's father maintained troubadour poets working in that language at his court. So, while we can probably safely conclude Eleanor spoke and read both her lands' vernaculars of *lengua romana* and *langue du roi*, and did so with facility and enjoyment, it is worth bearing in mind that the former was not her vernacular.

Consistent with this, as we will see throughout Eleanor's life, there is in fact no evidence to associate her with its promotion, nor with a particular fondness for it.

What else do we know about the group of young people who may have surrounded Eleanor during her formative years? When Duke William the Troubadour died, he also left behind him at least one illegitimate son (and probably a second) via Dangereuse, beside his heir, William. The only one who has made any real impression on history is Raymond, later Prince of Antioch, though contemporaneous sources suggest that Raymond had a brother, Henri. Raymond is, of course, conventionally stated to have been the son of William IX and Philippa of Toulouse, and hence a full brother to William X. However, it seems that the better view is that he was actually the son of William's affair with Dangereuse.

The starting point is the record of the proposed marriage of Raymond to Constance of Antioch in 1136. William of Tyre records that the King of Jerusalem proposed 'the young Raymond, son of William Count of Poitou', who was said to be living at the court of Henry I of England where he had been made a knight.[22] The word used in the chronicle, '*adolescens*', denoting 'not yet fully grown', is crucial. William of Tyre again records in a later passage that ambassadors from Antioch were sent to '*domino Raimundo ... adolescentem*', and brought him secretly from England to Antioch. If Raymond was not yet an adult in 1136, he must have been born sometime after 1115. This would also place his birth after Philippa separated from William, and also after William embarked on his grand passion with Dangereuse – whose history with her husband shows her to have been very fertile.

The next clue is in an oddly worded passage in the Chronicle of Saint-Maixent. This starts by recording the birth of Duke William IX's first son, 'also called William', and proceeds to state that he had five daughters from the same wife. The chronicler then adds, in a new sentence, a reference to Raymond. If Raymond was indeed the full brother of the other children, it would make far more sense to list him with the other children, and in the same sentence.[23] In addition, the chronicle rather oddly refers to Raymond as '*uterinum*', which makes little sense if it refers back to the same mother who is was earlier described as William's wife. The usual use of the word 'uterine' in this context, referring to children born from the same mother but who do not necessarily share the same father, seems impossible. More probable is that the chronicler is somewhat coyly referring to a child born to a notorious woman – which of course is exactly what Dangereuse was.

The conclusion is not perfectly safe. Too much turns on some ambiguities in the Latin. But it is certainly strongly arguable, and is given support by the fact that Raymond is never referred to in any other chronicles either as the legitimate son of William IX or as the full brother of William X. One final point in its favour: on William X's death there seems to have been no suggestion that Raymond should succeed to the title of count-duke instead of Eleanor. If he were legitimate, this would be surprising. After all, Philippa of Toulouse had been ousted by an uncle of very dubious legitimacy; and as noted earlier, the position as regard women's rights was moving backwards rather than forwards as the twelfth century progressed.

In any event, it would seem that Raymond, who may have been somewhere between five and nine years older than Eleanor, was probably in residence at court at the time of his father's death, and for some time thereafter. Although some biographers suggest that his time there barely overlapped with Eleanor's childhood, his age indicates that in fact he probably left for Henry I's court sometime around 1130 – when he was fifteen. If this is so, it is therefore quite credible that Eleanor knew him fairly well from childhood and that in her earliest years Raymond occupied the role of the glamorous big brother.

And what of young Henry? All that we know of him is that William of Tyre records a plan that he should come east with his brother and marry Constance of Antioch's mother, Alice. This certainly suggests existence, but phantom people are not unknown in the chronicles of the time. He did not appear to marry Alice, but she also disappears from the record at around this period. Nonetheless, it is worth noting that, given William IX's departure on Crusade in 1120, Henry, if he indeed existed, would probably have been born either in the period 1117–19 or in the last few years of William's life. If so, Henry would have been close to Eleanor in age and a likely close companion for her and her siblings.

Aside from these two young uncles, Eleanor is often gifted with two illegitimate brothers, Joscelin and William, as a result of references in the Pipe Rolls to 'the Queen's brother'. However, Elizabeth Chadwick has satisfactorily proved that these references never identify which queen they are talking about, while another source, the records of Reading Abbey, identifies Joscelin as the brother of Adeliza of Louvain, the second queen of Henry I. This Joscelin was well established at the English court and exercised considerable influence, and would reasonably have been referred to in shorthand even years later as Joscelin the Queen's brother.[24] Eleanor's reputed brother Joscelin therefore disappears in a puff of smoke.

Other close companions may well have originated from Dangereuse's family. Dangereuse's second son, Raoul, the Seigneur de Faye via his marriage to the heiress of Faye le Vineuse, had a number of children whose ages were probably close to those of the ducal children. Eleanor's later closeness to Raoul suggests that he was very present in her childhood and that she may well have shared some of her education with his children. This, indeed, may account for the queen's alleged brother William, referred to just once in the records; the youngest of the de la Faye children was a Guillame. It may be that in this case the secretary filling out the account books misinterpreted cousinship and closeness from childhood as a fraternal bond.

Outside the children with whom Eleanor was educated, who else is likely to have played a large part in her upbringing? Obvious questions hang over the involvement of the lovely Dangereuse. She disappears from the record after Duke William's death, but we can be confident that while her daughter lived Dangereuse was still welcome and often resident with the ducal family. Eleanor was therefore assured of a fascinating grandmother for her earliest years. Whether she remained after 1130 is uncertain; she may well have stayed, providing Eleanor with a fascinating female influence. However, it is also possible that she either followed her young sons to England or took up residence with her youngest daughter, Aimable, now Countess of Angoulême.

Another formidable female mentor was not likely to be lacking, however, for in 1127 Eleanor's father's sister Agnes of Aquitaine, wife of the Viscount of Thouars – an important vassal of the Counts of Poitou – was widowed. As the mother of three young sons, she is likely to have spent a good deal of time under the protection of her brother, who could ensure their position was safeguarded. Indeed, the charter evidence shows the boys making donations supported by their uncle, indicating a closeness between the families.[25] This also suggests that they may have been companions of Eleanor and her siblings in the schoolroom. Agnes was, as mentioned above, to remarry in 1135, being chosen as the bride of Ramiro II 'the Monk', the reluctant King of Aragon who was hauled out of his monastery to assume power on the death of his older brother. She thus became the mother of Eleanor's near contemporary Petronilla, Queen of Aragon. Also regularly accessible to Eleanor was another of her aunts, another Agnes, known as Agnes of Poitou, who had entered the abbey of Notre-Dame at Saintes, where she in due course became abbess. Female role models were not lacking, then; but there is no evidence of a single consistent female influence through Eleanor's childhood.

Much more consistent are likely to have been the predominantly male influences of the ducal household. In line with the royal origins of the dukes of Aquitaine, they maintained a considerable household, modelled on the Carolingian royal court,[26] featuring a range of clerics including a chaplain, a steward or seneschal in overall control of the household, a chamberlain in charge of the duke's private quarters, a constable in charge of the extensive stables and the retinue of household knights. In addition, the court would frequently visit or receive the principal nobles of the area. So people such as William de Mauzé, the seneschal of Poitou – in succession to his own father, Geoffrey de Rancon, Sire of Taillebourg and chamberlain of Poitou[27] – would have been regular figures in Eleanor's life during her childhood, and she would have come to know the chief nobles of Aquitaine.

For all this, an important part of Eleanor's education, albeit one which will have left no trace in the records, is her education as a noblewoman. During her mother's lifetime, Eleanor will almost certainly have been part of a group of girls being educated to their various female stations in life by Aenor, supported by Dangereuse. Eleanor and any other noble girls will have been instructed in the ways of running a household and comital court – the responsibilities of a noblewoman as administrator liaising with the various department heads to ensure the castle was adequately supplied and serviced, as hostess welcoming notable guests, and indeed as educator in her turn of the next generation. It was vital that Eleanor be schooled in these regards as she moved from her early childhood towards her teens and a beckoning marriage, which suggests most strongly that her aunt Agnes joined the court after her mother's death and took over this role.

Eleanor probably spent the majority of her time at the count-dukes' favourite residence at Poitiers. This would have made her particularly familiar with the town, the palace and the cathedral there. She would therefore have been intimately familiar with the saints who were particularly venerated in Poitiers, St Hilaire and St Radegonde. The church of St-Hilaire-le-Grand was outside the city's Roman walls and contained the tomb of the fourth-century bishop, who was a distinguished early theologian of the Church and the formal patron saint of the city.

St Radegonde was a German princess who was taken prisoner of war and married to Clothaire, King of the Franks. After the murder of her brother by her husband, she fled her unhappy marriage for a religious life, to which she had always been strongly inclined – Clothaire was reputed to have said, 'I thought I married a princess, but it seems I have married a nun.' She was a great friend to the poor and sick, providing out of her funds for their care and even nursing the sick personally. Her tomb was in the church dedicated to her on the other side of the city, near the river and close to the Abbey of Saint-Croix, which she had founded and where she worked as a humble nun, having declined the leadership of the abbey in favour of her foster daughter Agnes, later St Agnes of Poitiers. There the nuns practised a rather unusually academic form of religious life, spending several hours each day in religious study and copying manuscripts – a fitting tribute to Radegonde, who herself was highly literate, having left a number of poems and letters which survive. In keeping with this, she is portrayed repeatedly in art reading a book. Her abbey was one of the very earliest religious houses for women, and distinguished by the possession of a fragment of the True Cross.[28]

Eleanor would visit those churches often, particularly on the feast days of those saints, when special services at the relevant church would be followed by an assembly or feast at the ducal court. Furthermore, both churches were stops on the route to Compostela, attracting religious tourists to Eleanor's home town. The rhythms of the church year and the pilgrim season will certainly have been strongly felt in Poitiers, a major religious centre which was also home to a major religious school of high academic repute.

Eleanor would naturally have been left behind when her father went on his numerous campaigns, but at least the major festivals of the year would be spent with him, wherever the court then was. We know she spent time at Niort, where she witnessed a charter, and at Nieuil, where a modernisation of the church was being sponsored by the family and where her mother was to be buried. She will also have been familiar with Limoges and the famous Abbey of Saint-Martial, which was probably the major centre for church music within France at the time. Aquitaine, and in particular the Abbey of Saint-Martial, was at the cutting edge of polyphonic religious music, with the scriptorium at Saint Martial apparently operating as a valuable repository for polyphonic works as they developed.[29]

Certainly, although his visits to the southern part of his lands were fairly infrequent – no more than once a year – Eleanor will also have been familiar with the lands around Bordeaux, and the palace there, known as L'Ombriere owing to its shady situation at the end of a long avenue of large trees. But it is unlikely that she visited further into Gascony than the chateau of Belin Beliet, a little to the south of Bordeaux.

Perhaps as important as the individuals who surrounded Eleanor on a regular basis was the atmosphere and culture of the court. Biographies of Eleanor tend to assert the difference of this culture, but it has proved hard to conjure this difference convincingly or to contextualise it.

The starting point must be Aquitaine's relative proximity to the Iberian Peninsula, where the Christian monarchs of León, Castile and Aragon (Portugal was not yet a kingdom) were fighting hard to regain the territories which had been lost to the Islamic invaders in the eighth century, and where about half the peninsula remained in the hands of Islamic rulers. Close proximity to the Islamic invaders would have effects on the development of local cultures.

For these Islamic invaders were patrons of learning who transformed the part of the peninsula they inhabited, ushering in advanced agriculture, huge sophisticated towns, and seventeen universities (by way of comparison, there were two universities elsewhere in Europe). Their main towns, such as Toledo, became centres of excellence for medicine, architecture, agronomy, astrology and mathematics.

There were a number of knock-on effects which are significant as far as Eleanor is concerned, but perhaps the most important concerns beauty, design and domestic comfort. The Reconquista familiarised the Iberian monarchs and their allies, such as the dukes of Aquitaine, with true palaces crammed with items of beauty: vibrantly coloured or beautifully decorated bowls, ornately carved screens, jewel-coloured tiles and rich textiles that were used far more liberally than was common in northern Europe – as wall hangings, for example. Life was, in short, conducted in surroundings of beauty, using beautiful things.

One classic example of the cultural cross fertilisation outlined above is the one tangible link between Eleanor and her grandfather William the Troubadour. At the time of her marriage, Eleanor had in her possession – possibly as a christening gift – a remarkable rock crystal vase which he had brought back from his Iberian Crusade just before her birth. The vase – still in existence in the Louvre – is a simple pear-shape carved with a 'honeycomb' pattern composed of rows of small, hollowed-out hexagons – an adornment which was not uncommon on glass vases in Persia, but is apparently unique on rock crystal. Aside from its beauty and the value ascribed to rock crystal, which was believed to be crystallised water, it was already a valuable antique when it was given to Duke William, dating probably from somewhere between the sixth and eighth centuries and probably originating in Persia. As for its provenance, it was almost certainly a gift from Emir Imād-al-dawla, the last Taifa Emir of Saragossa, known to the Christian world as Mitadolus. He had been deposed by the Almoravids in 1110, and fought the 1120 campaign alongside Duke William as an ally of Alfonso 'the Battler', King of Aragon.

Thus we see an item of beauty from Persia, valued by an Islamic invader and passed by him to a neighbour with whom he was in alliance. This is just an isolated example which we can prove – and indeed still see. Many other examples of trade and gift over the centuries leading up to Eleanor's birth and throughout her childhood will have existed, and they had brought about a situation where Aquitaine, although nominally under the power of France, partook very considerably of its closer neighbour's culture. It was seen as more ostentatious and more prodigal than other comital courts; this is reflected in the testimony of Richard the Poitevin that Eleanor was brought up in an atmosphere of luxury and beauty.[30]

Nor was the Iberian influence confined to the material, for the very troubadour culture which had become a key defining feature of the Poitevin court had some at least of its origins in Arab culture. In fact, there is a credible argument that the very term troubadour derives from the Arabic words *tarab*, meaning music or song, and *dour*, meaning home, palace or castle. Aside from this, the tunes of some of the surviving troubadour works derive from Jewish or Arabic music as well as more traditional folk tunes – or from the religious works noted at Saint Martial. Further, the structure and themes of William the Troubadour's works appear to echo pieces which came into being a little earlier in the eleventh century in Spain, performed often in Arabic or Hebrew, with a Spanish refrain.[31]

It is perhaps worth noting here that troubadour culture, while certainly a defining characteristic of the Poitevin court under Eleanor's father, was still somewhat in its infancy during Eleanor's childhood, and the association with 'courtly love' and the adoration of an unattainable lady had not yet fully developed. There had been a very intense initial flowering during the reign of her grandfather, when he and Èbles, Viscount of Ventadorn, who was also a troubadour, competed to outdo each other in display and poetry. However, thereafter the pace of development slowed somewhat. Though distinguished poets such as Cercamon and Marcabru were in attendance at William X's court, it seems that their works tend as much to the bawdy style of William the Troubadour's early efforts as they do to the courtly love ideal. Scholars now suggest that the settling of the form into the courtly mode only occurred later in the century – at about the time that the second round of noble troubadours (and trobaritzes, such as Alamanda de Castelnau, the Comtessa de Dia and Garsenda of Provence) emerged. One should not assume that Eleanor's childhood inculcated her with the traditions which the later troubadour poetry created, of the devoted love of the worthy knight for the lady far above him.[32]

The picture of Eleanor's childhood which emerges, then, far more strongly suggests a clash or melange of cultures than one single strong culture. However, that clash itself cannot but have influenced her. The Church was at the heart of all Christian society, and it appears that her upbringing will have been strongly biased towards the Church's teachings – since wherever she was taught her tutors were overwhelmingly likely to be of the priestly class, and there is strong evidence of her father's innate religiosity. At the same time, her father's conflicts with the Church and his need for reconcilement with the Church must have been major themes in her life.

She also cannot have escaped knowledge of the increasing force of the Church's argument that women (unless they emulated the Virgin Mary) were inherently sinful, 'raging volcanoes of sexual desire', tempting men to the sin of lust; or the developing corollary of that argument that women, made less rational both by their lusts and their status as 'imperfect males', required to be subjected to male authority.[33] Just as her grandfather intended, such teaching sat uneasily with the developing troubadour culture, which placed men and women on a more equal footing as to power, lust and pleasure, and offered women the possibility of power over men by dint of their virtues – without requiring them to achieve the untouchable perfection of the Madonna archetype.

Taken together with her slightly male-dominated world and the rich cross-cultural resources which fell within the Poitevin court's ambit, it seems likely that Eleanor, at the time of her accession as duchess, was likely to be a young woman with a sophisticated, if not fully developed, knowledge of the world, and with perhaps more understanding of other cultures than many of her age. But it also seems certain that she had a very much greater religious background and a more profound religious education than she has traditionally been given credit for.

3

Duchess of Aquitaine, Queen of France

Franssa Peitau e Beiriu/Aclin' a un sol seignoriu...
[France subjects Poitou and Berry/to a single jurisdiction...]
Marcabru, XXII ll 55–6

Surely 1137 was a year to which Eleanor looked back as one of the most exceptional years of a long and full existence. At the start of the year she was twelve years old – on the cusp of what was then regarded as young womanhood. The year must have seemed to promise a fair but hardly exceptional degree of interest – her father's pilgrimage and remarriage, and perhaps plans for her own marriage. But what arrived was a year of complete upheaval and change.

The first harbinger of this was the death of her father – which will certainly have hit her hard as he had been her sole parent for the last six years, and accounts suggest the kind of larger-than-life figure to be adored by his children. Aside from the personal, however, William's death was a major political event. It is often taken as read that Eleanor, as the direct heir, became Duchess of Aquitaine on his death, but it should be recalled that female succession was by no means a given, even in the south; her own grandmother's story is proof enough of that. What is more, succession of a minor was also fraught with difficulty, particularly where a country or territory was likely to require active defence – as Aquitaine did. Already the south of France was dealing with one such issue, for in 1134 Viscount Aimery of Narbonne had died in battle in Aragon, leaving only two daughters. The eldest, Ermengarde, was only about six years old, and was currently being raised by an alliance of local lords to try to hold the Count of Toulouse at bay – a far from ideal solution in a troubled region.[1]

Unsurprisingly, therefore, William's favoured troubadour, Marcabru, mourned not just for the count-duke but for the future of his lands: 'Antioch, Guyenne and Poitou, Weep for his worth and valour. Lord God in heaven, Give peace to the count's soul; And may the Lord who rose from the tomb, keep safe Poitiers and Niort.' His co-favourite Cercamon sighed to similar effect: 'Famous and courtly Gascons, you have lost your lord, this must be terrible and awful for you ... for not one of you can find a place.'[2]

As the poet suggests, the future of Poitou and Aquitaine was definitely uncertain on his death, and its future security was regarded as requiring divine intervention. But William had acted prudently in his planning, albeit for what he probably regarded as a remote contingency. First and foremost, he had done well in removing his half-brother Raymond from the equation some years before. Raymond had since 1136 been married to Constance of Antioch; his brother Henry appears to have died, and, owing to the family's tendency to breed females rather than males in recent generations, there was not an obvious male heir.[3]

However, Eleanor's tenure as duchess was far from secure. The obvious concern would be that Eleanor and Aelis would be snapped up by ambitious vassals who would then fight each other for primacy in the names of their wives – it should be recalled that this was exactly the way in which Eleanor's own family had reunited Gascony with the northern parts of Poitou/Aquitaine. This, too, William had apparently anticipated as a possibility. While the exact terms of his dispositions do not survive, the later account of them by Abbot Suger of Saint-Denis, chief adviser to the Kings of France, marries well with the facts. The story for public consumption was that William placed his daughters in the care of Louis VI ('the Fat'), King of France, giving him the power to arrange their marriages. It is said that this plan was communicated to the king before his departure and that Duke William reiterated his wishes as he lay dying. There is also an apocryphal will of the duke – apparently produced at the French court. This is to similar effect but goes a little further, not only placing them in the king's care but seeking a marriage between Eleanor and Louis' heir.[4]

One might say that Louis, as the feudal lord of Poitou and Aquitaine, would in any event have contended that the marriage of the heir would have to be approved by the king, and there was unlikely to be anyone prepared to argue this point, so for William to leave his daughters in the king's hands was in one sense little more than acknowledging the status quo. However, as already indicated, such a clear sense of feudal obligation was lacking between Aquitaine and France at this period; William himself almost certainly did not acknowledge that he had any duty to get his daughters' marriages approved by the King of France.

If William made this provision, it therefore clearly did have a significant meaning. Furthermore, even accepting some sort of feudal obligation to seek approval, if William had had a favoured candidate for the marriage of Eleanor among his own vassals or neighbours (an Angevin boy, for example) he could have indicated this preference and left the girls in the neighbour's hands for the guardian to obtain approval or not as he saw fit. Thus what William did (or is said to have done) suggests that he hoped for – and maybe even, as the false will says, suggested – a marriage link between Eleanor and Louis' son, another Louis.

There is, however, an alternative narrative, which is that William made no such provision. Certainly no genuine document evidencing it survives, and the fact that what does survive is a will demonstrated to be a forgery might be said to be suggestive. So too is the fact that Duke William apparently made absolutely no provision for his second daughter, Aelis – an odd oversight. On this analysis, what happened was not a transfer of power intended by the Duke of Aquitaine, but a covert takeover of the duchy by the King of France. Interestingly, this is how the chroniclers recorded it – that by the marriage France 'gained possession of the duchy of Aquitaine, which none of his forbears had held before him'.[5]

Whether planned and agreed to by Duke William or not, we may perhaps detect the hand of Geoffroi de Loroux, who would be likely to look favourably upon a match with a dynasty which had very good relations with the Church, both for its likely stability after the upheavals of the recent years and also for the benefits to the Church itself.[6]

That either William took this step or that his advisers acquiesced in it is itself a sign of the achievements of Louis the Fat during his reign. As indicated previously, the power and prestige of the French monarchy had sunk to a very low ebb in the preceding centuries. Louis VI was the first Capetian monarch to make significant steps in rebuilding the status of his family and crown. He, like Henry I in England, had paid considerable attention to making the royal justice system actually work – a fundamental building block in bolstering public confidence in the institution. He had also gone out of his way to align the monarchy with the power of the Church, earmarking his second and third sons, Louis and Henry, for careers in the Church, upholding it in significant disputes with his vassals and (unlike the Aquitanian dukes) going out of his way to work harmoniously with the bishops who, following the Gregorian reforms, were no longer his nominees. A further link to the Church came via his marriage to Adelaide of Maurienne, the daughter of the Count of Savoy and granddaughter of the Count of Burgundy – but also the niece of the hugely influential Guy of Vienne, Abbot of Cluny, who was later to become Pope Calixtus II. The Church repaid him with support, and in the person of Abbot Suger, a profoundly talented churchman who made his way in the world despite his origins as a serf, provided him with both a supremely industrious and clever administrator and an admiring biographer.

Suger, who left his own account of the reign of Louis VI, gives the official version, which is that the formal offer of Eleanor's hand came to Louis at the Chateau of Béthisy together with the message conveying the news of Duke William's death in May 1137. Although apparently some of his advisers urged caution, for Louis the marriage offer was plainly one which had to be accepted. His work over the course of his reign had done much to repair the position of the King of France, particularly in the north of the country. But he remained short of land, short of money, and short of southern support. Furthermore, he remained pressed, particularly by the militarily successful Norman dynasty, who had acquired the status of kings via the conquest of England and one part of which (the Empress) was now allied through marriage with the other particularly successful northern military family, the Angevins. Following a brief alliance with Geoffrey of Anjou, Louis had just reached an accommodation with the other aspirant to the English throne and Duchy of Normandy, Stephen of Blois, and the Angevin threat was therefore particularly pressing.

The marriage with Eleanor offered land, at least during her lifetime, and hopefully for her French heirs a huge boost to revenues and a key southern power bloc which was conveniently placed to threaten the Norman/Angevin troublemakers. To make it all perfect, Eleanor was just of an age for marriage, and only a few years younger than Louis' second son, Louis, who was now in his seventeenth year. Young Louis had become the heir to the throne in October 1131 following the unexpected death of the eldest son, Philippe, who died after a fall from his horse when it was startled by a pig. Young Louis' status was confirmed days later in the mode preferred by the French kings, and deriving from the Roman Emperors, by coronation as the junior king. However, his status thus far was notional; the junior king, who had willingly embraced the cloister of Saint-Denis as a child, returned there to continue his studies while his father held the reins of government firmly in his own hands. From Saint-Denis he was now summoned to receive the good news of his forthcoming marriage.

Interestingly, while Suger gives many small details of the consideration of the marriage, one critical point – practically an elephant in the room – is nowhere mentioned. The elephant is consanguinity, or technical incest. The early Church, following Roman law, had prohibited marriage between couples related within four degrees of consanguinity (with a common great-grandparent or nearer relative). In the ninth century the Church – much to the horror of noble families everywhere, who relied on close ties of affinity as part of their means of maintaining power and peace in their regions – had raised the degrees of consanguinity within which marriage was forbidden to seven (second cousins once removed and closer). This was a very wide prohibition – indeed, it has been described by a leading modern scholar as unprecedented.[7]

Strong feelings on this subject had not died down, with controversies about kinship within the prohibited degrees extremely common. Louis VI himself, for example, had repudiated his first betrothal on this ground. Yet apparently no one thought to mention that the hugely important marriage between Eleanor and Louis was uncanonical – William VI/VIII had of course married a granddaughter of Robert the Pious of France, making the putative couple second cousins once removed. There were also two further arguable links within the prohibited degrees – via William II's marriage to Adela of Normandy, and via a Burgundian link.

In any event, it seems hugely implausible that brilliant, religious, thorough Suger (or even the religiously educated Louis) on one side and the brilliant and devout Loroux on the other missed this point. Which raises the question: did they deliberately ignore it, to leave the parties a route out if necessary? Or was it felt that since the reformist Innocent II, who within two years would emphatically reaffirm the Church's position on consanguinity, would not be amenable to a request for a dispensation, the parties should just keep their heads down? It is likely that the latter is correct. The question of consanguinity was already being seen as ripe for reform, and both families had form for ignoring the restrictions when they were inconvenient – William VIII's Burgundian marriage itself, for example, and the marriage of Robert II to Ermengarde of Anjou.[8]

Whatever the case, it must sensibly be concluded that the adults concluding the deal were well aware of the point and decided to press ahead regardless. Thus within a short period of time the messengers made their way to Bordeaux, confirming that Eleanor as duchess would receive French protection in the most emphatic form – marriage to young Louis. That marriage would occur in July, and Louis would begin the journey to Eleanor's domains as soon as possible. Louis VI's enthusiasm for the marriage is amply demonstrated by this act – sending his heir so far from territory where he held sway was a risky move. Louis might be killed or, more likely, taken hostage by any of the ambitious and hostile barons whose lands lay on the way.

Within two or three weeks, the plans at the French end were complete. Louis would ride south escorted by five hundred carefully selected knights. This itself gives some indication that a degree of controversy was expected as regards the marriage; as Jane Martindale notes, this sounds more like an army prepared to deal with trouble than a wedding escort. He would be chaperoned by three of the most important men at the French court: the forty-seven-year-old Theobald 'the Great', Count of Blois-Champagne; Louis' forty-year-old cousin and seneschal, Comte Raoul 'the Brave' de Vermandois; and the invaluable Suger himself. With them came the Bishop of Chartres and the Abbot of Cluny, Peter the Venerable. As the three most influential men at the French court, relations between Theobald, Raoul and Suger were predictably less than smooth, despite Raoul's marriage to Theobald's sister Eleanore. One can imagine therefore that the journey may have been less than enjoyable. Nor was it improved by the unusual heat of that summer, which meant that much of the travelling was done by night, and that most of the provisions were melted or spoiled by the heat.[9]

Eleanor awaited Louis in the stifling summer heat of Bordeaux, sending those of her principal vassals who accepted the marriage to greet Louis and his entourage at Limoges. This was by no means all of her vassals – the perpetually troublesome Count of Angoulême was absent, for one. Why did Eleanor not greet Louis in Limoges, and thereby gain a chance to get to know him more thoroughly before the wedding, one cannot help wonder? Probably a number of reasons played into this. First, her own preparations would have required her presence. But secondly, Eleanor's security almost certainly called for it. Until she was married, she would inevitably be a target for ambitious men who sought to seize her and gain marriage by the simple expedient of rape. Those of her vassals who did not welcome the match with France would have been bound to try to scupper it by these means. That this was probably the predominant reason is reflected in the fact that the Bishop of Chartres, a friend and confidant of Geoffroi de Loroux, despatched ahead by Louis VI as an emissary to Eleanor, reported back that she was staying in the Ombrière Palace under strong guard. Nicholas Vincent has memorably described Eleanor as a 'walking title deed'; as such, she of course had to be under lock and key until ownership had been safely transferred.[10]

To modern sensibilities, this idea of an arranged marriage with so little time for preparation or meeting of the parties beforehand seems outrageously cruel. However, this is one of the many points in Eleanor's story where modern sensibilities must be put aside. Eleanor will have been brought up to expect an arranged marriage. The who and the when of the marriage may have come as a surprise – though given her age a marriage was bound to emerge in the near future – but the broad outlines of the situation must have been something for which she had been prepared throughout her childhood. In some ways there was much to be grateful for. Few teenaged girls would be able to resist some sense of delight and triumph at being chosen as a future queen. And by way of bonus, her partner, young Louis, was close in age to her – by no means a given, of course. When Henry I of England's eight-year-old daughter Matilda was despatched for her first betrothal and marriage, her partner was over twenty years her senior. On the second occasion, for contrast, her father constrained her to marry a boy twelve years younger than her, and considerably below her in rank. Eleanor, while doubtless uncomfortably aware of being traded like a valuable piece of property, could count her blessings somewhat.

By 29 June the French party had arrived at Limoges, where Louis formally laid claim to the county of Poitou and the Duchy of Aquitaine, received a number of the more compliant vassals, and joined in the celebrations of the saint's day of St Martial, the patron saint of Limoges.[11]

As Louis made his way uneventfully from Limoges to Perigeux en route to Bordeaux, the first reports of his appearance and nature will surely have made it back to Eleanor. They will have done much to raise her spirits. Louis' late elder brother Philippe had apparently been something of a yob; Louis, by contrast, having spent much of his childhood as an oblate in the Abbey of Saint-Denis, was polite, humble and tended to be studious. However, the knightly training on which his father had insisted once he succeeded to his brother's honours had counteracted any tendency towards looking like a bookworm. In his late teens, he was now tall and muscular, with rather angelic fair hair and blue eyes. Suger described him as 'a very handsome boy'.[12]

On 11 July 1137, Eleanor had her first opportunity to meet him in the flesh. Louis and his entourage arrived on the far side of the River Garonne, where they set up camp. Here he was received by Loroux, who then accompanied him back across the river for his first meeting with Eleanor in the Ombrière Palace. The pair were then able to take two weeks to get to know each other a little before the wedding, since the presence of Eleanor's vassals at the event was deemed a necessary and a number of them were somewhat tardy in putting in an appearance. In fact, even by 25 July the full complement of vassals had not arrived, and reports were coming in that some might be assembling for a show of force. The decision was therefore taken to put the matter beyond argument, and proceed with the wedding.[13]

On 25 July 1137, a Sunday, Eleanor and Louis were married in the Cathedral of St André, presumably entering by the Porte Royale, the one part of the cathedral which survives from that time. As part of the marriage ceremony Louis provided Eleanor with a temporary coronation, emphasising her new status as 'the Young Queen' by crowning her with a golden diadem to match his own. Both were then crowned as Duke and Duchess of Aquitaine by the Archbishop of Bordeaux. The description of events, as usual, is disappointingly scrappy. Suger, though a keen author, failed to cover the day at all. The author of the Chronique de Morigny is our best source, but he adopts the frustrating convention of simply telling us that it was all too splendid for words – saying instead that it would have defeated Cicero or Seneca to give an account of the richness of the celebration, the food, the company and the general pomp.[14]

So nowhere do we have that basic building block of a biography – a description of Eleanor on her wedding day. In fact, despite gallant attempts by historians and novelists to fill in the gaps over the years, the blunt truth is that there is no contemporaneous description of Eleanor at this point in her life. Such descriptions as we have of Eleanor date from her years as a grown woman, and tend to indicate that she was regarded as being extremely desirable. But the absence of the kinds of detailed descriptions of her beauty which accompanied Henry I's second wife, Adeliza of Louvain, suggest that she was maybe not of surpassing beauty. Adeliza (also known as La Belle) was actually known as 'a singular beauty', 'the fairest woman on the earth' or 'the fair maid of Brabant'. No one ever says this of Eleanor. Yet we can be fairly sure that Eleanor was even at this age an attractive girl. We know that from an early stage in their acquaintance Louis gave every sign of being hugely smitten by Eleanor – and remained so even as the marriage hit problems. While at thirteen she might not yet have reached the height of her beauty, she was very possibly a worthy heir to her legendary grandmother Dangereuse.

It is reported that Louis gave Eleanor a range of rich and wonderful gifts, but we are told nothing about them. It was perhaps the richness of the gifts, or her relief at the first positive indications that her new husband would be well suited to her, that prompted Eleanor to give Louis the precious rock crystal vase left her by her grandfather. Meanwhile, among the gift giving there was one gift that would at once have brought home to Eleanor her relative powerlessness. As his gift to Geoffroi de Loroux by way of thanks for arranging this profitable marriage – and in hopes that the local church would therefore assist him in keeping the peace in the notoriously combative duchy – Louis VI renounced any claim to lordship over the diocese of Bordeaux, and Young Louis followed him by waiving his rights of homage and fealty from new bishops, and the right to take possession of episcopal lands during a vacancy. This was a very significant concession, described by one noted historian as 'a privilege of unprecedented lavishness'. All of these rights had, of course, been at the heart of Eleanor's father's fight with the Church. Eleanor's views on this concession are not indicated in any source; she may have regarded it as a derogation from her patrimony, but equally she may well have been persuaded by Geoffroi de Loroux that it was an appropriate approach.[15]

However, there would barely have been time for a feast and gift giving, or the account of a procession through cheering crowds given by the author of the Chronique de Touraine, for on the very day of the wedding the young couple's advisers put them on the road north. News apparently suggested that Eleanor's discontented vassals were moving to stake out the roads north, perhaps with a view to capturing the young royals and negotiating terms with Louis VI. The threat must have been deemed acute, for it is hard to believe that the consummation of this vital marriage would otherwise have been put off – as the sources reliably indicate that it was. The first night Eleanor and Louis spent together was apparently at the safe refuge of Geoffrey de Rancon's castle of Taillebourg, over 60 miles north. This was a distance which could not possibly have been achieved in one day.[16] Since marriage was considered not to be complete and indissoluble until it had been consummated, a powerful reason for delay must have been required. This and the highly surprising decision to leave Bordeaux on the actual day of the marriage – days of celebration would normally have been expected – indicates that there was a serious concern for security.

For a few days after the marriage Eleanor and Louis rode north, married but not bedded, and surrounded by Louis' probably highly nervous escort and Eleanor's closest supporters and her sister. The rush north suggests that such stops as they made were informal and cursory; there was no time or appetite for a completion of the wedding ceremonies. Periodically the party will have arrived at a safe place, eaten, grabbed a few hours' sleep, and pushed on as fast as possible. On such a programme it is possible that the party may have made Taillebourg within two days.

Thus before Eleanor and Louis were put to bed together for the first time, she will have had quite an unusual opportunity to see her new husband both under formal and stressed conditions. She probably had begun to grasp that she was now married to a complex, if not confused, young man. The records of the young Louis speak with two voices. On the one hand, there are those which speak of how suited he had been to his original vocation – how he was simple, humble, devout with a highly sensitive conscience. Yet equally there is the strand which indicates a strong thread of emotional instability – a tendency to burst into tears at little provocation, or to violent bouts of temper which might then be followed by periods of inactivity and depression. Those who find this duality hard to envision may like to think of an English monarch well known to most: Henry VIII. Also a handsome younger son, Henry was originally destined for the Church, loved his wife obsessively and was prone to violent outbursts of temper, and his religious training often sat uncomfortably with his nature. Be that as it may, however promising Louis had looked as he rode towards Eleanor for their first meeting on 11 July, it is likely that by the time they were bedded at the end of the month she had begun to see that marriage to him would not be a thing of perfect romance.

This impression was almost certainly compounded by their first few nights together. Both were virgins, but Eleanor had been brought up in an environment where, alongside the Church's teaching, sexual love between adults was celebrated and approved – sometimes at the expense of convention, as in her grandfather's poetry. Louis, by contrast, had been schooled from an early age only in the hard-line approach of the Gregorian Church, seeing abstinence as the true path and sex even within marriage as a lure to sin. However enchanted he was by Eleanor's beauty and charm – and observers then and later testified that he was besotted by her – that very inclination would set alarm bells ringing in his mind. He knew, from the Church's teaching, that anything more than a dutiful approach to paying the marriage debt was a sin; lust would corrupt his understanding, and to actually enjoy sex was to glory in a sin. Marriage, and sex within marriage, should be regarded as a distasteful necessity directed only at the procreation of children. It must be eschewed on Wednesdays, Fridays, weekends and feast days. Following St Jerome, loving one's wife with too much passion was seen as the sin of adultery; sex must be performed with restraint, and it was the responsibility of the husband to hold back and to repress the excessive passions of the wife.[17] Such competing imperatives in Louis' mind can hardly have made him an ideal husband, and indeed must have tended to increase his struggles with his temper.

But there was hardly time to make any serious study of her husband; on 1 August the young couple moved on to Poitiers, the heart of Eleanor's domain, where they were met by crowds 'transported by joy' and conveyed to the comfortable living area of the Maubergeonne Tower, formerly home to the trysts of Eleanor's grandparents William IX and Dangereuse. Following about a week of celebrations, on 8 August Abbot Suger presided at a grand formal investiture of the new Count and Countess of Poitou and Duke and Duchess of Aquitaine in the Cathedral of St Pierre.[18]

Interestingly, it is from this point – at which Louis became effective master of Eleanor's lands – that the use of the title Duke of Aquitaine (which was of course historically linked to the French monarchy) becomes the main style used and predominates over that of the more meaningful title of Count of Poitou. Indeed, Louis did not even adopt the subsidiary titles Count of Poitou and Duke of Gascony.[19]

At this point it must surely have seemed to Eleanor that the end of a series of major changes, challenges and upheavals was in sight. However, in a turn which no novelist would have dared to invent, within hours a messenger reached the celebrating court: Louis VI had died in Paris on 1 August, just as Eleanor and Louis were being welcomed into Poitiers. By the time the message had reached his heir, the funeral was long past. Louis was King Louis VII, and Eleanor, still probably aged only thirteen, was not 'the Young Queen' but the Queen of France.[20]

Taking into account the plans of Suger and the departed Louis VI, this turn of events was, if not a catastrophe, at least a serious issue. Louis had known his time to be limited, but had surely hoped to shepherd his son through a few more years and imbue him with more of the statecraft he would need to stand up to the nobles whom Louis had brought to heel by the force of his own personality and acumen. Instead, a teenaged royal couple were acceding to the throne away from the centre of power, and indeed in territory which might well be regarded as hostile. It follows that, quite aside from the genuine grief which will have afflicted young Louis and (probably more so) Suger, the acclamation of the new royals was rendered a little muted by the difficult circumstances likely to be faced in the future. Indeed, it seems likely that an uprising at Orleans, attempting to establish a commune there,[21] was a reaction to the death of Louis VI. Certainly, young Louis soon had to leave Eleanor for a period while he led a force to Orleans to suppress the uprising.

There was, however, some good news: while internal problems might be looked for within France, the opportunity for external meddling by the King of England and by the German Emperor was to be much limited by succession struggles in both jurisdictions following the deaths of Henry I and Emperor Lothair II. In England, the titanic struggle between Empress Matilda and her cousin Stephen of Blois had barely begun. In Germany, meanwhile, the death of the absent Lothair II saw a power struggle between Duke Henry of Saxony and the Hohenstaufen Conrad III of Swabia, ensuring that the Empire had to focus internally for some time.

The new king and queen were therefore relatively safe (once Louis' immediate military obligations had been fulfilled) to cut short their celebrations and make their way back to Paris to observe a period of mourning for Louis VI and plan their coronation as the senior royals. Eleanor would thus become acquainted for the first time with Paris, Louis' family and the full French court.

It is unlikely that Eleanor approached Paris with the degree of anticipation or excitement which has now been traditional for many centuries in the face of its long-standing reputation as a centre of beauty, learning and culture. It was not until the thirteenth century that Paris would really become accepted as one of the pre-eminent European cities – or even take on its recognised form with the construction of Philip Augustus' famous enceinte walls and gates.[22] In fact, Eleanor might more credibly have approached it with a degree of trepidation.

Paris had been an important city under the Romans, and was adopted as the capital of the Merovingian kings, who founded the basilica of Saint-Denis and were all duly buried there. But the Carolingians who succeeded them ruled not from Paris but from Aix-La-Chapelle (Aachen), and even the early Capetians spent little time there. Nor should it be forgotten that Paris had been besieged and threatened repeatedly by the Vikings and saved only by substantial bribes. When Anna Yaroslavna, the second queen of Henry I of France, arrived in the city shortly after her own marriage in 1051, she was utterly disgusted, writing back home to her father, Yaroslav of Kiev, 'What sort of a barbaric country have you sent me to? The dwellings here are dark, the churches misshapen, and the customs appalling!'[23]

The Ile de la Cité was the principal part of Paris, but it was hardly a great advertisement for the city. The sixth-century Merovingian church of Notre-Dame occupied the east end of the island. At the other end was crowded a fairly undistinguished royal palace, the Cité Palace, which showed the effects both of the years of disuse in its lack of repair and the defensive history of the Ile in its lack of windows – ventilation being supplied instead by arrow slits. Between the two were crammed a frankly insanitary warren of houses and shops. The whole was protected by a much-degraded Roman wall. On the Right Bank, the protection was a mere wooden palisade. The Pont des Planches de Milbray and the Petit Pont, still more rickety, were regularly swept away by floods. Perhaps the high point of the city was the single stone bridge, the Grand Pont, lined with shops, which connected the Right Bank with the Ile.[24]

Considerable improvements had been made since Anna Yaroslavna's day. The new Notre-Dame had still not been begun, but the palace on the Ile de la Cité had at least been partially restored, and a church founded where Sainte-Chapelle now stands. The abbey and church of St Germain-des-Près, burial site of the Merovingian kings south of the Seine, had been rebuilt in stone and a prosperous village had grown up around it. On the Right Bank, new buildings had recently more or less ousted the farming which had proceeded hand in hand with city life. On the Left Bank, however, where urbanisation was about fifty years behind, the slopes were covered with vineyards contained in walled closes, alongside the new buildings which were gradually being built on defunct vineyards. Nor were the vineyards alone; an illustration in the later Tres Riches Heures du duc de Berry shows that from the windows of the Palais de la Cité could be seen fields in which hay was grown.

Most recently, the old Carolingian church in the northern suburb of Saint-Denis had begun to be gloriously remodelled – the close relationship between its abbot (Suger) and the royals paying dividends. Such royal investment was beginning to pay off; it is estimated that in the fifty years before Eleanor came to Paris its population had doubled, although it was still only a little over 50,000. Pictures from thirteenth- and fourteenth-century books show us a Paris which was vibrant, with traders bringing a rich variety of merchandise into the city on foot, in carts or by river. And a letter from a friend to one of our principal witnesses, John of Salisbury, whose path first crosses with that of Eleanor now, suggests that Paris had at least taken the first steps to stake its claim as a centre of gastronomy, for he speaks of Paris at the time of Eleanor's residence as a place which overflowed with an abundance of good things, fine foods and amazing wines.[25]

Nonetheless, considerable evidence of the years of attack and neglect must have been apparent to Eleanor, most of whose childhood had been spent between Poitiers and Bordeaux. The former had been a cherished capital for her family for generations, and, as has been described above, had also been the beneficiary of a rolling programme of structural investment. The latter had been a vibrant trading centre since at least Roman times, as well as the capital of the dukes of Gascony; it too therefore had the patina of affluence and modernisation upon it.[26]

However, unlike the days when Anna Yaroslavna could despair at the prospect of finding a literate companion in Paris, the pursuit of learning in the city had exploded, with the schools that were to result in the University of Paris (later the Sorbonne) crowded with international students and fascinating and dangerous theories. Poitiers may a century earlier have boasted of being the centre of cutting-edge learning in France, but its laurels were in the process of being very thoroughly taken by Paris. The left bank was thronged with an international crowd of the intellectually hungry. For the scholars, at least, Paris was the place to be. Robert d'Arbrissel of Fontevraud had studied and taught here, and more recently the romantic and intellectual hero of his time, Pierre Abelard, was enrapturing his listeners and students at the school of the old church of Notre-Dame.

In reminding the reader of the story of Abelard and Heloise, it is easy to accept without question the romantic hero status which time has given him – doubtless helped by his publication, probably in the early 1130s and shortly before Eleanor's arrival in Paris, of his and Heloise's letters. But the story only ever gained the currency it did because of Abelard's intellectual megastar status. So famous and compelling a teacher was he that students flocked to him from all over the world; it is he who is most often credited with giving the schools of Paris the boost which transformed them into Europe's foremost university. A brilliant scion of the minor nobility, Abelard's genius and intellectual arrogance had brought him to the fore at a young age, when his combative approach – the germ of what would become his dialectic teaching style – had him expelled from the Parisian classes of William of Champeaux. His response was to turn for teaching elsewhere, and within a few years he had himself begun teaching and returned to Paris. His powers were astonishing – with Aristotle's works yet to be rediscovered, Abelard had come to similar conclusions to the great man by independent analysis. Like d'Arbrissel, he was magnetic and drew crowds of followers. He appears to have accepted the popular view of himself as a star, and in his writings he accepts that he was exceptionally pleased with himself. But nemesis awaited.

In about 1115, Abelard stayed in Paris with a lay canon, one Fulbert, within the precincts of Notre-Dame. Fulbert had a niece, Heloise, who was herself a notable scholar and apparently a somewhat radical thinker. Abelard agreed to teach her privately, but quickly become involved in an affair with her and got her pregnant. The arrogance of Abelard is perhaps well demonstrated by the fact that he composed and performed songs boasting of his seduction in which he actually named Heloise. The pair were caught by Fulbert *in flagrante* and marriage was posited to Abelard as the only honourable route. Abelard was initially resistant to the idea of marrying her, as marriage would impede his career. Heloise backed him up. She placed his career first, and also held the rather shocking view that marriage for worldly advantage was no more than legalised prostitution. The pair were eventually bullied into the marriage, and Heloise gave birth to a child she called Astrolabe, after the astronomical instrument (some children of the 1960s will doubtless sympathise with this kind of 'new age' witticism). But the scandal wouldn't die, and Fulbert, perhaps thinking that Abelard's placing of Heloise in a convent for the birth denoted an intention of forcing her into the religious life, and very probably seething with resentment at the notoriety the situation had created, arranged to have Abelard not simply beaten up but actually castrated.

All unknowing, he had thereby created out of a personal catastrophe a turning point in the history of religion. Abelard became a monk at Suger's Abbey of Saint-Denis, and he forced a furiously reluctant Heloise to take the veil. After a period of depression Abelard turned his formidable powers on the teachings of the Church, building on the works of such scholars as Geoffroi du Loroux to bring into being the full-blown concept of scholasticism. He also corresponded with Heloise (whose own abilities had raised her to the position of abbess of a new foundation called the Paraclete) on theological issues, and issues of monastic order. Their letters, in which their passionate past and the demands of their new discipline twine together, became immortal.[27]

However, Abelard's dialectic approach to religion soon landed him in trouble. In the early 1120s he was denounced to Bernard of Clairvaux by the leaders of the school of Rheims – on grounds which perhaps did not fairly reflect his work. Bernard, the core of whose theology was that true knowledge of God consisted of a personal, profound experience of Jesus Christ and of his love, was a natural opponent of those like Abelard who were seeking to introduce complex dialectical reasoning into religious thinking. To Bernard, Jesus was visceral: 'honey in the mouth, song to the ear, jubilation in the heart'; to Abelard, Jesus was to be found through disciplined 'Yes or No' examination of the writings of the Church authorities. Despite support from Geoffrey of Chartres, Abelard was found to have written a heretical work, and forced to burn it and retreat for some time to a monastery that appears to have been something of a borstal for monks. But nothing could keep Abelard down for long. By the early 1130s, the Chronicle of Morigny finds him back teaching in Paris, in the celebrity of his recently published Letters and surrounded by a crowd of admiring students. Among these was John of Salisbury, who writes that at this time he was studying under Abelard and his fellow scholastic theologian Gilbert 'of Poitiers', a graduate of the cathedral school in Poitiers.[28]

By the time of Eleanor's arrival in Paris in 1137, Abelard was drawing crowds to hear his theological lessons, and legions of the brightest young men of their generation to learn from him and his associates. If he is to be believed, the audiences for his lectures were not confined to official students but also extended to noble ladies and gentlemen of the court. He was also beginning to attract scholarly controversy again – William of Mortagne asked him whether he really advocated views so directly contrary to Church teaching as those indicated in an early draft of the work that was to be called 'Theologia' and would lead to the term theology.[29]

At the same time, preachers of brilliance were thrilling Paris with a new approach to the art. Turning their backs on the traditional approach of an exposition of the liturgy for the particular point in the Church's year, such preachers as Peter Lombard, Odo of Soissons and Peter Comestor were instead concentrating on detailed analysis of single texts as a prompt to their hearers' personal morality: 'every action of Christ is a lesson for the Christian'.[30] Gilbert of Poitiers had recently completed his commentary on the Psalms, and he and others were using it as a teaching tool which combined prophecy, history and exegesis to address theological questions.[31]

Eleanor's new city was, therefore, alive with interest, even if it was still far from being a place of beauty.

It is often asserted that Eleanor carried with her to Paris's dull court the troubadour culture of the south. However, this is wrong on two fronts. While it certainly seems to have been the case that the French court was not welcoming to jongleurs and troubadours, it would be inaccurate to describe the court's culture as dull when there was considerable crossover from the Paris schools, particularly as to religious learning. Furthermore, it seems quite clear that Eleanor did not take troubadour culture with her. As the excerpts from Cercamon and Marcabru quoted above indicate, her accession and marriage were seen as the ending of the troubadour culture in Aquitaine, not as the beginning of bright new horizons in her court in Paris. Marcabru himself would take service with the King of Castile and hymn the joys and merits of the Reconquista, and Cercamon's conclusion in his lament for the Gascons suggests a similar route: 'not one of you can find a place, except with the lord Alfonso'. The troubadours, as noted earlier, would migrate to comital courts elsewhere in the south: to Ventadorn and Provence, and to Narbonne as Ermengarde of Narbonne grew older.[32]

A point which has been less concentrated upon but for which there is (marginally) more evidence is Eleanor's possible influence on the religious musical life of Paris. As noted earlier, Aquitaine appears to have been the leading source of polyphonic musical arrangements. During the latter part of the twelfth century these spread both north and south, becoming fairly common by the start of the thirteenth century. Paris was to become the leading northern source for the development of polyphony, with Leonin and Perotin composing works which are still influential today. This was happening around the time of Eleanor's years in Paris, and this development may find some link to the teachings of Gilbert of Poitiers, which emphasised the musical context of the Psalms and the importance of poetry and music as being able to inspire delight.[33]

It has been credibly suggested that Eleanor was the natural vector for the transmission of this new musical style – in other words that she brought not troubadour music but cutting-edge religious music to Paris. There are two points which may be said to turn this point from an agreeable speculation into a real probability. The first is the matching later coincidence of the first English reports of polyphony with Eleanor's move to England – to find polyphony following Eleanor once might be an accident, but twice looks like design. The second is the report that one thing which Eleanor did do on her arrival in Paris was dismiss the choirmaster of the royal chapel of St Nicholas, replacing him with her own nominee.[34]

One plus point for Eleanor, arriving in a strange world with no time to orient herself out of the limelight, was that most of the French royal court will have been about as disoriented as she was herself. The court was not a cohesive entity that could withstand the loss of Louis VI without much strain. Louis had been the definite centre point, and with him removed nobody knew quite what their place was.

There was, for example, no definite family core. Louis VII's brothers and sisters were all still children – the eldest, Henri, was just old enough to have been tonsured as a monk at Saint-Denis; brawny Robert was entering his teens; and Pierre, Constance and Philippe were in steps down to five years old. In the older generation, Louis VI had been the sole surviving male of his family, having outlived his rebellious half-brother Philippe. His sisters had married abroad.

Raoul of Vermandois, a grandson of Hugh I and Anna Yaroslavna, was thus Louis' closest relative on the paternal side; and Philippe I's chequered marital history (repudiating his first wife to run off with Bertrade de Montfort) had ensured that there was no close tie to his grandmaternal family. Raoul was a near contemporary of Louis VI, having been born in the early 1090s. He fought loyally in his cousin's interests, losing an eye at the siege of Livry in 1129, an event prompted by the prominent Garlande family's attempts to transfer a prestigious court title (Seneschal of France) as a dowry. Raoul's reward was to be appointed seneschal himself in 1131. Because of his loyalty and his close blood tie to the Crown, Raoul was also used by Louis as the glue to bind his single most powerful vassal, Theobald of Blois, to the Crown.

Theobald, son of the Crusader Etienne of Blois and his formidable wife Adela of Normandy (daughter of William the Conqueror), was another near contemporary of Louis VI, against whom he had campaigned in the early part of the latter's reign. He eventually reconciled with Louis, but with his extensive holdings (he would succeed to his uncle's holdings of Troyes and Champagne, extending the count's actual control over the latter domain considerably) and his status, he was a prickly ally. Raoul was married to Theobald's sister Eleanore in 1120, but as of the date of Eleanor's marriage in 1137 the match had yet to result in any children.

Meanwhile, although Raoul had become ever closer to Louis, Theobald had become still more powerful – and dangerous. In 1135, on the death of his uncle Henry I of England without a male heir, Theobald was approached by a powerful faction within England and urged to assume the throne. This role was in fact taken by Theobald's amiable younger brother Stephen, who had stronger ties to the English nobility, courtesy of his habitual residence in England. But Theobald remained a powerful figure on the English scene, and was paid a substantial pension by his brother for his kindness in declining a throne.

Two other powerful figures remained at the heart of the French court. One was, of course, Abbot Suger. As Louis VI's principal adviser, his knowledge of affairs was encyclopaedic and his influence legendary. His personal clout was backed by a confederacy of other elderly clerics including Bishop Jocelyn of Soissons and Bishop Alvise of Arras.[35]

Finally, there was Queen Adelaide, Louis' mother. One of the interesting things to note about Eleanor's reign as Queen of France is the contrast it presents to the queenship of the previous incumbent. As we will see, Eleanor more or less disappears from the record for several years following her marriage. Her influence over Louis can never be seen overtly and has to be inferred; and as will be considered below, the extent of that influence can probably be considered very limited. Often this is explained away by reference to the lesser status accorded to noble women and queens in the northern parts of France compared to their southern sisters, but Adelaide of Maurienne demonstrates that this simple excuse cannot stand.

Adelaide, though somewhat younger than Louis VI, was permitted by him to exercise very considerable power. In part this conformed to the older French tradition, which was a partnership in ruling, but Adelaide took it to new heights. In addition to signing some royal charters alongside her husband, she appointed ecclesiastics, made legal determinations of rights, bestowed privileges and conferred safe-conducts, all in her own name. She even, on occasion, dated her charters by her own regnal year. How this paradigm changed so rapidly and completely for Eleanor's queenship is a key question for these years. However, in terms of context and introduction it is enough to say that Adelaide, as dowager queen, was plainly more accustomed to the exercise of power than either the new king or queen, and might well have expected to exercise very considerable influence at court for years to come.[36]

Eleanor therefore faced at least four well-established operators with extensive networks at court if she cherished ambitions to be a substantial influence on her husband's reign. This alone might render it unsurprising that she seems to have gained no traction at all as a political figure in the early years of his reign.

However, there are at least three further factors at play here. Abbot Suger and his religious allies at least would have been very inimical to the exercise of influence by a woman. As discussed earlier, the views of the Church on women had become more negative and hard-line since the Gregorian reforms effectively split the priesthood off from feminine influence. Suger had apparently disapproved of the influence of Adelaide of Maurienne at Louis VI's court, but Louis VI's consent to her role effectively prevented it from being eroded in his lifetime. Once Louis VI was gone, Suger and his religious allies would doubtless have determined to ensure that there should be no repeat of this state of affairs under the new king. And here Suger had an enormous advantage. That king was a boy whom he had essentially raised and trained – for the priesthood, no less. He might not have the affection of the new king, but he had formed his religious views and drilled him to obedience. It is therefore likely that he could rely upon Louis VII to be minded, despite any physical or romantic infatuation with his new wife, to keep feminine influence out of state affairs.

Secondly, there is the factor of Eleanor herself. She was just entering in her teens – a time at which even the most intelligent can be expected to make a number of missteps, and in particular to push too hard and too obviously for their own way. She hailed from an area which was not highly respected at the French court, and in all likelihood brought with her a sizeable household of Poitevins,[37] who would raise hackles in anticipation of favouritism when benefits came to be distributed. And she created an expectation that she would seek to exert her influence because, uniquely among royal brides for centuries, she was herself an heiress with extensive lands. Eleanor therefore almost certainly created a climate of resistance simply by existing, which would only strengthen with every attempt she made to exert power.

Finally, there is the factor of Louis himself. His lack of comfort with his new status is reflected in the account by Odo of Deuil that the king continued to study at Notre-Dame as he had before his elevation, keeping the vigils each day and singing in the cathedral choir. So too is it evidenced in his record for the early years of his reign; here there is every sign that Louis was both unready for rule and at the same time wanted to show he was personally ruling rather than being a puppet of his father's ministers. While Louis was, in the longer term, to go on to become a fairly well-regarded King of France, there is no doubt that his early years as king were, to put it politely, less than distinguished. Again and again the accounts paint a picture of a young man who struggled to impose authority, and who in his attempts to appear decisive instead often acted impulsively and unwisely. Caught between the various factions which his father's personal authority and experience had held in delicate equilibrium, he rejected the equilibrium and sought to show his personal authority by acting without consensus, inclining at times to one faction and then to another. Worse than this, his own temper inclined him to act impulsively and often in an extreme fashion – and the factor of his age in following this impulse should not be overlooked. In his first years of rule, he often behaved as the untrained teenager he was on his accession.

In terms of Louis' wish to demonstrate independence from the old guard, the moves of the first few years of his reign will illustrate this, but it can also be demonstrated a step or so down from the top players, where Louis instituted many changes. Stephen de Garlande, who had returned as chancellor after his falling out with Louis VI in 1131, was again discharged from the chancellorship soon after Louis VII came to power; his successor Algrin then had a tenure of only a few years and was himself followed only briefly by Noel, Abbot of Rebais. Louis also began to introduce his own advisers. Two of them, Thierry de Galeran and Cadurc, were to figure large in the years which followed, but at this early point in the reign it is hard to pinpoint who had come to royal notice. It seems likely that Cadurc was discovered by the new royals, but the Templar Thierry de Galeran, later a prominent treasurer in the Order, had already had some role under Louis VI.[38]

Enough can be inferred from the known facts to provide a backdrop to Eleanor's experience. However, what we know of that experience in the next few years is depressingly slight. There are relatively few surviving chronicles from the France of this period, and those that do survive are predominantly those concerned with the affairs of great abbeys rather than the wider politics of the day. Eleanor is not personally mentioned in such chronicles as exist for some years. The gap cannot be satisfactorily filled by charter evidence – there are issues as to the survival rate of charters, and certainly very few remain relating to Aquitaine, meaning Eleanor's charter evidence is at best thin. At best, one can track Louis and then ascertain the probabilities for Eleanor by reference to this evidence and what little remains in the charters and chronicles.

As for Eleanor's political ambitions, we have no information. It has been asserted that Eleanor will have expected to share authority over her ancestral lands and to play a part in ruling the kingdom,[39] but there is no evidence for this. Eleanor might have hoped to eventually play as significant a role as Adelaide of Maurienne, or have some role in governing her lands, but at thirteen, and not raised to expect a role in government, still less to be queen in such short order, this actually seems unlikely. Most likely she was simply uncertain and looking to find her feet, growing into her role as queen gradually. On the evidence, it must be counted an overreach to attribute to her a plan or fixed ambitions for the future.

The evidence also suggests that Eleanor suffered a miscarriage early in her marriage (she would later confide this in St Bernard). This would mean that she likely became pregnant either on the journey back to Paris or shortly thereafter. The pregnancy and subsequent miscarriage would indubitably have taken her out of the main political currents for some time. Given her age, the unsuccessful pregnancy and Louis' own age and inclinations, there is also a good chance that the decision was taken to cease cohabiting until Eleanor was older. This was not uncommon in marriages of young nobles; in the fourteenth century Mary de Bohun would be married at twelve, with consummation necessary to secure her inheritance. But after a miscarriage she and her husband ceased to cohabit until she was eighteen and pregnancy was deemed safer. But if this sensible approach was followed, it would only tend to marginalise Eleanor further.[40]

So far as the record carries us, for the first few months of the reign little seems to have happened in this uneasy new court. We know that the court went to Bourges for the Christmas season, and it was there that Eleanor was formally crowned on December 25 as Queen of France while Louis himself, already crowned in his father's lifetime, held a formal crown wearing. Orderic Vitalis describes this as a major event, 'attended by all the nobles and middling men from all over France and Aquitaine and other regions round about'. Everything we know about it suggests that it would have seen the French court at its finest. A letter from Bernard of Clairvaux to one Sophia, a young lady who had declared her intention to pursue a religious life, contains a fascinating pen portrait of the court:

> They are clothed in purple and fine linen, but their souls are in rags. Their bodies glitter with jewels, but their lives are foul with vanity. ... Consider it wholly beneath you to borrow your appearance from the furs of animals and the work of worms, let what you have be sufficient for you ... You see women burdened rather than adorned with ornaments of gold, silver and precious

stones, and all the raiment of a court. You see them dragging long trains of most precious material behind them, stirring up clouds of dust as they go. Do not let this trouble you. They leave it all behind them when they die, but you will take your holiness with you.[41]

This lavish Christmas court at Bourges is therefore likely to have provided the venue for Eleanor's first meeting with Geoffrey of Anjou, and very possibly also his wife, the Empress, who had still not sailed to England in support of her claim to the English throne. It is unlikely that they were accompanied by their sons, however, all three of whom were still under five years of age. Some of the Anglo-Norman barons (including the Beaumont brothers Waleran, Count of Meulan and Robert, Earl of Leicester) also attended the court. This reinforces the suggestion that this Christmas court was effectively a three-line whip to all major nobles, at which promises of fealty would be expected to be given. It seems possible that it was at Bourges that the cleric Cadurc, who came from the region, first recommended himself to Louis and joined his writing office.

It was apparently shortly after this that the jockeying for place among the old guard produced a windfall for Eleanor. Suger and Theobald of Blois aligned themselves together against the queen dowager and Raoul of Vermandois. Adelaide then played into their hands by creating a substantial fuss about financial affairs – probably including her dower arrangements, but possibly also the cost of the substantial seasonal celebrations or funding for Saint-Denis. It is not beyond the bounds of possibility that the affluence of Eleanor, with her own duchy, created a certain amount of heart-burning for the older woman. Some writers suggest that despite Eleanor's own resources formal provision was made for her by the French Crown by the expedient of taking revenues directly from Adelaide. Whatever the reason, the raising of this issue annoyed Louis very much, and Suger used this annoyance to engineer the effective dismissals from court in early 1138 of both Adelaide and Raoul.[42]

Raoul was to return and regain influence, but Adelaide never did come back to court for any length of time or return to any position of power. Retreating to her dower lands near Compiegne, she swiftly remarried Matthew de Montmorency, the possessor of lands that marched usefully with her own. Thus, Eleanor's exposure to her mother in law was fairly limited, and the dominant feature of her early years at the French court was not, as has often been suggested, an attempt to wrest Louis from the influence of his beloved mother.[43]

The year of 1138 in fact gave three main points of interest in terms of analysing Louis as a monarch and Eleanor's role as queen. The first was Louis' intervention in the election of the new Archbishop of Reims in January 1138. This was an early indication that despite his training, and despite the grant to the clergy of Aquitaine, Louis intended to take a hard line in the debate about royal rights over episcopal appointments.[44] It seems implausible that Abbot Suger would have approved this stance, so this provides another indication of Louis trying to take his own line. It also seems an implausible issue for Eleanor to advocate, given both her close ties to the Church and the prior experience of her father's unsuccessful dispute.

The second point is that despite this area of friction with the Church, for a period following the fall of Adelaide and Raoul the Suger/Blois alliance was in ascendancy. In the spring of 1138 they cooperated to arrange a joint visit between Louis and Theobald to northern Burgundy, in particular to Auxerre and Langres where a disputed episcopal election was in progress. Again Louis sought to impose his choice on the diocese (unsuccessfully), prompting Bernard of Clairvaux, who wanted his own secretary elected, to raise his first complaint of Louis:

> How sorry I am to hear things of you so contrary to the fair promise of your early days! But how much more bitter would be the sorrow of the Church, after having tasted first of such great joys, if she were to be deprived (which God forbid,) of the glad hope of having a shield in your good dispositions... I would rather die than see a king of such fair reputation and of even better hopes, attempt to oppose the will of god and stir up against himself the wrath of the supreme Judge![45]

Meanwhile, Aquitaine was apparently in Louis' mind – as it must have been in Eleanor's as the first anniversary of her exile approached. While a full visit to the province was not planned, in May Louis and Eleanor ventured as far as Le-Puy-en-Velay, near the borders of Aquitaine, to the shrine of Our Lady. This visit represented a considerable departure from the habits of recent French kings, who had tended to confine themselves to a northern round of visits, but also reflected the reality of France's expanded horizons courtesy of Eleanor's inheritance. It may also reflect a shared interest in things religious forming common ground between Eleanor and her new husband. But it also offered an opportunity for Louis to take the homage of the nobility of the region, emphasising his power.[46]

However, more political attention to the area was soon to prove necessary, and this raises the third and greatest point of interest in the year. In early autumn came a rebellion of the people of Eleanor's own hometown of Poitiers, and their attempt to establish a commune, as the Orleanais had sought to do the previous summer. Suger has left a fairly good account of the event, towards the end of the part of the account of Louis' reign that he is thought to have personally authored. From him we know that Louis and the Bishop of Soissons set off to re-establish control, with Suger following a little behind. From him too we know that Louis sought military support from Theobald of Blois, and was refused, perhaps because the Angevins had flared into life again in Normandy and England. Whatever the reason, this provided the first cloud over Louis' relationship with his premier vassal.

As Suger tells it, Louis proceeded with a force of two hundred knights and an array of siege engines to a position outside the walls of Poitiers, which the rebels had surmounted with wooden palisades. The sight overawed the rebels, and they immediately sought peace. Louis, still enraged with them and denied his show of force, dissolved the commune and ordered one hundred child hostages from the town's leading citizens. This was hardly an extraordinary measure – similar demands would be made by a number of English kings in England, including Stephen, Henry II, John and Edward I. However, in the absence of any attested violence it may have been somewhat of an overreaction. Suger certainly seems to have thought so on his arrival, and he claims that, touched by the pleas of the distraught parents, he successfully interceded for the Poitevins.[47]

Often it is asserted that this intervention by Louis was planned, superintended or directed by Eleanor. However, when one scrutinises Suger's eyewitness account and such other contemporaneous accounts as survive, nowhere is it suggested that Eleanor – a natural mediatrix for her own people – even formed part of the party. It would seem that Louis, again seeking to establish his control in his own right, deliberately chose to cut Eleanor out of the circle of influence in this key incident relating to her own duchy. Her absence might have been due to her pregnancy and miscarriage at around this time, but pregnancy would be no particular reason to avoid travel of this distance. This episode therefore provides an early indication of Eleanor's exclusion from the decision-making circle.[48]

This is supported by an analysis of the surviving charters issued by Eleanor and Louis relating to Aquitaine in this period of their marriage, which provides strong indications that Eleanor, while not completely deprived of a role in Aquitaine, wielded no substantive power over the duchy. Essentially, she was used as 'window dressing' by her husband when her involvement was deemed appropriate or useful. Thus, four charters issued by Eleanor alone in these years survive. All of these related to Aquitaine – but all were actually confirmations of earlier charters by Louis. The decision in each case had been made by him, and Eleanor's charter simply provided an extra layer of approval. Twelve charters were issued jointly, by Louis with Eleanor's consent or with her agreement or at her request (the wordings vary). All of these concern religious benefactions to the great religious houses historically supported by her family such as Saint-Maixent and Notre-Dame de Saintes.[49]

As such, these were all affairs likely to be considered very suitable by those (like Louis and Suger) adopting the modern Church views as to a woman's role. In the case of Notre-Dame, the suitability was bolstered further by the fact that the abbess was her aunt. This made the business both domestic and religious, and thus the perfect example of a female sphere of influence. In this charter Eleanor's donations are witnessed and approved by Aelis, reinforcing the family aspect of the donation. By contrast, all the surviving charters relating to Aquitaine from this period pertaining to politics, law or justice were issued by Louis alone, without any reference to Eleanor.[50]

In this respect, Marie Hivergneaux's conclusion that Eleanor's role in Aquitaine was 'far from negligible' appears to be a considerable overstatement. It is true that we are forced to draw conclusions from the surviving charters only, and cannot tell how many more existed, or how representative the survivors are; but it is interesting to note that the evidence of the surviving charters is echoed in the lament of Eleanor's father's favourite troubadour, Marcabru: 'France subjects Poitou and Berry to a single jurisdiction.'[51]

But what is particularly interesting about the uprising in Poitiers is that this was actually a perfect opportunity to present Eleanor in a suitable but influential role – interceding with her powerful husband for mercy as Queen Esther did in the Bible. This paradigm was much used by medieval monarchs to bolster a wife's perceived influence in an acceptable way. Often the intercessions were for individual favours, benefices or pardons, but the approach was also very thoroughly used by Edward III in Queen Philippa's intercession for the burghers of Calais.[52] That Eleanor was not presented in this role suggests that she exercised little influence even over Aquitaine, and furthermore that there was a deliberate policy in place – perhaps as a reaction to the considerable influence of Adelaide of Maurienne – to actively portray Eleanor as being without influence.

This appearance might not represent the reality behind closed doors, of course. Edward I was later to pursue a similar policy to defuse the hostility to powerful foreign queens engendered by his mother, Eleanor of Provence, but as far as we can tell from the limited surviving evidence it appears that Eleanor of Castile was nonetheless embedded in his central group of policy makers.[53] Whether this was also the case for Eleanor of Aquitaine is even harder to tell, given the paucity of the evidence. However, the earliest evidence we have suggests on its face that Eleanor was very deliberately kept out of the limelight and out of overt exercise of power. At this stage one might say that doing so was perhaps only to be expected – in 1138 Eleanor was still only fourteen. She may well have been unwell. She could have been busy with her education. However, the precedent which was being established would itself stand in the way of her later assertion of authority.

Consistent with this, Louis' next move was also within Eleanor's domains, was once more conducted without her and was again designed to portray him as a powerful ruler. Perhaps inspired by the Poitevin rebellion, a number of troublesome barons had also created trouble. One in particular, William de Lezay, had taken over the ducal chateau of Talmont, where the main ducal stables and mews was situated, including some precious gyrfalcons. Gyrfalcons were essentially seen as a royal bird, with people of lesser rank forbidden to own them – hence their annexation carried with it a symbolic challenge to Louis. Most of the troublemakers backed down in the light of events at Poitiers, but de Lezay did not, so Louis took his troops to Talmont where, following a skirmish with de Lezay's men, the castle was retaken. Louis himself was involved in punishing some of the rebels, cutting off the feet of at least one. Richard recounts with ghoulish enjoyment that Louis' youth and lack of muscular development meant that he took more than one stroke to accomplish the mutilation. The town was put to the torch, and de Lezay is inferred to have perished in the inferno.[54]

On his return to Paris, Louis seems to have reviewed his position – with interesting effects. Suger and Theobald of Blois fell away from prominence. Theobald's lack of assistance was not forgotten, nor Suger's association with him, or Suger's tendency to second-guess Louis – as he had done at Poitiers. Suger remained an adviser, and indeed would later become Louis' primary adviser again, but he never regained quite the eminence he enjoyed under Louis VI or in this first year of Louis VII's reign. Meanwhile, Adelaide's husband was appointed Constable of France – a partial rehabilitation for her, though there are no reports of her returning to court. More significantly, Raoul de Vermandois returned to court and was swiftly reappointed seneschal.[55]

This was not, however, to say that Theobald of Blois fell totally out of favour. Much of the next year, 1139, would be occupied with the English question, with the Empress commencing operations against Theobald's brother Stephen. At this time Louis' support for the family of Blois was clearly indicated by his agreement, in summer 1139, to marry his sister Constance to Stephen's son and heir-apparent, Eustace – an agreement which was effected by the marriage in 1140 and the investiture of Eustace as Duke of Normandy in early 1141. The year 1140 itself finished in Orleans, where what seems to have been a fairly full Christmas court assembled, and among those attending was a good Aquitanian contingent: Geoffroi de Loroux, Geoffrey de Rancon, Guillame de Mauzé and a number of knights in the train of the greater lords. Most of these were lords to whom Louis had given significant roles in the governance of Aquitaine.[56]

The years of the early 1140s were dominated by three themes, all of which had their origins in the first years of Louis' reign, and all of which offer some material for inference as to Eleanor's role.

The first theme was Louis' desire to control episcopal appointments, or at least to retain some rights as to investiture, a desire which conflicted with the Church's determination to take such matters out of the hold of temporal powers. Two such quarrels had, as we have seen, sprung up in the first couple of years of his reign. In both cases he had ultimately been forced to back down and had incurred significant odium from the Church, with which his father had maintained such a good relationship. His determination on this point was not to be shifted, however. The next flare-up occurred within Eleanor's lands – indeed in Poitiers itself. In 1140, the longstanding bishop William Adelme died and the canons elected an abbot named Grimoard without seeking Louis' consent and without offering him the customary opportunity to invest the bishop first. There was a question as to whether this was covered by the approval given by Louis VI of the rights of the churches of the archdiocese of Bordeaux, and Louis, standing up for his traditional rights, barred the new bishop from entering Poitiers and summoned Geoffroi de Loroux, who had installed the bishop, to appear before him in the King's Court.

Unsurprisingly, this brought protests from Bernard of Clairvaux and Pope Innocent, who both weighed into the dispute with hard-hitting letters upholding Geoffroi's position. 'What,' asked Bernard, 'has this poor man done that is wrong?' Louis was on the point of backing down, but Grimoald then tactfully died and the vacancy remained open for some time. This is yet another dispute where Eleanor is absent, though it did concern her duchy and involved a serious confrontation with her father's and her own mentor, Geoffroi. Certainly, Louis does not seem to have invoked her name by way of support; and this is consistent with his policy of keeping her interventions to uncontroversial subjects. But if, as seems particularly likely in this specific case, Eleanor was against the course taken by Louis, there is also no sign of her influence being effective.[57]

Can Eleanor's influence nonetheless be inferred in Louis' stance on relations with the Church? Some commentators suggest that her family's history of opposition to the Church, *inter alia* on episcopal appointments, suggests that she may have been the driving force behind this approach. This seems unlikely. The early interventions outside Aquitaine would have put in place a more favourable regime outside Aquitaine than pertained under Louis VI's dispensation within it; there would be no reason for Eleanor to want this. Also, while we cannot know, it seems unlikely that if Eleanor was exercising such power as to be the initiator of this line of action she would appear nowhere in the record, as is in fact the case. It also seems unlikely that Eleanor, who had seen her father brought down by the Church – and effectively over the same debate – would have encouraged Louis to pick this fight. She will surely have appreciated better than Louis that whatever the practices of the past, this was a fight which the modern Church would not permit him to win, and which could only damage his prestige.

So when we see Louis pursuing this policy again in early 1141, this time in relation to the bishopric of Bourges, which he wanted for his clerical servant Cadurc, whom he had recently promoted to the role of royal chancellor, it should probably be seen as a continuation of an initiative of Louis' own making, perhaps encouraged by Cadurc himself, who is described by Bernard of Clairvaux's biographer as a somewhat combative man. Bourges, perhaps the most geographically central bishopric in France, was also key politically, exercising as it did authority over practically the whole of the Massif Central. Traditionally its bishops had been approved by the Crown. Naturally Louis would want a man of proven loyalty in this strategic location, and Cadurc had apparently proven himself to Louis since the start of the reign. Against him in the lists was Pierre de la Châtre, nephew or cousin of Cardinal de la Châtre, Pope Innocent's own chancellor. Louis, however, maintained his right to nominate the bishop. Perhaps unsurprisingly, the canons of Bourges chose to dither over this delicate decision, and Pierre de la Châtre set off to Innocent to plead his case.[58]

In the interim, the burning questions of theology which had been enlivening conversation in Paris returned to the fore. In the late 1130s, Abelard had published most of his main works, including the famous 'History of my Calamities' and his 'Ethics'. Unsurprisingly he continued to have enemies, and in late 1139 and early 1140 William of St Thierry and Thomas of Morigny had denounced Abelard to Bernard of Clairvaux and the Bishop of Chartres. Apparently on the advice of a number of 'great men', including Suger himself, Bernard turned his attention to Abelard and discerned heresy.

In particular, Bernard, who was an extreme follower of simple monastic discipline, saw Abelard's analytical questioning approach as potentially confusing to the faithful and as tending to distract them onto unnecessary elaborations and queries which might shake their faith. Joseph McCabe says of Bernard: 'To him faith was the soul's first duty; ... To reason, to ask a question, was honestly incomprehensible and abhorrent to him.' To Bernard and his followers, he stood for spirituality against the destructive forces of rationalism.[59] He preached fervently against Abelard in late 1140, and meetings between the two failed to put the matter to rest.

The stage was set for a debate between the two religious stars of their day, and it was scheduled to take place in front of Louis and Eleanor at a church council in Sens in June 1141. Abelard, the skilled dialectician and debater, anticipated victory, but in this he was outmanoeuvred by Bernard, who arranged for all the bishops to sign up to a denunciation of Abelard ahead of time, which he then disclosed to stunning effect in public. Abelard, now old and broken in health, was unable to respond. The account of events has distinct echoes of Eleanor's father's final encounter with Bernard, and must have been traumatic for her to watch.

However, there was a distinction that would prove of significance in Eleanor's story. At the council, despite the bishops' condemnation, Abelard was defended with some spirit (indeed Bernard categorised it as aggression) by a fifty-year-old lawyer-priest called Hyacinth Bobone. A diplomat close to the papacy, he is generally thought to have studied under and been influenced by Abelard's approach to theology. Hyacinth insisted that Abelard should be allowed to appeal to the Pope, and with other supporters of Abelard (including one Berengar of Poitiers) helped to compile a dossier in defence of the great man, which Abelard presumably took with him when he commenced a journey to Rome shortly thereafter. The efforts were bootless, however. Abelard's health forced him to stop at Cluny, while Bernard's own dossier and representatives preceded him. Abelard was excommunicated just a month later, and, like Eleanor's father, died a few months after his defeat at Bernard's hands. Eleanor, and Louis too, had been given another demonstration of the force with which the Church under Innocent II would defend orthodoxy.[60]

But the evidence suggests that Louis was not moved by this display of Church force. During the prosecution, one of the places which continued to support Abelard was the school of Chartres, headed up by Gilbert of Poitiers. As noted above, this graduate of the Poitiers cathedral school had espoused the scholastic approach to theology and had become one of the most popular lecturers in Paris. It is therefore interesting to find that at exactly the time when Gilbert was highly controversially advocating the withdrawal of the excommunication against Abelard, he should be uncontroversially installed as the new bishop in Poitiers. Of course, as a distinguished teacher and native of Poitiers he was likely to be acceptable to the local canons. However, the absence of any contrary nomination by Louis this time around suggests that he too approved of

Gilbert – whether because he was controversial, or because he had heard him teach, or possibly on this occasion through some intercession by Eleanor. No direct link to Eleanor can be made, of course, but given his connection to her place of birth and her putative school, it is likely that if Eleanor sought teaching about the theological and intellectual debates of the time she sought it from Gilbert, who was certainly teaching in Paris in 1140.

On this point, is perhaps worthy of note that a much later story about Eleanor, in the Anecdotes of Stephen of Bourbon in the middle years of the thirteenth century, suggests a closeness between Eleanor and Gilbert. In the context of that time, when Eleanor's reputation was coming under threat, the story runs that she had propositioned Gilbert at the Council of Sens and he had (of course) refused her.[61] While this story is inherently unlikely, it may well reflect an oral tradition of a closeness between Eleanor and Gilbert. Certainly Eleanor's advocacy for the advancement of a man who was her townsman, her possible teacher and an opponent of Bernard of Clairvaux seems a distinct possibility.

This is perhaps reinforced when one considers the evidence from Chartres Cathedral. The jamb statues there, which date to this period, are very unusual, particularly in that they include no fewer than seven female figures – in contrast to the lack of similar figures in other sculptural programmes of the period (for instance at Vézelay or St Trophime in Arles). What is more, those figures are dressed in what was then the height of current fashion, with tight, figure-hugging draped clothes, meticulous long braids and intriguing smiles. At least one modern scholar has seen – particularly in the context of later similar representations in Angevin churches – grounds to deduce Eleanor's hand in the planning of this series in a location which had a history of patronage from her family. To this is added recent work which positively identifies Eleanor as a patron of the famous windows of Chartres made later, in conjunction with Henry II. An identification of Eleanor with one of the figures – variously identified as the Queen of Sheba or (more plausibly) Queen Esther – has also been made.[62] If Eleanor was indeed visiting Chartres in connection with the works there it would have provided further opportunities for her and Louis to converse with Gilbert, head of the School of Chartres, and for them to reach a consensus as to his suitability for the vacant see at Poitiers.

Meanwhile, Louis fell into further troubles elsewhere. The first of these is the action of his which is often deemed the most likely to suggest influence by Eleanor: in summer of 1141, Louis set off on a campaign to take the city and county of Toulouse from its incumbent, Alphonse Jourdain.[63] It will be recalled that Eleanor's grandmother Philippa had been the direct heir to Toulouse and that she and William the Troubadour had even briefly held it at the turn of the century. It is conventionally asserted, therefore, that Louis's attempt to invoke Eleanor's hereditary rights came at her insistence, and this fact is used to leverage an argument that Eleanor was the moving hand behind most of Louis' actions during this period. However, since the general idea of Eleanor as a strong influence on Louis can, on closer examination of the facts, be fairly convincingly rejected, we should consider whether the idea of her initiating the Toulouse campaign should also be treated with caution.

Overall, there are certainly grounds for scepticism. In the first place. Eleanor's own father and grandfather seem to have effectively abandoned their claims to Toulouse; it was not, therefore, a question of renewing a very active claim. In the second place, the decision to attack Toulouse seems to have been taken fairly suddenly, following the public relations disasters of the repeated interventions in episcopal elections. A good news story in relation to Louis' temporal power might well be seen as a useful counterweight to a bad news story on his religious role. In the third place – and importantly – acquiring Toulouse would be of enormous benefit to Louis; Toulouse was a key link to the trade on the Garonne, which was the most effective route between the Mediterranean and the Atlantic seaboard. Being overlord of both areas would provide a very substantial boost to revenues – always an issue for Louis with his limited landholding.[64]

Finally, there was a solid political motive that was purely French: at the very least, challenging Alphonse-Jourdain might encourage him to acknowledge Louis' overlordship, which he had not done thus far, and would tend to keep his ambitions in check; this was vital as Alphonse-Jourdain appears to have essentially taken control of the city of Narbonne, with its heiress, Ermengarde, his effective hostage.[65] In the greater scheme, then, this move should probably not be seen as evidence of Eleanor exercising a huge amount of influence. She may well have provided the initial idea, and she would almost certainly have supported it, but the plan should probably be seen as quite as much Louis' creature as hers.

In any event, Louis and Eleanor moved to Poitiers as he assembled his men and materiel for the campaign. Crucially,

Theobald of Blois again refused to assist Louis, thereby falling yet further in the young king's esteem. By late June, Louis had moved on Toulouse, leaving Eleanor behind in her old home, for on 21 June he is recorded outside the walls of Toulouse. However, Alphonse-Jourdain seems to have had sources of information, for he had reached Toulouse first and fortified it against attack. Faced with a very marginal campaign, Louis backed off. Yet the price Louis exacted may actually have been what he was playing for all along – Alphonse-Jourdain did acknowledge his overlordship, and did homage to him. On one level this may therefore be seen as both a qualified win and the first sign of the political subtlety Louis was later to demonstrate.[66]

Moving back into Gascony, Louis rendezvoused with Eleanor. As part of a summer spent in her domains, they paid a visit to her mother's tomb at l'Abbaye de Saint-Vincent at Nieul-sur-l'Autise, a little outside Niort – one of the locations posited as a possible site of Eleanor's own birth. It was on this site and at this time that one of Eleanor's rare exercises of power in these years is recorded – Louis, 'with the assent and at the request of Queen Eleanor at our side', made the abbey a royal abbey. The development of the abbey buildings at this period suggests that Eleanor and Louis also backed up the charter with solid financial support. At the same time, Louis made decisions in a number of legal disputes referred to him in his role as Duke of Aquitaine, including the question of succession to the lordship of Limoges, where Eleanor's former stepmother-elect Emma of Limoges was passed over by Louis in favour of her nephews. Eleanor's name appears nowhere in these important decisions about her vassals. Perhaps some ballast was added to the arguments against female succession in Limoges by the state of affairs not just in Aquitaine, where Eleanor was apparently exercising no power, but also in Narbonne, where the Count of Toulouse's takeover was, in late 1141, to result in his forcing Ermengarde – probably twelve and only just of canonical age for marriage – to marry him and sign a 'donation' giving him 'Narbonne and all that belongs to it, entirely'.[67]

This period, while a low point in Louis' monarchy, nonetheless marks perhaps the very limited high watermark of Eleanor's influence with him, for the next event to come to the fore genuinely provides some evidence of her involvement. By the time of the royal party's return from Aquitaine, Raoul de Vermandois had become romantically involved with Eleanor's sister Aelis.

Traditionally – and even in the sources closest to the period[68] – the relationship at the heart of the controversy which was to follow is depicted as a touching romance. A closer examination makes this story hard to accept entirely uncritically. Raoul (dismissed by John of Salisbury as one 'dominated by lust') was now approaching fifty years of age; Aelis was probably only fifteen years old and had been growing up effectively in the same household. The words 'grooming' and 'quasi-incest' spring to modern minds. While those modern sensibilities may be misplaced, the age gap and the circumstances are at best unattractive. However, at the same time, it seems likely that the reports have at least an element of truth and there was a real attraction between the two. Raoul's attraction to the youthful and probably beautiful Aelis is obvious, and hers to the dashing father figure who had been close to the sisters since their arrival in a strange land is scarcely harder to comprehend.

However, for Raoul – and Louis – the affair also had considerable political overtones. Indeed, those overtones are so strong that one is entitled to doubt whether the affair would ever have seen the light of day had it not been in the interests of both men. From Raoul's perspective, Aelis of course was also an heiress, and while she did not have a direct claim to Aquitaine, her husband would be well placed to acquire a position as de facto ruler under Louis there. What is more, a marriage to Louis' queen's sister would cement his position at the heart of the regime – and put his heirs in pole position to inherit Aquitaine if Louis and Eleanor failed to have an heir.

For both, too, the affair offered an opportunity to mark the apparent political eclipse of Theobald of Blois, the brother of Raoul's wife. Theobald had long been Raoul's main rival for influence at court. For Louis, Theobald had now repeatedly blotted his copybook in refusing to bring military assistance in Poitiers and then in Toulouse; what is more, his family did not at the moment require to be kept sweet in the context of England, for 1141 marked the high point of the Empress's long campaign against Stephen of Blois: in February 1141 his army had been routed by hers at Lincoln, and he was to remain her prisoner for most of the rest of the year.

Thus, while traditionally fingers have been pointed at Eleanor as the cause of Louis' support for his cousin, and this has been echoed in much recent scholarship, Louis' own motivations to reward Raoul and score points off Theobald cannot be excluded as causes in themselves. Another fact which seems to suggest that that dispute was not one dominated by romance and fuelled by Eleanor's support for her sister is that while Aelis was to prove notably fertile, producing three children in under five years, her first child by Raoul does not appear to have been conceived until after they were married. Despite the publicity, then, this was no shotgun wedding.[69]

So, towards the end of 1141 three bishops were convened to decide on the legality of the marriage of Raoul and Eleanore. The Bishop of Noyon was Raoul's local bishop – the bishopric of Noyon had previously been based at Vermandois itself. He was also Raoul's younger brother. The other two bishops were those of Laon and Senlis. The former's diocese also fell within Raoul's county of Vermandois and had been the gift of Raoul's mother, and its bishop was pressed for money to fund the building of two abbeys he had founded. The latter's diocese was within Louis' Ile de France territory. It may therefore be imagined that this was not the most impartial tribunal that could have been assembled. However, Church law, as fiercely defended by the incumbent Pope, was with them; Raoul and Eleanore were in fact related within seven degrees of consanguinity, there having been a Vermandois marriage five generations before. The panel declared the marriage invalid, and Raoul and Aelis were reportedly married in Eleanor's presence.[70]

Theobald of Blois was not minded to take this insult to his sister without due protest. He despatched envoys to the Pope seeking to overturn the panel's findings – and the dispute became live just as the Bourges dispute revivified.

Meanwhile, Pierre de-le-Châtre had reached Rome and had been consecrated personally by the Pope. The Church authorities had so far kept the gloves on in their dealings with Louis, but now they hit back firmly. Excoriating letters were despatched – and published. 'This King,' said the Pope, 'is a child in need of education. We must teach him to drop his bad habits.' For good measure, the Pope declared Cadurc unworthy to hold any benefice. An enraged Louis refused to give in, swearing a public oath that as long as he lived the new bishop would not enter Bourges. And Theobald of Blois was happy, given his own dispute with Louis, to offer Pierre a home in his lands.[71]

While Louis' intemperate response was winging its way to the papacy, the Pope's envoy in the matter of the Vermandois marriage arrived, convened a council at Lagny (perhaps significantly in

Theobald's lands) and in June 1142 duly declared Raoul still married to Eleanore. In the face of Raoul's refusal to separate from Aelis, the legate excommunicated him, Aelis and the bishops who had sanctioned their marriage.[72]

Within weeks, the final spark was set to the detonator. Letters arrived from Pope Innocent, exercising the papal nuclear option of putting Louis under interdict. Given the consequences of this decision, it was bound to provoke criticism of Louis and invite pressure on him. For a man raised to be a priest, it would also be a terrible personal punishment – and it was one which was to last for the best part of three years.

The immediate result was to cause Louis to lash out at the opponent within his reach: Theobald. He had now offended Louis repeatedly, and he was no longer the formidable opponent he had once been. While the Blois clan was not quite at its lowest ebb – Stephen had been released in November 1141 – Theobald was still hard pressed in his attempts to hold Normandy against the Angevins, and he would get no help from Stephen, who had enough to do to try to get some vestige of authority re-established in England. In summer 1142, Louis set out to vent his frustrations on Theobald by an invasion of Champagne. This was to give rise to one of the defining events of Louis' early reign.

Louis' first main target was the town of Vitry, situated on the banks of the River Marne. Louis' army took the simple step of pillaging and burning the unguarded lower town. One fire linked to another, and in the summer heat the whole town, and even the high chateau, was soon ablaze. Over a thousand people – a third of the town's population – escaping from the brutal pillage sought the traditional refuge in the church and were burnt alive when the fire, now out of control, consumed the church also. The town is still known as Vitry-le-Brulé in memory of the events of summer 1142. While this was a devastating blow against Theobald, who was reviled by his people for his failure to provide the protection expected of an overlord, it was an equal blow to Louis as it formed another ghastly offence against the Church.[73]

Louis was reported to be overcome by tears at the sight of the burning church. However, in an interesting hallmark of his stubbornness, he was not so overcome as to give up his campaign, and further devastation of the surrounding lands brought Theobald to the negotiating table. It was agreed that he would try to persuade the Pope to lift the interdict against Raoul and Aelis. A temporary lifting of the sanction was obtained, but the papacy, encouraged by Bernard of Clairvaux, revived the excommunication as soon as Theobald was restored in his lands, and the conflict dragged on, with Louis complicating the matter with disputes as to the proposed marriages for Theobald's children, which he condemned as consanguineous (largely because he felt they evidenced an alliance of hostile nobles against him). Meanwhile, Louis refused to allow episcopal vacancies to be filled and took the revenues of the dioceses for himself. Bernard of Clairvaux, acting for the papacy, excoriated Louis' approach to consanguinity 'when it is common knowledge that he is himself living with a woman who is kin to him in the third degree'.[74]

Following the death of Innocent in late 1143 and the installation of the more moderate Pope Celestine II, a council was convened at Corbeil in spring 1144 to try to bring about peace between Louis, Theobald and the papacy. An account of the conference, which appears to derive from St Bernard himself, records that Eleanor herself was present – and that for the first time she made her presence felt. As St Bernard's biography tells it, Louis was inclined for peace and was prepared to sign up to a deal which involved the excommunication against him being lifted but that against Raoul and Aelis being maintained. Eleanor, however, spoke out in favour of the peace being extended to the pair. While the biographer suggests this discloses her as the evil genius behind the whole affair, this is a logical leap. All Eleanor was doing was standing up for her sister, who on any analysis was one of the least causatively significant players involved, and still very young. But her intervention can certainly be seen to evidence the closeness and loyalty which she felt for her sister – and also her willingness to take a different course from Louis.[75]

Regardless, her intervention brought down on her the full force of Bernard's advocacy, leading to a fascinating exchange. He berated her and adjured her not to put an obstacle in the way of the welfare of her country. The force of his personality seems, as with her father and Abelard, to have provoked an extreme reaction – Eleanor is said to have confided in him about her grief that she had yet to bear a child apart from the single early miscarriage. As a quid pro quo for submission, Bernard promised solemnly to pray for her union with the king to be blessed. The deal was then concluded in principle, with the clerks left to hammer out the final terms. Louis' excommunication was lifted, and Raoul, at least, was left excommunicate. Since Aelis appears to have continued to cohabit with Raoul – their second child was born the next year – it seems likely that the sentence remained in force against her, too, and Eleanor's intercession was unsuccessful.

Eleanor's first emergence from the shadows since her marriage, now about twenty years old, provides a good point at which to pause and try to assess something of the relationship between Eleanor and Louis during these years. Very little can be said for a certainty, but the indications are that the marriage never developed into a particularly close one despite Louis' initial infatuation, and that by 1144 there was already considerable friction on more than one front.

As considered above, there are some hints in the events of the years which followed the marriage – and particular in the types of steps taken by Louis (the claim to Toulouse and support of Aelis' marriage in particular) that Eleanor was exercising influence; and some writers have sought to infer from that a role for Eleanor as the power behind the throne. But close examination turns up no clear evidence of Eleanor's influence, and the actual steps taken by Louis are usually at least equally explicable by reference to his own agenda. Certainly the evidence is clear that Eleanor was prevented from exercising any real power. It is therefore tempting to conclude that Eleanor was not at all influential over Louis.

Only in the documents of two key witnesses – the Pope and St Bernard – are there possible indications that contemporaries suspected Louis of being influenced by Eleanor. Some biographers refer to a papal letter in the context of the Bourges dispute in which it is said that Innocent voiced the suspicion that Eleanor was the prime mover. However, this is by reference to the chronicler Guillame of Nangis, who wrote at the end of the thirteenth century when Eleanor's reputation was under attack. There is no other support for this; Innocent's surviving letters to Louis contain no such suggestions. Other writers refer to Bernard of Clairvaux's letter 297, in which he upbraids Louis for kicking aside good and sound advice 'under I know not what devilish advice' and hastening back to evil ways, referring to 'those who are urging you to repeat your former wrongdoing'. However, a fuller reading of the other Clairvaux letters around this period indicates that in fact Bernard drops no hint of influence by Eleanor – rather he is pointing a finger to the king's 'elderly advisers', and letter 297 should be seen as a reference to them, not to Eleanor. Bernard, therefore, was seeing

Louis as influenced by others in his battle against Theobald – probably Cadurc, Raoul and Joscelin de Soissons, who notably received separate letters of admonition.[76]

Overall, therefore, the better view, which has gained ground in academic writings in recent years and which is amply supported by the account above, is that Eleanor's role in these years was that of a conventional queen and she cannot be seen as the person responsible for Louis' behaviour. If Eleanor was exercising any influence over Louis it was at a very marginal level, and in some major areas of policy Eleanor's advice, if heeded, would have been likely to be directly contrary to the course which he actually took. The reality is that Louis' primary advisers were older male councillors, desirous of shutting out feminine influence.[77]

So far as Aelis's position is concerned, Eleanor's initial involvement in procuring Louis' support cannot be verified. In any case, there were ample political factors to prompt Louis to support, if not to initiate, a link between his closest aristocratic supporter and the throne. The only place where Eleanor's influence can be seen in this incident is actually in opposition to her husband at the end of the debacle. This passage suggests not only Eleanor's loyalty to Aelis, but also her willingness to contradict and disrespect her husband by speaking against a line of action he supported in public – far more likely if she considered he had used Aelis as a political pawn than if the problem had been one of her own making. Whatever the origins of the problem, however, Eleanor's first attested appearance in the records after her marriage plainly shows a significant fault line in the marriage by 1144.

This indication of problems in the marriage is supported by the other information, limited though it is, that one can glean from the record. Nothing can be reliably inferred from the reported separation of the royal couple when Louis went on campaign – though it is noteworthy that some of Eleanor's descendants were to habitually accompany their menfolk to within scant miles of the battlefield. However, even in peaceful years one can see hints that the couple were often apart. So when Louis made a grant in 1139 to the Templars in Paris under his and Eleanor's names, the charter had to be carried to Eleanor at Lorris near Orleans for her to sign it. It is not clear what Eleanor was doing at Lorris, but the signatures (which, apart from Raoul de Vermandois, who inferentially brought the charter, are of members of Eleanor's household) indicate that she was not at this time surrounded by a formal court.[78]

This gives pause for thought as to how Eleanor did occupy her time if, as seems the better view, she was not fulfilling any real role as a ruler of her own lands or adviser to her husband. She will have had plenty of time for reading and study, for the enjoyment of music, for the observance of religious offices and for patronage of both artists and dressmakers.

Which of these interests occupied her time the most cannot be reliably discerned. Despite repeated suggestions on this front in the biographies, there is simply no evidence for Eleanor as a leader of fashion, or as scandalising the French court with her southern fashions. The Clairvaux letter in translation by Amy Kelly, which is relied on by some biographers, is both a poor translation and lacks any reference to Eleanor – it is the simple condemnation of courtly finery quoted above.[79] In fact, the absence of any such comments seems rather to indicate that Eleanor did not stand out from the women of the court in this respect, which is hardly consistent with her as a leader or innovator of fashion and luxurious consumption.

Louis' own habit of retreating to monastic routine rather suggests that religious observance probably played a considerable part in Eleanor's own, necessarily somewhat parallel, routine. There are certainly grounds to believe that Eleanor, most probably educated to a high standard in a cathedral school, took a real interest in the intellectual debates which so galvanised Paris during these years, and that such affairs would not be uncongenial to her. There is also some basis for considering that she was not merely interested in but also influential in the matter of music. Reading backwards from the future, we can see that Eleanor's children by Henry would be interested and well-educated in music. Further (and reinforcing the view that she was strongly religiously observant), there are also indications that Eleanor was a primary vector for the spread of polyphonic music from Aquitaine. Thus the evidence points more toward a life heavy on education and religion than one mired in frivolity and fashion.

However, nothing suggests a very crowded programme. Eleanor's later life indicates that she was a woman who enjoyed being busy; the relative peace and lack of focus of these years will probably have been a source of friction in her marriage in and of itself.

But the political disputes which so filled this period also gave rise to one issue which was to loom ever larger over the marriage. With questions of consanguinity very much alive, Bernard of Clairvaux had, as noted above, made sure that Louis was aware that his own marriage was consanguineous. And as Louis himself took points on the consanguinity of marriages proposed by Theobald of Blois for his heirs, the question must have been more and more present to both parties' minds as the years drew on.

Adding to this concern was the absence of any heir – the point which Eleanor could not forbear to raise with Bernard of Clairvaux in 1144. The overwhelming evidence is that, even allowing for some period of grace while Eleanor reached physical maturity, in the prime of sexual life in their late teens and early twenties Eleanor and Louis were not regularly cohabiting. We know this because we know that Louis was not infertile – he would eventually have five children – and that Eleanor, given the chance, was very fertile – in her next marriage she would conceive almost at every opportunity. Yet in seven years of marriage to Louis, Eleanor had conceived only once before 1144.

Admittedly, it is more than likely that while he had been excommunicated Louis did not cohabit with Eleanor. However, even so, there were five years between the marriage and the excommunication in which no child had resulted. Nor can the absence of progeny be blamed on religious observance. While the Church forbade sexual relations during the great feasts of the Church, when a woman was menstruating and before she was 'churched' after childbirth, as well as on various other occasions, thereby considerable reducing the 'available' days for procreation, fertile couples who regularly cohabited produced more children than this. A few generations later, for example, we can find Eleanor's descendants Edward I and Eleanor of Castile provably observing sexual abstinence as prescribed by the Church, and yet still averaging a pregnancy every eighteen months.

The report that Eleanor claimed to have realised she was married to a monk, not a king, is a later account by a historian who was rather ill-disposed to Eleanor, and may be apocryphal, but it appears to embody a truth, as well as to allude to St Radegonde's story in a way which suggests Eleanor may well have said it. Indeed, a more neutral source, Stephen of Paris, says, 'You would never think he was a king, rather than a monk, unless you knew it.'[80] There seems to be a good case that Louis, by reason of his early training to celibacy and his indoctrination to consider women dangerous, was either unable or unwilling to pay the marriage debt on a regular basis. Guilt arising from an inability in this direction would gel well with his observed childish obsessive regard for Eleanor.

This narrative would also explain why Eleanor, infuriated by this – not least because the absence of an heir materially diminished her status – would ventilate their marital embarrassments to Bernard of Clairvaux. Thus from this same story we see the second major fault line in the marriage laid bare.

It is therefore permissible to infer that by 1144 and her twentieth birthday Eleanor knew that her marriage was far from ideal – and always would be.

However, it is equally plain that neither Eleanor nor Louis had thoughts of ending their marriage at this point. In her exchange with Bernard of Clairvaux, Eleanor did not hold out for what she wanted but gave ground important to her to secure the deal which her husband sought; she still regarded herself as aligned with him. However, Eleanor did also achieve something of what she wanted too: following the meeting, and the guidance which Bernard doubtless gave to Louis (though sadly in this case not in the form of one of his letters), Louis did obviously steel himself to have sex with Eleanor; for by the end of 1144, Eleanor was finally pregnant.

Was this unmitigatedly good news for Eleanor? Without a baby she would be presumed to be infertile, and a question would hover over the marriage – carrying with it the possibility of escape from life with Louis. The pregnancy was therefore both a desired vindication for Eleanor and also (it must have seemed) an end to any question of separation and greater freedom.

It is thus that we find Eleanor, realigned to her marriage as she endured the first months of what was to be her first successful pregnancy, present when a grand ceremony was convened at Saint-Denis in October 1144 to mark the conclusion of the peace between Louis, the papacy and Theobald of Blois. Saint-Denis was progressing towards its final glory – the soaring complex choir had been dedicated on 11 June 1144. Louis, Eleanor, their principal counsellors and a bevy of bishops (Suger, Jocelyn of Soissons, Hugh of Auxerre and the bishops of Amiens, Arras, Chalons, Chartres, Reims and Meaux) attended. Bernard of Clairvaux, who felt the Gothic style so beloved of Suger was, in effect, the architectural equivalent of Abelard's approach to theology, was not apparently present either on this occasion or in June.

It also seems very likely that either the June or the October ceremony was the occasion when Louis – marking his gratitude to Suger for his assistance in bringing about the peace with Theobald and the Church at large – gave to Suger the rock crystal vase which

Eleanor had given him as a wedding present. Suger's delight in it is evident in the inscription which he added when he mounted to it on a gold base – 'As a bride, Eleanor gave this vase to King Louis … King Louis to me, and Suger to the Saints' – and its significance as a mark of the reconciliation between mentor and mentee is evidenced elsewhere where he describes it as 'a tribute of his great love'. Many biographers suggest Eleanor felt grief at the re-gifting of her wedding present.[81] She may well have done so; but the assertion is based on no evidence. If we are to speculate, we might equally imagine that Eleanor, at long last contemplating the possibility of fulfilling her role as queen and providing an heir to France, would have considered it a very suitable gift to the Church from both of the royal couple – even if Louis chose to call it a gift from him.

Although the baby did not turn out to be the desired heir, Eleanor's harmony with the Church – and in particular with Bernard – is suggested by the name given to her daughter: Marie. This was a new departure as a name for a French royal princess or a daughter of Aquitaine. Its most likely inspiration was Bernard, who was, for his generation and many to come, the primary exponent of Marian theology, and a well-known preacher in praise of the role of Mary, the Mother of God as a mediatrix for fallible humanity.[82]

Meanwhile, as Eleanor celebrated the birth of her first child, and all she represented as the end of a very difficult period in Eleanor's marriage and her husband's kingship, the next storm was brewing on the far horizon of the Holy Land. At the end of 1144, the Crusader city of Edessa had fallen to the infidel.

Crusade

*Ki ore irat od Loouis/ja mar d'enfern n'avarat pour/Char s'alme
en iert en pareis od les/angeles nostre Seignor.*
[Who now will go with Louis need not have/any fear of hell/For
his soul shall go to paradise with the/angels of our Lord]
Troubadour song of the Second Crusade[1]

*e·l criz per aqel lavador/versa sobre·ls plus rics captaus,/fraich-
faillit de proessa las, que non amo joi ni deport.*
[the public outcry relating to [the Holy Land] pours down on
the highest-ranking leaders; broken failures, weary of valour,
who love neither joy nor delight.]
Marcabru

The First Crusade was still seen as a huge success story in France and western Europe, and indeed it had been – at least in the short term. Jerusalem had been retaken, and a web of Christian Crusader states – Jerusalem, Tripoli, Antioch, and Edessa – had been established. But by the 1140s the exposed nature of these principalities was becoming apparent as the Muslim forces brought themselves into order for a resurgence. The call to jihad was in the air.

The risk was higher for some than others. In Jerusalem, Queen Melisende was married to the doughty warrior Fulk of Anjou, father of Geoffrey le Bel, and they also had the support of smaller principalities. In Antioch, the smallest of the Crusader states, Queen Constance had her warrior husband, Eleanor's uncle Raymond, and a strong strategic position as well as a very small Muslim presence in the area. The county of Edessa, however, was nearly an island in Muslim territory. It suffered repeated attacks, during which its ruler, Joscelin of Courtenay, was captured and later killed. Its next ruler, Joscelin II, was forced into an uneasy alliance with his Byzantine neighbours as well as with Fulk of Jerusalem; but in 1143, both Fulk and Byzantine Emperor John II Komnenos died, leaving Edessa even more exposed. Joscelin therefore made an alliance of expedience with one of the local Muslim rulers, Kara Arslan. In pursuance of that alliance he left his capital with his entire army to support a campaign against another neighbour, Imad ad-Din Zengi, ruler of Mosul and Aleppo. In Edessa there remained 'only shoemakers, weavers, silk merchants, tailors and priests'. In Joscelin's absence, Zengi hurried to Edessa and besieged it, bringing the full force of his army's ingenuity to bear on reducing its defences. Believing that relief would come, its ragtag defenders rejected repeated offers of terms.[2]

But no relief did come – neither Joscelin nor Melisende could get a relief force to Edessa in time. On 23 December 1144, Zengi fired a massive mine; a long section of wall yielded, and the invading forces rushed into the city. Thousands died. William of Tyre reports the panic:

> The more prudent or more experienced citizens rushed to the citadel … so that they might at least preserve their lives, their children, and their wives, if only for a short time. At the gate there was such a crush of people trying to enter that, because of the press of the crowd, many were suffocated and died miserably.

The chronicler l'Faraj writes that 'about five thousand people died atrociously; twisted, suffering, pressed together into a single compact mass'. The citadel provided but a short respite. On 26 December, the city formally yielded to the invaders. Craftsmen were spared to work as Zengi's own slaves, notables were despatched in chains to Aleppo, and men of no distinction were simply slaughtered. In the interim, thousands had been tortured and killed. 'Neither age, condition, nor sex was spared,' wrote William of Tyre. Those women and children who survived the random violence of the sack were enslaved – it is estimated that ten thousand children found their way to the slave markets.[3]

Word trickled out through the Middle East to the West only gradually. In the winter weather it took weeks for the news to reach even Jerusalem and Antioch, whose rulers then had to digest the implications for themselves and the Crusader States as a whole. Then an envoy had to be despatched by ship against the prevailing winds. Realistically, the news probably only reached Rome in May or June, where it was received by a new Pope, Eugenius II, formerly a monk under Bernard at Clairvaux, and probably not the leader for whom the leaders of the Christian East would have prayed. Eugenius was kind, gentle and unworldly, elected only because the position of the papacy was so desperate that no one really wanted the job. Bernard (perhaps in part with Eugenius' own wellbeing in mind) regarded it as an unfortunate choice: writing to the college of cardinals he expostulated, 'May God forgive you what you have done! ... What reason or counsel, when the Supreme Pontiff was dead, made you rush upon a mere rustic, lay hands on him in his refuge, wrest from his hands the axe, pick or hoe, and lift him to a throne?' He took a similar tone with Eugenius himself when he invoked the Bible in describing him as a 'beggar raised from a dunghill to sit with princes'.[4]

The news from the East will then have progressed to France, arriving in early summer. But by late summer, shortly after the birth of Marie, letters from Raymond and Constance, and other correspondents in the East, would have told Eleanor and Louis that there was a crisis and that help was being sought from the papacy and the countries who had contributed Crusaders to past efforts.

France was one of the most important targets for the calls for help, perhaps the most important. The bulk of the leading First Crusaders had been French, so the support of the King of France was an obvious stepping stone to recruitment. Louis had strong blood ties to the Crusaders – his great-uncle Hugh 'the Great' had led the French contingent and his aunt Constance had been grandmother to Constance of Antioch. Then there was Eleanor's close familial link to Antioch through her uncle Raymond. Constance and Raymond will therefore have had good hopes of interesting Louis and of ensuring Eleanor's intercession in so doing.[5]

What they cannot have anticipated was the quite absurd synchronicity in how Louis received the shocking news and the pleas for help. Following his long alienation from the Church, he had felt in need of some form of pilgrimage to cement his good accord; no better pilgrimage than one to Jerusalem could be offered. His actions at Vitry required expiation too – again a demanding and lengthy pilgrimage to the East would offer opportunities in this respect. He had sworn a public oath in the matter of Bourges and was now technically perjured; although that oath was against the Church, it was still a sacred undertaking from which he required powerful blessings to feel released. As a further makeweight, his brother Philippe had sworn an oath to make a pilgrimage to the Holy Land before his death, which Louis had assumed along with Philippe's other responsibilities. Time away from the political sphere would also be expedient in light of his recent disasters, and on Crusade he could perhaps restore his status. Having had to abandon war at home, an opportunity to win his spurs elsewhere would be opportune.[6]

There were also personal aspects. For both Louis and Eleanor, now seeking an heir after seven years of marriage and the 'failure' of producing only a single girl child, the ultimate in pilgrimages, with the additional blessings accruing for fighting for the cross, would surely help to secure the heir they needed. And if, as the evidence suggests, their personal relationship was not as harmonious as would be ideal, a joint focus on an important problem might offer a way to mend that too.

Added to this impetus was the positive fashion for pilgrimage which was then current in France, fed by the appearance of the *Gesta Francorum* (a highly thrilling account of the deeds of the First Crusaders written from the viewpoint of an anonymous lower-ranking knight), by other narratives inspired by it and by *chansons* such as the *Chanson D'Antioch* and *Chanson de Jerusalem*, which had begun to circulate a few years previously. There was, too, a burgeoning pilgrim industry heavily promoted by the original Crusaders, who saw pilgrimage as part of the route to economic success for the Crusader States. The early years of the century had therefore seen visits to Jerusalem by such high-status individuals as King Eric of Denmark and his wife, and the counts of Portugal and Champagne, along with noble visitors from France, Germany, Britain and Iberia, and clerics from all these places – as well as Russia and Iceland. All returned with tales to tell. Some of them, on their return, even wrote books about their experiences, or guides for pilgrims. Either way, as 1146 approached, their experiences were again stoking interest in the Holy Land as a destination.[7]

Scholars have puzzled about Louis' keenness, which was so intense that he seems to have anticipated the receipt of the papal response, promoting a call to Crusade at his Christmas court at Bourges in 1145. The papal bull *Quantum praedecessores* (roughly: 'How hard did our predecessors labour for the liberty of the Church in the East?') was published on 1 December at Vetrella and almost certainly could not have made it across the Alps before the new year. However, these facts simply demonstrate that for Louis this was an idea which called to him strongly from the first, and that he was unwilling to waste the opportunity of the large assembly which the seasonal court offered. And in this enthusiasm, we can infer Eleanor would have supported him, as it fulfilled her own duty of support towards her own close family as well as evoking her own family's crusading history. It may even have offered a period of reconciliation in what was otherwise becoming a troubled marriage.

In terms of the timeline to taking the Cross, what appears to have happened is that at some point in late summer, having received the call for aid, Louis and Eleanor decided to make a pilgrimage or Crusade, and set the stage for their Christmas court to launch the endeavour. Having corresponded with the Pope in the autumn, Louis probably knew that a response was in the process of production, and therefore anticipated the receipt of the Papal Bull before Christmas and made his preparations accordingly. The production of *Quantum praedecessores* was in fact slower than expected, and by December it was not yet to hand; but Louis, committed to the project, pressed ahead. Odo of Deuil says that, having invited more attendees to the crown wearing than was usual, he confided in them the 'secret of his heart'. Bishop Godfrey of Langres preached a powerful sermon, evoking the devastation of Edessa and the sufferings of its people, while Louis, 'shining with faith', called on his vassals to aid their brothers in the East.

But the call met with fairly tepid enthusiasm, and the verdict of the assembled nobles and churchmen was to defer the issue. The departure of a crowned king on Crusade was seen as a radical step and possibly a step too far. Principal among the naysayers was Suger, who somewhat tactlessly mentioned Louis' lack of military success and the continuing lack of a male heir as reasons indicating that the venture was too risky. He might well have added, and doubtless also thought, that the country was too unstable, in the light of the recent years' upheavals, to be safely left by the king and many of its principal nobles. He and many of the nobles whose support would be necessary will also have had cause to be concerned about the costs of a Crusade as well as the personal risk to many of the noble houses – which itself constituted a risk to the entire family affected. Eleanor's own nobles, many of whom lost key family members in William the Troubadour's first Crusade, will not have forgotten this negative side of the endeavour. Despite repeated statements in biographies of Louis and Eleanor, there is no evidence that enthusiasm for the Crusade was driven by Eleanor or the lords of Aquitaine. Louis therefore had to content himself with the qualified victory of a determination to reconvene and debate the matter further at Vézelay at Easter 1146. By then the papal response would have been forthcoming and it was even possible, given the precedent of the First Crusade, that the Pope himself would preach the Cross.[8]

Soon after Christmas, Louis will have received *Quantum praedecessores*. At that point, the campaign for the Crusade took fire, for (despite Bernard of Clairvaux's doubts about his abilities) Eugenius and his advisers had put together a remarkably effective manifesto. A number of key themes were deployed. The first, and key to any understanding of the Second Crusade, was the selling of it as effectively a sequel to or continuation of the First Crusade, deliberately evoking the literature of the First Crusade, which so enthused so wide an audience. Effectively, he trailed the prospect of becoming a fabled hero like those of the *Gesta Francorum*, and the opportunity which the Crusade offered of visiting the sites of their heroic deeds. Secondly, he trailed the familial and heritage aspect of the endeavour, counteracting the risks to families by reminding them of the family heroes of the previous generation with two very pointed questions: do you want your fathers' sacrifices to have been in vain? And are you going to fail to live up to their heroism? Thirdly, he evoked the horrors of the fall of Edessa, bolstering it with oblique reference to the thousands of Christians enslaved and the appalling acts of the infidels. In the long final paragraph he turned to spiritual practicalities, and here he revolutionised crusading, for he offered what was probably a better deal than that offered by Pope Urban to the First Crusaders – a full remission of sins, as opposed to a remission of penance, as well as protection for the Crusaders' close families and property and immunity from suit for the entire family of a Crusader during his absence.[9]

The Pope had therefore put in place an incentive which should help to commit waverers; and to assist in selling his message he despatched Bernard of Clairvaux to overwhelm listeners with his oratory. What he had not done, of course, was to set out any coherent plan of action. While he called for men to volunteer and to travel East to support the Holy Land, he did not set out goals or even explain in broad terms what the Crusaders should do when they got there. It may be that the failure of the Second Crusade can in part be traced back to this omission.[10]

Before turning to the events which followed, it is necessary to spend a little time examining the sources for the Second Crusade. This is because Eleanor's biographers have traditionally taken a somewhat credulous approach to some rather dubious sources, and readers may therefore be surprised to find some stories given as gospel elsewhere will be rejected in what follows.

Unlike the First Crusade, the Second Crusade offers poor pickings in terms of contemporaneous chroniclers – very probably because of its conspicuous lack of success. The quasi-official historian of the German contingent, Otto of Freising, is of little use. He gave up his account in 1147, on the grounds that he had not set out to write a tragedy.[11] Moreover, his crusading contingent was largely separated from that which Eleanor joined. The sole contemporaneous account of the rest of the Crusade comes from Odo of Deuil, the French army's official historian (and later Suger's successor). However, while he is a very useful source for the journey out, he actually ceases his account in March 1148 – before the key events at Antioch and Damascus. Further (and for reasons which scholars continue to debate), he seems to go out of his way to avoid mentioning Eleanor – where the odd mention of her survives it appears to have been an accidental inclusion. There are therefore suggestions, which seem to be persuasive, that once Eleanor's marriage to Louis was over Odo went through his account and deliberately expunged her so far as possible from the official record. This action might derive from simple disapproval or from an apparent belief that a place in his account of the holy endeavour provided a form of immortality and only the worthy should benefit. Whatever the reasoning, the result is that practically all that has been said of Eleanor and the Second Crusade therefore depends on later accounts.

These include Henry of Huntingdon in his *Historia Anglorum* in 1154 – the next closest account in time, but very brief – and William of Tyre, writing under the aegis of the King of Jerusalem in the 1170s but based on eyewitness accounts from participants. William of Tyre has strong claims to be the most reliable account, aside from Odo of Deuil. Far more influential for Eleanor's memory, however, has been the account of William of Newburgh, written in around 1196–98 – i.e. around fifty years after the Crusade – and based in part on his recollections of conversations in his youth with a monk who had once been to Antioch.[12]

The date for the official preaching of the Crusade was set for Easter Day, 31 March 1146, at Vézelay. Word was sent to Louis' nobles and spread fast, leading to a huge number of people converging on the town. Since there was no building which could contain the crowd, a wooden platform was built for Bernard in a field outside of Vézelay, enabling him to speak from on high to the audience clustered at his feet. Before the main event began, Louis received his own cross, kneeling before Bernard. Bernard then mounted the platform together with Louis and spun his familiar magic. Before long, people on all sides began to cry out to be allowed to take the Cross, and Bernard threw pre-prepared crosses to the crowd as if he was scattering alms. Soon stocks were exhausted, and still the people cried for crosses, leaving Bernard to tear his own clothing into crosses. Bernard reported back to the Pope, 'I opened my mouth and I spoke – at once the Crusaders are multiplied to infinity. Villages and towns are deserted, and one can scarcely find one man for every seven women.'[13]

What of Eleanor? Her participation in the Crusade has long been part of 'the Black Myth' which has tarnished her name. Some accounts have her scandalising the court by her response to Bernard's preaching, or following taking the Cross, by dressing with her women as Amazons and galloping among the crowd to encourage recruitment. Almost all regard her participation in the crusade at all as something highly unusual, bordering on scandalous. But the truth is that it was only later events – and particularly the work of later chroniclers such as William of Newburgh – which resulted in Eleanor's action in committing to the Crusade being cast as transgressive.

While the Crusade was in part designed as a military expedition, it was also in large measure designed as a pilgrimage. There was nothing unusual about women going on pilgrimage to Jerusalem and the Holy Land. Indeed, William of Tyre, writing of the First Crusade, speaks of women as not merely present but fighting in emergencies as well as occupying support roles near the front line and bringing water and food to fighters. Similarly, some Muslim writers record female participants fighting for both sides. On the Second Crusade, too, Otto of Freising describes the presence of many women and children in the German contingent laconically, plainly regarding it as unremarkable. There was therefore nothing at all out of the way about Eleanor's decision to take the Cross; and this is exactly how the only contemporaneous account treats the occasion. Suger, in his history of Louis VII, records Louis taking the Cross and then adds flatly that his wife Eleanor took the Cross too, before going on to list the nobles who followed in their footsteps.[14]

Why did Eleanor take the Cross? A number of reasons have been offered, and the truth will never be known. The idea that she did so for political reasons or under coercion, to enable recruitment of her vassals, seems unlikely; Louis had been exerting his influence over Eleanor's lands for nearly a decade now, and did not require Eleanor's influence to ensure recruitment. While the fact of Geoffrey de Rancon's participation is sometimes seen as a result of loyalty to Eleanor, it can equally be seen as an attempt by him to gain prestige with Louis. The other Aquitanian lords who participated (de Sanzay, de Lusignan and Thouars) were of lesser standing, and Crusade offered an obvious chance to improve their position. The Lusignans indeed were to succeed, becoming a major force in the East. The troubadour Jaufre Rudel, Lord of Blaye, went as well, but as part of the Count of Toulouse's retinue.[15] Another theory has Eleanor coerced into participation to prevent her exercising power as regent. However, absent an heir, with a surplus of experienced candidates for regent, and given the determined approach of Louis and his advisers to keeping Eleanor out of the limelight, this was never a realistic possibility. William of Newburgh put Eleanor's participation down to Louis' doting fondness for his wife, suggesting that he could not bear the long separation. However, as we have seen, this does not seem to fairly reflect the state of the royal marriage at the time. We can therefore probably safely assume that Eleanor went voluntarily.

As for positive reasons for participation, these can hardly have been lacking. The value of the pilgrimage and the opportunity to visit the East should not be underestimated, nor the perceived spiritual benefits. But for Eleanor there were two strong personal reasons. One was to see her uncle Raymond again, and the other was to continue to try to do her primary duty as a queen. Aged twenty-two, she still had only one child, a girl, to her credit. Louis would be absent for at least a year (the Crusade in fact lasted nearly two and a half years). He was planning to participate in military action, in the course of which he might die. Quite simply, if she did not accompany him she would be neglecting her duty to try to conceive an heir to the throne – which was also her only means of strengthening her own political position. One might add to this that with Louis' apparently ambivalent attitude to sex except under religious sanction, a successful holy journey might well, despite the expectation of chastity for pilgrims, seem to offer her the best chance she would ever have of conceiving that vital heir. This practical approach to conjugal duty can be seen in later crusading women, for in the next century, Marguerite, Queen of France; Eleanor of Castile, Queen of England; Isabella of Aragon, Queen of France; and Beatrice of England, Duchess of Brittany all chose not to waste valuable child-breeding time by letting their husbands go off on Crusade for years. All either bore or conceived children on Crusade.

Nor is there any reason to accept the delightfully picturesque accounts that Eleanor, having taken the Cross, re-robed herself as Penthesila, Queen of the Amazons, and with her companions rode among the laggards handing out distaffs (the medieval equivalent of the white feather) to encourage recruitment. This story has been painstakingly debunked by Jean Flori, the leading French biographer of Eleanor. Its earliest origins lie in the passing reference (dealt with later in this chapter) to a striking woman riding with a lance through Constantinople. To be clear: there is no near contemporary account of Eleanor taking the Cross, other than Suger's brief mention. In the seventeenth century, Isaac de Larrey elevated this passing reference to an unnamed woman into an assertion of female squadrons of crusaders, with Eleanor among their number. His account was then amplified in Suger's eighteenth-century biography by F. A. Gervaise, which itself was seized upon by Agnes Strickland in her *Lives of the Queens of England*. She (with characteristic lack of scrupulousness) attributed it to 'Suger and contemporaneous historians'. Similarly, in France, Michaud's *Histoire des Croisades*, published in 1829, has Eleanor taking up sword and lance, and introduces the distaff aspect, apparently by misquoting from an account of the Third Crusade and various seventeenth- and eighteenth-century historians. Later historians have generally tried to have their cake and eat it, by casting doubt on the provenance of the story but suggesting such a thing might have been; largely, it would seem, because they would so much have liked it to be true. In fact, it can safely be assumed that if Eleanor had tried any such antics in front of St Bernard, he would have left an appalled and disapproving record of it.[16]

A related question is that of participation of other women on the Crusade. As may have been noticed, the official recruitment via the

Pope and Bernard of Clairvaux was directed at men only. While we know that many women joined the First Crusade, the picture is much less clear for the Second, again because of the paucity of sources. Some of the slightly later historians, such as William of Newburgh, tend to attribute the failure of the Crusade to hordes of women encouraging moral laxness. This, as we shall see, is rubbish. But it is very hard to be clear about how many women and of what ranks did accompany the Crusade. At the top end, apart from Eleanor we can only be sure that one young unmarried female relative of Louis was in the queen's retinue, because apparently the Byzantine Emperor Manuel Komnenos demanded she be given as a wife to one of his nephews, leading to Louis' brother Robert abducting her from Eleanor's retinue to save her from this fate.[17] However, the story does tell us that Eleanor had a retinue. Of whom it consisted we do not know.

Accounts in the works of respected historians state that Eleanor was accompanied by Sybilla, Countess of Flanders; Mabille de Roucy; Faydide, Countess of Toulouse; Florina of Bourgogne; and the countesses of Bouillon and Blois.[18] Kostick has picked apart the assertions for each of these ladies and concluded that the Countess of Flanders did not travel to Jerusalem with her husband until 1157, and that Mabille de Roucy, the Countess of Bouillon and Florina of Bourgogne were much earlier visitors – during or shortly after the First Crusade. The only one who might have been present was Faydide of Toulouse, whose husband did accompany the Crusade, albeit in a different contingent than Eleanor. However, the evidence tends to suggest that Faydide was divorced by 1142, when Alphonse of Toulouse married Ermengarde of Narbonne, Eleanor's fellow comital heiress.

As for the possibility of Ermengarde's presence, the marriage, as noted above, was one made under duress. By now Ermengarde had been rescued by an alliance of local barons led by the Trencavel family and the Count of Barcelona (who was de facto King of Aragon following his marriage to Eleanor's infant cousin Petronilla) and the marriage had been dissolved. Indeed, the Count of Toulouse's participation may have been in part down to this significant tactical reverse.[19]

But even without names, we can be sure of this: Eleanor was accompanied by a number of relatively high-ranking women, and all of them will themselves have been accompanied by female servants. As for women of other conditions, the Crusade was not without these either. The First Crusade had famously attracted great crowds of people, men and women from all walks of life. The Second Crusade was less disseminated by popular preachers, and the message conveyed was more strictly military and less seeking migrants to colonise the Holy Land than had been the case then. Accordingly, the numbers of women were almost certainly correspondingly lower, though aside from Otto of Freising more than one chronicler of the German recruiting round speaks of large numbers of both sexes taking up the call.[20] Eleanor, then, was far from being alone in accompanying the Crusade; women of all ranks of life were also present among the Crusaders who ultimately set off in summer 1147.

In the intervening period there was much to do, not least in completing the work of recruitment and making administrative provision for the absence of the king and queen, and such a segment of the aristocracy. It is in about this period that charter evidence, and particularly evidence of Eleanor sealing documents, becomes more plentiful; this in turn suggests that at the age of twenty-two or twenty-three, and with her status improved by the provision of a child, Eleanor was beginning to seek greater recognition. A number of the religious charters into which Eleanor and Louis entered date from this period, particularly from their circuit of Aquitaine, the Auvergne and Velay in late 1146, which combined recruitment, making appointments for administration in the absence of such stalwarts as Geoffrey de Rancon and others, and collecting contributions to the Crusade's war chest. It is no great leap to suppose that the religious houses to whom grants were made by the royal couple – including charters in favour of the great abbeys of La Trinite-de-Vendôme, Saint-Maixent and Fontevraud – reciprocated with generous donations to the funding of this religiously inspired exercise.

There seems to have been some upheaval in the royal households at this time, for now we find Bernard of Clairvaux writing to Eleanor in terms which mix the friendly and peremptory so as to indicate both familiarity and reasonable accord. He disclaims any right to be heard but trusts in 'your most famous generosity and kindness'; yet at the same time he makes clear that he expects Eleanor to restore possessions to a recently dismissed member of her household, who is to enter a monastery, and to show favour to the Abbot of Beaulieu, who carries the letter.[21]

Bernard of Clairvaux then turned his primary attention to Germany, where he recruited not just huge crowds of humble

Crusaders, but also a second crowned head to the endeavour – the German ruler Conrad III found his status was not proof against Bernard's compelling words. At the same time, the French Jewish community, while not suffering the anti-Semitic attacks which took place during the preaching of the Crusade in Germany, were forced to make a substantial contribution through taxation.[22]

By early 1147, the participants were committed. A conference was convened at Étampes to decide on the route, and here one sees more evidence of the lack of geopolitical knowledge and planning which was to doom the exercise. A vibrant debate took place as to whether the journey should be by sea (a proposal lobbied for by Roger of Sicily, whose territory would be a natural stopping-off point) or by land via Constantinople. Despite the preferences of Conrad, the recommendation of Raymond of Antioch and the availability of detailed accounts of the massacres suffered by the First Crusaders on the land routes, the decision was taken to prefer a land approach to a maritime route. In the end, it came down to the papal wish to please Roger's adversary, Manuel Komnenos, with a view to cooperation on the ground and possible rapprochement between the Western and Eastern churches.[23]

Likewise, despite the provisioning difficulties encountered by the First Crusaders – even with their approaches divided over a number of routes – the decision was made for the vast majority of the host to follow a single route, with only a minor contingent under Alphonse of Toulouse coming a different way. However, the decision to co-operate with the Byzantines rather than Roger was by no means uncontroversial, and set the scene for the hostility on the part of some of the party which was to mark the crusaders' stay in Constantinople. The departure date for Louis' contingent was set for June 1147. Approaches were made to the King of Hungary and the Byzantine Emperor seeking safe passage and provisions. But two crucial things remained undetermined: who was to govern France in Louis' absence? And just what was the purpose of the Crusade – was it a pilgrimage, was it to liberate (what remained of) Edessa, or was it part of something bigger?

While the second issue remained in the air, without any serious attempts even being made to consult the local Christian authorities as to what they wanted the Crusade to do, the first question was soon settled. At the Easter court at Saint-Denis, Louis handed custody of his kingdom over to the Pope, who was himself in attendance to make religious appointments to the Crusade.

Eugenius, predictably, appointed Suger. Two associates were also named. Louis chose Raoul de Vermandois – a tactless choice given that he was still excommunicate. The Pope, via Suger, nominated the Archbishop of Reims, Samson of Mauvoisin, a man with a foot in both royal and papal camps. This apparently uncomfortable triumvirate would succeed better than the Crusaders.

These discussions with the Pope reflect the fact that he and his entourage had arrived in France on 30 March, and would stay there until the royal party's departure on Crusade. The Pope was accompanied by his legate, the new cardinal Hyacinth Bobone, whom Eleanor and Louis had probably met at the Council of Sens in 1141. This closer meeting was to mark the start of a friendship between the cardinal and both Louis and Eleanor.

On 11 June, Eleanor, Adelaide of Maurienne, the Pope and his legates, Suger and doubtless every other name of importance processed to Saint-Denis for the religious ceremony to mark the Crusaders' departure. They are likely to have included the main participants from Aquitaine, the Count of Auvergne and his knights as well as representatives from the forces of Brittany. The Templar contingent, including the Master of the Temple, Everard of Barres, would also have been there. Louis, eager to present himself in the role of the humble pilgrim, stopped on the way at a leper hospital, leaving the distinguished crowd to await him in the June heat at the cathedral. Once arrived, he prostrated himself before Eugenius and Suger (in his role as Abbot of Saint-Denis) and was permitted to venerate the relics of the saint. Thereafter he was presented with the sacred Capetian banner, the Oriflamme, and received the blessing of the Pope together with a pilgrim pouch and staff – another indication of the nature of the expedition, as Louis saw it. Louis then retreated to the monks' refectory, leaving his womenfolk to await him again, until they were nearly fainting from the crush and the heat. Adelaide, of course, could retire to comfort later that day. Eleanor, on the other hand, was off with the Crusaders in the direction of Metz by the later afternoon.[24]

Eleanor's experience of the Crusade can be broken down into a number of phases: Paris to Regensburg; Regensburg to Constantinople; Constantinople itself; the journey to Antioch; Jerusalem; and the return. Each appears to have been fairly distinct and to have offered huge novelties for a young woman who had never before left France and had never, apart from the few days after her wedding, accompanied an army. In the course of the journey, Eleanor laid the foundation for becoming one of England's two best-travelled queens before the current incumbent, and apparently gained no dislike of travelling. The fact of her having undertaken the journey successfully also suggests strongly that she was a keen horsewoman and physically fit – the journey was not one to be undertaken by anyone not in good health, and there is no sign that Eleanor suffered any illness or difficulty on the journey out (had she done so, we can trust this failing would have been seized upon by Odo).

At the same time, the period of Crusade marks the effective death of Eleanor's marriage to Louis. Before the Crusade it was imperfect, probably even troubled. By the time of their return it was clear to both that it would have to be terminated. Each stage of Eleanor's Crusade may therefore also be said to mark a step towards the end of the marriage.

The precise size of the force Eleanor accompanied is very uncertain. Between the various armies (those of Louis, Conrad, the Count of Savoy and the Count of Toulouse) modern historians have estimated that the total roll call was between 25,000 and 50,000, of whom maybe half were fighting men. Louis' army therefore numbered perhaps 10,000 to 20,000 in total and had to proceed at a pace which could accommodate both the baggage train, the pedestrians and the litters and carts which were used by some ladies and invalids. The progress to Metz, then on to Worms and Regensburg, was slow and doubtless tedious. The first phase, in France and then in Imperial territory, would offer scope for considerable comfort for the royal party. Most likely pre-planned halts were made in the vicinity of well-equipped abbeys, where Louis and Eleanor and their immediate circles would have enjoyed rooms, decent food and something approximating the comforts of their everyday life.[25]

At Metz, the French forces rendezvoused with the armies of Thierry of Alsace, Renaud of Bar, Amadeus II of Savoy and his half-brother William V of Montferrat, as well as those of Burgundy and Lorraine, the majority of which were to follow a land route through Italy to Brindisi. At Worms, the French contingent was joined by Crusaders from Normandy, northern France and England, including William de Warenne, Earl of Surrey, his brother in law Guy of Ponthieu and Guy's cousin Gerard, Vidame of Amiens. Most of the remainder of the English contingent were making their way to the Holy Land by sea. This route via Worms raises the tantalising possibility that the party may have been able to pay a visit to the Abbey of Disibodenberg, where the celebrated female polymath Hildegarde of Bingen – a future correspondent of Eleanor – was abbess.

At Regensburg, they were met by Manuel Komnenos' envoys. The Emperor Conrad had departed with his own party already. At once, fault lines began to appear. The Greek envoys' smooth, flattering approach raised hackles, as Odo de Deuil's account makes clear, with mutterings of '*timeo Danaos*' only just being kept in check. So too did their master's request for assurances that any formerly Imperial lands won by the Crusaders would be held as fiefs of the Eastern Emperor, with appropriate homage being rendered. The idea that crowned heads of state, if they conquered territory, should make themselves subject to an Emperor who had not managed to hold the lands on his own account was unsurprisingly unwelcome to Louis and Conrad, and would become a festering sore in the relationship with the Byzantines. Louis and Eleanor and their contingent stayed in Regensburg for some time, during which time they made arrangements for the bulky baggage to be sent on to Bulgaria down the Danube since the carts were struggling with the terrain, even in summer. Later accounts suggest that much of the baggage was Eleanor's, but none of the contemporaneous accounts assert this, and it is perhaps best regarded as part of William of Newburgh's stance on the Crusade, which attributed its failure to female involvement and was notably hostile to Eleanor.[26]

It had been agreed that Louis' contingent should allow Conrad to depart with his force first, the idea being to ensure that provisioning was not made impossible by sheer force of numbers. Predictably, however, the result was that the French crusaders faced a countryside stripped bare and a hostile populace. Wealthy Crusaders might have sufficient provisions laid in, but those forced to find food en route were reduced to desperate straits – as were the horses, for whom no fodder could be found. The problem persisted along the banks of the Danube and all the way though Hungary into Bulgaria – the start of Byzantine-controlled territory. To keep the Crusade going, Louis was forced to buy provisions and write home to Suger seeking more money. The Lorrainers, in the vanguard, overlapped for a time with the tail of the German army and hostilities erupted. 'The Germans were unbearable, even to us,' says Odo.[27]

There was still greater hostility from the local populations in Bulgaria, echoing the increasing caution of Manuel Komnenos, who feared that the Crusaders might prove hostile, even to the point of making an attack on Constantinople. Matters were hardly improved when some of Conrad's German troops under his nephew, the future Emperor Frederick Barbarossa, attacked an Orthodox monastery near Adrianople (modern Edirne).[28] All in all, this stretch of the journey, though it did not expose her directly to any violence, will probably have provided Eleanor with her first experience of living in a military camp, in all likelihood in a fairly basic tent, and will also have provided regular encounters with the evidence of recent violent death. It was to be good training for the later phases of the voyage.

One point of interest should be noted with regard to this stage of the journey: Odo of Deuil notes that Louis did not travel or sleep with Eleanor on the journey. Rather he travelled with his inner circle, including Odo himself and the Templar monk Thierry de Galeran,[29] while Eleanor and her women were part of the Aquitanian contingent. Some might say that this reflected prudence, in that the long journey was no time to risk a pregnancy. However, this was not a view endorsed by past or future Crusaders. Eleanor's descendant Eleanor of Castile, for example, would depart on Crusade pregnant and breed two more children on her travels. The situation is therefore better seen as a continuing separation between the couple, and likely evidence of dysfunction in the bedroom. Furthermore, this separation was the more dangerous in that placing a now mature Eleanor with her vassals offered her an opportunity to hear their unexpurgated complaints about royal administration, and revive her ties with her homeland. It can only have contributed to further alienation between the royal couple.

By early October, the French contingent was finally approaching Constantinople, prior to crossing into hostile Turkish territory. As they did so, the news reached them that their nominal ally Manuel Komnenos had just signed a truce with the Turkish Sultan of Konya. In fact, the move was necessitated by his concerns about the resurgence of the Muslim forces which surrounded his lands, and threats from Roger of Sicily – as well as the need to have his hands free to deal with any further hostility from the massive Crusader army now encamped on his doorstep. In particular, on 10 September 1147 the German army had followed up their actions at Adrianople by commencing hostilities against the Byzantine guards posted to protect the city and plundering the Emperor's private game reserve. The German force had consequently been barred from the city altogether. Eleanor therefore arrived among a French contingent which was seething with hostility to the Byzantines. Odo offered an explanation: 'Our people considered that they were not really Christians, and that killing them was of no consequence.' Apparently, as they approached the city some of the party were actually advocating an alliance with Roger of Sicily against the Emperor.[30]

Yet in some ways the French visit went considerably better than the approach had led them to expect. Odo of Deuil's account leaves no doubt that the French were hugely impressed by the city, its churches and even the lavishness of the welcome they received. Odo's descriptions are, despite his hostility, breathless. There is no reason to doubt that Eleanor, though somewhat more familiar with Eastern luxuries via her childhood proximity to Iberia than the northern French, will have been similarly impressed, and that the weeks in Byzantium were a highlight of the otherwise fairly miserable Crusade.

The visit commenced in style. As Louis and his army approached Byzantium, they were met by a large deputation of stunningly dressed nobles and priests, all displaying the elegant manners which were such a feature of a court where everyone had a reverence for grades of hierarchy, where Sebastos competed with Nobelissimus, where the depth of a bow to each person was the subject of deep and troubled study and could make or break a career. To Louis and his monks, all devoted to simplicity, this was at first breathtakingly impressive. Louis permitted himself to be led by this crowd to the Blachernae Palace, which Odo describes as of 'almost matchless beauty'. We do not know what Eleanor's itinerary was. However, it is most likely that she was met by the Empress Irene, and either given a palace reception or conveyed by her to the residence that was put at the French royals' disposal. The likelihood of this is reinforced by a stray reference in Odo of Deuil to correspondence between the two queens, which suggests that Irene had been corresponding with Eleanor on the journey – perhaps since Regensburg.

The Byzantine royals provided an interesting contrast to the French visitors. While both kings were of a similar age and both reputedly tall and handsome, Louis adopted a monkish reticence about his looks and other sensual matters. Not so Manuel Komnenos. Although only the fourth of John II Komnenos' sons, and (like Louis) therefore raised with no expectations of the throne, he revelled in his role. He cultivated his good looks, dressing with grandeur and richness, and was equally devoted to the pursuit of arms as to study – in particular of medicine, in which he had gained considerable expertise. He delighted to practice healing foreign rulers and dignitaries, and would conduct bloodlettings himself if no physician were available. As his later history was to show, his intellectual interests included theology – he was to play an active part in the debates which marked the latter part of his rule and was to publish a paper defending the discipline of astrology from a theological perspective. Even Odo of Deuil concedes that he was charming and charismatic, equally at ease displaying the majesty of the Emperor, participating in intellectual talk or conducting an informal man-to-man conversation. In another contrast to Louis, he excelled in charming women; his mistresses included his own niece. Moreover, even the wife to whom he was routinely unfaithful spoke of his kindness and consideration to her and how nothing was too much trouble for him if it would please her.

If Manuel was more obviously attractive than Louis, his wife would be placed very much in the shade by Eleanor. Born Bertha of Sulzbach, the sister of Conrad III's late wife, she boasted a very distinguished lineage descended from Charlemagne. However, her family lacked the high status which would have been required for a marriage to the heir to the Byzantine Empire. The marriage came about because she was betrothed to Manuel when he was simply the Emperor's fourth son, and shipped to Constantinople, where, as was habitual for foreign brides, she was renamed Irene, and schooled in Greek and the elaborate ceremonial of the court. Her marriage was ultimately delayed until two years after the accession of her husband-to-be, and was made possible by her being adopted by Conrad to give her the necessary status. The years of training had failed to take the down-to-earth German approach of Bertha out of Irene the Empress. No chronicler offers even the most cursory compliment on her beauty, and we can infer that she did not excel in this regard. However, the chroniclers are unanimous in their enthusiasm for her philanthropy and her piety – while they also make sure to mention her neglect of her appearance and refusal to use the cosmetics regarded as *de rigueur* in Constantinople.

There is some controversy about whether Eleanor caught the imagination of the Greeks. The Greek chronicler Niketas Choniates, writing in the closing years of the century, recounts the arrival in

Constantinople of one particular woman, who has come to be often identified with Eleanor:

> ... even women travelled amongst the crusaders, boldly sitting astride like men, dressed like men and armed with lance and battle-axe. They held themselves like soldiers, bold as Amazons. At the head of these women was one, more richly dressed, who because of the gold embroidery around her dress's hem was called by us 'Lady Goldenfoot'. Her elegance and freedom of movement called to mind Penthesilea, the famous Queen of the Amazons.

Very few of Eleanor's biographers – even Flori – have resisted the temptation to identify Eleanor with this exciting woman. However, their enthusiasm is probably misplaced. Quite apart from the fact that Niketas was not an eyewitness but was rather writing fifty years later about events which took place before he was born, and that in a number of other respects his account of the Second Crusaders is demonstrably erroneous, he seems to identify Lady Goldenfoot with the German contingent (Alemanoi) rather than the French crusaders, and he says nothing about his heroine being a queen. Moreover, at the time Choniates was writing, Eleanor was still famous – or possibly infamous. It seems unlikely that he would have failed to identify Eleanor if indeed this character was known to be her. The better argument therefore is that Eleanor is not Lady Goldenfoot – and that the Crusade boasted some other rather memorable ladies.[31]

Although the conventions of Constantinople will have kept Eleanor more cloistered with other women than was usual in the West, Eleanor's experience of the city may well have been more congenial than her husband's. Not only would she not have been put in the shade by her hostess, as Louis was by his host, but the queens were both well-educated women who would become noted patrons of the arts.

And we know that Empress Irene was not the only person with whom Eleanor struck up a bond, for there is clear evidence that she and Manuel had the opportunity to get to know each other during her stay. This evidence can still be found in the library of Trinity College, Cambridge, where there is a book on women's medicine, the *Gynecia Cleopatrae*, which clearly states that it was translated for and sent to Eleanor in later life by the medically knowledgeable Manuel.[32] This suggests that a friendship commenced between the two in 1147 and persisted in correspondence for some years. Given the nature of the book, which covers women's diseases, contraception, conception, birth and abortion, it in fact suggests that the friendship between the two was somewhat confidential. It also seems likely that it was from Eleanor and her household rather than from Louis that Manuel gained an interest in Western chivalry – he was later to shock his subjects by taking up the practice of jousting, in which he excelled.

The French royal residence was either the Blachernae Palace or the Philopation (recently vandalised by the Germans). Odo's feeling account of the views afforded to the inhabitants of the Blachernae out over sea, fields and city suggests the former. He speaks of its lovely exterior, but finds his superlatives fail him when he speaks of the interior: the gold, the colours, the cunningly patterned marble floors, the art, the taste – in short, everything. Eleanor will have enjoyed the surrounds, and quite possibly some licensed hunting in the Emperor's game parks, as well as trips to the many beautiful churches wherein rare religious relics – the reputed Holy Lance, the Crown of Thorns, a fragment of the True Cross, among others – were to be found. She will have been able to see the magnificent funerary traditions of the Emperors. She may have participated in the formal service at St Sophia and the lavish banquet and reception which followed in a room whose floor was covered in rose petals, and where food was eaten using that most novel of instruments – a fork. There is, however, no basis for later writers' suggestions that the visit to Constantinople was a watershed moment for Eleanor 'lifting the accidie ... from her soul', as Kelly puts it.[33]

On 9 October, Manuel ensured that the French could celebrate the festival of St Denis in style, sending a band of clergy equipped with richly decorated candles to boost the celebrations. Even Odo admired the beauty of their chanting, the eunuchs' voices blending harmoniously with the tenors and basses and even the grace of their bearing as they clapped and genuflected with their song; and Louis wrote warmly of the service to Suger at home.[34] Briefly, it seems, Odo and Louis were lulled into believing the Emperor to be in full sympathy with them. But Manuel's spies had doubtless informed him that others, including the Bishop of Langres, were agitating for the army to be turned on Constantinople; and the detail with which Odo speaks of these arguments evidences clearly both the serious traction they were gaining and Louis' inability to manage his own team. Within days, the subtle Manuel had concocted a plan to remove his difficult guests from the immediate area. Louis was informed that the Germans, who had already crossed into Anatolia, had conducted their first battle against the Turks, slaughtering 14,000 of them, and that the terrified populace of the city of Iconium (Konya) had fled from their advance.

Not wanting to miss all the action, Louis ordered an immediate departure of his troops, though he himself awaited the arrival of the remainder of the forces he was expecting – the Savoyard contingent under the command of Louis' uncle the Count of Maurienne and the Marquess of Montferrat. Meanwhile, he continued to arrange the purchase of supplies in the limited markets made available to the crusading forces, to negotiate terms of support from Manuel and to urge Suger to send yet more money. With Louis now desperate to leave, Manuel asked two things: homage from any of Louis' barons who retook lands previously within the empire, and one of Eleanor's ladies (a relation of the king) as a wife for his nephew. The first point was agreed, but the second was put out of his power by Louis' brother, who arranged the abduction of the young lady in question so that she need not be left behind alone.

This episode is highly interesting from Eleanor's perspective. Firstly, it makes clear that Eleanor must have had a significant number of ladies accompanying her; a single young lady with blood links to the king would hardly have formed part of the party otherwise. It also demonstrates that the misconception of the trip as a risk-free pilgrimage had been prevalent before the party set out. Thirdly, it shows that by this point Eleanor had crossed the Bosphorus with the army, while Louis remained in Constantinople – yet more evidence of the growing separation between them. That this is so is made clear by the fact that Robert, on taking the girl, is not said to have fled across the Bosphorus but to have 'moved on ahead of the army'. Finally, it raises a strong inference that Eleanor, despite her good accord with Manuel, had conspired with Robert to ensure the girl was not sacrificed to Louis' weakness or political machinations. Again, the alienation between Eleanor and her husband crosses the years to us.

The identity of the girl and her subsequent fate is shrouded in mystery. That she did not marry Robert is clear – he was already married to Hawise of Salisbury, and would marry another widow on her death. What is clear is that the price of this defiance was that the guides for whom Louis had negotiated were never forthcoming – a point which cannot have assisted relations between Louis and his brother or Eleanor.

However, the deal, such as it was, was done, and Louis and his party finally moved to join his army, coincidentally at almost the exact time that a partial eclipse of the sun took place. Naturally this was taken as portending some disaster, and rumours swept the army that Louis was dead. While this was not true, there was indeed a disaster in the wings. News began to arrive that the Germans, far from triumphing, had been heavily defeated. Nine-tenths of their army had been slaughtered, and Conrad himself was seriously injured with a head wound. The French army finally caught up with the feeble remnants of the German army at the castle of Lopardium, where Louis, 'vigorous but tearful', welcomed Conrad with open arms.

Understandably made nervous by the Germans' experiences following an inland route, the main party decided to proceed by the more roundabout but safer coastal route, via Philadelphia, Smyrna, Pergamon and Ephesus. The route was dramatic, slow and tiresome. Odo refers to nearly daily encounters with steep, stony mountains and deep channels of mountain streams which were hard to ford. Food was hard to come by; often the inhabitants of the towns along the way barred their gates to the army. Some fell by the wayside. Others – even among the noble contingent – sickened and died, including Count Guy of Ponthieu, who was buried in the church of St John in Smyrna. By the time they arrived there in December, Conrad himself was unfit to journey further. He journeyed back with messengers sent by the Emperor, who warned the Crusaders against proceeding further. Louis' contingent, dominated by those hostile to the Emperor, dismissed his warnings, insisting that the army could defend and support itself on the road ahead.

Just before Christmas 1147, Louis and his army moved out of Ephesus along the nearby valley. A few minor raids took place but were repulsed. The heavy rains and snows set in, and, concerned about impending floods, Louis turned into the Maeander valley, which, as its name suggests, offered a wide plain with gentle slopes to the river, which curves to and from along the valley floor. The Turks gathered in the mountains and across the river, awaiting their moment to strike. Eleanor, with the baggage train and the wounded, was almost certainly in the centre of the army, with well-armed knights on every side. On the second day of this march, a Turkish strike was successfully repulsed by Theobald of Blois' son Henry of Champagne on one front while Louis led another charge to the rear. Continuing on their journey, the army reached Laodicea by 3 January 1148. The town was closed and deserted. There was no food to be had. Once again, Louis demonstrated his failures as a leader by convening a council to debate the next move.[35]

In the end, they had little choice but to move on as fast as possible through territory where the second section of the German Crusaders had recently been subjected to murderous attacks – blood still adorned stones along the roadside and unburied bodies lay in plain sight. Louis at least had the sense to proceed in battle order – the cavalry led the vanguard, the footsoldiers surrounded the baggage train and other vulnerable persons, and Louis brought up the rear with his royal guard. On the second day of this journey, the vanguard was under the command of under Eleanor's vassal Geoffrey de Rancon and Louis' uncle Amadeus of Maurienne when the party faced the challenge of transiting Mount Cadmus. It had been agreed that the army would spend a whole day reaching the passage by the summit, but the vanguard made better progress than anticipated and pulled ahead, moving over the crest, where they made preparations for the night's camp. The reasons for this decision are unclear, but it appears likely that, as William of Tyre suggests, the ground near the peak revealed itself to be unsuitable for a full camp, and the leaders followed the advice of their guides that a better site lay a short way ahead.[36]

Meanwhile, the heavy and slow baggage train, which stretched over 6 miles of precipitous single-track paths, followed ponderously behind. As for the rear guard, anticipating making faster progress uphill than the baggage and invalids, it had not set out at all. The most vulnerable part of the army was therefore left isolated from two parts of its protection. Predictably, the Turks struck with devastating effect. They seized the peak, striking with lightning speed from either side, thrusting and slashing and darting out of reach, leaving behind dead, injured and panicking civilians. The panic itself added to the fatalities, as horses and people lost their footing in trying to escape and plunged to their deaths. The numbers of attackers were large – Odo describes the French overwhelmed among the enemy 'as if drowned in the tide of the sea'. Odo himself was sent post-haste to summon Louis and his royal guard, who were with the rear guard.[37]

Louis and a relief force rode in haste to the battle and a ferocious contest ensued. Louis himself barely escaped with his life, having to flee to hide among the rocks, where he was able to take advantage of his higher position to fend off his pursuers. It was only after dark that they left him and he was able to scramble down and make his way back to his devastated army. The seriousness of the battle is attested by the admittedly incomplete list of noble deaths which Louis sent to Suger: Count William of Warenne, Everard of Breteuil, Manasses of Bulles, Gautier of Montjay, Reynald of Tours and Itiers of Meingnac. It is reinforced by the statistic that Louis' own guard lost forty men. And the death toll would only rise as sick men, far from comfort and required to keep moving, died en route. Gerard of Amiens was one of these; and the Damascene chronicler Ibn Al-Qalanisi reported that fresh reports of French losses continued until the spring of 1148.[38]

Where was Eleanor in this debacle? Many biographers, relying on an unsupported assertion in Richard's *Histoire des Comtes de Poitou*, deriving from the seventeenth-century historian Maimbourg, place Eleanor with the vanguard, and credit her with the initiative in pressing ahead of the rest of the army in order to make camp in a pretty green valley. However, none of the contemporaneous sources suggest this, nor any of those made shortly after. Both Odo and William of Tyre point the finger elsewhere. And we can be tolerably sure that those unfavourably disposed to Eleanor would surely have mentioned this had it occurred – some mention would be bound to appear either in Louis' correspondence or in Odo's account. Furthermore, as Ralph Turner rightly points out, it would have been completely contrary to accepted practice for Eleanor (or any other vulnerable person) to be exposed to the greater danger of the vanguard rather than travelling in the middle section of the army, which benefitted from the double protection of the vanguard and the rear guard.

What this means is that in all probability Eleanor was in the very section of the army which first came under attack, that she saw the Turkish assault at terrifying proximity and spent the battle sheltering as best she could, while the nearest troops fought to defend her. If this is the case, she cannot have avoided seeing up close the deaths and mutilation of a number of people she will have come to know well in the many months since the party left France. Until late in the day she will not have known whether or not she was a widow; until late in the day she may well have feared capture or death herself.[39]

The Turks eventually retreated, carrying off much loot and many of the surviving horses. The recriminations could then begin. Louis, of course, could not be openly criticised, but there can be little doubt that many, including Eleanor, will have held him primarily responsible, since it was by his decision-making that the party was there at all. The other main targets of ire were Geoffrey de Rancon and the Count of Maurienne, the leaders of the vanguard – and given the status of Maurienne as the king's uncle, and traditional hostility between northern and southern contingents, Rancon was the primary target. He was spared any proper punishment because any meted out to him would necessarily have applied to Maurienne also. However, there is no sign that the king stood up for Geoffrey; on the contrary, the king's mouthpiece, Odo, planted blame firmly at his door, saying that 'the entire people judged that Geoffrey should be hanged because he had not obeyed the king's command'. This failure to stand behind her vassal will have fed into Eleanor's grievances against Louis. It is likely that her ire would have been still greater had she been aware that the blame which lay on Rancon would gradually attach itself to her; William of Tyre, writing twenty years later, speculates that Rancon acted on Eleanor's orders, and from here grew the story that Eleanor had been with the vanguard, and in effective charge of it – a key piece in the 'Black Myth' which was to grow up around her in the years to come.

In all the excitement about the detail of the battle, the blaming of Geoffrey de Rancon and the fevered speculation about Eleanor's role, one very important point seems to have been neglected by those writing about the battle – and about Eleanor. It is this: if de Rancon was to blame for allowing the vanguard to lose touch with the central portion of the expedition, was not Louis, the leader of the rear guard, not (at least) equally to blame for doing likewise at the other end? Logically, the answer must be yes. This was a colossal dual failure of leadership by Louis. He had failed to ensure his orders were obeyed by the vanguard, but even more shockingly he had failed to observe basic discipline in the leading of his own contingent. One reason why the finger was so firmly pointed at Geoffrey de Rancon must have been that, at least in Odo's account, blame could not be placed on Louis's shoulders. On the ground, however, everyone involved would surely have understood this; and if Eleanor, fresh from a terrible ordeal, did not blame her husband firstly for allowing the incident to occur and secondly for allowing the bulk of the blame to be assigned elsewhere, she would hardly have been human. This is only amplified by the knowledge that her uncle Raymond's had urged the use of a maritime route.

Although Louis catches none of the blame in Odo's account, the reality of the feeling towards him is shockingly revealed by the fact that now, reeling from the assault, Louis apparently abdicated further responsibility for leading the Crusade, and instead placed the party under the command of the Templar contingent. Every Crusader was required to 'establish fraternity with the Templars, rich and poor alike swearing that they would not flee the field and that they would obey the officers of the Templars assigned to them in every respect'. The party was broken up into groups, each under the command of a Templar knight, and all of them under the command of a knight called Gilbert. Each officer drilled every fit person in his contingent. One way of looking at this event is that it reflected a fairly startling acceptance of Louis' own inability to lead, which is reflected in John of Salisbury's verdict that the army had 'neither military discipline, nor a strong hand to dispense justice and correct faults'.[40] Another is that Louis' resignation as commander was not entirely voluntary but reflected a general loss of confidence in his abilities, which would hardly be surprising in the circumstances. If so, this humiliation provided a still further reason for Eleanor to be alienated from Louis. And to make matters worse, everyone will have had ample opportunity to nurse their grudges over the next weeks as the party limped on, lacking most of its comforts and with few horses – many of which were eaten when they failed from exhaustion and hunger.

The terrain continued to be extremely challenging: an expanse of wetland traversed by two substantial rivers surrounded by mud, from which tired horses had to be pulled by force. Nor had the attentions of the Turkish raiders ceased – they attacked the party as it moved beyond the rivers, and a small battle took place as the two armies sought the more favourable positions from which to snipe at each other. On this occasion, inspired by the more martial leadership of the Templars, the French had the best of it. But as more and more of the horses died, more and more of the baggage had to be carried by its owners, or abandoned. Clothes, tents and valuables, all were abandoned by the wayside as the weakened force made its painful way towards the coast. Behind Odo's relatively brave face lies another hellish month.

The sheer desperation of the situation can be discerned by the detail let slip by Odo that when, late in the month, the beleaguered party arrived at the small port of Attalia, seeking supplies for their onward journey, their requirements included clothing for the ladies and shoes for the bishops, who had ended up walking barefoot. Eleanor of course will have been better supplied than most, but she cannot have escaped considerable privations, a diet which seems to have consisted substantially of recently deceased horses, and seeing many in the party reduced to desperate straits – if not to death.

All of the party will have reached Attalia hoping that things were to take a considerable turn for the better, but this city, long past its glory days and recently the subject of Turkish raids, could by no means furnish the requirements for even Louis' now considerably diminished army. Nor could it provide a sufficient fleet to transport the whole force by sea to Antioch. The party was at a dead end. The army camped outside the walls rapidly fell a victim to disease, exacerbated by their weakened state. In the end, after further weeks of indecision and unsuccessful negotiation, during which time the death toll rose to alarming proportions, Louis hired ships to take himself, Eleanor, their immediate circles and his best knights to Antioch. Even this decision appears to have been forced on him by his vassals, the chief of whom announced to him their election to travel by ship, rather than, as Louis would have preferred, to continue to follow in the footsteps of the First Crusaders. The rest of the army he abandoned to make their way as best they could overland, which was a forty-day march at the best of times; only half of the force he left behind was to make it to Antioch. Still worse was the fate of the pilgrims accompanying the Crusade, who were expelled by the Attalians as useless mouths. Most were massacred by the Turks as they struggled to follow the remains of Louis' army; some few thousand survived by converting to Islam.[41] Another shameful failure was added to Louis' account.

Even apart from the horror which must have been felt as to the fate of much of the crusading force, Louis and Eleanor's own troubles were not over as they embarked at the start of March for Antioch. The journey, which should have taken three days, was severely impeded by bad weather; and while Louis' ship apparently made landfall to schedule, storms meant that for others, including Odo, and possibly Eleanor, the transit lasted instead some two weeks.[42] The bedraggled state of the self-appointed saviour of the

Holy Land on arrival can well be imagined – and indeed some of the party, including Eleanor's vassal the Viscount of Limoges, were to die in Antioch.

What the party found was long-awaited relief from the privations they had endured. There was more of the same sorts of luxury which they had experienced in Constantinople – a city rich in beautiful residences decorated with marble columns and vibrantly beautiful mosaics, in hanging gardens, orchards and water sources. It was the perfect place to recoup their much-tried strength; and yet, ironically, it was Antioch's call for help which had put the Crusade in train, for this oasis of beauty and civilisation was precariously placed.

Eleanor's stay in Antioch has dominated accounts of her Crusade experience and the perception of her life. While it was a key moment in her story, there is no evidence to suggest that it marked any 'sudden revelation of a world in accordance with her heart and her dreams', as Pernoud would have it; nor that 'Antioch was to her the essence of poetry', as Kelly claims.[43] It is important to recall that while her Crusade experience was to last from Easter 1147 until November 1149, she was in Antioch for no longer than a few weeks. The final division which emerged between Eleanor and Louis at this point needs to be viewed in the light of the events of the Crusade, and indeed the marriage, to date. The stay at Antioch is much better seen as a point when Eleanor, recovering from the terrible ordeals of the past month, had time to take stock – and the opportunity to do so with a more than sympathetic ear available.

What would Eleanor have been forced to conclude about her position and her marriage? While Odo reported that Louis had met reverses with firmness and courage, the picture which Eleanor and the vassals (including her own) will have taken from the journey was that Louis was a poor leader, riven by indecisiveness, and with an unenviable talent for taking the wrong decision when forced to make one. The weeks of hard travelling will have provided an unusual opportunity for Eleanor both to evaluate what decisions she would have taken at each point and to take the temperature of informed male opinion on military and political matters. By Antioch, Eleanor seems (from what was to occur) to have decided that her views were at least as sound as her husband's. So much she might have been obliged to tolerate if the physical side of the marriage – which was essential for her to be in a position to provide an heir – had improved. But far from it; there had been no improvement at all in their intimate relationship. Odo reports how God was 'the Alpha and Omega' of Louis' enterprise and speaks of the rigour of his religious observances. Apparently never once had Louis failed, throughout their terrible journey, to hear Mass and observe the canonical hours.[44] Eleanor therefore knew by now that she was married to a weak man whose mind was set on God and for whom marriage would never be more than a rather distasteful necessity.

Against this background, the reunion with uncle Raymond of Antioch, her exceedingly handsome, virile cousin – described by one chronicler as the handsomest man of his day and accepted by all as an exceptional warrior and horseman – could not fail to provide much food for thought, and it is quite clear that Eleanor was drawn to him. He was just thirty-five years old – much the age her father was in Eleanor's memory. He was the kind of compelling giant of a man that her father and grandfather seem to have been. He was her closest male relative, who knew the stories of her childhood. Save in sharing a tendency to immoderate outbursts of rage, here was a man who was everything that her husband was not. He was also, however, a desperate man who had an agenda and a use for his niece.[45]

Raymond had sought aid from the West following the fall of Edessa because his principality was next in line for the attention of Zengi's heir, Nur-ad-Din, whose extreme Muslim piety fostered a desire to extirpate the entire Christian empire. Raymond had accompanied his plea with rich gifts to Louis to ensure that the French king was on board with his plan. Raymond was therefore disconcerted (to say the least) to discover that Louis had not only rejected his advice as to how to reach the Holy Land, but that he was also by no means committed to Raymond's plan. This plan was to move towards a recovery of Edessa via an attack on the city of Aleppo, and by that means to safeguard the entire Frankish Outremer empire, including Jerusalem. Naturally, it carried with it a substantial collateral benefit: it would increase the power of his own principality and provide him with a much stronger bargaining position vis-à-vis Manuel Komnenos, who claimed the right to rule Antioch.[46]

Yet Raymond found that Louis' attention was far more fixed on achieving his pilgrim aim of visiting Jerusalem; and to be quite fair to him, from the moment of his decision to depart on Crusade he had been badgered by all the Christian princes of the region for assistance and was in no position to make any early moves, having exhausted his funds, with only a small band of followers in Antioch and the position of his remaining army still uncertain.[47] Further the Emperor Conrad was to arrive in Jerusalem shortly and it made sense for the two leaders to agree a way forward. But, equally, Louis' extensive group of advisers included not a few who will have worked out that Raymond was in fact looking to use French troops to increase his own empire – and this would, strictly speaking, benefit his overlord Manuel Komnenos. With the bulk of the party minded to blame Manuel for their recent experiences, on the basis that he should have provided them with more help, it is likely that this factor weighed heavily with the advisers.

So Raymond, though doubtless honestly pleased to renew acquaintance with his niece and her vassals, many of whom he would have recalled from childhood, was bound to try to persuade Eleanor of the merits of his plan, hoping that through her curtain lectures Louis might be brought to accept Raymond's way of thinking; doubtless he had heard, as William of Tyre and John of Salisbury attest, of Louis' continued 'almost excessive' love for Eleanor.[48]

For Eleanor we can infer the pleasure of reunion with this glamorous big brother figure, and his numerous Poitevin ministers, in a court where she could once again hear the *lengua romana* in use, was further enhanced by the unusual treat of having her views sought on political matters. The two spent much time together, and Eleanor became a convert to the Aleppo plan and advocated it strongly. Perhaps predictably, this seems to have driven Louis more firmly into the anti-Aleppo camp. He quickly made it apparent that he was minded to move directly to Jerusalem, and that he expected his queen, as a good obedient wife, to submit to his decision.[49]

In the early years of their marriage, back in France, Eleanor may have been prepared to adopt this expected mantle. Now aged twenty-four or twenty-five, and having been on a revelatory journey, she was not so minded. She refused to change her view and met Louis' and his entourage's diatribes about wifely duty with a shocking counter-move: she suggested that Louis go to Jerusalem while she – and her vassals – stayed in Antioch. When he refused to agree, she said she would nonetheless stay – and she would initiate proceedings for an annulment of their marriage on the grounds of consanguinity.

It is from these events that the stories of Eleanor's affair with her uncle (inflated in the next century into attempts to elope with an unnamed Turk or the currently ten-year-old Saladin[50]) derive. Within the sizeable world of Eleanor scholarship, 'the Affair at Antioch', as it is known, has developed into a mini-school of its own, with multiple papers by renowned academics debating the subject.[51] In the light of all that debate and consideration, what credence should we give to the stories?

In answering this question, we do not have Odo's evidence – his account comes to an abrupt end just when the Crusaders arrived in Antioch. The reason for this cessation is not clear. Flori speculates that Odo decided that he could not with any degree of honesty tell the story after this point consistently with his mission to protect Louis' reputation.[52] This seems logical, but is unhelpful, as on any analysis the denouement of the story is one which would justify this approach. Louis' own surviving letters of the period tell us little – apart from the fact that he was desperate for funds and that Suger was keen for him to return, with Louis putting this off. A letter which plainly did cover what occurred at Antioch is lost – probably destroyed by Suger.

However, we are extraordinarily fortunate to have a reliable, almost first-hand account from John of Salisbury, who had now moved from Paris and was in the service of Pope Eugenius when Eleanor and Louis visited him on return from Crusade. In around 1164,[53] he wrote his honest account, which he assures us is 'nothing but what I myself have seen and heard and know to be true, or have on good authority from the testimony and writings of reliable men'.

His account was drawn from the personal accounts of both Louis and Eleanor to the Pope on their return journey. John may have been personally in attendance, or else he heard the two accounts direct from the lips of Eugenius. He tells us this:

> the attentions paid by the Prince to the Queen, and his constant, indeed almost continuous, conversation with her, aroused the King's suspicions. These were greatly strengthened when the Queen wished to remain behind although the King was preparing to leave, and the Prince made every effort to keep her, if the King would give consent. And when the King made haste to tear her away, she mentioned their kinship, saying that it was not lawful for them to remain together as man and wife, since they were related in the fourth and fifth degrees. Even before their departure a rumour to that effect had been heard in France … At this the

king was deeply moved; and although he loved the queen almost beyond reason he consented to divorce her if his counsellors and the French nobility would allow it. There was one knight amongst the king's secretaries called Thierry de Galeran, a eunuch whom the queen had always hated and mocked, but who was faithful and had the king's ear like his father's before him. He boldly persuaded the king not to suffer her to dally longer in Antioch both because 'guilt under kinship's disguise could lie concealed' and because it would be a lasting shame to the kingdom of the Franks if in addition to all the other disasters it was reported that the king had been deserted by his wife, or robbed of her. So he argued, either because he hated the queen or because he really believed it, moved perchance by widespread rumour.[54]

From this we see that the story John was told was based on unfounded jealousy on Louis' part – while there were plainly a lot of lengthy meetings between Eleanor and Raymond, there is no suggestion that Eleanor had done more than spend a rather excessive amount of time talking to him. In short, and unsurprisingly, she evinced pleasure in being in his company. That this prompted disquiet on Louis' part echoes the early stories about his possessiveness regarding Eleanor, and also chimes with the fact that there is no suggestion in Louis' own correspondence or in Odo's account of any actual impropriety by Eleanor. The account does not suggest that Louis thought that Eleanor had been unfaithful – or even that de Galeran suggested that she had been. What was in issue with Louis, who despite his devotion had been agreeable in principle to a divorce, was in reality worried about the effect a separation and divorce at this point would provoke.

The big question here is what should be read into the paraphrasing of Ovid about sin being hidden under kinship's cloak. Flori sees this as an explicit signalling of actual incest. However, it can be convincingly argued that this is reading too much into the phrase, and that such an interpretation conflicts with what John explicitly says. Further, the phrase may be said to be equally referable either to the issue of perception (i.e. what people would say) or to the sin of wifely disobedience being covered by the colourable excuse of remaining with her own family.

Is there any better ground for believing the incest story? It would seem not. The other near-contemporary chroniclers carry no such suggestion. For example, Lambert of Wattelros tells us that Louis picked a 'childish quarrel' with Eleanor on Crusade which lasted until the year of the divorce, while Henry of Huntingdon, Hugh of Poitiers, Richard le Poitevin and Robert of Torigny do not have anything negative to say about Eleanor's conduct on Crusade. The first possible suggestion of physical unfaithfulness in the chronicles (as opposed to undutifulness) comes thirty years later, in the account of William of Tyre, whose verdict was that Eleanor was a 'foolish woman ... [who] disregarded her marriage vows and neglected her duty to be faithful to her husband'. William's account has to be treated carefully, as he condemns Eleanor by reference to her conduct 'before and after this time' and is thus avowedly coloured by hindsight. But it should be noted that his account does not mention physical infidelity – as he could easily have done if that is what he meant – but rather breach of the marriage bond. This in fact suggests that to William, as to John, Eleanor's sin was that of disloyalty to her husband – put simply, disobedience.

William's ambiguous verdict was nonetheless influential and echoed in later writers' accounts, even those who were generally favourable to Eleanor, such as Richard of Devizes, who while generally praising Eleanor refers to something that arose on Crusade and was 'better not spoken of'.[55] Later French writers in the pay of the French kings such as Hélinand de Froidmont and Aubri de Trois-Fontaines seized upon it to found a claim that she behaved on Crusade 'not like a queen but like a common whore'. Gerald of Wales (again influenced by the French) works to similar effect, accusing Eleanor of infidelity on Crusade and also after her return to France. From there it is but a short step to the thirteenth-century account of Matthew Paris, which reports that Eleanor had been accused of adultery 'with an infidel' and the Minstrel of Reims 1260 version which has Eleanor falling in love with Saladin and offering to desert her husband and recant her faith for him.[56]

The ambiguity of the account and the later development of the story chimes with the fact that John's carefully worded account does indicate strongly that even if Louis did not consider that Eleanor had been unfaithful with Raymond, there were widespread verbal rumours to that effect at the time, which Thierry de Galeran cited in order to influence Louis. This inference is sometimes said to be supported by the lines of the troubadour Cercamon, formerly a favourite of Eleanor's father and now in service to the Count of Toulouse, who speaks of an unfaithful woman: 'Better that she should never have been born than that she should commit that fault which will cause her to be the subject of gossip from here to Poitou.' It is fair to say, however, that Cercamon's poem appears to reference infidelity generally with no specific basis to point it at Eleanor.[57] With such stories doing the rounds at the time, it is hardly surprising that as the facts receded into the past the more salacious story gained currency – perhaps fuelled by the prominent, far from submissive roles which Eleanor came to play in her later life.

What, in the final analysis, is the best reading of the evidence? In my own view, which coincides with the majority of those recently writing on the subject (though not with Flori), the subject of the Antioch incident was not infidelity and incest but jealousy and wifely disobedience. This is most consistent with the earliest and most reliable sources. It is also surely the most likely answer. Quite apart from the shortness of the period when Eleanor was in Antioch, the taint of incest and the practical and logistical difficulties for two such eminent (and accompanied) people to arrange an affair, it is highly unlikely that Eleanor, her duties as bearer of a French heir still undischarged, would have imperilled the royal bloodline – or risked becoming pregnant with a baby which would trap her in her marriage. What Eleanor did do, in the eyes even of more sympathetic viewers, was to transgress her duty of wifely loyalty and obedience. For the Church was quite clear on this: the Decretum of Burchard of Worms – a leading text on canon law – prescribed an oath for a wife which included the following passage: 'I will be subject to [my husband] obedient, in service, in love and in fear, as according to the law the wife ought to be subject to the husband.'[58]

At the time, the consequence of the rumours and de Galeran's advice was summarised by John of Salisbury: '... she was torn away and forced to leave for Jerusalem with the king; and their mutual anger growing greater, the wound remained, hide it as best they might'. These slightly understated words cover a shocking truth, which seems likely to have been a part of Odo's reason for ceasing his account on the arrival at Antioch. What John means is that, having been told that Eleanor had chosen not to go on, Louis forced Eleanor to accompany him, presumably by ordering his men to physically compel her. Although as her husband he had the right to discipline his wife, using his soldiers to manhandle her would have been viewed fairly dimly, even at the time.

In light of these events, it is no surprise that the marriage was effectively past repair, at least from Eleanor's side, from Antioch onwards. However, it appears that the alienation was profound on both sides, for Suger writes to Louis shortly after (in reply to the lost letter from Louis):

> ... as regards your wife, the Queen, we venture if we may to endorse your decision to conceal whatever rancour is in your heart, if there is any, until you return to your own kingdom ... and you can attend to this and other matters.

Plainly Louis, too, was furious, and talking of taking action.[59]

Ironically, given that the reason de Galeran suggested the removal of Eleanor was to prevent rumours, a further consequence of the abduction of Eleanor would have been to add fuel to them – why, people would be bound to ask, did Louis have to abduct her if there was not something in the story?

The episode is therefore less colourful than it is often said to be. But it does tell us some important things about Eleanor. The obvious one is that she was done with her first marriage by the spring of 1148. But it also seems to indicate that, at least at this time, she had a tendency to headstrong action. The deployment of the annulment argument at this point has all the hallmarks of a badly controlled row; this was neither the time nor the place for that line to be taken. Another thing it suggests is that Eleanor was determined and ruthless with herself as well as others. After over a decade as a queen, she cannot but have been well aware of how greatly her conduct would be scrutinised, and she doubtless had early indications from Louis or his advisers about his discomfort with her close companionship with her uncle and the resulting gossip. Although she may not have cared about Louis' personal feelings, she must have continued on this course with her eyes open as to the consequences for her reputation. Talk would inevitably become scandal – as indeed it did. Yet, having decided to depart from the course set by her marriage, it appears that Eleanor was prepared to sustain the long-term collateral damage this entailed.

In the short term, however, what Eleanor's conduct resulted in was a quasi-abduction and a closely supervised journey to Jerusalem, followed by a long sojourn there. The arrival of the French Crusaders, whom it was feared might have been lured away by Raymond's plan, was hailed with joy by a large crowd led by Queen Melisende, her sixteen-year-old son Baldwin III and the newly arrived Emperor Conrad (now recovered from his wounds, thanks in part to the personal efforts of Manuel Komnenos). They were conducted into the city by the Patriarch and the Frankish nobles of the kingdom, and taken in a joyful procession accompanied by religious music to worship at the Holy Places.[60] For these few days, at least, Eleanor and Louis will have been able to share in the pleasure of having completed their pilgrim journey to Jerusalem and having been privileged to see the city's shrines and churches, and the scenes familiar to them from the accounts of the First Crusade.

Eleanor was to have the opportunity to become properly familiar with the great city, for shortly after their arrival Louis left Eleanor under supervision there while he attended a conference in late June at Acre which included all the leaders of the Crusader kingdoms – apart from Raymond and the Count of Tripoli, who had refused to attend. Raymond understood by now that any plan he put forward would be ignored, and washed his hands of the Crusade he had been instrumental in calling into being.[61]

The result of this conference was a somewhat surprising agreement to attack Damascus – the principal city of Syria, and although Muslim, a key buffer between the Crusader States and the Turks. Its ruler Mu'in al-Din even had a treaty of alliance with Jerusalem. In geopolitical terms, any modern reader will probably immediately spot the action of the council as a mistake; far more likely than stopping a unification of Muslim Syria under Nur-ad-Din was the actual outcome, namely that Damascus would be driven straight into his arms. However, while most scholars have derided the decision, a sensible geopolitical case can be made for it, not least in that a campaign in Aleppo could no longer save Edessa, and would only strengthen Raymond, whereas Damascus had historically been a threat and a successful campaign against Damascus would nip in the bud any signs of growing cohesion among the Muslim leaders.[62]

In any event, Louis cannot bear the blame for the decision alone – it was the considered view of a group that included Conrad, the rulers of Jerusalem and representatives of the Knights Templar, and it reflected an earlier agreement apparently reached by Conrad with the Templars in May. It also may well be reflective of the fact that Conrad was now bankrolled by Manuel Komnenos. Indeed, the outside perception was that this was Conrad's decision; the Arab chroniclers barely mention Louis, and Conrad is seen by them as the undoubted leader of the Crusade.[63]

The armies of Louis, Conrad and Baldwin of Jerusalem moved at once; but by the end of July their great attack was over. Mu'in al-Din got wind of the plan and fortified the city while also sending for help from Nur-ad-Din. The Crusaders arrived on 24 July 1148, and this first day of the campaign was a great success. The second was equivocal, with the Crusaders repelling sorties from the city but making no progress with taking it. On the third day, everything fell apart. Nur-ad-Din's advance cavalry arrived, as did news that two armies, those of Aleppo and Mosul, were just behind them. Mu'in al-Din offered the Crusaders an ultimatum: withdraw or he would hand the city over to Nur-ad-Din. Unable to agree to press on, with dissension flourishing among the various factions making up the army, they ended up having no choice but to withdraw. To add insult to injury, the Turkish cavalry harried them all the way back into their own borders.[64] The active part of the Second Crusade, on which so much money and so many lives had been wasted, was over. It is hardly surprising that neither Odo nor Otto of Friesing were prepared to write about this denouement.

While Louis was embarking on this disastrous campaign, Eleanor may well have been making better use of her time. Following the council at Acre, Queen Melisende of Jerusalem returned to her city. Eleanor could scarcely have sought a better companion to advise and assist her in the position in which she found herself. Melisende was a great heiress too: the daughter of Baldwin II of Jerusalem, and aunt to Raymond of Antioch's queen. Now in her mid to late forties, she had been raised to rule and had been queen since 1131. However, she had had to fight her own husband, the formidable Fulk of Anjou (father of Geoffrey le Bel), for her right to rule. Fulk, it should be noted, was a man of such wealth, talent and power that it was widely considered that he was recommended for the role of King of Jerusalem by Louis VI to ensure he could not dominate French politics – particularly after Louis VI's anticipated death. Like Eleanor, Melisende's political influence in the early years of her marriage can be seen to be limited based on the paucity of charters issued by her. Melisende too was no stranger to controversy and damage to her reputation; one of the weapons her husband had deployed against her was an accusation that she had had an affair with one of her most prominent vassals – to whom she was also related. Melisende, however, had fought back and over a period of five years had put herself into a position where she was effectively able to wrest dominance from Fulk and rule with him, but very much in her own right. After his death she was now ruling alone – despite Bernard of Clairvaux's advice to her that such a state of affairs was so unnatural as to be impossible and although her son Baldwin had been crowned co-ruler with her.[65]

If Eleanor was to emerge as a duchess in her own right from her marriage with Louis, Melisende was a God-given source of advice. Eleanor also had good opportunities to see the means by which Melisende was ensuring her own legacy and fame in Jerusalem through substantial building projects, including the remodelling of the Church of the Holy Sepulchre and the rebuilding of the Church of St Anne – both projects which were underway during the French visit. Another point of interest may well have been the necropolis which was developing for the royal house, with four Crusader kings buried there in grandeur.[66]

And Eleanor had plenty of time to get Melisende's advice, for while the bulk of the Crusader army – including Louis' brother Robert – melted away quickly after the Damascus debacle, Louis determined not to sail before the winter weather set in, and thereby ensured that he and his immediate party had to remain in Jerusalem until spring brought weather which was safe for sailing. Louis' motivations have been much speculated on; it seems likely that, with the kudos of a successful campaigner denied him, he wanted a period of time for the embarrassment to die down. Moreover, this extension of his stay enabled a full pilgrimage tour, and he could at least return home with that form of glory. Some rationale is called for, since plainly an earlier return was possible and Suger's letters implore a speedy return, not least once Robert of Dreux came back and started to share his frank views on Louis' failings as a leader.[67]

It therefore seems likely that Eleanor will have accompanied Louis on some if not all of his visits across the Holy Land – to sites such as Bethlehem and the Jordan River, providing her with many tales to tell her future children.[68] These, however, were not coming any time soon. Louis' biographers inform us that as part of his pilgrimage Louis was continuing to remain celibate.

Finally, Louis and Eleanor set off for home on 3 April 1149. In the light of the vicissitudes of the outward journey and the shortcomings of the Byzantine Emperor as an adviser and ally, the return was to be made by sea, and under the aegis of Roger of Sicily. While a sea voyage was definitely seen as the safer option, it should not be confused, even in spring, with a modern cruise; the writings of the era make it plain that sea travel was unpleasant and often dangerous if storms blew up. There was also the real threat of piracy – and indeed war, for Sicily and Byzantium were recommencing hostilities. It is perhaps predictable, given the bad luck which had dogged the entire expedition, that these risks were not evaded.

What Louis and Eleanor first encountered was a sea battle between the Sicilians and the Byzantines near Corfu, into which their little fleet somehow blundered. Louis' ship evaded the encounter, but Eleanor's was captured by the Byzantines. What happened in the ensuing three weeks is unclear – the account given by John of Salisbury is far from easy to follow, suggesting that Eleanor's capture was used as a bargaining chip to persuade Louis to journey back via Constantinople, and the sources from the Empire are no better.[69] It seems clear, however, that Eleanor and all those travelling with her were held prisoner 'for a time'; but whether they were released by Manuel or freed only after another battle is the subject of conflicting accounts. While it is unlikely that Eleanor herself will have been offered any violence or even discourtesy, she will certainly have had another occasion to see violence at close range, and was very possibly unable to stop violence or insult being offered to her travelling companions and female attendants. She will have been unsure as to whether she would be held hostage for some hours or even days. In the event, either the Sicilians regained control of the vessel or Manuel Komnenos ordered its release on account of Eleanor's presence on it.

But this was not the end of the vicissitudes of the voyage. Once the fleet was reunited, it encountered terrible – and somewhat unseasonal – storms. Louis' vessel eventually made landfall at the end of July 1149 in Calabria, while Eleanor's sought refuge in early August at Palermo. The extremity of the journey is vouched for by the fact that this is the only time, apart from towards the end of Eleanor's long life, when the records suggest that she was seriously ill; she was not fit to continue on her journey for another three weeks.[70] Doubtless stress and prolonged seasickness had left her in a very delicate condition, but she may also have suffered some injury in the storms. However, the agents of Roger II of Sicily ensured she was well cared for, and escorted her to his beautiful palace to regain her strength, while a message was sent to Louis to inform him that his wife was still alive.

Eleanor was still unwell when she rejoined Louis at the end of the month in Calabria and they journeyed together to Roger's court at Potenza.[71] At some point in this period, news will have reached the couple of the fate of Raymond and Antioch. It can hardly have assisted either Eleanor's recovery or the pair's relationship.

After Eleanor and Louis had left in 1148, Raymond had pursued his Aleppo strategy with some success. However, the next year Nur-ad-Din was back – this time in alliance with the Damascenes, alienated by the actions of Louis and his Crusaders. They besieged the fortress of Inab. Raymond was unable to secure support from Jerusalem or Edessa, and though he was initially successful in driving them off with a small force, the Muslim troops believing that his attack was the spearhead for a larger army, he neglected to secure his camp overnight, and awoke to find his enemies had realised the true weakness of his army and surrounded it. Raymond refused to leave his army and flee, but even his most heroic efforts were bound to fail in the face of the enemy's numbers. Nearly the entire army of 1,500 men was slaughtered, Raymond's head was taken as a trophy for the Caliph, and the key fortresses protecting Antioch were besieged. Antioch, which the Crusade had been supposed to save, was in worse case than before they set out. It survived a siege by Nur-ad-Din, but at the price of offering him covert allegiance in the form of coinage and mentions in daily prayers.[72]

When we next hear of Eleanor travelling north with Louis, it is again at a slow pace and reportedly because of her ill health; while she had probably not fully recovered from the vicissitudes of her abduction and sea voyage, it seems plausible that the shock and grief occasioned by her uncle's terrible death caused a relapse. Pausing here, we should perhaps reconsider just how much Eleanor had endured physically and mentally over the course of the Crusade. Later in her life, Eleanor's resilience in the face of troubles can be seen to be remarkable. Surely this resilience was in large part acquired from the concatenation of terrible experiences she survived in this period. But here, too, we can see the Eleanor who was to emerge, who would never be passive in the face of adversity. What happened next suggests that Eleanor already felt her marriage to Louis was finished and that she was looking forward to obtaining a formal release once they returned home.

But this was not to be, for on their path lay Pope Eugenius. Their first stop en route to him was at Ceprano, where they were greeted by papal legates who would escort them the rest of the way. Among these was the royal couple's friend Cardinal Hyacinth Bobone. Hyacinth also had the merit of being able to bring Louis and

Eleanor up to date with the religious controversies which had been exciting France in their absence. In particular, Bernard of Clairvaux had sought to indict Gilbert of Poitiers for heresy. But in Gilbert he had faced an adversary who not only had Hyacinth's, and hence the Pope's, support, but who was also at the height of his powers and prepared to enter into theological disputation with Bernard. The result had been a rare ignominious defeat for Bernard.[73]

Following the short journey with the legates, a visit was made to the Pope at Tusculum (now Frascati) on 9 or 10 October 1149.[74] It appears that Suger had already briefed him on the disharmony in the marriage and on Eleanor's wish for an annulment, as well as on Suger's view that it was imperative that the marriage should survive. For Eugenius, that monk whom Bernard of Clairvaux had regarded as too unworldly for the role, cooked up a truly astonishing attempt at reconciliation. It is to this remarkable event that we owe the testimony of John of Salisbury, who was present.

Having heard both parties' different accounts of their estrangement, 'he commanded under pain of anathema that no word should be spoken against their marriage and that it should not be dissolved under any pretext whatsoever. This ruling plainly delighted the King for he loved the Queen passionately, in an almost childish way.'[75]

This is an interesting point to consider. This is the only eyewitness account we have of Louis' supposed love for Eleanor, though it is echoed in William of Tyre's later charge against Louis of 'immoderate' affection for Eleanor.[76] Its source is good, but it seems odd coming at a time when the couple were plainly contemplating divorce – Louis had apparently agreed in principle to this in Antioch – and at a time when Suger's correspondence suggests that Louis' letters spoke of considerable bitterness against Eleanor. Which account should be preferred? Actually, it seems very possible that both were true. Louis may well have admired Eleanor excessively, perhaps the more desperately and guiltily for his apparent difficulties in the bedroom. But his failures with her, and her increasing unwillingness to conform to the Church's template for good wifedom, plainly stoked considerable resentment in him too.

As for Eleanor, John does not tell us what her complaints were, but there is a strong inference that not only did she reiterate her case on consanguinity but she also complained of Louis' failures to pay the marriage debt. Were it not for this it is hardly credible that

Eugenius would have, as he apparently did, 'made them sleep in the same bed, which he had decked with priceless hangings of his own, and daily ... he strove by friendly converse to restore the love between them'.[77] That Eleanor's complaints were justified, and that Louis generally had difficulty in performing his marital duty, is also supported by the fact that this interlude did apparently result (as had the Bernard of Clairvaux-sanctioned coupling) in a pregnancy.

Quite why Eugenius took this course has been a matter for speculation. Eleanor and Louis were plainly related within the prohibited degrees, and their marriage was clearly neither fruitful nor happy. However, contemporary teaching said that the consanguinity rules were ones which the Pope could dispense with as they were part of man-made law, not natural or divine law.[78] While Bernard of Clairvaux, Eugenius' mentor, despised the jurists' works, Suger may well have pleaded with Eugenius in advance as to the political nightmare which would be caused by the divorce.

It is also possible that Eugenius, already aware of the criticisms circulating against him and Louis *inter alia* for the failure of the Crusade he had encouraged, felt that a divorce between two of the major figures in the Crusade immediately on their return could only cause more problems for all involved. As it was, Marcabru was writing that 'the public outcry relating to [the Holy Land] pours down on the highest ranking leaders; broken failures weary of valour who love neither joy nor delight'.[79]

While a tearful Eugenius heaped the royal couple with gifts and sent them on their way to Rome for a rendezvous with the shrines and the Senate, it is overwhelmingly likely that Eleanor departed from him in rage, resentment and misery. The door to freedom had briefly opened; he had closed it in her face. Once her pregnancy began to manifest itself, she will have felt the walls closing about her, apparently trapping her in an arid and increasingly hostile marriage.[80]

Louis and Eleanor finally returned to France in November 1149, after an absence of over two years,[81] only to find that pleas from the Holy Land for further support or for another Crusade were waiting. Fortunately, Eugenius and Bernard of Clairvaux, stung by the criticism directed at them, were lukewarm about the endeavour. However, rather oddly, Abbot Suger, contrary to his negativity about the Second Crusade and the tone of his correspondence with Louis, seems to have embraced the call with enthusiasm, seeing in it a suitable final project for himself.[82]

It was therefore Suger who was the driving force behind an assembly to discuss the Crusade in May 1150 at Chartres, which many of the most eminent churchmen did not attend. Bernard himself was an absentee, although he sent his companion and secretary Geoffrey of Clairvaux, the Bishop of Langres. Contrary to Suger's intention of leading the Crusade himself, the assembly elected the absent Bernard the leader of the endeavour. However, Bernard was in a cautious mood. Having been burnt by both the failure of the Second Crusade and his unsuccessful trial of Gilbert of Poitiers, he preached an unusually humble and resigned sermon, calling the failure of the Crusade the will of God and refusing to take leadership of any new Crusade into his own hands, although privately he urged Eugenius and others to take some steps. With such muted enthusiasm, the plan soon crumbled.[83]

The other major factor on the horizon at the French court was dealing with Geoffrey of Anjou and his seventeen-year-old son Henry. Specifically, while Stephen of Blois had been occupied trying to hold England against Geoffrey's wife, the Empress, Geoffrey himself had concentrated, with considerable success, on gaining control of the County of Normandy, which both claimed as an adjunct to the English throne. Contrary to the accounts of certain biographers, Geoffrey was thus occupied during the years 1147–49, and did not accompany the Crusade.[84]

Then, in January of 1150, Henry returned from England where he had been supporting his mother's efforts to gain her throne, and was deemed by his father old enough to be vested with the hypothetical lordship of Normandy. This transfer of power, however, should have been marked by an offer of homage to Louis – which did not come. Further, the Angevins had made encroaching movements in other directions, ensuring Geoffrey's sister's election (contrary to Gilbert of Poitiers' preference) as Abbess of Fontevraud and clashing with Louis' brother Robert in the county of Perche. Thus, when one of the lords who was holding out against Geoffrey, Giraud of Montrueil-Bellay, appealed for help to Louis, Louis saw an opportunity to gain some much-needed credit as a military man and led an attack against the Norman town of Sées.[85]

While this cloud gathered, Eleanor approached her confinement in the summer of 1150 and reacquainted herself with her elder daughter, Marie, now over five years old. There is every sign that Marie, a future patron of the arts, commissioner of religious works and effective ruler in right of her absent son, was an intelligent child and that she was influenced by her mother in the brief period that they spent together. Like Eleanor's later children, she showed a keen appreciation for poetry and music. Her court with her husband was to be the major centre for the development of chivalric themes, nurturing Chretien de Troyes, Andreas Capellanus and others. Since she was to spend the rest of her childhood in a convent, it seems most likely that she acquired her taste for these, including a fondness for troubadour poetry, from her mother. And it may be that it was from Eleanor's interest in the debates still swirling about in the wake of the heresy trial of Gilbert that Marie first became acquainted with the concept of scholasticism, which she imbibed so thoroughly as to call one of her daughters Scholastica.

For Eleanor, the pleasure of getting to know her daughter again must have been somewhat affected by the uncertainty surrounding the impending birth of her second child; if it was a son, her position as Queen of France would be both secure and irremediable. While Louis must have been convinced that he would soon have a son given Pope Eugenius' intervention, it must have been to Eleanor's considerable relief that she gave birth to another daughter, to be named Alice, after Eleanor's sister – who herself had recently named her third child Elenor in her sister's honour. Had the child been a son, Eleanor, as the successful producer of an heir to the French throne, would have been locked into her dead marriage for life. However, the birth of a daughter offered at least a hope of escape.

This is because Aristotelean analysis asserted that the birth of a girl child, which was seen as a defective male child, resulted from some wrongness in the mother. There were two theories as to how this came about, as to whether babies originated from a single seed or from both parents. However, by whatever mechanism, a female baby was a less than ideal outcome and proceeded from the fact that the mother's defective femaleness somehow overwhelmed the pure male seed planted in her by her husband.[86] With only two pregnancies to her credit in over ten years of marriage, and both of them resulting in female babies, Eleanor could expect to be criticised as somehow physically defective; only a very few academics held that failure to conceive or the production of defective babies could be down to the man. While criticism could never be congenial, it offered Eleanor her best opportunity of freedom. And such criticism duly began to circulate.

Meanwhile, another factor arrived to help Eleanor. On 13 January 1151, Abbot Suger, the architect and strongest defender of her marriage to Louis, died at the age of seventy after an illness which had confined him to his bed since October 1150.[87] It was Suger, the 'Father of the Country' as he was called by many on his death, who had advocated the benefits of absorption of Aquitaine into the French Crown, and who had seen divorce as leading to a power struggle which was likely to be of immense harm to the Crown. With him gone, the voices of criticism and pure theology as to the consanguinity between Eleanor and Louis would have greater scope.

In summer 1151, with the very first steps towards an annulment being considered in the corridors of power, Louis decided to return to action with his other priority – the Angevins. He assembled an army and set off down the Seine towards Normandy. Before military action could commence, however, two things intervened. First Louis caught a fever, and then Bernard of Clairvaux prevailed on both sides to declare a truce and negotiate.[88]

So, in summer 1151, Geoffrey and Henry came to the French court, as did Bernard, who was determined to ensure a peace.[89] Eleanor had of course met Geoffrey before, but it was her first meeting with Henry. All of Eleanor's biographers (including the scholarly Turner) opine that Henry made a considerable impression on Eleanor and that she found him attractive. There is no factual basis for these assertions, but given later events it is a tempting inference that she found him at least not unattractive.

One might also wonder whether Eleanor was struck by the contrast in types presented by her husband and the Angevins. At more or less this time, Hildegarde of Bingen in her *Causae et Curae* categorised men into types by reference to their vitality and fertility. The description of the least vital type, with weak veins and a pale complexion, sounds very like Louis; the personification of her ideal, meanwhile – hardy with reddish skin and fiery blood – would appear in Geoffrey le Bel and his son.[90]

However, it should be borne firmly in mind that Eleanor was faced with a form of Hobson's choice. She will have known that her marriage to Louis was in its dying days. She will have known that she had to marry again, for her own protection if for nothing else. As Duchess of Aquitaine and Countess of Poitou, she realistically had to marry someone whose lands were either within or proximate to her own. Her advisers will doubtless have reiterated the conclusion to which her father had come – that a marriage to a vassal was unworkable, and would simply lead to unrest (although a marriage of convenience to a vassal was ultimately the solution which worked in the medium term for her contemporary Ermengarde of Narbonne). She therefore had to identify a husband with lands near hers. The Angevins were the prime candidates – as her family's marital history for centuries had demonstrated, and as her own father's discussions with Geoffrey of Anjou illustrated again. Henry was therefore the obvious candidate – and unlike other candidates she was presented with an opportunity of ascertaining at least a limited amount about him. Henry, then, may simply have been less of an unknown quantity than Eleanor's other options.[91] Having said that, it is likely that the fact that Henry already had a reputation as a man of action and a creditable warrior and leader of men will have proved a point in his favour to Eleanor, who had endured an extensive demonstration of Louis' failures in these respects.

It is often asserted that a marriage between Eleanor and Henry was settled during this period. Again, there is no evidence that this was the case. While it seems likely that the decision that Eleanor and Louis should divorce was taken over this summer, and therefore Eleanor would have been turning her mind to her next marriage, all of this is inference. Certainly it is unlikely that Eleanor and Henry – or indeed Geoffrey, who is more likely at this point to have taken the lead in any negotiation – will have had much, if any, opportunity for private meeting or to ascertain more than whether each side was willing to seriously consider a match if the divorce came about – which could not be guaranteed.

For the present, however, the focus was on reconciliation between the Angevins and the Crown. They were initially intransigent, refusing to release de Bellay as Louis demanded; but finally they conceded his release and the cession of the Norman Vexin to Louis. Henry did homage to Louis for Normandy, and the pair departed. This *volte face* provides the closest thing to evidence that some form of understanding had been reached between Eleanor and Henry and that the Angevins had taken the view that peace was well bought with Eleanor's lands in the offing. If there was a deal, it turned out to be rather better than Eleanor could have anticipated: within weeks the thirty-eight-year-old Geoffrey was dead, and Henry was Count of Anjou.[92]

The news will have reached Eleanor and Louis as they made a tour, their last as a married couple, into Aquitaine. The events of that tour suggest strongly that a final decision to separate had already been taken by then, for Louis demolished fortifications and withdrew troops – a symbolic withdrawal of power. With Suger dead, and Bernard in attendance, he will doubtless have advocated a separation which Louis would himself have begun to see as a necessity if he was to procure an heir. Yet apparently Louis was still ambivalent about the separation, for the records of this period record that his behaviour was marked by jealousy and possessiveness.[93]

Christmas 1151 was spent together at Limoges, and probably represented Eleanor's last opportunity to see her daughters before the annulment. It is usually said that this was unlikely to have been much of a wrench for Eleanor, as it was unlikely that she was close to her children.[94] But this should by no means be assumed. Eleanor was very close to her second family, as will be seen. There is no reason to believe that things would have been different for her children of her first marriage; indeed, as she seems to have had less of a political role in her first marriage, she had more time to devote to her children. As noted earlier, there is evidence that Eleanor, despite her limited opportunities, influenced Marie considerably – only likely if they were close. The much better assumption is that leaving her children behind was one of the hardest things Eleanor ever had to do.

From Limoges, the royal couple moved on to Bordeaux before arriving at the abbey of St Jean D'Angely on 2 February 1152 for the Candlemas celebration. Each had their own retinue. Eleanor's included Geoffroi de Loroux, Gilbert of Poitiers, the Bishop of Saintes, and abbots of a number of favoured abbeys as well as her temporal lords: the Count of Angoulême, her cousin the Viscount of Châtellerault, Hugh de Lusignan, and Geoffrey de Rancon. Louis's entourage included his chancellor, Hugh de Champfleury, and Thierry de Galeran. Here they formally separated. Louis headed back into Paris and Eleanor remained in her duchy, most likely basing herself in Poitiers.[95]

Eleanor almost certainly turned her attention to making a decision about her remarriage once her divorce was finalised, and it is to this period that we should most likely look for correspondence with Henry concluding their plans to marry once she was free.

The assembly at Beaugency which opened on 18 March 1152 was therefore not, as Louis' official historian tries to suggest, one which came about because he only discovered the position on consanguinity then. Most likely this official historian did not want to acknowledge the truth – that Louis had known of it at least since his disputes with Theobald of Blois in the early 1140s, and most certainly since Eleanor's outburst at Antioch. Nor did he wish to deal with the fact that the parties had decided to ignore the ruling of Pope Eugenius. The reality is that Louis had consulted his diocesan ordinary, the Bishop of Paris, in the summer of 1151 and following consultation with the Archbishop of Sens, head of the ecclesiastical province, a synod was convened.[96] The synod included the Archbishops of Reims, Rouen and Bordeaux, as well as some bishops. The laity was also represented via a selection of barons. Beaugency as a venue reflected a more or less neutral venue close to the borders of both parties' territories.

Some taste of the level of gossip and scandal which surrounded the event comes down to us through the partial accounts of proceedings which survive. Technically, an inquiry into consanguinity was all that was necessary. Markale suggests that the Bishop of Langres – a mouthpiece for the absent Bernard of Clairvaux – proposed that the assembly inquire into allegations of Eleanor's adultery, and that Eleanor's position was defended by Geoffroi du Loroux, who argued that the consideration should be limited to the question of consanguinity. However, no subsequent author has been able to verify a source for this allegation.[97] Whether or not this dispute occurred, in the event the proceedings were based solely on consanguinity, with Louis the technical claimant and Eleanor not opposing the claim. This of course greatly simplified the trial, as the facts were not in issue and could be proved via two or three witnesses, detailing the family trees of the pair. The central issue could thus be easily decided, and on 21 March the Archbishop of Sens declared the marriage annulled. It was also held that, since the parties had married in good faith, their children were legitimate. Interestingly there is no record of whether the synod grappled with Pope Eugenius' ruling just over two years before – or whether the members of the synod were even aware of it. Nor is there any record of what Eugenius – who was to die the next year – had to say about this outcome.

The effect of the annulment was, as a matter of French law, that Eleanor left the marriage with her family lands. Technically, lands acquired during the marriage and moveable property should have been equally split. There is no record as to whether this was done.[98] What is clear, however, is that, in line with the prevailing law and practice, Marie and Alice were regarded as Louis' property, to be retained in his custody and disposed of at his will, without Eleanor having any input into their futures.

Another final separation which Eleanor probably had to endure at this time was from her sister Aelis, who was married to Raoul de Vermandois. Although we catch sight of Aelis in October 1151, confirming a grant by Eleanor to Abbess Agnes at Notre-Dame de Saintes, Aelis's name never emerges in the records again; and Raoul de Vermandois was to remarry at around this time.[99] It therefore seems likely that Aelis died late in 1151 or early in 1152.

One final vignette casts some light on Eleanor's position at the end of her marriage to Louis. It is a story recorded in two separate Norman vernacular histories, probably of the thirteenth century – one in Cambridge and one in the Bibliotheque de l'Arsenal in Paris.[100] The story they tell goes like this:

> Now, King Louis hated his wife Eleanor, who was the heir of Aquitaine and Poitou ... The king had himself separated from his wife, at Étampes. Her men of Poitou came to her there to take her away .... After she had been divorced, she surveyed her own people, she disrobed and said, 'Gentlemen, what kind of beast am I?' 'By God,' they said, 'there is no more beautiful woman alive today.'
>
> 'Then gentlemen,' she said, 'I am not the devil that the King of France called me just now.'

Of course, we cannot take this account literally. While textual analysis, and the fact of two separate versions of the story in two separate locations suggest that the story had been current for some years before it was written down in either manuscript, there is no version of the story in any surviving contemporaneous source, and its account of Eleanor actually disrobing is in line with the 'Black Myth' of the thirteenth century. It is plainly inaccurate in at least one other respect, namely the location of the divorce – although it does agree with contemporaneous sources in placing Poitevin barons at the synod for the purpose of escorting Eleanor back to her lands.[101]

It is, however, interesting as a sidelight on perceptions. It conveys a suggestion, in line with the unconfirmed reports of the Bishop of Langres' approach to the synod hearing, that even if the event was as procedural and anodyne as the majority of sources suggest, the accounts of it which circulated were not. Whether with Louis' sanction or not, the rumour mill almost certainly went into overdrive and the effect would have been to blacken Eleanor's name – quite apart from the questions over her fertility which the annulment proceedings would in any event have provoked.

It also gives some sense of the challenge that Eleanor now faced. As of spring 1152, she might be free from her miserable marriage, but she would enter any new one in some sense as 'damaged goods', with a need to prove herself not just to any new husband but also to his vassals.

Success Is the Best Revenge

*Huguet mos cotes massatgers/Chantatz ma canso volonters/A la
reina dels Normans.*
[Huguet, my courtly messenger, sing my song eagerly to the
Queen of the Normans.]
Bernart de Ventadorn, poem 33 ll. 43–5

When Eleanor left Beaugency in March 1152, she will have known
herself to be a marked woman. Once again, she was the richest
marital prize in France. Despite the damage that her reputation
had suffered over the past years, there would be no shortage of
men who wanted to take control of her lands via marriage to
her – with or without her consent. She duly took precautions. It
seems that before she left Beaugency she sent a messenger to Henry
of Anjou, just turned nineteen years old, who was at Lisieux,
preparing to depart for England. And when she left Beaugency she
was accompanied by a selection of her own lords as she rode back
along the Loire.

And rightly so, for within a short period Eleanor was warned
of a gang lying in wait to abduct her on behalf of the twenty-
two-year-old Count Thibaut of Blois – Count Theobald 'the
Great' having died at the start of the year. These men having
been evaded – according to one account by barge – they came
under threat from another determined suitor, Henry of Anjou's
seventeen-year-old brother Geoffrey, who had planned an ambush
at Port de Piles, on the direct route to Poitiers. However, some
word of the plan was leaked to Eleanor and she took a different
route – very possibly via Dangereuse's family town of L'Isle

Bouchard. The Chronicle of Touraine describes the message as a warning by her angels, which may import a hint that the source of the information was Henry himself.[1]

Once in Poitiers, Eleanor could start to exercise her independence, setting up a household of her own. From this point there is slightly greater visibility of those who were working for Eleanor. Two men seem to have made the transition from her household when married to Louis: Saldebreuil de Sanzay and Harvey le Panetier or Panetarius. Saldebreuil was present at one of her donations while married to Louis, and appears to have held the key position of steward, while Harvey's name indicates that he headed up the pantry section of Eleanor's household. Both would be rewarded for past services: Saldebreuil became Constable of Poitou and Harvey the Provost of Poitiers. Her chamberlain was one Bernard de Chauvigny, who was a distant relation of Eleanor's through her Châtellerault maternal family.

Interestingly, Eleanor also seems to have had a significant number of churchmen in her retinue: there was her chaplain, Peter; another Peter who appears to have been her scribe; and her butler Philip. There was also a second Bernard – Master Bernard, a clerk who was later to become her chancellor. One point to note here, which remains valid throughout Eleanor's life, is the extent of her patronage of clerics. Nicholas Vincent's work on Eleanor's surviving charters highlights just how often the witness lists are dominated by those known to be, or who can be inferred to be, churchmen – suggesting that Eleanor's household may have contained rather more clergy than was usual.[2]

Eleanor also began to show her position in external matters, issuing charters, though it is probable that her seal from this period does not survive. Interestingly, there are some indications that she had a plan to assert her authority by auditing grants made under Louis' aegis. She seems to have revoked a grant which Louis had made with her assent to a tract of woodland; in all likelihood some other grants were revoked at the same time.

She also began to plan her marriage, in particular summoning her vassals to swear allegiance to her and Henry while she awaited her chosen husband. She did not have to wait long. By mid-May Henry had arrived, accompanied by a small escort. Less than two months after Eleanor's divorce, on 18 May 1152, Whit Sunday, the couple were married in the cathedral at Poitiers. This time there was not the endless pomp and ceremony of Eleanor's first marriage;

William of Newburgh specifically says that the marriage was entered into without the level of such things appropriate to their station in life. Perhaps this was because considerable efforts had been made keep the match under wraps until it was accomplished. And these efforts had succeeded – the tone of surprise at the news is apparent even in the chronicles.[3]

Perhaps ironically, but more realistically underlining the artificiality of the debate which had underpinned Eleanor's divorce, Eleanor and Henry were at least as closely related as had been she and Louis. Both could trace their descent both from Fulk 'the Black' of Anjou and Robert II of France, as well as by two other proscribed routes; indeed, an earlier plan to marry Henry to Eleanor and Louis' daughter Marie had failed for precisely this reason.[4]

It would later be suggested that Eleanor and Henry were doubly consanguineous, in that she had had a relationship with his father, Geoffrey le Bel. Despite the many references to this, the story can be dismissed as an opportunistic fabrication. There is no contemporaneous report of such an affair, or even the rumours of it. The first suggestion of it emerges in the work of Walter Map (who was a student in Paris at the time of the divorce) in about the 1180s or 1190s, saying that 'she was secretly reputed to have shared Louis' couch with [Henry's] father Geoffrey'. Gerald of Wales (born 1146), another fairly negative commentator in the latter part of the century and who was then advocating the claims of Louis VIII to the English throne against Eleanor's descendants, adopted the story and placed the liaison 'when Geoffrey le Bel was Seneschal of France'. He gives Henry, via St Hugh of Lincoln, as the source. There is therefore no contemporaneous evidence for the story. Further, while the seneschal's role had been in the Anjou family, and a claim would later be advanced on Henry's behalf, there is no evidence that Geoffrey was ever Seneschal of France; indeed, his frequent opposition to the Crown would seem to disqualify him from the role.

Another account suggests that the affair could have flourished on Crusade; but since (as noted above) Geoffrey did not go on Crusade, instead fighting his wife's claims in Normandy throughout, that one can safely be dismissed. Another biographer posits an affair in 1146, while Eleanor and Louis were in Aquitaine and Geoffrey was (supposedly) Seneschal of Poitou. However, Geoffrey was not Seneschal of Poitou, and there is no evidence to even place him in

Aquitaine at the time. Whichever version of the story one looks at, it is not credible.[5]

It is often said that the couple should, as vassals of Louis, have sought his permission to wed – and Louis may indeed, as Robert of Torigny suggests, have asserted this right. But this is not accurate; the reality is more nuanced. The power to veto vassals' rights was one which Louis asserted, but which was denied by nearly all his vassals – as the debate regarding the marriages of Theobald of Blois' heirs had made clear. There was such an understanding of feudal obligation in England and Normandy, and perhaps in other parts of northern France, but this did not extend to southern territories of France and probably not even to Louis' own directly held territories. He was certainly looking to extend this obligation to his vassals, but there is no evidence that at this point in time he had successfully done so. Still less could it be said to extend to Gascony or Aquitaine – as noted earlier, Eleanor's grandfather had refused to do homage to the French king, and the separate use by Louis of the title Duke of Aquitaine during his marriage to Eleanor indicates a tacit recognition that this honour was separate and independent of his.

Thus Eleanor almost certainly recognised no such obligation at all, and Henry himself would probably regard it as being owed, if at all, only in respect of Normandy. And given that the match was bound to be highly unwelcome to Louis, it is only to be expected that no permission was sought and the marriage was kept as secret as humanly possible. After all, with Theobald of Blois dead, and his lands split between his two eldest sons, Louis' two greatest vassals were none other than Eleanor and Henry. The Chronicler of Touraine says that the marriage caused discord between Louis and Henry more or less from the start of their relationship. Both Eleanor and Henry must have anticipated this, but determined that the gains from the match were so great as to outweigh even this grave disadvantage.[6]

We know what Henry was acquiring in Eleanor, but it is worth reflecting what Eleanor would have found herself harnessed to following her marriage. Henry was, physically, no Geoffrey le Bel; but he was at least equally magnetic. Walter Map described him as a man whose face one would still feel drawn to gaze upon after a thousand meetings – perhaps the result of the fierce glowing grey eyes which figure in more than one account. Despite the fact that he cropped his red hair short, witnesses still cannot resist describing him as leonine in appearance. His appearance was combative, a tendency to which his thrusting forward of his neck contributed. He was stocky rather than tall, just above middle height, with a thick neck and broad chest supporting powerful arms. At the time of his marriage he will have been wiry, owing to his incessant activity and noted agility. Later he would struggle, unsuccessfully, to keep his weight down.

Many facets of his personality sound strongly appealing. He was a practical man, with no tendency to enjoy the trappings of rank. His preferred clothes were hunting clothes, and he would mend them himself. He worked phenomenally hard, keeping late hours to keep up with the press of business. While liberal to others he was frugal in private, and did not overindulge in the pleasures of the table – though this meant that he also made poor provision for his household, with Peter of Blois complaining they existed on 'half-baked bread, sour wine, stale fish and meat'. He often took honest opposition in good part, and was capable of great loyalty to those he liked. Peter reports that 'if he forms an attachment to a man he seldom gives him up'.

But Henry was no mere man of his hands; it is quite clear that he impressed the generally sniffy clerical chroniclers. Even Gerald of Wales, who actually clerked for Henry, accepts that he was 'remarkably polished in letters' – a legacy of early schooling at the feet of a noted academic, Peter of Saintes. His later schooling under Master Matthew of Loudoun (later Bishop of Angers) and William of Conches was equally distinguished – the high-level education that might be given to a clerk who had to live by his academic abilities. The legacy of this excellent education was a lifelong passion for learning and the company of scholars, an encyclopaedic memory and a store of academic and practical facts as well as an ability to read several languages and speak at least two – French and Latin. Despite his distaste for formality, he did not lack social graces – when he was in good temper, that is. The chroniclers are clear that in such circumstances he was the politest of men, patient to a fault and 'exceedingly good and lovable'.

But he had a very significant dark side, which Eleanor was to discover over the years. While generally polite and even capable of courtesy in the face of considerable provocation, he had a volcanic temper in the course of which he would even roll on the floor or bite the mattress. Such rage might well be provoked by being disturbed when he was sleeping or focussing all his attention on another matter. Which mood Henry was in was a hair's-breadth business – Peter of Blois reports that he would scan his master's face carefully before uttering a word, so fearful was he of invoking the man's explosive wrath.

And yet while this was his most striking fault, it was not the one most inimical to a contented relationship. Four facets of his personality would prove more difficult to endure in the long term. One was his intolerance for delay or inactivity – 'except when riding a horse or eating a meal, he never sits'; and even the second qualification was inaccurate, for he would often scoff his food standing up to return to some other more pressing interest. When he had to be in one place for a time – at Mass or at a formal dinner – he would fidget constantly, fix something, whisper to his neighbour or get on with writing notes about some matter of pressing business. He was, quite simply, hyperactive. Secondly, despite being technically religiously observant (hearing Mass at dawn to make time for it in a busy day) and a great supporter of the ascetic Grandmontine Order, he appears to have had a somewhat combative attitude to the Church, being happy to sketch, work or gossip in church, to harbour heretics (in particular Albigensians) and to break even solemn oaths when it seemed to suit his purposes. To Eleanor, whose religious beliefs appear to have been firm, if on the modern side, and who maintained close ties with prominent churchmen throughout her life, this must have been food for dispute. Another problem was his excessive decisiveness; untroubled by doubts or ambiguities, able to take decisions and to execute them competently himself (at greater speed than others would do it), he loathed delegating anything which interested him or which he considered important. Finally, undoubtedly a legacy of his unhappy childhood and his mother's bitter experience of betrayal, he was cautious, unconfiding and trusted virtually no one, while being ready to break his word when it suited him. The percipient St Hugh of Lincoln described Henry as being volatile, crafty and unfathomable. In short, Henry presents with a number of the hallmarks of the successful psychopath.[7]

This dark side, however, was probably far from sight in the first days of the marriage, and Eleanor would have congratulated herself on the acquisition of a dynamic, interesting life partner as the pair of them began to tour a portion of her lands with a significant entourage of her lords. Certainly the grants in celebration of her marriage would indicate contentment, but the terms of the grant to Saint-Maixent, renewing a week or so after the wedding, the grant of the woodland originally made with Louis and which she had recently revoked, speak more clearly: 'This gift which I at first made reluctantly, I now renew with a glad heart, now that I am joined in wedlock to Henry, Duke of Normandy and Count of Anjou.'

At the same time, she alone confirmed historical grants made by her family, placing herself in the context of the ruler of Aquitaine and successor to her ancestors, without any apparent insistence by Henry that he be included as Duke of Aquitaine. For example, a confirmatory grant to her family abbey of Montierneuf speaks thus:

> I Eleanor, by the grace of God duchess of Aquitanians and Normans, signify to the future as well as the present, ... and for the redemption of my soul and those of my father and my grandfathers, all those things which my ancestor gave, granted and confirmed, ... and my father and grandfather similarly gave, granted and confirmed, I give, grant, and confirm.... I grant also and confirm all the protections which my ancestor, grandfather, and father gave to that monastery...

Some size of the Poitevin entourage with the couple appears from the witness list to this charter: Ebles of Mauléon and his brother Ralph, Hugo of Châtellerault and his brother Raoul, Segebrand Chabot, Saldebreuil de Sanzay 'and many others'.[8]

The couple's itinerary for these first few weeks seems to have been flexible, for in June, in a grant to Fontevraud, Eleanor speaks of being prompted by divine inspiration to want to make the visit. The grant in question is a confirmation of a grant made with Louis of 500 sous of Poitou, but Eleanor also speaks of approving and affirming all previous grants made by her father and forebears. This grant has two interesting facets. One is that she asserts her own regained power, placing it in the context of her heritage and consigning Louis 'in the days when he was my husband' firmly to the past. Yet one can also see an emotional connection – if Louis was the past, Fontevraud was already a link for her new family. Sited at the borders of their respective lands, founded with her grandmother's money and supported by both her family and Henry's, it was now headed by Geoffrey's sister Matilde, who was also widow of the Empress's brother William the Atheling. Here, their stories had entwined before their marriage; it seems that they decided early on to make it a focus for joint patronage as a place which was symbolic of the union created by their marriage. So it is not surprising to find Eleanor speaking of her 'heartfelt emotion' at making the gift. Other charters from the period echo Eleanor's sense of regained power, turning her back on the past and re-engaging with her heritage. In most, Henry is not referred to as Duke of Aquitaine. And the witnesses Eleanor uses for these documents nearly all appear to be Poitevins.

Also of interest, in the context of modern tendencies to downplay any idea of an Angevin empire, is the charter in which Eleanor refers to Henry as 'ruling the Empire of the Poitevins and Angevins'. Eleanor herself therefore saw her new marriage as creating an empire.[9]

Another noteworthy factor in this period is the emergence of the first surviving version of Eleanor's seal. It is a pointed oval, similar to that used by Bertrade de Montfort as Queen of France and very probably derived from Eleanor's own seal as Queen of France (no copy of which survives). In it, Eleanor is standing facing forward, dressed in a tight-fitting bliaut gironé – a fitted overgarment, tight in the body and to the elbow but with long hanging sleeves and a full skirt, similar to fashionable court dress at the time and demonstrably a move away from the dresses depicted on the seals of earlier queens. Her hair is bound – unlike that of some earlier depictions of queens – and obviously she is uncrowned. She appears to have her head uncovered, though a slightly later seal in slightly better condition suggests that the original may have depicted her veiled. She appears slight, surprisingly girlish, and hopeful. Like many queens and noblewomen of the period, she carries on her seal a *fleur de lys*, and a bird – possibly a dove of peace.

Echoing Melisende of Jerusalem, Eleanor seems also to have embarked on a round of church development. It is known that at some point she and Henry commissioned improvements, including to the ducal palace (now the Palais de Justice), and ensured that Poitiers was finally surrounded by a defensive wall. But there are also a number of representations of kingly and queenly heads on churches of this period in the area – at Langon's Notre-Dame du Bourg, heads from the south wall of the choir are frequently said to represent portraits of Eleanor and Henry. But others exist at Saint-Andre in Bordeaux and in Notre-Dame de Saintes, where Eleanor's aunt was abbess.

Many of these may date from after Henry's departure; he apparently stayed in Poitou for just over a month and then left, with the intention of crossing to England to assert his claims there. Eleanor was left in Poitiers, where she established a court of her trusted vassals – her uncle Raoul de Faye and Saldebreuil de Sanzay being particularly to the fore; Geoffrey de Rancon is not much in evidence, very probably reflecting poor health – he was to die the next year.[10]

Eleanor's influence was to stay with Henry, however, for her disappointed suitors Thibaut of Blois and Geoffrey of Anjou had convened with Louis as soon as the news of the marriage had broken. Making common cause with Thibaut's brother and his cousin Eustace of Boulogne, King Stephen's son, whose position was particularly threatened by Henry's sudden accession to even greater wealth, power and status, a decision was taken to attack Henry's Norman lands. Abandoning his plans, Henry rode back at top speed to deal with this problem. It would appear that the royal expedition force had reckoned that he would have departed by now, because by the time he reached them they were already in retreat. Denied an open battle, Henry attacked the Vexin and lands belonging to Louis' brother Robert, before disciplining his brother Geoffrey by taking the three castles left to him by his father. At the last one, Montserrat, Louis was also to be found; at such a disadvantage, he was bound to agree a truce.

By August, with the French side of the equation put in order, Henry was able to rejoin Eleanor and tour Aquitaine with her while he made plans for an invasion of England once winter was over. This tour enabled Eleanor to familiarise herself with her lands again and introduce them properly to Henry. Records remain of visits outside Poitou to the Limousin, Saintonge and to Talmont. They also went to the Landes in Gascony and also to some of the ports, where Henry recruited men and hired ships for his invasion force. But at Limoges, where Henry was apparently formally installed as Duke of Aquitaine, Eleanor encountered Henry's temper. Limoges had been a troublesome vassal for years, and with the status of the Abbey of Saint-Martial it was supported in a slightly superior outlook. Trouble flared between the royal entourage and the locals, but the real crisis point came when the abbey, which would traditionally bear the costs of royal visitors to Limoges, declined to pay up because the royal party had camped outside the city walls. A classic Henrician tantrum resulted – reinforced with an order to tear down the walls of Limoges, to destroy that particular pretext.[11]

Henry and Eleanor emerged from this tour late in 1152 at Angers, en route for Henry to make a departure for England as early as possible in 1153 so as to take Stephen by surprise. Eleanor was already pregnant – a further provocation to Louis. It seems likely that Henry and Eleanor stopped on their way north at Rouen, now home to his mother, the Empress. It is tempting to speculate (as some biographers have) that Eleanor and the Empress would not have been congenial companions, but in the decade and more during which they were to be part of the same family there is in fact not a hint of the disharmony which was said to exist – with about similar factual basis – between Eleanor and Adelaide of Maurienne. In the absence of any record of friction, and with some evidence of co-operation, as well as the naming of Eleanor's first daughter for her mother-in-law, the evidence much better supports the thesis that the parallels of the two women's lives made for a fairly harmonious and supportive relationship. They were, after all, the pre-eminent heiresses of their respective generations, married young to a monarch, with a second marriage to a much younger husband, and experienced in the difficulties of holding and exercising power in a male-dominated world. Furthermore, Eleanor was short of role models, and the Empress had encountered few female mentees. Even if her notoriously lordly manners may have tempted Eleanor towards conflict on occasion, she appears to have understood that Henry's mother formed part of his very limited inner circle – Henry indeed called himself Henry Fitz-Empress – and therefore that if she wished to establish a role for herself in that circle she could not afford to be at odds with the Empress.

But when Henry left the continent on 6 January 1153, Eleanor did not take up residence with her mother-in-law.

It seems likely that she returned to Angers, where she held a court including Henry's sixteen-year-old brother, William, some of her Aquitanian lords and a good number of Angevin lords including William FitzHamo and Geoffrey de Clères. Charters issued in this period appear to reflect Eleanor exercising the powers of a regent over her own lands, where she is said to be 'presently governing the duchy' as well as over Anjou. This would make sense, since the Empress was left by Henry in charge of Normandy.[12]

The summer would be a period of enormous change for Eleanor, for as she approached her confinement news would have arrived of the death of Pope Eugenius, who had so earnestly tried to trap Eleanor in her first marriage. But it was August which was to prove truly momentous. From Eleanor's perspective, the first as well as the greatest event was the birth of her first son, William – a name equally appropriate as a Count of Poitou or a Duke of Normandy and King of England – on 17 August. Eleanor's role as a provider of heirs was finally fulfilled, and the criticisms made of her by Louis and his circle triumphantly rebutted. But hard on the heels of this news came two other great events. The first was that on the very day in which she went into labour to provide Henry's heir, Stephen's heir, Eustace, died, aged about twenty. While Stephen had another son, Guillame, it was Eustace whose claims had been so strongly asserted against Henry. Secondly, on 20 August 1153, Bernard of Clairvaux, the giant who had bestridden Eleanor's childhood and first marriage, finally succumbed to the physical frailties which had bedevilled him for so many years.

As Eleanor recovered from childbirth, she resumed business. A petition from the Abbot of Holy Trinity de Vendôme can be tied to this period, as Eleanor references her 'dearest husband' Henry and her wishes for his success in England, as well as seeking prayers for the safe rearing of 'my son William'. And just as she thought of Henry's success, the stage was being set for her to become a queen again. Henry had gained the upper hand militarily in England. Eustace was dead, Guillame was too young to assert his rights, and the English Church had swung over to support Henry. On 6 November 1153, Stephen agreed to name Henry as his heir although he would retain the crown for life. The disinherited Guillame would inherit the lands held by Stephen at the time of Henry I's death (principally the county of Mortain). A treaty putting all this into writing was drawn up by Archbishop Theobald of Canterbury and was ratified by the parties at Christmas in Westminster, witnessed by a plethora of bishops and earls.

At more or less the same time, Louis arranged the disposition of his and Eleanor's daughters – now no longer heiresses to Aquitaine and Poitou. Little Marie was engaged, aged eight, to Theobald of Blois' eldest son, Henri 'the Liberal', Count of Champagne, already at twenty-seven a veteran of the Second Crusade and well known to Eleanor. Baby Alice, at three years of age, was engaged to Eleanor's unsuccessful suitor Thibaut of Blois. The little girls were handed over by Louis to their new family, who sent them to be raised by the nuns at Avenay.[13]

Interestingly, it was not until March 1154 that Henry returned to the continent – some fifteen months after he had left Eleanor. This period of time is not much considered by Eleanor's biographers, but surely offers a key place to assess two questions which hang over the relationship between Eleanor and Henry.

The first is the question of the emotional relationship between them. While they had married in haste and with little knowledge of each other, before Henry left they had had the opportunity to spend the best part of half a year in each other's company. It is overwhelmingly likely that the extent of their emotional attachment became clear in that period. Therefore, this first period of absence should be looked at as a key signifier. While Eleanor was to refer to Henry as 'my dearest husband', one should be careful about reading too much into this. Actions speak louder than words, and the actions of the two shed doubt over any theory of deep emotional attachment. The first part of the period might well be one where separation was necessary – Henry still had a war to fight and Eleanor was pregnant with what might be an heir. Having said that, however, Henry had safe lands in England and more than one of Eleanor's descendants was to accompany her husband very close to the field of battle while pregnant. If there were a love story here, one might expect to see even this separation evaded. However, once Eustace was dead and *a fortiori* once the November settlement was in place, there was no reason why either Henry could not come back, or, if his business of finalising the deal reached and learning the ropes in England was too pressing, why Eleanor could not cross to join him. His itinerary for this period does not suggest any good reason. This hiatus therefore speaks volumes and provides a strong suggestion that, while a close alliance might have been forged between Eleanor and her new husband, it was not a relationship founded on or strongly supported by an emotional tie.

On the other hand, there is evidence which provides grounds for belief that Eleanor and Henry had come to a good preliminary agreement about affording her an active role in managing their already extensive lands. Indeed, the failure to take up the opportunity to reunite as early as possible also signals them as operating as a partnership, with Eleanor taking charge of one department while Henry took charge of another (the Empress minding a third). The conclusion of some of Eleanor's biographers that Henry was determined to keep Eleanor out of power and relegated to a traditional female role seem somewhat wide of the mark. For as noted above, Eleanor was despatching business over an entire geographical division of their lands. The charter in which she refers to Henry as her dearest husband shows her granting a request of the Abbot of La Trinité-de-Vendôme, an abbey north of Blois, in the heart of Henry's lands. She was again therefore demonstrably personally exercising power over his lands, not just her own.

This should not of course be surprising on one level – Eleanor was older than Henry and, while lacking first-hand experience of power, had been at the centre of French politics for nearly fifteen years. Further, Henry was not likely to be sceptical of a woman's ability to rule, with his mother as an exemplar and exercising power for him in the northernmost parts of his lands at this time, confirming the elections of prelates and dealing with property issues. However, it does indicate that Eleanor is likely to have come into the marriage with an agenda of wanting to be more actively involved in ruling, and that with the choice open to him once they were married, Henry formed the view that she was capable of doing so. All of this said, one should still note the reservations on this apparent trust: Eleanor's court at the time contained not just Henry's younger brother William, who would himself be learning the ropes, but also a number of experienced administrators from Henry's court: the Seneschal of Anjou, William fitzHamo, and Geoffrey de Clères, whose family had served Henry's father. Eleanor was therefore exercising power, but under guidance. She was not acting fully independently and in her own right. This view is reinforced when one adds that it is likely that Eleanor was also already served by 'Master Matthew', her new chancellor, who was a long-time servant of the Plantagenets, having acted as Henry's tutor, taught Henry's two aunts and drafted charters for Geoffrey le Bel. Eleanor was therefore given status as a senior Plantagenet executive, but very much in training with safe hands to guide her.[14]

Against this background, Henry returned across the Channel in March 1154, celebrating Easter in Normandy with his entire family, including his new son and his mother. Eleanor and Henry then made their way into Aquitaine to deal with unrest among the lords of Limousin and Perigeux. While in the south they visited Saintes, where they jointly renewed ducal protection for the Abbaye aux Dames, where Eleanor's aunt Agnes was abbess. On this occasion they were accompanied by bishops from Norman territories and from Bordeaux and Agen, as well as key members of Eleanor's Poitevin entourage, including Saldebreuil de Sanzay and Ebles de Mauléon.[15]

It is quite possibly in this period that Henry acquired the services of the only famous troubadour who can be definitively linked with Eleanor – Bernart de Ventadorn. Bernart would write one brief lyric (recited above) which is indubitably addressed to Eleanor 'the Queen of the Normans', and various others which have been speculatively associated with her. From these limited facts has been erected a massive romantic edifice which, in some writers' hands, even involves theorising that Bernart was Eleanor's lover. Much blame goes to a thirteenth-century biography of Bernart by Uc of Saint-Circ, which some biographers rely upon for their account of Eleanor's relationship with Bernart. That account appears to be the hearsay, via a comital family's oral traditions, of nearly a century later – and moreover put into writing at a time when Eleanor's reputation was very low. It can also be proved to be inaccurate in a number of respects – Uc places Bernart at Eleanor's court before her marriage, and terms her the Duchess of Normandy in her own right. He refers to Henry only as the King of England, and as being a king at the time of his marriage. It should therefore be treated as unreliable.

In fact, based on recent scholarly investigation, it seems likely that Eleanor's association with Bernart was relatively brief, and that Bernart was in Henry's service, not that of Eleanor. In poem 26, he speaks of seeing his love before winter 'if the English King and the Norman Duke allows' and proclaims himself 'for the king's sake' both English and Norman. In poem 21, he sends apologies and good wishes to Henry when his passion keeps him with his love. Both of these are consistent with his being in Henry's service. There is no evidence for the story that he joined Eleanor's court before her marriage or during Henry's fifteen-month absence. Bernart hailed from the Limousin and apparently at about this time had need to leave his initial patron, the Count of Ventadorn, owing to too close an association with the young countess. This would place him in the path of Eleanor and Henry on this summer foray of 1154. Bernart later refers specifically to Henry as his lord and to crossing the Channel at his command. His direct reference to Eleanor as 'Queen of the Normans' places her in his circle simply as the wife of his patron, not as his patron or as his object of affection. Indeed, the critical quote which does identify her does not suggest he will be singing his own song to her; he does so through his 'courtly messenger'.

What, then, of the tradition that she is the focus of his poems? Again, this is massively unsafe. Bernart does refer in his poems to a woman or women as his 'magnet'. However, there is nothing specific to associate that magnet with Eleanor as opposed to Ermengarde of Narbonne (to whom he definitely did dedicate one poem) or another, nameless, patroness or love. Furthermore Bernart, the son of a baker, was a professional poet – he literally sang for his supper. One should not be surprised to find in his poetry flattering depictions of the noble ladies of the household who paid him; it would be wrong to infer from this that he loved any of them from a distance, still less that he had any physical relationship with them.[16]

May brought the royal couple to Normandy via Fontevraud, where Eleanor was still accompanied by some Poitevins, including Geoffrey de Rancon, the son of the Geoffrey who had accompanied Eleanor on Crusade. The older Geoffrey had died in 1153. It seems likely that the new Seigneur de Taillebourg was being sounded out by Henry and Eleanor during the journey north to establish his qualities and his reliability.

On reaching Normandy the party reunited with Empress, who would have had charge of young William. In the absence of Henry, she had also confirmed one Robert of Torigny, formerly prior of Bec, as abbot of the famous monastery at Mont St Michel. He was to be one of the foremost chroniclers of Henry's reign, and it is likely that Henry and Eleanor will have met him when this appointment was further confirmed by Henry on his return.[17]

At about this time, too, probably slightly before the family celebrated the feast of St John the Baptist in Rouen, Eleanor conceived her second child, the future Henry the Young King. When, in August, Henry met with Louis at Vernon to settle the remaining border disputes between them and for Louis to formally relinquish his claims to the Duchy of Aquitaine, Henry will have had the pleasure of being able to apprise him of the fact that Louis' supposedly infertile ex-wife was now once again expecting. Louis himself had by now acquired a replacement for Eleanor, the sixteen-year-old Constance, daughter of Alfonso VII of Castile and León, and was doubtless hoping for similar good news.

In September 1154, Henry fell seriously ill. Suddenly, Eleanor was facing the possibility of widowhood with a baby and another on the way. However, Henry pulled through, and by early October was back in action leading a campaign against rebellious vassals in the Vexin.[18]

Eleanor, based in Rouen with the Empress, will just have been looking forward to a peaceful Christmas when in early November the news came that King Stephen had died, aged sixty, and that she was once more a queen. There could be no question of waiting for spring, so a trip in rough weather had to be faced – a prospect which doubtless filled Eleanor with horror based on her experiences in the Mediterranean returning from the Crusade.

With the speed characteristic of Henry, the household was prepared for a trip to England. While he completed the reduction of the castle at Torigny, where he was in action when the news reached him, the party which was to accompany him assembled at Barfleur for 7 November. Eleanor's contingent apparently comprised about thirty-six servants, and necessitated a number of vessels to transport them and the goods deemed necessary for travel. But when Henry joined them, they waited. This was either because of the winds (the general belief, and fairly credible given the time of year) or because Henry would not set sail until an auspicious day had arrived – and 7–8 December, the Feast of the Conception of the Virgin Mary, who was looked to as the 'Stella Maris', or protector of those at sea, was deemed by Henry a perfect date for such an important crossing.[19]

The theory of the Marian-influenced crossing is supported by the fact that Henry apparently did not wait for a quiet sea, for when the royal couple arrived on 8 December 1154 they made landfall not at any of the usual ports but on the Hampshire coast, probably somewhere near Southampton. Despite the six-week interregnum, all was peaceful – England was tired of war and ready to accept Henry with joy and respect. One chronicler speaks of the love the nation felt for the king who was to come to them, while another opines that no one would dare break the peace because Henry's reputation meant that he was held in awe. The party then proceeded via Winchester, which was still regarded as one of major cities of England, if not the foremost, and where they were met by several nobles to do fealty. From there they proceeded to London, where on 19 December 1154 the couple celebrated their joint coronation.[20]

Quite who formed their party is unclear. The Empress did not come to see her son and his wife crowned in her place. She remained in Rouen, and took up the reins of day-to-day government throughout Normandy and Anjou. Although Aelis is suggested to be present by some biographers, no chronicler names her, and as already indicated other sources suggest that she was dead by this date. It is unclear whether William was taken to England at this time, bearing in mind the likely roughness of the crossing at this time of year, but he certainly joined his parents by the next spring. Ralph of Diss, albeit writing later, records that Henry was accompanied by his brothers Geoffrey and William. Although Ralph was not yet as well placed as he would be later, he was already Archdeacon of Middlesex, and will have had good sources of information.

What is relatively certain is that they will have been met either at Winchester or before by Thomas Becket, a clerk to Archbishop Theobald (who was temporarily holding the reins of government). Becket appears to have aligned himself closely with Henry during the period when the settlement with Stephen was negotiated. Becket's rise is mysterious. He was the son of a London tradesman, so with no strong family connections to recommend him. He was clever, but far from being the genius that was John of Salisbury – by now his associate in Theobald's household, following a recommendation from none other than Barnard of Clairvaux. The decision of Theobald to take Becket into his household is itself puzzling; still more so is his rise to favour with Henry. The best one can say at this distance in time is that Becket plainly had a personal magnetism; John of Salisbury strongly liked and admired him, despite the younger and less shrewd man's advancement ahead of him. Becket's later history provides repeated illustrations of this quality. Otherwise Becket appears to have been, like Henry, a man of broad rather than purely scholarly interests and above all a man with useful and practical talents.[21]

Becket was to form an integral part of the Angevin court for the next decade, and Eleanor will inevitably have interacted closely with him. However, very little trace remains of their relationship. Contrary to many accounts, there is nothing to suggest any hostility between them; equally, there is nothing to suggest she formed any close personal bond with him. That may be the less surprising, for one good reason. Eleanor and Henry had formed a good working relationship, and Henry plainly trusted her to some degree – as evidenced by her role in his absence. However, as we have seen, that trust was limited; Henry would leave Eleanor with some of his own close circle as 'advisers'. But what is quite plain is that Becket, whose association with Henry started at much the same time as Eleanor's, was admitted into Henry's perfect trust. Becket was much that Henry was not – tall, handsome, personally vain, fond of luxury – but some combination of his qualities had, by the time Eleanor was to first meet him, gained him Henry's unqualified trust, esteem and affection.

It was probably thanks to Becket's considerable practical talents that so soon after their arrival the pair were able to enjoy a magnificent and well-organised coronation. The organisation is attested to by the line-up of those present, including both archbishops, over fifteen bishops from as far afield as Chester and Lisieux, and the earls of Cornwall, Norfolk and Leicester.

We know from Gervase of Canterbury (writing somewhat later but with impeccable sources) that, owing to the dilapidated state of Westminster Palace, the recently improved Bermondsey Priory, opposite the Tower of London, provided the lodging place for the royal party. From here Eleanor would be able to look out over the city. North of the Thames lay an odd hybrid city – the Roman walled city colonised and spreading along the Thames in both directions, but most substantially to the west.[22]

We are blessed in having a more or less contemporaneous description of the city as Eleanor would have seen it, written by Becket's biographer William FitzStephen, a proud Londoner himself:

Among the noble cities of the world that Fame celebrates, the City of London of the Kingdom of the English, is the one seat

177

that pours out its fame more widely, sends to farther lands its wealth and trade, lifts its head higher than the rest. It is happy in the healthiness of its air, in the Christian religion, in the strength of its defences, the nature of its site, the honour of its citizens, the modesty of its matrons; pleasant in sports; fruitful of noble men.

He goes on to describe how the city appears, mentioning the Tower (very great and strong) to the east and the two strongly fortified towers of Baynard's Castle and Montfichet's Castle on the western walls of the City, with the high and great wall running between these points. The Thames is described as a great and fish-bearing river. Further to the west, the royal palace, 'an incomparable building with ramparts and bulwarks', was visible 2 miles from the city, and joined to it by a populous suburb featuring spacious and beautiful gardens with trees. To the north one could see rich pastures, well-stocked barns and meadow land through which flowed river streams (the upper reaches of the Fleet, the Hole Burn, the Westbourne and others) by which sat mill wheels. From about modern Islington onwards lay a huge forest, with stags, fallow deer, boars and wild bulls. The other sight which must have struck the eye was the forest of spires – London boasted around 140 churches, including abbey churches.

Also of note were the city's healthful amenities. FitzStephen speaks feelingly of the 'excellent suburban springs, with sweet, wholesome, and clear water that flows rippling over the bright stones; among which Holy Well, Clerken Well, and Saint Clements are held to be of most note; these are frequented by greater numbers, and visited more by scholars and youth of the city when they go out for fresh air on summer evenings. It is a good city indeed when it has a good master.'

Trade was good, the wharves to the east of the city and as far along as the Fleet being crammed with ships from every trading nation, and shops were to be found selling everything under the sun. There was a huge public cook shop offering a variety of every sort of seasonal food, and such a range that anyone could find a meal to their taste.[23]

The richness and pleasantness of the city – and its inhabitants ('conspicuous and noteworthy for handsomeness of manners and of dress, at table, and in way of speaking') – were FitzStephen's pride and may be somewhat overstated, but even his *amour propre* cannot paint a picture of cultural richness to compete with the Paris of the time. London was richer and better served, but it had only three proper schools, with others cropping up 'by favour'.

So far as arrangements for the coronation are concerned, lodging to the south of the river and opposite the old Roman city, Henry and Eleanor had some way to go to reach the abbey for their coronation. They will have entered the Roman city via the then existing iteration of London Bridge, which was probably substantially wooden – it had been destroyed by fire under William Rufus and would be extensively repaired in 1163 in wood. From there a procession will have been undertaken, probably via Cheapside and St Paul's, for a thanksgiving ceremony and along the riverside Strand to Westminster. None of this, however, is covered by the chroniclers.

The accounts simply tell us that Henry was crowned and consecrated with becoming pomp and splendour. In fact, Eleanor's role in the event continues to trouble scholars. The majority of contemporaneous chroniclers who bring up the coronation do not mention her at all, and those who do refer to her make no explicit mention her being crowned. Gervase of Canterbury, who does say she was crowned with Henry, was writing later. This has raised a controversy about whether Eleanor was ever specifically given an English coronation – it may have been considered that with Eleanor already been anointed and crowned as Queen of France, no further coronation was needed. This might account for her being left out of the account – Henry's chroniclers may not have liked the idea of Eleanor walking crowned into the abbey next to her still unconsecrated husband. The ritual of consecration did not much affect Henry himself; typically, he managed to seal at least two charters on the day of the coronation itself.

There is one other potential source for a description of the coronation: Wace's *Roman de Brut*, which was composed under Henry and Eleanor's patronage just a few years later. This speaks of a king being conducted into the church with one archbishop on either side of him, and of four swords borne before him. This matches with what we know of coronation ritual from accounts of later coronations. Interestingly, consistently with the theory that Eleanor was not publicly crowned, Wace tells of the queen putting on her crown in her chamber and proceeding crowned through the streets, preceded by four ladies bearing doves, and followed by a fair company of damsels from the noblest families of the realm. Also of interest is the account which Wace gives of a polyphonic service 'when the Mass had commenced, which was of exceptional proportions, the sound of the organ was heard by many, and clerics chanted in polyphony, with voices subsiding and lifting, song rising and falling'. Here again we may have an indication that Eleanor's taste for the new polyphony was following her.[24]

Some time will have been spent over the following days returning to Westminster, for Henry immediately charged Becket (himself a Londoner and doubtless with good trade connections) with ensuring that the royal palace there was put back into repair. Most of Christmas was spent there or at Bermondsey, where Henry and Eleanor are recorded as holding court. It was at this point that Henry named Becket as his chancellor. This post – head of the royal chapel and secretariat – had not hitherto been a post of the highest status. However, under Henry and Becket, two men with a passion for hands-on detail and administration, it was to rise to such eminence that the nominally superior justiciarship faded into the background.

In the New Year, Henry went via Oxford north through Northamptonshire, Nottinghamshire and as far as Staffordshire, making his desire to ensure access to justice for all England's citizens apparent to as many people as possible. This reflected his declaration in his coronation charter of his intent to restore the laws and customs of Henry I which had been in abeyance in the anarchy of the war between Stephen and the Empress. It seems unlikely that Eleanor, by now well into her final trimester, accompanied him on this trip. More likely she remained at Bermondsey, whence she could take gentle trips into Smithfield to see the famous horse market which took place every Friday or to explore a little of London and the surrounding country. She may even have interested herself in assessing the state of the Tower, which would be the subject of considerable works in the coming years.[25]

However, the last day of February most definitely saw her at Bermondsey giving birth to her second son, who was named after

Henry and his grandfather Henry I and was baptised by Richard de Belmeis, the Bishop of London. Henry himself was at work in Northampton. Young Henry was provided with a wet nurse called Christina. Interestingly, there is reason to suppose that this lady was of the middle classes, rather than the working woman which was the norm; in 1167 she would have a debt of £69 pounds remitted by Henry – a sum way beyond the indebtedness of a working-class woman. This provides a first indication that Eleanor chose to surround herself with women of a class she could befriend.[26]

By the end of March, Eleanor had apparently been churched and was back in circulation, taking part in Easter festivities at Merton Abbey. She was also establishing her status as a decisionmaker among her husband's new subjects, for she features as a witness at a great council which Henry held shortly afterwards in London for the purpose of renewing and confirming charters to various churches. Eleanor witnessed grants to the canons of Holy Trinity London and Christ Church London together with Becket, Richard de Lucy and Eleanor's new steward, Ralph de Hastings – a long-time royal servant and a relative of Queen Adeliza's steward. Also witnessing were William Fitz-Hamo – Eleanor's adviser from her time in Anjou – and a new Anglo-Norman adviser, Joscelin de Balliol, who was to become her most frequent witness for the next five years or so. Balliol also had form as a trusted adviser to the Plantagenets, having served Empress Matilda. The witness list shows that a major gathering of nobles was present; in addition to those present at the coronation, there were the Earl of Gloucester, the previously disaffected Earl of Hereford, John Marshal and Humphrey de Bohun.[27]

On 10 April 1155, Eleanor will also have featured large when Henry held a great council at Wallingford – a key location in his mother's battle for her rights – to recognise the successional rights of William and Young Henry. Interestingly, it appears to have been understood at the time that William would succeed to both England and Poitiers, and Young Henry to Anjou. This was obviously a different arrangement to that reached in Eleanor's first marriage, and was not obviously to the benefit of her lands. It is possible that this issue, which was to loom up again in later years, formed an early cause of friction between Henry and Eleanor.[28]

After this council, Henry rode north to suppress the rebellion of Hugh de Mortimer. Where Eleanor was during this period, or when Henry subsequently held a major council at Bridgnorth, is uncertain. William of Newburgh places her in Westminster in early summer reviewing the work which Becket had not yet completed on Westminster Palace. Most likely, given the recent arrival of Young Henry, she remained in London, moving out to another property with the children in summer. She must have rejoined Henry either at Worcester in high summer or Salisbury in early autumn, because by the time her name appears again in the context of a major council, at Winchester in late September (also attended by the Empress), Eleanor was pregnant again. It seems that Eleanor and the Empress had joined together to persuade Henry to make a grant to the Knights Hospitallers – an interesting but by no means isolated example of their co-operation. Eleanor would of course have been familiar with their work from her time on Crusade.

There are suggestions that Eleanor and Henry remained at Winchester until Christmas, but in fact the scanty documents which survive suggest that they visited Cirencester, Northampton, Salisbury, Worcester, Cricklade, Woodstock, Newbury and Windsor. At Newbury a grant was made to Ralph de Hastings. This grant was witnessed by a number of the very great and good, including three of England's most senior earls: Robert Beaumont, Earl of Leicester, whom Eleanor knew from her time as Queen of France; Reginald, Earl of Cornwall, an illegitimate son of Henry I; and Henry I's grandson William FitzRobert, Earl of Gloucester. This provides an indication that Eleanor's own status within the court was high, as her domestic business rated such senior witnesses – and also that Ralph's role was seen as a significant one.[29]

Christmas was held with another great court at Westminster, and from there the party progressed via Canterbury to Dover to make preparations for Henry's departure for the continent. Eleanor remained behind as Regent of England, albeit supported by the justiciars. During the period which followed, she issued writs with royal authority relating not just to her own expenses (now not covered by Henry's finances as they would be if they were residing together) but also dealing with matters pertaining to royal revenues. While none of Eleanor's charters of this period survive complete with their seal, we know that following her coronation Eleanor updated her seal to reflect her new status as Queen of England – the commissioning of a seal following coronation was standard practice for English queens. That seal was interesting in a number of respects. First, it was apparently the first queen's seal to be two-sided, much as Henry's was the first double-sided king's seal. In part, the reason for this may have been practical – it had now become impractical to contain all of Eleanor's titles on one side of a seal. So, the front of Eleanor's seal proclaims her marital status: Queen of England, by the grace of God, Duchess of the Normans; the back then completes the roster: Duchess of Aquitaine and Countess of Anjou. But it was an innovation in terms of the combination of oval shape (female) and two sides (male).

In stylistic terms, the seal appears mostly to hybridise her own existing seal and that of her predecessor Queen Matilda (whose own seal was derived from that of William I's wife). Her dress remains the fashionable *bliaut girone* seen in her earlier seal, but she adopts the regal cape worn in the English seals. The small *fleur de lys* which she held, derived from the style of the queens of France, becomes longer, more like a full lily with leaves, similar to that held by Queen Matilda. She is crowned, the style of the crown being very derivative of the English mode. However, there is one very interesting innovation: the bird which she had held as Queen of France, and which also was held by the queens of England, appears perched not on her hand but on an orb surmounted by a cross. This is a combination which derives from seals of the English kings – including Henry – who portrayed themselves with this combination to symbolise the combination of power (orb) and wisdom (dove representing Holy Spirit). Previous English queens (other than the Empress) had at best held the orb alone, with the bird perched on a sceptre in their other hand. Eleanor's appropriation, as consort, of male symbolism was something new.[30]

Eleanor also appears to have adopted something of the same approach to royal business as Henry, in that she plainly was not static, despite her progressing pregnancy. While we do not have her itinerary clearly evidenced, we know that in the first six months of Henry's absence she had her expenses paid twice by the Sheriff of London (indicating two stays there) and once each by the sheriffs of Surrey, Essex, Buckinghamshire, Hampshire and Kent. Given the fact that she was due to give birth in June, this is an impressive record.

To some extent we can link these expenses to particular periods. So, we know in particular that Eleanor was at Wallingford Castle in April, just about a year after the Council of Wallingford, when her eldest son, William, fell ill and died. June is sometimes given for this date, but since Eleanor was to give birth in June, her presence in Wallingford in the same month is hardly credible. William was the first of Eleanor's children to die, and it must have been a terrible blow to her; not least as she approached the end of another pregnancy, and the fragility of babies' lives was brought home to her. She then visited Reading Abbey, where William was buried in company with his royal great-grandfather Henry I, and Eleanor began to establish a close relationship with the abbey, entering into fraternity with it, and asking Henry to issue a charter in favour of Hurley Priory for William's soul.

Her relationship with the abbey is perhaps evidenced by one of her few surviving letters, in which she deals decisively with an issue which has been troubling them:

> Eleanor, queen of England, etc., to John, son of viscount Ralph of London, greetings. The monks of Reading have complained to me that they have been unjustly dispossessed of certain lands in London which Richard, son of B, gave them when he became a monk, namely from the holdings of the abbot of Westminster and of St. Augustine of Canterbury. I therefore order you to investigate without delay if it is so and if you find it to be true, to have the monks repossessed without delay, so that I hear no more complaint about the want of right and justice. And we wish also that they in no way lose anything unjustly that belongs to them. Fare well.

We know that Eleanor was at Windsor Castle by the time she gave birth to Matilda (named, of course, for the Empress, but also with resonances of earlier English queens) in June 1156. Matilda was christened in London by Archbishop Theobald of Canterbury and, echoing the royal past, this took place at Holy Trinity Aldgate, which was a foundation of Henry I's wife, Edith-Matilda.[31]

The mention of Archbishop Theobald demonstrates that he was not infrequently with Eleanor during this period, and the evidence suggests that they became close. As a result, Eleanor will also have had exposure to members of Theobald's extensive household, but in particular John of Salisbury, who had taken up duties as Theobald's secretary at about the time that Eleanor came to England. He speaks of 'the faithful care of the archbishop of Canterbury' for the queen, and of his own assistance in 'the safe custody of the illustrious queen of the English and the king's sons'. Theobald will have been invaluable to Eleanor not only for his knowledge of the country, its ways and the various people with whom Eleanor had to deal, but also his learning generally – he maintained something not dissimilar to the cathedral school of her childhood, attracting many ambitious young men who later emerged as learned future bishops. He was of a similar age to Geoffroi de Loroux, and may well have filled something of the same role in Eleanor's life during her time in England. It is also worth noting here that as a result of this closeness John himself counts as a witness with good first-hand knowledge of Eleanor. It is significant that, while not praising her much, he never says a harsh word about her. We can therefore assume (particularly given his later antipathy to Henry and his empire) that John formed a favourable view of Eleanor from his dealings with her.[32]

The Earl of Leicester, the senior justiciar and an elder statesman of the English nobility, was sure to have been present often, and with him his son Robert, a near-contemporary of Eleanor and a highly intelligent and well-educated man who, like Eleanor, had received an excellent education under the aegis of the Church (in his case Abingdon Abbey). Robert was married shortly after Henry's accession to Petronilla de Grandmesnil, herself a major heiress and forceful personality. She and her husband formed a close bond and she was to become one of his closest advisers. Like the Empress, her son would choose to call himself after her (Fitz-Pernel). By age, situation, temperament and location, Petronella would be a natural close associate of Eleanor. Similarly, Richard de Lucy, the junior justiciar, although travelling extensively, will have been often in her company, and by this means she will have come to know his second son, Godfrey, who was destined for the Church.[33]

Although Eleanor's court will not have been as extensive as the full court which surrounded Henry, it is likely that she had a substantial retinue of servants and advisers. The role which she had to play will have involved daily discussions with counsellors, decisions as to actions to be taken, and approval of letters drafted on her behalf. A fine example, which evokes not just her assurance in this role but the theme of good government which had formed part of Henry's coronation oath and which her advisers would be keen to see Eleanor name-checking, is a letter sent to the tenants of Abingdon Abbey:

> To the knights and men holding lands and tenures from Abingdon Abbey, greetings. I command that in all equity, and without delay, you provide Vauquelin, Abbot of Abingdon, with those same services which your ancestors provided in the days of King Henry, grandfather of our sovereign lord; and if you do not do so, the King's justice and my own will make you do so.

To similar effect is a letter to the Sheriff of Suffolk indicating that his failure to carry out a previous order had 'much displeased my lord the king and me' and that 'if you do not wish [to act] the king's justice will be made to be carried out'. So too another to the Sheriff of London chasing him to act to enforce the king's justice and saying that until he does 'I do not wish to hear more complaints about default of justice'.

At the day-to-day level, Eleanor confirmed settlements of actions in the local courts or confirmed writs issued by the king abroad and brought to England by petitioners. Also, it was for her to issue 'licenses to depart' – effectively passports permitting the king's subjects to leave the realm. Without one it would be impossible to take ship legitimately.[34]

There is also every sign that Eleanor's court continued, among the press of business, to showcase the new polyphonic style in church music. For it is to this period that John of Salisbury's description of a polyphonic service dates. In his *Policraticus*, he describes feelingly how the singers seek to astound the simple listening souls; though an innovator theologically, he speaks with the old-fashioned cleric's disapproval of 'these caressing melodies, starting, chiming in, resounding, falling away, intertwining and twittering'.

As for Eleanor's female companions, we know very little. One major controversy which continues to rage is whether Aelis was alive in this period and with Eleanor. However, as already explained, the records plainly indicate that she died earlier. These records are backed up by the evidence of John of Salisbury, who refers to Aelis as having predeceased Raoul. The controversy is caused by some limited records in the Pipe Rolls (the term given to the surviving financial records of the Exchequer, which were stored rolled up tight, like a pipe). There is one mention of the name Petronille (by which name, it will be recalled, Aelis was sometimes known) in close proximity to Eleanor's name; but this person is not identified as Eleanor's sister. She could simply be a member of the household. There are three other records which refer to 'the Queen's sister' or 'the King's sister'. In fact, we know that at some point Henry's illegitimate sister Emma joined Eleanor's household, and was later married to Prince David of Wales. She might therefore be referred to as the sister to either Henry or Eleanor. For these reasons it seems to be a far more consistent assumption that Aelis died young, that the Petronille in the records is a member of the household, and that the sister referred to is Henry's sister. This is not the less so in that Emma seems to have been very much younger – probably born not long before Geoffrey's death. She would therefore be a natural companion for Eleanor's children.

While considering Eleanor's household, the question of the presence of Henry's son Geoffroy arises. Geoffroy was born in 1151 to a woman Walter Map calls Ykenai and describes as a harlot. However, one possibility is that she was from the quasi-noble Akeny or Acquigny family, a name used in the slightly better known de Tosny family, who owned the castle of Acquigny in Normandy as well as lands in Hertfordshire and Clifford in the Welsh Marches; certainly Geoffroy was well educated, as might be expected of a son with quasi-noble blood. It also appears that a lady of this family received lands 'for her service' to the king. Geoffroy was somewhat older that Eleanor's sons, but may well have been included in the royal nursery, at least until he was old enough to move into another house to commence his formal education.[35]

It is also worth noting while Geoffroy is under consideration that in this period of the marriage there is no clear evidence of Henry being unfaithful to Eleanor. However, three things suggest that he was. The first is that the chroniclers are united in saying that he was unfaithful, though they do not, until much later, name names. For example, William of Newburgh says that he 'was much inclined to concupiscence and extramarital relationships'. The second is that Henry was demonstrably and repeatedly unfaithful to Eleanor in the later years of the marriage. The third is the purely practical one; apart so much and for such long periods, sexual continence was hardly to be expected. There is no sign, however, that it constituted much of an annoyance to Eleanor at this stage. It is unlikely that Eleanor, raised to expect an arranged marriage, would actually have expected fidelity from her husband.

Eleanor and the children rejoined Henry in France in summer, once she had recovered from Matilda's birth. In autumn 1156, the two of them made a progress through her duchy of Aquitaine, taking in Limoges, La Grande-Sauve and Bordeaux, and the surviving evidence suggests that some seeds for future strife were already sowed. The first area involved a second visit to the troublesome Limoges, where Henry upheld the male succession over the claims of Emma of Limoges but insisted on taking the young heir into his guardianship and leaving two of his own men to run the viscount's lands – a custom contrary to local rules of succession. In addition, he arranged the heir's marriage to Sarah of Cornwall, the daughter of his uncle Reginald of Cornwall, in an affront to the neighbours who would expect a chance at this marriage. The second is the evidence as to Eleanor's decreasing role in her own lands. Five surviving documents were sealed by Eleanor during this visit, suggesting that a good deal of business was done. But the charters are interesting; far from showing her governing in her own right, they tend to show her as governing within limits set by Henry – they are confirmations of Henry's acts and fairly routine orders to local agents concerning her father's grants of privileges to religious houses and they are witnessed by only a few Poitevins accompanied by Ralph of Hastings, Master Matthew, Thomas Becket, Warin fitzGerold (a long-time associate of Henry's) and William fitzHamo. Indeed, following the taking of homage by Henry directly from Eleanor's vassals during this visit, Henry's grip on the duchy tightened. Following this visit, Eleanor completely disappears from the surviving charters of Aquitaine between 1157 and 1166. From here on in, Henry issued charters in matters concerning Poitou, Aquitaine and Gascony as if Eleanor did not exist.[36]

Another interesting feature of these charters is the fact that the confirmations follow actions by Henry a few days earlier, which indicates that Eleanor and Henry were not always travelling together, even though they were touring her lands. This in turn suggests a degree of estrangement between them – or maybe that Henry preferred not to travel with a nursery party, as the absence of any records for the children in England suggests that Eleanor had taken them with her.

Harmony was probably not assisted either by the fact that Eleanor's cousin, the Viscount of Thouars, had assisted Henry's brother Geoffrey in his most recent revolt. As a punishment, Henry expelled the viscount from his lands and destroyed his castle. Henry must have seen Eleanor's closest male relatives in Aquitaine as a potential threat to an absentee ruler, and he did not have the time to make subtle points; with a vast empire to govern, he could not remain in Aquitaine for long, or return soon. In light of this, Henry felt a clear declaration of authority made sense – though the French chroniclers, commencing their work of demonising Eleanor, place the blame for Henry's actions at her door. For Eleanor, however troublesome her cousin was, these steps and her increasing marginalisation from decisions relating to the governance of Aquitaine are likely to have been a vexation. Henry was not only taking over authority, he was imposing alien norms on her lands. Furthermore, as it is quite likely that her cousin was among her childhood companions, she may well have considered Henry's reaction as excessive, as many of her vassals did.[37]

Even if Eleanor and Henry's four-year marriage was already faltering, the tour offered Eleanor the chance to restock her household with talented Poitevins. With Saldebreuil de Sanzay promoted to constable, her steward was Porteclie de Mauzé, whose father had been seneschal under her father and Louis. New clerks in the form of Jordan and John Pinero joined her at this time. And again, she can be seen actually supporting churchmen – 2 marks was paid to one of her clerks in 1156, and a gift of land was made to another in the 1160s. Such active clerical patronage reflects the substantial records in the Pipe Rolls of the period for incense and other expenses for Eleanor's chapel.[38]

Other reminders of her childhood came to the fore at this time: arriving at court were ambassadors from the Moorish King of Valencia seeking an alliance with Aquitaine against the Almohads, and bringing as a sweetener gifts of gold, silk and other precious wares from Africa – though not, it would seem, a replacement for Eleanor's lost rock crystal vase.

By the time the couple held a Christmas court at Bordeaux, again in the company of her old mentor Geoffroi de Loroux, Eleanor was once again pregnant – her fourth pregnancy in as many years. This did not stop her from commencing the long journey back to England shortly after Christmas, and she arrived there via Southampton by the end of February 1157, accompanied by her children, and proceeded to London via Winchester. One of those eagerly awaiting her return was John of Salisbury, who had received word that Henry's wrath had grown 'hot against me in full force' for supposed challenges to royal powers which he was accused of making while at Rome. Eleanor was able to put his mind at rest, telling him that 'the storm ... has abated'.

Henry followed later, arriving around 8 April 1157 in time for the royal party to move into East Anglia, where visits were made to Norwich and Thetford before passing to Bury St Edmunds for a great council of the realm on 19 May, at which there was also a ceremonial crown-wearing. The following days were spent with many of the great council at Colchester, following which further sites in Essex were visited. It is likely that the pregnant Eleanor now returned to London – though whether she was formally regent, as some accounts suggest, is open to doubt.[39]

Meanwhile, Henry's party moved north via Northampton to Peak Castle (Peverel Castle) to rendezvous with King Malcolm of Scotland, who had come south expecting Henry to make good on an oath he had made before his accession to cede Newcastle and Northumbria to Scotland. Henry had no intention of making good on this oath, pointing out that it would clash with his overriding duty, repeated in his coronation oath, to preserve his ancestral rights. Malcolm must have been furious, but, faced with Henry's military dominance, shortly afterwards did homage to Henry and accepted the earldom of Huntingdon. While Eleanor obviously continued to maintain Henry's line as regards his coronation oath and aims, this flouting of a solemn oath by her husband cannot but have given her pause for thought.[40]

Henry then commenced his campaign against Owain Gwynedd, Prince of North Wales. During this period the Pipe Roll evidence suggests that Eleanor spent her time in Hampshire, Devon, Berkshire and Wiltshire. Although Eleanor's dower from Henry is unclear, the locations of dower properties which were later listed indicate that she probably had some in these areas, and that she may well therefore have been reviewing them. It is perhaps to these early travels that we can trace the charming story of Eleanor, on her travels, finding a destitute boy at the side of the road and sending him to be educated at Abingdon Abbey.

Eleanor moved to Oxford in early August, remaining there until the birth of Richard on 8 September. The birth took place just north of the city's walls, in what was then known as the King's House, but later became Beaumont Palace. The Pipe Rolls note the expenses of Eleanor's confinement at 20s. Richard was then put in the charge of a wet nurse, Hodierna, the mother of the future Abbot of Cirencester and Oxford academic Alexander of Neckham. Although traditionally her son's advancement is attributed to royal generosity after her role, the substantial pension she received both from Richard and John, her location in Oxford at the time of Richard's birth and her son's abilities combine to suggest that again Eleanor may have chosen a wet nurse for her son who was herself an intelligent and interesting woman. Mentions of Woodstock in the accounts at this period suggest that Eleanor may have moved the short distance there to spend her recovery time after giving birth.[41]

The choice of the name Richard remains something of a puzzle; it was not a name which had resonance in Eleanor's family, which was dominated by Williams, nor in Henry's immediate family where Fulk, Henry, Geoffrey and William were the dominant names. The best guess is that Richard was named for one of the early dukes of Normandy, 'Richard the Fearless', who may well have been a role model for Henry II as he had had to fight from a young age to wrest his inheritance from the crown of France and other predatory noble houses, including that of Blois. Richard was also credited with the introduction of feudal customs into Normandy. Finally, it was his daughter Emma who had married both Aethelred the Unready and Cnut, forming the basis for William the Conqueror's claim to England. If this is so, it offers a hint that, contrary to many speculations (but in line with Henry's earlier indications vis-à-vis William and Young Henry), Richard was not originally planned to be the inheritor of Aquitaine – it seems possible that his name was given to invoke legitimacy as a ruler of Normandy. It would also, of course, come in handy if he were needed as heir to England. What is particularly interesting, though, is the positive decision not to use William, the superlatively resonant and royal name given to their firstborn, and now once again available after his death. The failure to use this name again, now or later, strongly suggests that one or both parents had bonded strongly with young William, and could not bear to see another child take his name.[42]

Shortly after the birth of Richard, Eleanor began her first journey to the north of England with Henry. The party proceeded via her probable dower town of Stamford to Lincoln, where the Christmas court of 1157 was spent, with another crown-wearing. Although Eleanor's presence is not directly mentioned, we can be sure she was present as her next child, Geoffrey, was conceived over the Christmas period – just two months after his brother's birth.

It is also to this period that we should look for the arrival of the *Gynecia Cleopatrae* sent by Manuel Komnenos to Eleanor. This is because the book bears the legend, 'Henri friend of the Emperor Manuel, carried this book from Constantinople and copied it for the Queen of England.' It can be no coincidence that at this time there is a record of an embassy from Constantinople headed by one Henri Aristippe which brought other books from the scholarly Byzantine Emperor to Henry's court.

Following this, the movements of the court are unclear. Some records suggest that Henry headed north, visiting Carlisle, Wark in Northumberland and Newcastle upon Tyne before the journey south began via Yorkshire (staying at York) and Nottinghamshire, where there were visits to Nottingham Castle and Blythe Priory, though Judith Everard's recent auditing of the itinerary materials demonstrates that these are not wholly reliable. In any case, a record of Eleanor moving between Winchester and London in February 1158 suggests that she was not on any such journey.

This period is perhaps the best fit for an affair which Henry had at around this time with Annabel de Balliol, the sister of Eleanor's clerk Joscelin de Balliol, and daughter of a lord whose landholdings were near the Scottish border. Unless this young lady was actually in Eleanor's service, this period of time seems the only likely window for Henry to have met her. Annabel would later receive the manor of Coniscliffe in Durham as her dowry with thanks 'for her service'. Then the court moved south, with stays at Clarendon Palace and Woodstock, before moving on to Brockenhurst and Salisbury and then north again via Winchester, this time to Worcester. At Worcester, there was another crown-wearing. It was after the Easter Mass here that Henry and Eleanor laid their crowns on the shrine of St Wulfstan, vowing never to wear them again. Crown-wearings having been traditional, this marked two things: Henry's satisfaction that his authority was established; and his determination to establish a new mode of kingship.[43]

From Worcester, the court proceeded to Malmesbury and then south again through Gloucestershire and Somerset. While the progress generally seems to have been aimed at showing the king and queen to as much of the country as possible, the move south at this time seems to have been aimed at dispatching Thomas Becket off on a diplomatic mission of some considerable sensitivity. Louis VII had finally been presented with a child by his new wife, Constance of Castile, early in 1158. The child, Marguerite, was now co-heiress to Louis with Eleanor's daughters, and must therefore be taken off the marriage market before a prejudicial match could be arranged. Becket was sent as a charm offensive, travelling with such scale and magnificence that the French were astounded and reluctantly impressed: 'Marvellous is the King of the English whose chancellor travels so very grandly.' And indeed Becket's allure temporarily distracted Louis from remembrance of how little he liked either Henry or Eleanor, and the match between Marguerite and Young Henry was agreed. Eleanor's thoughts on this remarkable turn of events are not recorded, though it seems highly unlikely that it can have been welcome to her.[44]

Meanwhile, in England, there had been no rest for Eleanor as she entered the third trimester of her pregnancy; again she seems to have accompanied Henry through Somerset, visiting Wells and Cheddar, into Devon and then back to Dorset before moving to Kent and then via London north into East Anglia, Northamptonshire, Rutlandshire, Gloucester and back to Carlisle by late June. No stay of any length was made in any of these places, and by August the royal party had returned south to Winchester, where it seems likely that Eleanor stayed while Henry departed to meet Louis, finalise the marriage alliance and the arrange for the return of the Norman Vexin, which was the bride's dowry. He would also take custody of Marguerite and settle her with the family who was to have custody of her (Louis having vetoed her entry into Eleanor's household). This visit would afford Henry another opportunity, since Louis authorised him as hereditary High Steward of France to deal with Brittany, which had been settled under his brother Geoffrey's control but now required handling since Geoffrey had died inconveniently in July 1158.[45]

The result of this summer tour was to give Eleanor as good a view of England as a country as any Queen of England had ever had – and better than any was to have again until her descendants Edward I and Eleanor of Castile took to regular peregrinations around England as a feature of his reign. It also appears to have reinforced Henry's view of Eleanor as a capable delegate, as she was left as regent, despite her pregnancy, albeit jointly with Richard de Lucy. But she did not remain in one place after Henry left. We do not know the place where, on 23 September 1158, Eleanor gave birth to her fourth son (named Geoffrey for his grandfather and his recently deceased uncle – and possibly for Eleanor's mentor Geoffroi de Loroux, who had died on 11 July 1158), but we do know that between Henry's departure in August and Eleanor's own departure some time in December, Eleanor managed visits to Hampshire, Oxfordshire, Devonshire, Dorset, Berkshire, Wiltshire, Kent, London, Buckinghamshire, Bedfordshire and Warwickshire. In other words, Eleanor appears barely to have stopped, despite her pregnancy and childbirth.

During this period, although Richard de Lucy was sitting as Justiciar of England, Eleanor issued precepts and certificates as regent – one of them in favour of Maud, Dowager Countess of Chester. Maud was, despite her title, likely to have been close in age to Eleanor. She married in 1141 and was to live until 1190. She was a granddaughter of Henry I via her father Robert of Gloucester, and managed her son's lands until his majority. She also, though of marriageable age on her widowhood in 1153, never remarried; possibly her relationship to Henry and Robert of Gloucester protected her from importunities. It is also possible that, since her husband's death had been murder, and her name was associated by rumour with that of the murderer, William Peverell, would-be suitors exercised discretion. Whether Eleanor and Maud were close is uncertain; Maud's custody of her son's northern lands may well have required her presence there for most of the year. However,

Maud provided a very good example of the type of formidable widow who was not uncommon in England and the northern parts of the continent, when women generally came into power over their lands only with their widowhood. These are women with whom Eleanor would have met and done business.

The consideration of women exercising power over property also links to the travel which we can see that Eleanor undertook in the period after her first arrival in England, and despite the inconveniences of repeated pregnancies. Although the exact extent of Eleanor's dower lands is uncertain, we do know that Henry had given her at least some of the lands which had been held by Henry I's queen Edith-Matilda and that, unlike later queens and many noblewomen, she was able to utilise their revenues during Henry's lifetime. In terms of the content of the dower, we know that later Berengaria of Navarre's dower was listed as being the same as that given to Eleanor, albeit after Richard had supplemented what he considered to be inadequate provision made for his mother. At that point her dower included lands both sides of the Channel. In France she held Falaise, Domfront and Bonneville-sur-Touques in Normandy, Loches and Montbazon in Touraine, and Chateau-du-Loire in Maine. In England she held some twenty-six properties across thirteen English shires, including considerable lands in Somerset (Incester), Devonshire (including Exeter, Kenton, Leston, Alescot, Slocombe), Berkshire, Wiltshire (including Malmesbury, Stanton), Oxfordshire, Rutland, Lincolnshire (including Grantham and Stamford), Northamptonshire (including Rockingham and Northampton), Hampshire ('Vulfinton') and Hertfordshire (both the town of Waltham and the barony of Berkhamstead whose properties were spread over a wide territory). Eleanor's dower from Henry will therefore have contained some, though not all, of these properties. A review of these properties against Eleanor's known itinerary as set out above, indicates a high degree of co-incidence, suggesting that she was keen to take the reins of these properties into her own hands.[46]

However, by Christmas 1158 Eleanor was back in Normandy. Christmas was spent at Cherbourg, and after Christmas the royal couple moved to Rouen and Argentan before setting off on another trip to Aquitaine. This was by way of preparation for a more substantial visit later in the year, where Henry planned to assert Eleanor's right to Toulouse. As with Louis' attempt to take

Toulouse, the assumption that this was at Eleanor's urging (Turner, for example, asserts it was the high point of Eleanor's influence on her husband) cannot be supported by any evidence. It may be so, but there were sound political and economic reasons for the move, completely unrelated to Eleanor's own feelings. There were also tactical reasons in the relative youth of the new Count Raymond V, just twenty-four years old, and the presence of his wife, Constance, who was sister of the King of France and widow of Eustace of Blois and thus an admirable potential hostage.

In fact, the idea that Eleanor was directing affairs in the south runs directly contrary to the tide of actual charter evidence in this period. The evidence seems to suggest much more strongly that the idea was one originated by Raymond's other enemies, and that Henry essentially jumped on the bandwagon – with a little encouragement from them. Ramon Berengar, Count of Barcelona, and King of Aragon via his marriage to Queen Petronilla, was an enemy of the new Count of Toulouse by virtue of their competing claims to the county of Provence. He had already, in late 1157 or mid-1158, allied himself with Eleanor's rival heiress Ermengarde of Narbonne and Raymond Trencavel, Vicomte of Beziers, as well as William of Montpellier, in a league against Raymond; war was, if not formally declared, plainly intended. Henry, in Eleanor's interests, was a natural ally – and provider of manpower. Thus, by the time Henry and Eleanor made for Blaye, where they met Ramon Berengar, writs were being issued in Normandy and England for service in Henry's army to attack Toulouse.

The initial meeting with Ramon Berengar was a qualified success; an agreement was made for him to support Henry's claim to Toulouse, the price being an agreement to marry Richard to his daughter. This is the first extant instance of Richard being designated as the heir to Aquitaine – and possibly only because he was the only available son for the match. Meanwhile, Ermengarde of Narbonne, Raymond Trencavel and William of Montpellier consented to offer support to a campaign led by Henry.[47]

Meanwhile, Louis VII was moving diplomatically to try to avert the attack on Toulouse, whose countess had recently provided the county with an heir who combined the French royal bloodline with that of the current regime in Toulouse.

In June 1159, the army assembled in Poitiers. It is likely that Eleanor remained there when Henry, Thomas Becket and the army moved south at the end of the month. Becket, typically, threw himself into the plan – indeed, there is far more evidence of his urging the move than there is of Eleanor doing so. Nor was his enthusiasm confined to the council chamber; he personally rode on campaign with a battle hammer and leading a company of knights. This is also probably the period in which he obtained his personal copies of the Roman strategist Vegetius' classic manual on military tactics, found in his library in Canterbury. Certainly John of Salisbury was sending extracts from those copies to Becket, who was at Henry's side.

After initial success, with Quercy being taken with little trouble, matters became more complicated. Louis himself moved to Toulouse, leaving Henry in the position of having to attack his feudal lord or commit to a siege. Having opted for a siege, the army then fell ill with dysentery. Attempts to draw Raymond of Toulouse out with raids on outlying territories failed, and by autumn Louis' brother Robert threatened attacks on Normandy which forced Henry to abandon the campaign for Toulouse. A truce was agreed, with Henry taking possession of the lands he had won in the area between Cahors and Toulouse. But the deal was concluded at speed, and Henry had to head north without even stopping to visit Eleanor[48] – if, indeed, Eleanor had remained in Poitiers.

Nearly all of Eleanor's biographers assume that Eleanor remained in Poitiers for much of the latter part of the year while Henry was about the business of Toulouse, before proceeding north to join him for Christmas at Falaise in Normandy. However, some charter evidence suggests that Eleanor was actually sent back to England to do business there.

A story in the history of St Albans Abbey dated to this period tells of a dispute between the abbey and Peter of Valognes regarding a wood which both claimed was theirs. After hearing argument, the Earl of Leicester ruled in favour of Valognes, who then took possession of the wood and 'committed waste' upon it. The abbey appealed to Eleanor, who issued an injunction requiring Valognes to desist until the matter could be further argued. Following a final hearing, directed by Henry in the new year, the abbey's case was successful. This story is interesting not just in relation to placing Eleanor but also because it provides quite a clear contextualised picture of her exercising her authority. Two things are particularly notable. The first is that she plainly does operate as a superior authority to the justiciar – and thus as regent, exercising the authority of the king. But the second is that Eleanor does not exercise that power fully. She grants interim relief, pending the matter being referred to the king himself – who duly does himself give directions for a trial. It therefore offers a clear picture of the way Eleanor's power was notionally great, but in fact often marginal or nominal. Despite these records, there is some doubt about Eleanor's presence in England before late December since the Pipe Roll records demonstrate her presence only after her return at the turn of the year.[49]

Whatever the case, Eleanor was certainly with Henry for Christmas at Falaise in 1159, and with them were some or all of the children. For we know that on 29 December Eleanor crossed back to England with Young Henry and Matilda in the royal *esnecca* – a long and swift galley with a crew of sixty named after the Scandinavian word for a snake. She accompanied the children from Southampton to Winchester, where she took charge of funds urgently needed for Henry's campaigns in France, accompanied it back to France to hand over to his Treasury officials before crossing back days later. By January 1160, Eleanor was back in England ruling on Henry's behalf.

We have no account of how she spent the next nine months, other than that the Pipe Rolls show that she was again travelling – expenses are noted in London, Wiltshire, Berkshire, Hampshire, Worcestershire, Surrey, Cambridgeshire and Huntingdonshire as well as Winchester. But the letters of Theobald of Canterbury written by John of Salisbury indicate that she was seen as ruling on behalf of the king. One letter complains that another cleric is seeking to 'kindle the indignation of the king or the queen to crush the innocent'. Others show her working hand in glove with the archbishop and John. So Theobald, through John, writes to pressure the Bishop of Worcester into appointing one of Eleanor's clerks as archdeacon, covertly warning him that failure to do so will be seen as an affront to Eleanor. In another letter, the Abbess of Amesbury is rebuked for not heeding a mandate by the queen to restore a cleric to his church and warned that the archbishop will endorse the queen's further actions if the abbess does not comply.[50]

As for Eleanor's spending, there is mention in the Pipe Rolls of money spent on domestic luxuries: regilding of cups, repairs to premises, and the queen's garden in Winchester. Money was spent on clothing and shields for attendants. It was spent on clothes for herself and her household – all of whom would naturally look to her for such supplies. She also spent money transporting such clothes and accessories when her household moved (as we have seen it often did). However (despite one biographer's description of it as 'extravagant luxury'), none of this is particularly notable in amount – the impression is of a well-supplied and elegant household on a very substantial scale. There are, however, two outstanding features. The first is the very regular mention of wine, which practically forms a refrain in the Pipe Rolls. Eleanor (like the later commentator Peter of Blois) appears to have had no great opinion of what Henry kept in stock, and imported supplies in some quantity from her own lands. The second is the amount of money spent on matters to do with her chapel. We have already noted how many trained churchmen Eleanor employed in her household, so it is perhaps not surprising therefore that it was apparently a very observant one. However, the expenditure which can be seen in the Pipe Rolls for chalices, incense and other church-related matters suggest a positive interest on her part; that is, the allegedly scandalous queen was in fact a very religiously inclined woman.

Whether that religious inclination extended to major patronage outside her household is an open question, and will likely remain so. There is no firm evidence for it; no surviving charters or financial documents tell us that Eleanor founded any religious houses. Some biographers claim that she was the hand behind the foundation of daughter houses of Fontevraud at Eaton and Westwood. However, there is no mention of her in connection with any of the surviving documents for these establishments; whereas Henry's involvement is plain and would later be repeated in another daughter house. More tantalising is the synchronicity of the emergence of institutions dedicated to St Radegonde in England. Over the next few years there would be founded a priory dedicated to the saint at Longleat, an appropriation of another at Cambridge, and three churches in Scruton, Maplebeck and Whitwell; meanwhile, chapels to the saint appeared in Old St Paul's, Gloucester, Lichfield and Exeter Cathedrals. So too did a hospice in Canterbury. Harmonising with this, another fascinating glimpse of Eleanor's serious interests is provided by the entries which show an increase in funding for the 'Queen's hospital' founded by Queen Edith-Matilda. This suggests that, like St Radegonde, Eleanor took a keen interest in ameliorating the position of the least fortunate in society in a practical way.

Of course, Eleanor was not dependent on what we see in the Pipe Rolls for money, so what we do see is perhaps the tip of a substantial iceberg. Aside from what came via the Pipe Rolls, Eleanor had the income from her dower properties, though much of that may have been occupied in developing and improving the properties. But in addition to that substantial income, Eleanor also had access to income from tin mines in Devon, a fair at Exeter and the payment rights arising from the dockland area of Queenhithe in London and queen's gold, essentially a cut of fees paid to Henry on inheritance. Altogether Eleanor's income seems to have been a little over £400 per year, putting her financially on an equal footing with all but the very richest of the earls and barons.[51]

Eleanor's travels, her regency and her religious views combine in one interesting mystery which hangs over this period: Eleanor's involvement in and reaction to the forced marriage of Mary of Boulogne. In October 1159, Stephen of Blois's disinherited younger son, Guillame, had died in his mid-twenties. He had inherited from his father only the lands Stephen had held on Henry I's death; but Queen Matilda had been Countess of Boulogne in her own right, and Guillame held this title until his death. On his demise, however, the title *prima facie* went to his sister, Mary, who had entered the convent at Romsey Abbey in her teens and had recently attained the rank of abbess there. The prospect of Boulogne being taken over by France in the absence of a ruler was unacceptable to Henry, and he had decided to marry Mary to his cousin and reliable ally Matthew of Flanders. The plan, which seems to have been ventilated fairly soon after the death of Guillame, provoked outrage from the Church, which outrage was endorsed by Becket, leading to one of the only major rows between Henry and Becket before the 1160s.

Henry was adamant, and in May 1160 Matthew came to England and forcibly removed Mary from her abbey and married her. Of course, this occurred under Eleanor's regency, and Matthew presumably had to present his credentials to Eleanor and have them endorsed before making any move. This means that Eleanor must have co-operated in this, one of Henry's most scandalous and maligned ideas. This does not of course mean that she subjectively approved the plan; but it does show that she was not prepared to take a step against his wishes, and indeed that she was deemed to be sufficiently on-side with Henry to have been left in a position where she could have thwarted the plan. It does not reflect credit on her; but technically and legally she was bound to obey her husband's instructions, and the Church itself was apparently equally powerless. Yet it is tempting to suppose that one of Eleanor's trips to Hampshire was spent pre-warning Mary that the decision was made and seeking forgiveness for her part in it.[52]

As for the children, they are noted in London, Winchester and Hampshire, which suggests that they travelled some of the time with Eleanor. The presence of the children with Eleanor is also supported by an interesting letter of Archbishop Theobald, who wrote (via John of Salisbury) to Henry during this period. The letter reminds Henry that it was a long time since he had seen his children; indeed, it is far from certain that he had even laid eyes on young Geoffrey, who had been born only weeks before Eleanor's last journey to France. Theobald, who had acted as godfather to all of the children, seems to have been close to them, again suggesting that he spent a good deal of time in Eleanor's company. He speaks fondly of them and gently chides Henry that 'even the most hard-hearted father could hardly bear to have them out of his sight for long'. It seems likely that Eleanor had some hand in the sending of this letter, and that here we see a first manifestation of her own dissatisfactions with Henry as a father to their children.

The letter, and any private letters Eleanor herself sent, did not bear fruit; and even when Henry sent for Eleanor in September 1160 he asked her to bring only the two elder children, Young Henry and Matilda. Nor was the summons one of affection. The purpose of the summoning of the children was manifestly political: Queen Constance of France was due to bear a child, which might be a son, to whom Matilda could be expeditiously engaged; at the same time, preliminary discussions were taking place for a marriage with her into the Empire, in imitation of her namesake grandmother, who was very keen on such a plan. As for Young Henry, the overt plan was that he could be deployed as the heir to Normandy to do homage to Louis.[53]

Whether Henry had in mind the scheme that he eventually executed is uncertain, though some indications suggest that he may have done so. For at this point Henry was able to exercise unusual leverage vis-à-vis the papacy, and did so in an interesting form. In early 1160, there had been a papal election. The majority verdict was for Alexander III, but the Emperor's supporters elected another candidate, Victor IV. During the rest of 1160, the question as to which of these popes would be recognised by the kings of France and England remained open. Legates were despatched to plead the case of the respective candidates. Henry ultimately did recognise Alexander, but the price of his doing so was a dispensation allowing Young Henry's marriage to Marguerite to take place before canonical age – and also agreement to the canonisation of Edward the Confessor.

However, on 4 October Queen Constance gave birth to another daughter, Alys, and died within hours. Louis was now thirty-nine years old and still lacked a male heir, while Henry had three living sons. Within a few days, rumours were circulating that Louis was to marry Adela of Champagne, the sister of Henry of Champagne and Thibaut of Blois (the fiancés of Eleanor's daughters by Louis). With the Blois/Champagne faction effectively in power in France, the match between Young Henry and Marguerite might well fall to the ground – taking with it the Norman Vexin. Henry therefore moved at once to ensure the marriage took place without delay and the key castles were delivered up. Marguerite was brought from the house of her guardian, and on 2 November the five-year-old prince wed the three-year-old princess, bringing Marguerite naturally within Henry's household – or more accurately that of Eleanor, since she had charge of the nursery. Not unnaturally, Louis was enraged by this course. The best diplomatic skills of the papal legate, Cardinal Bobone, were required to smooth over his anger against both the Pope for granting the dispensation and Henry for his sleight of hand.[54]

Eleanor proceeded to Le Mans with Henry, Matilda and Marguerite. Henry ensured that the Vexin castles were surrendered to him by the Templars, and moved to take Thibaut of Blois' castle of Chaumont as a warning against hostile moves from France. There may have been a plan to spend Christmas in England, but the contrary winds prevented it, so the royal party spent Christmas 1160 at Le Mans; and it is likely to have been over this period that their next child, Eleanor (Leonor), was conceived. Some time was probably spent making a visit to the Empress, too, who around this time began giving away her possessions to churches, monasteries and the poor – according to her on Henry's advice.[55]

There is very little evidence of Eleanor's activities in 1161 at all. Some biographers suggest that she stayed in Normandy all year. However, while the records in England do not yield much, they suggest at least one trip on Eleanor's part since expenses of £12 are noted for her in London at some point before Michaelmas. It seems likely that she insisted on attending the funeral of Archbishop Theobald, who died, with John of Salisbury at his bedside, in April. Eleanor would surely have been unimpressed by the fact that Becket had conspired to evade Theobald's heartfelt requests for him to visit his old patron on his deathbed. A decision to honour his funeral with her presence would be a subtle way of marking her affection and her displeasure at their discourtesy. On this trip it is equally possible either that she brought Matilda back to join the other children along with Marguerite, who would now be raised with them, or that she brought Richard and Geoffrey to spend time in France – and finally get to know their father. It is also possible, given a suggestion in Robert of Torigny's chronicle which places Henry in Aquitaine in summer, that Eleanor was able to spend some time in her own lands.

However, by October she was at her dower castle of Domfront in Normandy giving birth to Leonor, who was given Abbot Robert of Torigny as a godfather. He, too, can therefore be counted among the genuine first-hand witnesses to parts of Eleanor's life. And like John of Salisbury, he is among the most positive of the chroniclers on the subject of Eleanor. The christening was carried out by the papal legate Cardinal Henry of Pisa, and the Bishop of Avranches also stood as Leonor's godfather.[56]

Young Henry did not go back to the nursery. The year 1161 marked the point when he was expected to move into a lordly household and commence his formal education, and this matter was drawn to Henry's attention by the Archbishop of Rouen, writing on behalf of all Henry's bishops, who called on him to ensure that Young Henry should henceforth apply himself to his letters so that he might succeed to his father's wisdom as well as his lands. This idea dovetailed with Henry's plans to crown Young Henry in the near future; having himself been brought in on decisions by his mother at an early age, and increasingly aware of the burdens of singlehandedly running his empire,

Henry was looking to pave the way for Young Henry to take over in England at some time in the future. With this in mind, he bought £38 of gold for making a crown and regalia. In addition, by the use of some fairly heavy-handed tactics with the papal legates of Pope Alexander (who still depended heavily on Henry's support), he obtained a dispensation for the Archbishop of York to perform coronations, arguing that with the see of Canterbury still vacant it was effectively necessary for the other archbishop to be licensed.

This and the subject of who should fill Archbishop Theobald's shoes in Canterbury were under discussion at the Christmas Court at Bayeux in 1161. It may be as a result of disagreements over one or both of these subjects that Henry did not despatch Eleanor back to England after Christmas but kept her under his eye in Normandy. As a result, she was at his side when he ordered the disinterral and reburial of Counts Richard I and II of Normandy at Fécamp in February 1162 – a powerful indicator that they were indeed the inspirations behind young Richard's name. In the meantime, Richard's marriage to the daughter of Ramon Berengar and assumption of Aquitaine was still on the cards. Indeed, when Ramon Berengar died in mid-1162 he constituted Henry her guardian, although Eleanor's cousin Petronilla was left to rule Aragon and dispose of their other children alone.[57]

In April 1162, a major gathering of English bishops was entertained at Rouen in the presence of Henry and Eleanor as well as the Empress, doubtless to discuss the vacant archbishopric as well as the bishopric of London, which had just fallen vacant. Theobald himself had suggested Becket – a nomination which was appealing to Henry, who considered that having his chancellor and best friend in the role could only make easier his plans to deal with what he felt to be excessive power in the Church. The Empress and Gilbert Foliot, the respected Bishop of Hereford, however, urged him to make another choice (both likely had Gilbert in mind), considering Becket to be too worldly a man for the role. Henry agreed to consider this, but he and Eleanor meanwhile announced their decision to place Young Henry in Becket's household for the next stage of his education 'to bring up and instruct in good conduct and courtly ways'.

Becket, of course, was a natural choice for instructing a young prince in courtly ways; anyone who could have impressed the

French to the extent he had was a worthy instructor. Less obvious is his role as a mentor to a future knight and warlike king; but that neglects Becket's extensive military retinue, which he had taken to war in Toulouse and also in the Vexin. He was also reputed to be a talented fighter on his own account, having defeated the famous knight Enguarrand de Trie in single combat. Even if he were to become archbishop, Henry had it in mind for him to remain chancellor, so his household would not change significantly. Furthermore, it was far from unheard of for royal heirs to be raised in the houses of archbishops: William Rufus had been raised in the household of Archbishop Llanfranc of Canterbury.

By May, however, Henry had made up his mind. He commanded Becket to take Young Henry to England and present him to the barons as the heir to the throne for an oath of fealty. He also commanded Becket to go as archbishop designate.[58] It is generally speculated that Eleanor opposed this course of action. She may well have done. However, Theobald's recommendation probably weighed more heavily with her than with the Empress, and her own family habit of having a senior churchman as chief temporal adviser (a practice also common in the Empire – and which Eleanor had seen with Suger in France) would ensure that the plan seemed less outré to her than it does to modern readers. In the end, there is simply no contemporaneous material to tell us what her views were, one way or the other.

Becket genuinely seems to have been reluctant to take up the role; had he wanted it we can be sure that the interregnum between Theobald's death and his appointment would have been shorter, and the records of his protests are clear and speak of genuineness. Becket realised, if Henry did not, that he would be put in an impossible position, given Henry's already uneasy relationship with the power of the Church; bound to further the king's ends as chancellor and to represent the Church as its primate in England, he could not please both. What is more, being Becket, he had to play his new role to the full; hence, having given way on the appointment, he returned the Lord Chancellor's Seal in autumn 1162 and transformed himself from a worldly and luxurious warrior-clerk into an ascetic priest given to the wearing of a hair shirt, acts of self-flagellation, and extraordinary charitable gestures.

Meanwhile, the recommencement of records for the cost of upkeep of the king's children in the Pipe Rolls indicates that at some point the nursery party of children was returned to England – probably in anticipation of Henry and Eleanor's own return, which was scheduled for September. However, the return was stymied by bad storms in the Channel, and Eleanor and Henry were forced to spend Christmas 1162 in Cherbourg, waiting for the weather to clear. The journey was finally made to Southampton in January 1163, where the king and queen and Matilda, who had apparently remained with her mother throughout this trip, as well as young Leonor, were met by Becket and Young Henry. Given Henry's rage at Becket's resignation, it was expected that the meeting would be an awkward one. However, on the surface the two met as the greatest of good friends, and barons who had already started to complain about Becket's high-handed approach to the regaining of Church property began to fear that Henry would not support them. But one keen-sighted observer noticed a sign of royal displeasure. Ralph of Diss, standing among the crowd of churchmen, noted that the king kept turning his face away from the archbishop. To Ralph, this was a sign of trouble ahead.[59]

So, looking at this period, there is ample evidence of Eleanor's activities on the political front, as a wife, as a mother and as the head of a household featuring large in both children and clerics. What, then, of her later distinguished reputation as a patron of literature? Her links with the troubadours – or lack of them – have been mentioned already. But Eleanor's reputation is not simply that of a patron of troubadour literature but a patron of the literary arts in general. Indeed, her reputation as such, championed by Rita Lejeune and gleefully adopted by such biographers as Kelly and Pernoud, has become practically a given. It is repeatedly asserted that Eleanor 'must have' infused the sophistication and culture of her southern court into first the bleak Parisian and then the rude Norman/English courts. However, more recent scholarship casts considerable doubt on this assumption. The Paris of Louis VII was, as we have seen, already a vibrant cultural centre, more intellectually cutting-edge than Poitiers. And Henry II was no unlettered warrior, but something approaching a polymath, who won strong praise from the intellectual elite, many of whom were employed at his court. The only safe thing to do, therefore, is to evaluate the surviving evidence of dedications and patronage to evaluate to what extent an association with Eleanor can properly be discerned.

Two works have been said to be dedicated to Eleanor alone, but questions hang over both. The first is Wace's Norman-French *Roman de Brut* (the story of England from Brutus, via Arthur to the recent past), which Layamon, in his English version, claims was dedicated to Eleanor. However, none of the surviving manuscripts of the *Roman de Brut* bear this out, and doubts have been cast on this credit. Despite this, the balance of evidence does seem to support the argument that this work was probably dedicated to Eleanor. However, a dedication does not necessarily identify a patron who commissioned the work; and the likely timeline for the composition of the work, which took place in France during the period when Eleanor was regent in England, suggests Henry is the more likely patron.

The other book which can be traced as dedicated to Eleanor is Philip of Thaon's *Bestiary*, which speaks of Eleanor as 'the arbiter of honour, wit and beauty, Of largesse and loyalty'. However, that book was written well before Eleanor's marriage to Henry, and was in fact originally dedicated to Henry I's second queen, Adeliza, so it can only be a later manuscript copy which is dedicated to Eleanor.[60] The Nun of Barking's life of St Edmund was dedicated jointly to Eleanor and Henry; but not only is this a joint dedication, it is also not a literary work as such, but one associated with promotion of the English throne.

There is therefore almost nothing in the dedicated books to assist Eleanor's reputation as a great patron.

There remain two other well-known sources which demand attention. The first is the *Roman de Rou*, Wace's follow-up to the *Roman de Brut*, this time focussing on the history of the Normans and produced around 1160. While there is specific praise for Eleanor, this is a more obvious commission for Henry than for Eleanor, and consistently with this the praise of Eleanor contained in it is not for her alone but for her in conjunction with her husband. Overall, there is no compelling case for inferring Eleanor's role in commissioning it.[61]

Perhaps the focus of most discussion is Benoit de Saint-Maure's *Roman de Troie*, composed in the late 1160s, where the author refers to the 'rich lady of a rich king, without evil, without sorrow, without anger', a lady 'in whom all knowledge abounds'. Although this is probably a reference to Eleanor, it does not amount to a dedication, still less to evidence of patronage. It is a reference made following what has been described as an 'anti-feminist diatribe' castigating faithless women who change their affections quickly, to apologise to an intended reader. As Michael Evans has argued, it reads more as an attempt to avoid alienating a hoped-for future patron than as a reference to an existing one. Further, given the likely identification of Saint-Maure as the Benoît later commissioned by Henry to write the *Chronique des Ducs de Normandie*, which describes Eleanor in somewhat unflattering terms, any patron is more likely to have been Henry than Eleanor; and supporting this theory, the flattery of Henry is even more marked than that of Eleanor.[62]

Another name associated with Eleanor's patronage is Marie de France, the author of the *Lais*, a set of tales about love and adventure inspired by Breton legend. But Marie de France specifically dedicates her works to a 'noble king' – probably Henry or Young Henry. In relation to her works, as with Saint-Maure and Wace, Eleanor is probably best seen as a celebrity figure of inspiration, not as a patron. Certainly there is absolutely no evidence to back up Lejeune's assertion that Eleanor commissioned the *Lais* herself. There is, however, some cause to believe that Marie moved in court circles and would have been personally known to Eleanor; her education and familiar references to aristocratic life place her somewhere near the top of the social hierarchy, and her use of vignettes of court life on both sides of the Channel suggests strongly that she travelled either with Henry's court or with that of Young Henry.[63]

The surviving documents therefore provide very little in favour of an argument that Eleanor was a literary patron. Nor can a rear-guard argument based on lack of survival of material be credibly accepted; in fact, the evidence of Eleanor's patronage is noticeably absent by comparisons with earlier English queens, and consequently one cannot simply blame the passage of time for the absence of evidence. Running down the list of recent queens, Queen Edith commissioned a life of the then king, Edward the Confessor (and by extension the Godwin family). Queen Edith-Matilda commissioned and may have contributed to William of Malmesbury's *History* and a biography of her mother, St Margaret of Scotland. Adeliza of Louvain commissioned Robert of Torigny to compose a life of Henry I, and lives of her own mother and grandmother. In this context, the absence of evidence for Eleanor's own literary patronage is startling.[64]

In truth, Eleanor in this period presents more credibly as an inspiration of arts rather than as a direct patron, Most obvious is the well-known lyric from the *Carmina Burana*: 'Were the world all mine, From the sea up to the Rhine, I'd give it all up, If I could hold, The Queen of England in my arms.' Another Minnesinger offers this: 'The sweet young Queen, draws the thoughts of all upon her, As sirens lure the thoughtless mariners, onto the reef.' More sophisticated is Benoit de Saint-Maure in his *Roman de Troie* calling her 'Highborn lady, excellent and valiant, True understanding and noble, Ruled by right and justice, Queen of beauty and largesse'. So too is the *Tristan* of one Thomas, probably writing for Henry and Eleanor in these years, who creates for Iseult an ineffectual first husband whom she abandons for the younger, more masculine Tristan. Similarly, in the *Roman of Thebes* it is hard not to imagine that the line that 'the laughter and kisses of two pretty girls is more valuable than London or Poitiers' was intended for Eleanor's delectation.[65]

Further, one can also properly see Eleanor via the prism of her children's literary interests as at least a consumer of artistic endeavour, and thus an indirect patron, since a queen's enthusiasm would promote investment in the arts she appreciated. The interests of her children in later life must surely give some indication of the interests inculcated by their mother in the years when she had primary control of them. On this front, Richard's appreciation of poetry is well known and Geoffrey was also to write a couple of well-regarded poems. But there is also reason to believe that Leonor was despatched to her marriage with a copy of Geoffrey of Monmouth – the source material for Wace and Layamon in their *Bruts* – indicating that this book was common reading material among Eleanor's children. What is more, Leonor sent back one of her clerks to receive an English education – effectively disproving Turner's suggestion that her own education was undertaken primarily after her marriage. This shows that Leonor, based on her own experience, regarded an English education as the best. As for Marie of Champagne, Eleanor's eldest daughter, her joint patronage of chivalrous literature with her husband is well known. She also features as the commissioner of de Troyes' le *Chevalier de la Charette*. Based on this evidence, the case for Eleanor as an enthusiastic reader and educator of her children in literary interests is compelling.[66]

Thus Eleanor's life in the first ten years of her marriage may not have been one rich in artistic patronage, as it has often been portrayed. But her life was plainly full of interests – her political responsibilities as frequent regent, her core duties as bearer of heirs, her role as head of a household of young people being educated for distinguished roles in public life and as employer of many talented clerics.

And still there was room for enjoyment of other interests, such as the consumption of the works of Geoffrey of Monmouth and more modern writers as well as musicians – religious and lay – and other entertainments. Wace's description of the court of King Arthur must surely have been based on Henry and Eleanor's court: 'at the court were many … singers and instrumentalists; There one could hear many songs, rotrouenges, and new tunes; Lais for veille, lais for rote; Lais for harp, lais for pipes, Lyras cymbals and shawms; Hurdy-gurdies, psalteries; Monochords, timbrels, bagpipes … Some tell tales and fables; Others ask for dice and backgammon'. We of course know that Eleanor enjoyed music, and we infer that she enjoyed the tales; but it is also interesting to note that one of her grants to a clerical member of her household was made subject to his annual provision to her of three ivory dice.[67]

So, after years where patience, restraint and resilience seem to have been much called for, it seems that the first decade of Eleanor's second marriage offered her scope for many different sorts of fulfilment – and even fun.

6

Disillusionment

*Ego quod sum, quod possum, totam mentem meam, omnes
facultates meas vobis devote fideliterque expono.*
[I reveal to you what I am, what I can, all my mind, all my
faculties devotedly and faithfully.]
Letter from Eleanor to Cardinal Bobone

By 1168, Eleanor and Henry's marriage would have deteriorated
to the point that they would separate semi-formally. By 1173, she
would be involved in a rebellion against him. So, over the next ten
years the question hangs: what went wrong? This is a question few
biographies have been prepared to tackle meaningfully, ignoring
the question or preferring simplistic 'one-note' reasons. This is
perhaps understandable, given the paucity of the material dealing
directly with Eleanor for the next decade. It is genuinely difficult
to make sense of her life in this period. But without an attempt to
unpick the demise of her second marriage, Eleanor's story becomes
incoherent and unsatisfactory. The two chapters which follow
attempt to isolate and explain a number of factors that seemingly
point towards a complex but comprehensible marital failure. Some
clues can be picked up in the record, but much has to remain
speculation.

The starting point is this: already in the preceding account of the
first, apparently triumphant and harmonious years of the marriage
to Henry, one can see emerging fault lines: Henry's unwillingness
to fully delegate, his insensitivity to local norms within Eleanor's
lands, his lack of religious scruples, his lack of interest as a father,
his lack of emotional engagement and (possibly) his infidelities.

As we try to follow Eleanor through the next five years, all of these factors can be seen in play again, providing evidence for the deepening of those fault lines. As time progressed, into this heady mix was added perhaps the most toxic issue of all – the future, and the status, of Aquitaine.

We know that Eleanor seems to have remained in England for the whole of 1163, and with no records of separate accounting for her household, the strong likelihood is that she spent much of the year in company with Henry – which of course meant a very peripatetic year. While Henry took the Young Henry on a swift tour of the south, Eleanor and the younger children appear to have been resident first in Hampshire until February and then in Wiltshire before moving to London, where expenses for Richard are specifically noted. Another outlay on pork and sheep for the children's food at Young Henry's eighth birthday party (a rare insight from the records that such celebrations did exist) suggests that he was not entirely resident with Becket despite the formal handover earlier in the year.[1]

From Westminster the court moved to Canterbury and Dover followed by Windsor, Reading and Wallingford before moving to Woodstock while Henry campaigned in Wales. It is here that we find the first clear traces of Henry's infidelity since his marriage to Eleanor; Nest, the daughter of the lord of Carleon, became pregnant by him, and he married her to a tenant of Richard de Clare, Ralph Bloet. Their son, Morgan, may well have been taken into Eleanor's household, for he was certainly educated for the Church, in due course becoming Bishop-elect of Durham.

Following the campaign, Henry returned to Woodstock to take the homage of the King of Scots, alongside that of the defeated Welsh Princes, in July. This was a set-piece occasion in which homage was also offered to Young Henry as heir, and Young Henry made his first appearance as a charter witness. For Eleanor, too, this marked an epochal moment as it was a rite of passage for her eldest son towards a role in government. August then appears to have been spent in Windsor before a move back to London.[2]

The reason why Eleanor remained at Henry's side throughout this period is unclear. One obvious possibility is that she was pregnant and suffered a miscarriage and was deemed unfit to travel to France; the indication, by the usually well-informed Ralph of Diss, that she had six sons by Henry, when the record only yields five, suggests this may be the solution. However, the extent of geographical movement within England seems incompatible with that. Another is that Henry wished to ensure that, with himself fixed in England, she was pregnant again before sending her to rule abroad. But with three sons and two daughters, the acquisition of more children was unlikely to be an urgent priority now. Also credible is the possibility that increasing friction between Henry and Eleanor meant that he was simply unwilling to leave her even in nominal charge of a portion of his empire. If this is so, it can only have added to her building discontent.

Reasons for this can be discerned in passing. In Aquitaine, Henry was continuing to show his power. When the Bishop of Poitiers died in March 1161, there was a considerable hiatus, inferentially filled with disagreement, until Henry's English nominee, John of Canterbury (later known as John Belles-Mains), a former clerk to Theobald of Canterbury and close associate of Becket, was appointed. Henry doubtless came to regret the electors' compliance as John would become one of Becket's most wholehearted and influential supporters.[3]

Two key pieces of Eleanor's correspondence from about this time also seem to show a difference of approach between her and her husband. Henry had recently been ruthless with the new Pope and his envoys in the matter of the dispensation for Young Henry's coronation and his continued support for Pope Alexander III. He would continue to exert pressure on Alexander, who had taken refuge in Henry's lands and was to stay between Tours and Sens from late 1162 until mid-1165. Yet at about this time Eleanor separately wrote to the Pope, reflecting on the pleasure she had in the company of his envoys and begging him to restore Paul Raymond, the abbot of her family abbey at St Maixent, to whom she refers as a relative, to his benefices. Describing herself as 'Eleanor, humble queen of England', she offers 'due service with all devotion'. She reflects on the schism which has caused so much trouble and indicates that she has been firmly on the side of Alexander throughout:

Wherefore, whenever there is talk about factions in my presence, I am not afraid to do battle against the attempts of the enemy power but subdue them with my arguments, confidently defending your side. I had in any case most justly rejoiced in and embraced your successes before, but the glorious condescension of your writing and the greeting of great commendation and finally of truest promise were enough to obtain all the favour of my smallness. I cannot describe the spiritual sweetness of deepest delight I drew out, receiving the individual words as separate rewards of divine blessing most happily and devotedly.

This may have been mere political flannel, but it most certainly does not read that way; and if it does reflect Eleanor's own views it places her in a very different place from her husband, who had so ruthlessly bargained for his adherence. Again a suggestion emerges that Eleanor's real faith, which sees her here, and elsewhere in correspondence with the Church, emphasising the Church's precedence and her humility, was putting her at odds with her increasingly anti-clerical husband.

At the same time, demonstrating her keen personal interest in the fate of the Abbot of St Maixent, she wrote to Cardinal Hyacinth Bobone, this time referring to the abbot as her brother. What is more, this exchange of correspondence gives us a further insight into Eleanor's religious stance, revealing her as a close correspondent of a major figure in papal diplomacy. Her letter alludes to a continuing correspondence and even friendship with the cardinal, which we can infer to have dated back to their early meetings in the 1140s:

The favour of your excellence is neither new nor doubtful; always habitual, always exhibited, it does not admit of diminution or interruption. I rejoice that I have and have had such a friend in such a person, by whose sole authority and with my diligence, whatever and however much business can be happily transacted by his coming. For your letters and my knowledge of those letters testify that by intention you strive for my honour and my magnificence. I reveal to you what I am, what I can, all my mind, all my faculties devotedly and faithfully.[4]

The question thus arises of what Eleanor thought of the major topic of the year, which was the escalating row between Henry and Becket and in particular the issue of 'criminous clerks' – in other words, how to deal with priests and members of the minor orders who were guilty of a crime which for a layman would attract a sentence of death or mutilation. On the surface there is no sight whatsoever of Eleanor. Her own view of the topic never emerges openly. However, taken against the background of her experiences as daughter of William of Aquitaine and wife of Louis VII during their times of conflict with the Church, it is likely that she anticipated greater difficulties than did Henry. This, her apparent closeness to the papal hierarchy and her interest in religion suggest that she at least counselled moderation and may even have clashed with Henry on the subject. Later events, too, reinforce the view that Eleanor was not entirely on-side with Henry's approach.

The breakdown in the relationship between Henry and Becket first emerged in July 1163 at an event to inaugurate the new hall at Woodstock, a former hunting lodge in the process of being transformed into a palace. There Becket opposed Henry's taxation plans on behalf of the Church. There, too, the issue of criminous clerks was ventilated, with Henry taking up the position that justice should be the same for all on such charges; though the clerks might be tried by religious courts, and could be subject to religious discipline (such as defrocking and stripping them of their preferments), they must then be handed over to the secular authorities for punishment.

The debate intensified over the summer, with a good example of the issue arising in the case of the cleric Philip de Broi, an acquaintance of Becket, who had been accused of murdering a knight and acquitted by the Bishop of Lincoln's court. Becket supported the position that all alleged offences by members of the clergy should be tried in a Church court. To add to this, Becket picked two other quarrels with Henry, asserting his right to appoint clergy on the archbishopric's manors, and opposing Henry's latest attempt to bring about a technically incestuous marriage (that of his brother William to Isabelle de Warenne, the widow of Guillame of Blois).

Thus matters stood on 13 October 1163 when Becket notionally presided over, but was in effect sidelined at, a piece of theatre designed to assist Henry in his quarrel with the Church. This was the official translation of the newly canonised Edward the Confessor's bones. A part of this occasion, which involved the exhumation of the saint and his reinterment in a glorious tomb suited to his new status, involved the recovery and preservation of the saint-king's regalia to act as part of the royal regalia – props for Henry's arguments in favour of the quasi-sacerdotal nature of kingship. As the bones of Edward's wife, Edith, were part of the ceremony, there was doubtless some formal role for Eleanor to play in the pageantry.

The visit to London involved another round of debate, in which Henry's position on criminous clerks was supported by Gilbert Foliot as well as Roger de Pont-l'Évêque, the Bishop of York. Becket began to deploy a double jeopardy argument which John of Salisbury had developed. Henry sought a confirmation of allegiance, which Becket (now supported by his bishops) would only give subject to the rider 'in every way – subject to our order'.

With no progress in the argument, the event saw a formalisation of the rift between king and archbishop, with Becket being deprived of a number of castles previously in his custody and – just eighteen months after he assumed it – the tutorship of Young Henry.[5]

Where Young Henry was placed at this point is not clear, but it is unlikely it was with Eleanor; his age meant that he would be expected to be in another household. It appears most likely that he joined the court; certainly Walter Map speaks of Young Henry being educated 'by us and among us' and paints a vivid word picture of the young prince hanging on the words of those who interested him, asking endless questions and copying any passages in documents which he thought interesting.

From London, the court headed north to Northampton, Gloucestershire and the Peak before returning back via Woodstock and Oxford to spend Christmas at Berkhamsted, whose barony was part of Eleanor's dower and whose castle had just been reclaimed from Becket. Becket had spent lavishly in updating the castle; and that not all the money was spent in defensive works is suggested by the fact that numerous items of plate were sent from the royal treasury at Winchester to dress the rooms, suggesting a domestic refurbishment had been completed at the same time. This ensured that the Christmas season was spent in luxury and emphatically in a place which evidenced the king's power over Becket.[6]

Here, however, we see another glimpse of Eleanor within the context of this dispute, for Becket, understanding Henry's rage and fearing that he would have to flee England for his principles, had asked John of Salisbury to go to France to scope out possible places of refuge for him. Yet John could not leave the country without a royal licence. Strictly this should have been obtained from Henry; yet it was Eleanor whom John approached. The fact that John, apparently on Becket's express advice, sought out Eleanor, asking her to do what she could to mediate, and asking her to grant him the necessary licence to travel, surely indicates that Becket and John both considered that Eleanor was not ill-disposed to their side of the argument. But they had misjudged the position; Eleanor could not be seen to defy her husband on a matter so close to his heart. She therefore refused, and told Henry of the approach. John was forced to travel *sub rosa*, and while he was away Henry seized John's revenues, leaving him destitute when he returned.[7]

Early 1164 was spent in the south. The Council of Clarendon took place in January, with Young Henry notionally co-chairing the debate with his father. The meeting was to prove a turning point. An impasse having been reached, Henry reputedly locked the bishops up together for two days in an attempt to cow them. Once they had agreed, at Becket's instance, to declare to keep the customs of the realm 'in all good faith', Henry insisted those customs be codified and the bishops agree to them. Richard de Lucy, John of Oxford and Joscelin de Balliol were put in charge of drawing up the document, known to posterity as the Constitutions of Clarendon. Once it was read, this document was found to be utterly inimical to the clergy, but with the pass sold by Becket's verbal agreement, and the clergy exhausted by days of debate, no firm stand was taken that day.

Was Eleanor involved in these events? John Guy suggests her support for Henry is seen in the involvement of Joscelin de Balliol, whom he identifies as a 'key figure in Eleanor's household'. However, there appears to be no solid basis for this assertion. Balliol had indeed been assigned as an adviser to Eleanor in the 1150s, but he was not formally a part of Eleanor's household. And while during that period he is very evident as a witness to Eleanor's charters, he does not appear after 1160 except on one occasion. It appears far more likely that, having served his apprenticeship in the service first of the Empress and then of Eleanor, he had by now been promoted to Henry's service, and there is no evidence of Eleanor's involvement at all.[8]

Following Clarendon, there are indications of a stay at Windsor before Eleanor took her own household on a voyage through Wiltshire including stops at Marlborough, Hampshire including Winchester and then on to the Isle of Wight, Salisbury and Devon. Perhaps she was rendered uncomfortable by the continuing acrimony and the gathering negativity towards Henry's position within her Church contacts. Certainly as early as October 1163 her correspondent Cardinal Bobone had developed a friendship with Becket which was to see him become the foremost supporter of Becket in the Curia – he is mentioned more often in the surviving Becket correspondence that any other cardinal.⁹ By spring 1164, Pope Alexander had signalled clearly – if only in private correspondence – that Henry had overstepped the mark and that Becket would be right to resist anything hostile to the liberty of the Church. He had also indicated that the Archbishop of York should cease trying to assert priority over Becket.¹⁰

Eleanor was probably present at the hallowing of the Abbey Church at Reading on 19 April 1164, and rejoined Henry that summer at Woodstock, where Becket was briefly entertained for the final time. Meanwhile, Henry's henchmen – notably John Marshal, a long-time supporter of the Empress – were finding ways to bring Becket to trial. Marshal summoned Becket to court over a property dispute in September. Becket refused to appear and the king, who had chosen to hear the matter, reissued the summons for 6 October at Northampton. At Northampton, Becket was duly ambushed on a portfolio of charges, following which he was condemned and exiled.¹¹

Christmas 1164 was spent at Marlborough. It cannot have been a merry one. Eleanor would have learned about this time that Aelis' son Raoul had been diagnosed with leprosy; his wife repudiated him and he was forced to renounce his title in favour of his sister Isabelle, the wife of Philip of Flanders. On Christmas Eve, Henry received his envoys to the Pope. Enraged at the discovery that the Pope had allowed Becket to establish himself in a refuge at Pontigny, he spoke openly of renouncing his recognition of Alexander. On Christmas Day, he sequestrated Becket's property and that of his clerks and the archbishopric of Canterbury. On Boxing Day, he exiled all Becket's relatives, their servants and families and all those known to have harboured or assisted him. He froze all revenues due to the Pope, forbade all appeals to the Curia and ruled that anyone corresponding with the Pope or the archbishop was to be summarily hanged or cast adrift in an open boat without oars. Having got this off his chest, however, by New Year his spirits had recovered sufficiently to be doing his duty in the marital bed: Eleanor conceived her ninth child early in 1164.¹²

While Eleanor, now aged forty, was still facing the perils of childbirth, her first two daughters by Louis were of marriageable age. Engaged to the Blois-Champagne brothers since not long after Eleanor's second marriage, in 1164 they married (inferentially in a joint ceremony) their respective fiancés. Marie was eighteen or so, and Alice just fourteen. Marie would take as her seal an almost exact copy of Eleanor's seal as Queen of France, suggesting that she had not forgotten the mother she had not seen now for about twelve years.[13]

It was perhaps the early stages of her pregnancy which prevented Eleanor from returning to France with Henry in early 1165. Possibly also she wished to see Young Henry settled with his new household. Instead of being placed with a magnate, Young Henry's household was now formed under the charge of William FitzJohn, a trusted royal administrator. In any event, Eleanor remained behind until May. On this occasion, and giving weight to the indications of disharmony, there is no evidence that she was appointed as regent. During this period she and the children's household can be placed in Winchester, possibly elsewhere in Hampshire or the Isle of Wight, and making a short trip to Sherborne Castle; Young Henry's itinerary, so far as it can be discerned, overlaps with hers, suggesting that there was a reasonable amount of family time.[14]

In May, however, Eleanor returned to the Continent with Richard and Matilda – and probably also with the younger children. The reason for Richard's named presence is not apparent, but Henry had received an offer for eight-year-old Matilda's hand from Henry the Lion, Duke of Saxony and Bavaria, the cousin of Emperor Frederick 'Barbarossa'. Her presence and that of Eleanor was therefore needed to progress this promising avenue further.[15]

Both had already met in Berkshire (probably Windsor) with the Emperor's chief adviser, who was sent on to Eleanor by Henry after an initial interview. The match, aside from its obvious charms, had one more for Henry in his present mood: Barbarossa was a supporter of Alexander's rival for the papacy, Victor IV. Such a match would therefore indicate an intention to abandon Alexander III unless he mitigated his support for Becket. In a supplementary move aimed at Louis (whom Henry also blamed for his support of Becket), Leonor was to be betrothed to Barbarossa's son.[16]

On this occasion, Eleanor and Henry were barely in the same town at the same time. Very shortly after she arrived, ambassadors were despatched to the Emperor to move the match on, and Henry returned to England, leaving Eleanor in charge of Anjou and Maine, and resident at Angers, apparently with a number of the children. Which of them remained with her is uncertain. Young Henry, we know, was not with her but in his own household. However, both

Richard and Geoffrey had now reached the age where they would be expected to move into a noble's household and learn military skills, Richard being over eight years old and Geoffrey seven. It is therefore likely that they accompanied their father back to England, and most likely that the household in which they were then brought up was that of Young Henry, which would have ample provision for teaching boys of their age.

Eleanor stayed in Angers, acting as Henry's regent in Anjou and Maine until after the birth of her third daughter by him, Joanna, on 5 October 1165. The thinking behind this name is entirely unclear, with no obvious references either in Eleanor's family or that of Henry. Very possibly this was a wry reference to Joanna, like John the Baptist, being a child of Eleanor's old age. Alternatively, the name may invoke the male patron saint of Fontevraud, St John, whose line 'Behold thy mother' was the inspiration for the foundation.

At this time we see another indication that Eleanor was not seen as being completely on-side with Henry's approach to the Becket affair. For shortly before the birth, John Belles-Mains, a friend of Becket, visited her in Angers, at Becket's own suggestion. Again it was hoped that Eleanor might be prepared to intercede with Henry. But John reported that she was very much under the influence of Raoul de Faye, who was an ardent opponent of Becket and appears to have partaken somewhat of Henry's anticlericalism – Eleanor would hear complaints about him in this respect once she returned to her lands in 1168. But consistently with Becket's hopes, at the same time another letter from John of Salisbury in summer 1165 reports the Count of Flanders to be working at reconciling Henry and Becket, 'at the request of the Empress and the Queen', indicating that the Empress and Eleanor were co-operating in trying to defuse the quarrel. Matilda, indeed, had gone so far as to refuse to see the Emperor's ambassadors on religious grounds, despite her long attachment to the country of her first marriage.[17]

It may also be to this period that Eleanor's reputed role in the promulgation of the Rolls of Oléron (the first text of which is dated around 1166) can be attributed. This document was the first formal statement of maritime law in medieval Europe and drew heavily on propositions developed in the Holy Land, which Eleanor would have encountered while on Crusade. There is no surviving proof of Eleanor's involvement in its appearance, but the appearance of these laws first in Aquitaine and then in only slightly modified form in England a few years later does seem to indicate a real possibility that Eleanor was involved in this key development in maritime law.[18]

Towards the end of the year, three significant events occurred. The first, which was to cast a long shadow over Eleanor's later years, was the birth to Louis and Adela of Blois of a healthy son, Philip, in late August. After such a long wait, Philip was rapidly nicknamed 'dieu-donné', or God-Given. By dint of his birthday in August he was also called Augustus – a name he would subsequently justify at the expense of Eleanor's sons. The value of Young Henry's marriage to Marguerite was thus thrown into doubt, as she moved further down the line of accession.

Secondly, in southern France the political tectonic plates were moving; since a failed attempt to negotiate peace in early 1164, following which Henry had allowed his southern vassals to raid Toulouse freely, Raymond V of Toulouse separated himself from Constance of France. The timing of this move was somewhat transparent, occurring as it did shortly after Louis had finally acquired an heir, thereby removing Raymond's children from the possibility of succession. Almost simultaneously Raymond made a significant step in realigning himself decisively away from Louis, reaching an agreement with Count Ramon Berenguer of Provence (brother of the King of Aragon) as a result of which Raymond's heir, the future Raymond VI, would marry Ramon's heiress-apparent, Douce. She would bring as her dowry lands in and around Avignon – and possibly (depending on the birth of further children) a claim to the county of Provence.[19]

Thirdly at something like the same time, Henry, recovering from another less than successful foray in Wales, was being offered the hospitality of Bredelais Castle by Sir Walter de Clifford. That hospitality seems very possibly to have been the occasion for the seduction of his daughter Rosamund, since the occasion for meeting her is otherwise difficult to find. She would prove a more enduring attraction than Henry's other mistresses to date.

Meanwhile, around Eleanor we can see further straws in the wind. Perhaps consistently with the division which Becket seems to have seen between Eleanor and Henry, Eleanor was plainly being given less responsibility than previously by Henry – the period spent at his side, and the absence of a formal regency at the end of it, show this. There is evidence that this loss of faith on Henry's part was understood quite widely, as an incident from this period shows. Left in charge of Maine and Anjou, Eleanor sought to raise a force to deal with a threatened border rebellion by the counts of Ponthieu and Sées (the Talvas family). She was thwarted because her orders were simply ignored by the commanders. She also had difficulty dealing with further unrest in Maine and Brittany. Robert of Torigny is clear that it was her failure to deal with this serous unrest which led to a need to summon Henry to the continent. And of course this problem was self-fulfilling; Henry's confidence and trust would tend to be eroded by the failure.[20]

Equally, Eleanor was turning away from Henry; John Belles-Mains' letter, in saying she placed all her trust in her uncle, by implication places Henry beneath him in Eleanor's emotional hierarchy. After years where not a whisper about her conduct seems to have been raised, Belles-Mains also alludes to the relationship with Raoul with a degree of suspicion, saying that 'conjectures about it grow day by day and seem to deserve credence'. Thus, after years as a quiet officer in Henry's regime, Eleanor appears to have been exerting her individuality once more.

Meanwhile, two comets appeared in the sky above England. French historians were to associate them with the arrival of Philip Augustus. But comets, which are more often seen as harbingers of death and destruction, would be better suited to warning of the end of the accord which had held Eleanor and her second husband together for over a decade.

As the clouds gathered around Eleanor and Henry's marriage, they did not meet for the Christmas court of 1165 – the first time since their coronation that they had failed to do so. Eleanor remained at Angers while Henry was in Oxford. Of course, there is no evidence that this break with tradition had anything to do with Rosamund Clifford; but it raises a question about the state of affairs in the royal marriage. There is also a question over what appears from the records to be Henry's uncharacteristic immobility (at Woodstock or nearby Oxford) over the whole period from September 1165 to March 1166. There is no evidence of serious illness, so another cause has to be found for this break with Henry's usual restlessness. Some biographers suggest that it can be explained by Henry's attention to his law reform programme. However, this seems unlikely; Henry was, as we have seen, a highly talented multitasker who could have combined this work with his more usual peripatetic existence. What is more, if immobility were required, London, where more lawyers were resident to assist in the project, was a more obvious location.[21]

While the truth may simply be that records of his movements have been lost, there is one other suggestive point. It is at this time that the royal accounts first mention work on the spring at Everswell that was later reputed to have been built as 'Rosamund's bower'. Another question also hovers over the end of his residence in England in March; some biographers mention a story that Henry was due to sail to Normandy early in March to deal with the rebellion in Maine but, having set off, changed his mind and returned to Woodstock (not an obvious base for awaiting weather), not returning to Southampton until 16 March. This cannot be verified in the records and remains speculative, but a serious affair with Rosamund Clifford – the only one of Henry's sexual partners for whom he ever recorded his love – provides a credible answer to an anomaly in the records.[22]

On arrival in France, Henry moved immediately to deal with the Talvas rebels and as usual met with success, reducing their castles in fairly short order. The result was that he only met Eleanor over Easter at Angers, at which all their children appear to have been in attendance.[23] It was over this period that their last child, John, must have been conceived. But it was the calm before the renewal of the Becket storm. On Easter Sunday, a suspension placed by the Pope on Becket's powers of excommunication expired.

In May, the court moved to Le Mans; by June they were at Chinon. There news reached them of Becket's sermon at Vézelay (where Eleanor had taken the Cross twenty years before), during the course of which he excoriated Henry, released his fellow bishops from any obligation to observe the Constitutions of Clarendon and excommunicated Henry's principal supporters, including Joscelin de Balliol. There are some suggestions that in so doing he made a lasting enemy of Eleanor. Again, however, the basis for this assertion is lacking. Eleanor's close association with Balliol seems to have been some years in the past, and there is no evidence of her regarding Becket with enmity.

Henry moved to Brittany in July to deal with his restless vassal Count Conan IV. Following a short military campaign, an arrangement was reached whereby Conan's very young daughter Constance would be betrothed to Henry and Eleanor's third son, Geoffrey, now eight years old. Following this agreement, Henry formally claimed the 'Duchy' of Brittany (elevated by association with the royal house) on behalf of Geoffrey. Meanwhile, Geoffrey was sent for from England, where it appears that he was resident. Interestingly, three names appear in association with Geoffrey's movement: Joscelin de Balliol, Alan Neville and William Fitzjohn. The reference to the latter, who was Young Henry's *magister*, reinforces the supposition that at this point Richard and Geoffrey were being brought up with their older brother. The reference to Balliol again demonstrates his independence from Eleanor and suggests he had by now been assigned to Young Henry's household.[24]

It seems likely that Geoffrey was then sent to join his father in Brittany. Henry had spent the intervening period dealing with more trouble in Thouars, where the deputy holding the castle in lieu of Eleanor's cousin had himself revolted. Following Geoffrey's arrival, visits to Redon, Combort, Dol and Mont St Michel are recorded in August and September. There is no evidence as to whether Constance was handed over to be raised in Eleanor's household along with the similarly aged Leonor. Although the agreement placed Constance in Henry's charge, she was still very young – certainly no more than five years old and according to some accounts still a baby – to be sent away from her mother. Marguerite of France had been handed over at such an age, so it is not impossible; but Marguerite's mother died at roughly the time of her betrothal, whereas Constance's parents were alive.[25]

The family was reunited in October, when Henry returned to Normandy and installed himself at Caen. This was the location for one of Henry's most famous bouts of temper, when Richard de Humez, Constable of Normandy, spoke up for a person with whom Henry had just quarrelled. The chronicler recounts that Henry 'tore his hat from his head, undid his belt, hurled his cloak and the clothes he was wearing far away from him, tore the silken covering from the bed with his own hand and began to eat the straw on the floor, as if he were sitting in a ditch'.[26]

Over this period, it seems likely that Eleanor and her daughters were resident in Angers, for Gervase of Canterbury records her as being there when she received news of the unrest in Poitou which her loyal lords feared would lead to her vassals withdrawing their allegiance from Henry 'because of his pruning of their liberties'. Indeed, news may also have reached her that the Poitevin clergy now sought to draw the attention of the papal legates to the fact that she and Henry were related within the prohibited degrees of

1. Nieul – one of the possible locations for Eleanor's birth. Also the site of her mother's burial and a recipient of grants by her in later life. (Selby May)

2. Palais D'Ombriere, Bordeaux. Another possible location for her birth, and the place she stayed awaiting her first marriage.

3. Maubergeonne Tower in Poitiers. William the Troubadour had it built for his mistress, Eleanor's maternal grandmother Dangereuse. As Poitiers was the main centre of the dukes' activity, it is perhaps the most likely location for Eleanor's birth. (Gerd Eichmann)

4. Eglise Sainte-Radegonde, Poitiers. Formerly the Church of Saint Marie 'outside the walls', it was built by Eleanor's great-grandfather and was a focus for the family's worship. (Remi Jouan)

5. Saint Radegonde from the *Vie de sainte Radegonde* (BM Poitiers MS 250) by Venantius Fortunatus. The saint, a poetess, encouraged learning and is often depicted with a book. (Bibliothèque municipale de Poitiers)

6. Bernard of Clairvaux forces Eleanor's father to repent of his heresy. By Jean de Saint-Igny. (© RMN-Grand Palais / René-Gabriel Ojéda)

7. The Porte Royale at the Cathedrale St Andre Bordeaux. One of the only remaining pieces of the twelfth-century structure, it is the door Eleanor would have used to enter the cathedral for her first marriage. (Argentinensis)

8. The Eleanor vase. Given to Eleanor by her grandfather and by her as a wedding present to Louis VII. (© Genevra Kornbluth)

9. Eleanor vase base: records the chain of donations. '… Sponsa dedit A[lie]nor Regina …' (© Genevra Kornbluth)

10. Gilbert of Poitiers. A native of Eleanor's hometown, he was one of the foremost scholastic thinkers, training John of Salisbury and Jordan Fantosme (the latter pictured at his feet). Eleanor and Louis appointed him to the bishopric of Poitiers.

11. Abelard and Heloise. By the time Eleanor arrived in Paris, Abelard was enjoying his status as the intellectual rockstar of his generation before his fatal clash with Bernard of Clairvaux. (Musée Conde MS 482/665)

12. Hyacinth Bobone. A member of the Orsini family, this charming diplomat-lawyer-priest defended Abelard and developed a friendship with Eleanor.

13. Bernard of Clairvaux preaches the Crusade to an admiring Louis and Eleanor in a twentieth-century French schoolbook.

14. Manuel Komnenos. The Emperor of Constantinople was everything Louis was not. (Tokle)

15. The disaster on Mount Cadmus by Gustave Dore. (Author's collection)

16. The area around Mount Cadmus conjures a vivid picture of the hardships of the journey. (Ingo Mehling)

17. Eleanor's seals (above left *c.* 1152, above right *c.* 1154, below the dual face of her later seal – two sides were needed to cover all her titles). (Drawings made for Roger de Gagnieres, Bibliotheque Nationale de France, Paris)

Above right: 18. Marie of Champagne, Eleanor's eldest child, became close to her half-brother and adopted a seal eerily similar to Eleanor's own.

Right: 19. Seal of Empress Matilda.

Below right: 20. Seal of Edith-Matilda of Scotland.

Below: 21. Seal of Joanna Plantagenet, Queen of Sicily, Eleanor's youngest daughter. (Ealdgyth)

22. Geoffrey 'le Bel' of Anjou, Henry's father. Pictured on his grave, wearing a cloak lined with vair (squirrel fur).

23. Henry II, as Eleanor chose to portray him at Fontevraud. (Aurore Defferriere)

24. Eleanor's children by Henry. (British Library, Royal 14 B VI)

25. Heads said to depict Eleanor and Henry at the church of Notre-Dame de Langon dating from shortly after the marriage. (Metropolitan Museum of Art Rogers Fund, 1934)

26. Queen Petronilla of Aragon, Eleanor's cousin, pictured with her husband Ramon Berengar, Count of Barcelona. (Genealogía de los Reyes de Aragón o Rollo de Poblet)

27. A coin minted by Ermengarde of Narbonne, ruler in her own right of a powerful county neighbouring Aquitaine.

28. Hildegard of Bingen. The renowned German abbess and polymath offered Eleanor advice. (Miniatur aus dem Rupertsberger Codex des Liber Scivias)

29. A ring given by Eleanor to a childhood companion, Richard Animal. An example of the small gifts regularly given by Eleanor and Henry to suitors and dependents. (BL Cotton Nero D1, ff 146v-147)

30. A copy of the *Gynecia Cleopatrae* (a manual on women's health) sent by Manuel Komnenos to Eleanor as a gift. It says, 'Henry, friend of Manuel Comnenus brought this book from Constantinople and copied it for the Queen of England.' (Courtesy of Master and Fellows of Trinity College, Cambridge)

31. Poitiers Cathedral. (Misburg3014)

32. The stained-glass window in Poitiers Cathedral commissioned by Eleanor gives us one of the only 'authorised' images of her, probably dating from Eleanor's years in Aquitaine, 1168–73. (Danielclauzier)

33. Young Henry, a handsome paragon of chivalry whose revolt would lead to
Eleanor and Henry's final alienation. (© Paul M. R. Maeyaert)

34. A reconstruction of Old Sarum. Eleanor's main location during her imprisonment, it was also a frequent stay both in her early years as regent for Henry and in her final years in England. (Kurt Kastner)

35. The seal of Geoffrey, Count of Brittany, Eleanor's fourth son by Henry. Like Young Henry, he died during Eleanor's long imprisonment.

36. Eleanor and Rosamund as imagined by Burne Jones. One of many imaginative depictions of Eleanor procuring her supposed rival's death. In fact, at the time of Rosamund's death Eleanor was a prisoner. The suggestion Eleanor was involved dates to centuries after her own death. (Yale Center for British Art, Paul Mellon Fund)

37. The 'Eleanor psalter': some time in around 1186 it appears that Eleanor commissioned this psalter in Fécamp, and had herself depicted on the donor page opposite the 'Beatus' page. (Koninklijke Bibliotheek, Den Haag 76 F 13 (donated in the context of a partnership program), f.28v)

38. Commentators have noted strong stylistic similarities between the psalter depictions and other visual imagery linked to the Plantagenet family. Here the April depiction of a noble shows a vair-lined robe similar to Geoffrey of Anjou's tomb and a flower similar to that carried by Eleanor on her seal. (Koninklijke Bibliotheek, Den Haag 76 F 13 (donated in the context of a partnership program), f.4v)

39. Matilda, Duchess of Saxony, Eleanor's eldest daughter by Henry. She visited England in the early 1180s, bearing her last child in Eleanor's presence. After her return to Germany she commissioned a psalter which depicts her on the donor page. (Walters Art Museum)

40. The famous 'Plantagenet fresco' in the chapel devoted to St Radegonde at Chinon. There is a huge range of theories about who is depicted – and whether Eleanor is the regal figure in the centre. (Chinpat)

41. The mural in context. The chapel adjoins the cell and tomb of St John of Chinon. (Chinpat)

Right: 42. By the time of Richard's accession, Eleanor's long residence in England made her a natural authority figure. This church in Barfrestone, Kent, built in the late years of the century, places the queen (inferentially Eleanor) on the right hand of Christ – the position of power. (Author's collection)

Below: 43. Eleanor ruled in her own right in Richard's absence. Here, from the archives of Canterbury Cathedral (an institution to which she had close ties), is a letter commanding defences to be raised against an invasion by John supported by Philip Augustus of France. (Courtesy of the Chapter of Canterbury)

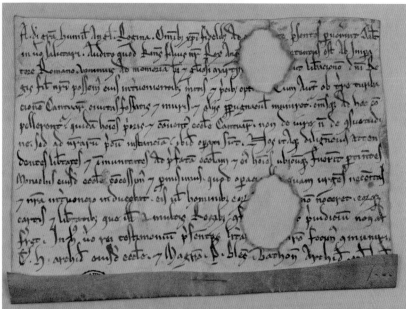

44. Eleanor's rule coincided with the foundation of an abbey in honour of St Radegonde (Radegund) on land near Dover which formed part of her granddaughter Mathilde's dowry. (© Ian Capper CC BY-SA 2.0)

45. Eleanor raced to attend Richard's deathbed, and oversaw his burial and remembrance. (AYArktos)

Left: 46. The tomb of William Marshal in Temple Church. Eleanor was his first patron, and he would go on to serve Young Henry, Henry II, Richard, John and Henry III. His loyalty to Eleanor never faltered. (Author's collection)

Below: 47. John. Eleanor repeatedly demonstrated her own loyalty to and affection for her last child. (Hugh Llewelyn)

Above and below: 48 & 49. Fontevraud, the location of Eleanor's retirement. With ties both to her family's past and to that of Henry, it was the perfect location for the Plantagenet matriarch. (Matthias Holländer; Manfred Heyde)

50. Leonor ruled jointly with her husband Alfonso VIII of Castile and was left regent on his death. (Tumbo menor de Castilla, Courtesy Biblioteca nacional de Madrid, España)

51. Leonor's eldest daughter, Berengaria, was the means of reuniting Castile and León and was the mother of St Ferdinand. (Tumbo de Toxos Outos; Mhmrodrigues)

52. Leonor's third daughter, Blanche, was de facto ruler of France for much of her widowhood, and mother of St Louis. This tomb was probably commissioned by her for herself, but later gifted to her niece Marie of Brienne, formerly Empress of Constantinople. (Author's collection)

53. Via her eldest daughter, Marie of Champagne, Eleanor's line would include two formidable countesses of Flanders, Jeanne and Margaret. Both at one point had custody of the Eleanor Psalter. (Valenciennes BM 0320)

54. Eleanor had full control of how she would be seen by us – she commissioned her own tomb image, the first recorded instance of a lay woman reading. (Touriste)

kinship, and the validity of their marriage was therefore open to question by the Church.[27]

At some point after this, Eleanor, accompanied by her daughters and household, returned to England to await her confinement. It may well be that she either missed or hardly saw Young Henry, who was summoned to his father's side, and the costs of whose expenses in crossing (£100) suggest that he was accompanied by his full household or something very like it. However, the fact that Eleanor was paid money to discharge Henry's expenses suggests that there was some limited crossover between the two.[28]

Eleanor's despatch to England so late in her pregnancy may well have had been brought about by a major disagreement between Henry and Eleanor regarding the future of Poitou and Aquitaine. For the reason behind summoning Young Henry was to present him, and not Richard, at a Christmas court in Poitiers as Henry's heir in respect of Eleanor's lands. Henry had summoned Eleanor's vassals to Chinon in November and announced his intention of holding his Christmas court in their lands the next month.

It appears that a full court was indeed assembled, though no account of the presentation of Young Henry remains. In truth this may all have been a clever piece of manoeuvring by Henry with an eye on Louis VII, whose worst nightmare was the transmission of all the Angevin lands to one lord. But there is no sign that Henry deigned to share such a plan with Eleanor. This new approach was, as she could have told him, unlikely to find favour with her vassals, who were restive in large measure because of their resentment at being part of a large empire based elsewhere, and Henry's seeking to impose universal customs which conflicted with long-standing local practice.[29]

It was also near certain to meet with Eleanor's own considerable displeasure as, with the exception of the short interval after William's birth, she had since the time of her marriage to Louis expected to leave her duchy to her younger son, if any. And for some years Richard had been acknowledged as the heir apparent, with a suitable marriage arranged for that role; thus it is likely that she and others about him had raised expectations in him. The despatch of Eleanor away from her homeland at this point (again without the compensating status of regency) should therefore probably be seen as a naked display of hostile power on the part of Henry. Another interesting question is whether Richard, who appears to have been part of Young Henry's household, was brought to France with his brother, to watch Young Henry being acknowledged as heir to the territory he probably already thought of as his own. Overall this seems likely, since with Geoffrey in France already there would remain no real purpose for the household in England.

Meanwhile, tradition has it that Eleanor, after some preliminary travelling in Oxfordshire, returned to Beaumont Palace in Oxford. This was the place where she had given birth to Richard, and it was said to be here that her last son, John, was born late in December 1166. There are a number of difficulties with the details of John's birth. In the first place, the location of the birth cannot be verified; it derives from a late text which may well have transposed details of Richard's birth.[30] Secondly, while the date of 1167 is given by Robert de Torigny this is a rare error by him (or at least by those reading an oddly interpolated bit of text) as neither conception or birth dates can be made to match with the known movements of Eleanor and Henry in 1167. 1166 therefore has to be preferred. As to the date, 24 December is the date suggested by the chronicle evidence, whereas the feast day of St John the Apostle, the most credible source for the name, is on 27 December. But for the coincidence of Joanna's name it would be tempting to prefer the date of 27 December as offering a conventional explanation for the choice. Given the coincidence and the chronicle evidence, however, 24 December is probably the safer date to accept.[31]

Eleanor seems to have stayed in England during early 1167, while Henry moved against her recalcitrant vassals – first in Angoulême and then in the Auvergne, where he attempted to deal with a dispute between the Count of Auvergne and his son. While this was delayed by one of the parties seeking the decision of their mutual overlord, Louis VII, Henry paid a visit to the Abbey of Grandmont, an ascetic order which was to become a particular favourite of his. There it is reported that he also met with Raymond of Toulouse, now detached from Louis' influence and seeking Henry's support. It seems it was at this meeting that the suggestion of becoming a vassal of Henry's was first discussed, though the resumption of hostilities by Louis prevented the idea from coming to fruition at this point.[32]

It may well be to this period and Eleanor's influence that we can trace the commencement of works to the Tower in London; although the majority of works were to take place after Eleanor left England, the first expenditures appear in the Pipe Roll for this year.[33]

However, the principal focus for Eleanor in 1167 was domestic. In the early part of the year we see her in England, visiting Carisbrooke Castle with her children. Eleanor was again scrupulous when it came to the employment of a wet nurse for John; as already noted, one of Richard's wet nurses was the mother of an Oxford academic. John's wet nurse Agatha, to whom payments are recorded in early 1167, was the common-law wife of Godfrey de Lucy, the son of the chief justiciar, Richard de Lucy, and himself a judge and the future Bishop of Winchester. His relationship with Agatha would be maintained for years, suggesting that she was an interesting woman.[34]

The main feature of the year, however, was preparation for the wedding of Matilda, who would turn eleven in June 1167. Quite what Eleanor thought about dispatching her daughter at such a young age we do not know, though of course this possibility was a given for every heiress; Eleanor had Marguerite of France in her own household to prove it. What is more, the Empress would doubtless have taken a bracing view, having left for her own marriage at an even younger age.

For a wedding to a duke reputed to be possessed of forty cities and sixty-seven castles, some serious preparation was required. Matilda's bridal wardrobe cost over £63 pounds, with £28 being spent simply on gilding of plates. Twenty-eight pairs of silvered and jewelled coffers were commissioned. She was sent away with seven saddles, covered with scarlet and with gilded reins – requiring an expenditure of another £14 – and of course several palfreys then had to be bought. Other expenses evidenced by the Pipe Rolls are further household goods as well as several scarlet-covered chairs, and a courser for Matilda's use in Saxony.[35]

July saw envoys, including the Elector of Cologne, arrive from the Duke of Saxony in preparation for taking Matilda to her new home. They appear to have stayed some time and to have travelled with Eleanor and Matilda to give her a chance to become familiar with them – and to enable the final preparations to be completed. Over this period, the records show expenses being incurred in their entertainment in London, Middlesex and Oxfordshire.

In September, a large party including Eleanor and the earls of Arundel and Pembroke (Richard de Clare, later known as 'Strongbow'), accompanied Matilda to Dover for her embarkation, though further wedding goods were sent on separately from Southampton. Originally it was probably intended that Eleanor should stay in England when Matilda left; however, it appears likely that Eleanor actually crossed to Normandy, where she met with Henry.

With her first daughter about to fly the nest, we have a useful platform from which to view Eleanor as a mother; by this stage she has seven live children by Henry, ranging from Young Henry, rising twelve, down to little John in the cradle. The need for this pause is that tradition has anathematised Eleanor as a bad and distant mother. More recent scholarship has been little more charitable, offering that she was distant but no more so than was the cultural norm. However, the account given above of Eleanor's marriage to Henry thus far raises considerable doubt as to whether the charge of distance is really well founded at all.[36]

It is true that Eleanor was not the type of parent that a normal modern family would see – washing the children's clothes, tying their laces and overseeing every meal. Turner suggests a parallel of Olympian distance by reference to George VI's experiences of his parents. However, one should be careful of inferring this simply because of the royal connection; both the time, the demands on royalty and the relationship of the parents in question are rather different. One should look for a closer parallel with a highly affluent family who can afford all help imaginable. In such a case, whether there is true closeness depends very much on the choice or ability of the parents to spend time with the children. Rich parents may subcontract their children's care almost entirely, or they may be very involved, simply looking to the staff to deal with time-consuming routine while they provide genuine parenting.

A fine example of this a mere century later is Eleanor of Provence, queen of Henry III. It is possible to see her making a positive choice to spend the majority of her time with her children (in preference to her husband), achieving co-residence with them for most of the year, and evidencing her day-to-day care by placing detailed orders for the children's clothes in her own accounts. The result is a well-evidenced affection between her and all of her offspring, including Edward I. By contrast, in Eleanor of Castile one sees the obverse side of the coin – a prolific mother who ensured that first-class care was available for her children but who prioritised her relationship with her husband over that with her children, meeting with them at regular intervals as her itinerary with Edward permitted.[37]

The more detailed picture we have for the two later Eleanors can usefully be compared with that for Eleanor of Aquitaine. While the picture as regards the children is not clear, owing to the paucity of the surviving sources, what is demonstrated by the account so far is that when we can reliably locate the children in the records there is a very high rate of coincidence between Eleanor's residence and theirs. So young William dies in her custody, Eleanor bears many of her children alone, the children are placed with her when Theobald berates Henry for his long absence from their lives, and Eleanor is repeatedly summoned to bring one or other child as Henry's plans call for their deployment. What is more, until Young Henry gets his own household (a cultural norm of the time which cannot blamed on Eleanor) there are only occasional references to the expenses of the royal children – which suggests that for the rest of the time they were part of Eleanor's household. They appear to travel with her often, including across the Channel, and from very young ages. A recent scholarly article concludes that 'for no other noblewoman do we have similar evidence of such close contact with her children'. So, the evidence actually demonstrates fairly clearly that Eleanor was not an absentee mother at all; on the contrary, she was highly present in the lives of her older daughters until their marriages and in those of her three eldest sons until their translation into Young Henry's household aged about seven. Joanna and John, the youngest, require separate consideration, owing to the coincidence of their youth with Eleanor's move to Aquitaine and what happened afterwards.[38]

Co-location, of course, does not necessarily mean that she played any real part in the children's lives, but two factors suggest that she did. First there is the fact that she did keep them with her, dealing with the joys of moving their household with hers, when she could easily have had them parked at a static location for all or much of the year, as did Eleanor of Castile the next century. The second is incontestable evidence of her children's fondness for her and the influence she had on them.

As for the fondness with which her children beheld her, we need only look to her later relationship with Richard, who regarded her as a key adviser – and even John, who would exercise unusual exertion to come to her aid in 1202. Young Henry was to intercede for her as one of his last acts. Matilda, too, would later choose to be by her mother's side for the birth of one of her children, and to send two of her children to be raised for periods by her. As for her influence, Colette Bowie has recently made a powerful case, by reference to Eleanor's daughters by Henry, that their childhood experiences with her had a strong influence on all of them and that the emotional bond they formed with their mother was both powerful and long lasting. It can sensibly also be argued she had such influence on her eldest daughter, Marie.[39]

One might perhaps also take into account Eleanor's repeated references to her daughters in charters as *dilectissima* or *carissma*, and the wording of her later alleged letters to Celestine III in the context of Richard's captivity. However, care should be taken on this front: the wordings are fairly standard for charters and are not safe for such deep reading. The Celestine letters are, as will be explained later, almost certainly not Eleanor's work.

In essence, it should be concluded that Eleanor, up until her return to Poitou, should be given much higher marks as a parent than has been traditional, and that the evidence to date (which later evidence only goes to support) suggests that she enjoyed having children and young people about her.

As indicated above, Eleanor was originally to have remained in England following Matilda's departure. However, the account of Gervase of Canterbury states that Eleanor crossed with Matilda to Normandy. Given that we know she was back in England within a few weeks, most biographers dismiss this account. Nonetheless, there are two good reasons to think it may be true. The first is that the Empress died on 10 September, aged sixty-five, either at the priory of Rouen or the convent of Bonnes at Nouvelles. Eleanor would indubitably have wished to pay her respects to her remarkable mother-in-law. Secondly, Eleanor's actions on her return suggest strongly that it was actually around this time (that is, as early as September 1167) that a decision was made for Eleanor to leave England and live for the foreseeable future in Poitou; in particular, the records show her having packed up six ships' worth of goods by the time she left for Normandy early in December 1167 with her children.[40] That suggests that a long-term move rather than a short stay was intended even before Christmas 1167. Since Henry ceased hostilities with Louis, reaching a truce until Easter 1168 to enable him to ride north and mourn his mother, it is likely that it was at the funeral of the Empress that Eleanor and Henry addressed the future of their union. The final details of these arrangements were then probably settled over Christmas court at Argentan, along with plans for the older children in the coming year.

The nature of the decision to post Eleanor to Aquitaine and the reasons behind it have been much speculated upon, but drawing together the strands at the time of the Empress's funeral sheds some light. Henry had missed his mother's deathbed because he had been occupied with unrest in Brittany. Before that he had been forced to reach a truce with Louis VII to quell more unrest in the Auvergne, and it was uncertain how long that area would remain peaceful; and even before that he had spent nearly a year in trying to reach a peaceful solution among Eleanor's vassals. While Henry's sons were growing old enough to visit him on campaign – and indeed a letter sent by Henry's bishops at this time reminding him of the importance of ensuring a good education for Young Henry suggests that the clerics considered that they were spending too much on campaign and not enough with their books – none of them was old enough to be of any actual assistance. And in the background, the dispute with Becket – formerly his most trusted deputy – rumbled on.

As the funeral party gathered to put the ultimately pragmatic Empress Matilda in her grave in the abbey at Bec, Henry must have begun to appreciate that, even with his superlative gifts and work ethic, he could not hold his empire together alone. And he will have appreciated, too, that the Empress had been, even in her declining years, an invaluable executive on his behalf in northern France. What he had formerly deputed to her he would now have to run himself. In essence, he needed to use his resources as effectively as possible, and with his own attempts to run Aquitaine having proved less than successful, the obvious solution was to use Eleanor there.[41]

It is hard to imagine that this news was unwelcome to Eleanor. Her children were starting to move from the nursery department over which she exercised influence. Of the boys only John remained in the nursery, and Leonor would be old enough to be married within a few years. This role, which had occupied her almost non-stop since her marriage, was winding down. And yet of recent years Eleanor's political and administrative role had sharply lessened rather than increasing. She was in fact being nearly entirely confined to domestic duties.

A move to Aquitaine would not only be a move to her childhood home, but would also offer her a hitherto unattainable chance of self-realisation. Eleanor by now was forty-three years old – a good way along the anticipated life expectancy of the time. As she watched the Empress laid under a slab which trumpeted her 'Henry's daughter, wife and mother: great by birth, greater by marriage, but greatest by motherhood', she must surely have wondered how her own life would come to be summarised. The role in Aquitaine was thus timely in the extreme.

Was it a formal separation sought by Eleanor, as some have speculated? The answer to this is a qualified no. There is no evidence of anything as formal as a separation at Eleanor's instance. The first suggestion of this comes in 1173, when such a case was consistent with the feeling that Eleanor had betrayed her marriage.[42] It must be recalled that, as argued above, this marriage had probably been not a love match but a political alliance, combined with an agreement to produce heirs for their lands. This second role could now safely be said to be done – their first child was married, the next three were betrothed, the eldest girl had left home. What is more, even with such an empire, finding lands for all the boys (particularly John) would be a challenge. What remained was keeping the lands at peace and, in due course, passing them safely to the heirs.

Less contact between Eleanor and Henry was needed in this phase, whereas more consistent attention to the southern lands was vital – not least with Raymond of Toulouse plainly restive and dangerous. He had recently met Henry at Grandmont, and he was strongly suspected to be behind the recent murder of Henry's former ally Raymond Trencavel in Beziers. The effects of that event were highly significant in the power politics of the south. It meant that Ermengarde of Narbonne, left without powerful allies, was effectively obliged to make peace with Raymond. This is why she can be found, just as Eleanor prepared to separate herself from her husband, welcoming her former enemy to Narbonne.[43] Such a change surely required greater vigilance in the south of the Angevin empire.

So far for the positive, practical, case. It was possibly even boosted by Henry's own contingency planning for his 'empire', which was to come to the fore within the next year. While some of this would not yet have been shared, the plan to crown Young Henry had been in gestation for some time, and once that came about it would make sense for him to be based in England as notional ruler, making Eleanor's presence there unwelcome. Purely practical reasons can therefore be constructed for seeing the move as a new posting as a Plantagenet executive rather than a marital separation.

But at the same time there seems no doubt that the pair were not seeing eye to eye. Eleanor had apparently sided with the Empress in seeking reconciliation with Becket. She was in correspondence with Hyacinth Bobone, Becket's strongest supporter in the Curia. Henry regarded any attempts to assist Becket as betrayal, and as of late 1167 Eleanor no longer had the Empress to side with. Eleanor could no longer have been comfortable as the position between the warring sides entrenched further, as it was to do over autumn 1167.[44]

There is also reason to suppose that Eleanor had disagreed with Henry as regards Henry's plans to present Young Henry as heir to her lands, and very possibly for some time in his approach to governing it. For this, it seems likely that she had paid the price of being dropped from the charters pertaining to Aquitaine and was excluded from the Christmas court at Poitiers. Elsewhere, that her regencies were scaled back rather than progressed, that she had ceased to appear on Henry's charters as a witness and that Henry's local barons disrespected Eleanor were all facts attesting to Henry's ambivalent approach to his wife.

If, as seems likely, Henry was also in the throes of a serious affair with Rosamund Clifford, there was now another divide between them. While Eleanor had doubtless been alive to Henry's frequent infidelities, she had thus far probably regarded them relatively lightly, given the amount of time they spent apart; yet an affair of a seriousness to see Henry change his habits would hardly conduce to harmony. Furthermore, the most patient of wives entering her mid-forties might well find herself exasperated by a husband infatuated with a girl barely into her twenties.

Indeed, a letter from the German polymath Abbess Hildegarde of Bingen to Eleanor, which seems likely to date from this period, responds to one sent by Eleanor seeking help in a time of unhappiness and turbulence. Eleanor's letter is sadly lost, but the context can be gleaned from Hildegarde's advice to her: 'Your mind is like a wall which is covered with clouds, and you look everywhere but have no rest. Flee this and attain stability with God and men, and God will help you in all your tribulations. May God give you his blessing and help in all your works.'[45]

The move therefore had (at least in prospect) the advantage of stopping a couple no longer cooperating well from rubbing each other up the wrong way. Trust had apparently broken down in significant respects, and it must have seemed that they were better apart. This theory, of course, did not entirely play out in practice over the next few years.

This more negative perspective on the move may well also explain the fact, often used to denigrate Eleanor, that John and Joanna were probably placed at Fontevraud for around five years at a very young age. Numerous biographers assert this this placement as fact. However, there is no contemporaneous or near-contemporaneous evidence for Joanna's residence there, nor is there (as is sometimes suggested) evidence of any of the other children residing there. Even for John, the evidence is one single line of text in necrology of Fontevraud of uncertain date, which states that he lived there for five years.[46]

However, John's residence can probably be accepted, and Joanna's residence there for at least some of the period is probably a reasonable inference, given their closeness in age and the fact that Eleanor's young children, male and female, seem previously to have been raised in one household. So, while at the other extreme some biographers contend that Henry permitted Eleanor to have her children with her at Poitiers, this does not seem to conform to the records of Fontevraud, and is unsupported by any reference. Bowie's argument has more force, referring to Eleanor's habit of keeping her young children with her to suggest that Joanna was with her mother; but an explanation which covers both children is probably intellectually more robust.[47]

But even if the fact of residence at Fontevraud is accepted, is the negative connotation as regards Eleanor logical? Some recent scholarship sees it simply as a sensible childcare arrangement when Eleanor was 'absent in Poitou and Aquitaine' – perhaps akin to parents posted abroad sending children to boarding school. There is a problem with this: it need not have followed that the children should be thus cared for; as we have seen, Henry had been happy for Eleanor to have effective custody of the older children in England or in Normandy when she was resident there. As he was also Duke of Aquitaine, why not also have Eleanor care for them in Aquitaine? There seem to be three possibilities. The first is that Eleanor had had enough of childcare duties and chose to divest herself of responsibility for these two late children to concentrate on her responsibilities in Poitou. The second is that one or other of Eleanor and Henry considered that Poitou was not safe for the children. The third is that Henry was not prepared to sanction Eleanor taking these last two children and raising them in Aquitaine because of a concern about Eleanor's reliability.

Eleanor's later positive approach to caring for other people's children suggests the first is unlikely. This is also lent some force by the note in the Fontevraud necrology being clear that the placement of John was Henry's decision. On the other hand, both the latter two possibilities are to an extent confirmed by the location of the children. Fontevraud was, as we have seen, very much on the borders between Poitou and Anjou, but technically in Angevin territory. It was also a place to which both Eleanor and Henry had long-standing links. It was therefore neutral as between them but technically in Henry's lands, putting the children as close to Eleanor as they could be while they remained technically and legally in Henry's power. Whether the main reason was security or lack of trust, one may therefore perhaps regard the children as being – ever so slightly – hostages for the good behaviour of their now imperfectly trusted mother.

7

'The duchy ... in her power'

Rejoice O Aquitaine! Be jubilant O Poitou!/For the sceptre of the
King of the North Wind, Is drawing away from you ...

Richard Le Poitevin

Even as arrangements for the separation were finalised, Aquitaine
flared into revolt again. The Count of Angoulême had only been
temporarily pacified, and now he and the Count of Thouars, together
with some recalcitrant Bretons including Eudes, the Vicomte of
Porhöet, made common cause with a rapidly strengthening house,
the Lusignans. This family boasted seven sons to provide for and
a strong Poitevin heritage – including descent from a sister of
Geoffrey de Rancon. But on one level now was a good time to deal
with them; their father, Hugh 'the Brown', had gone on Crusade in
1163 and had been taken captive, leaving only the youthful sons
(none much older than twenty) to deal with his lands.

So Henry and Eleanor hurried south, very probably leaving the
younger children at Fontevraud on the way. Eleanor, accompanied
by at least Richard and Leonor,[1] was left by Henry, probably at
Poitiers, under the care of Earl Patrick of Salisbury, who was to act
as Henry's military governor in Aquitaine. Earl Patrick was a man
with good connections in England and Normandy, being married
to the daughter of the Count of Ponthieu and having sisters married
respectively to the famous English warrior John 'the Marshal' (the
hereditary Marshal of England) and the Count of Perche.

Taking the rebellion at its head, Henry first took the chateau
of Bridiers, and installed a safe man there. He then attacked
the supposedly impregnable castle of the Lusignans at Lusignan

and took it, razing it to the ground and devastating the lands for miles around. The Lusignans fled, apparently to seek shelter with King Louis, to whom they had been threatening to transfer their allegiance. In late March, Henry therefore moved back to Normandy to meet with Louis and secure a settlement which would restore Eleanor's vassals to her in peace for sufficiently long to allow her to take steps to establish a government in Poitou.

Henry's involvement at this point raises a theme which is worth noting. Generally, it appears to be taken that Eleanor was alone in command in Aquitaine for the next five years; but as the story will demonstrate, this is very far from the truth, with the change from her previous *modus operandi* not at all marked until 1171. Until then, the separation is not so clear as is often thought. One sees her and Henry spending a reasonable amount of time in the same place – and indeed Eleanor spent significant portions of the next few years out of Aquitaine, pursuing the family's wider agenda.

The negotiations for this peace were progressing well, between the Count of Flanders for Henry and Eleanor's son-in-law Henry of Champagne for Louis, and Henry was on his way to meet Louis at Pacey, on the border with Louis' lands, when, on about 27 March, Eleanor, Earl Patrick and a small escort including the earl's young nephew William Marshal (son of John) were travelling along a road near Lusignan. The events of the day are described in detail in the *Histoire de Guillaume le Marechale* ('the Histoire').[2] This source is one of the most interesting resources for the latter part of Eleanor's life. It is near contemporary, having been written by a member of the household of William (by that stage himself 'the Marshal') and based on his own recollections as told to his family. It is therefore the nearest thing to an eyewitness account that survives of the era. However, it needs to be treated with caution as the author, deriving his material from an earlier account of John D'Erlay, William's devoted squire and writing for the family, was hugely admiring of the Marshal – and also because the relentlessly upwardly mobile William seems to have become quite talented at running his own PR over his long career.

However, there is no reason to doubt the essence of this story, fiercely exciting though it is. Considering the threat of the Lusignans to have been dealt with, the party was small and the men wore no armour – save for William, who adopted a 'better safe than sorry' approach to the wearing of armour throughout his career. He would also have wanted to appear diligent, having joined his uncle's household recently after being 'let go' by another Norman lord, William de Tancarville. However, the Lusignans, in particular two of the younger brothers, Guy and Geoffrey, had returned to the area and planned to abduct Eleanor and hold her to ransom. As the attackers bore down on the party, Eleanor was despatched by Earl Patrick on the fastest of the horses to seek safety in what remained of the castle of Lusignan, while the earl and his men held off the attack. As he struggled to put on his hauberk, the earl was stabbed fatally in the back. William places the responsibility firmly at the door of Geoffrey de Lusignan, as the leader of the band, though Geoffrey was apparently not himself the striker of the blow. Only young William put up much of a fight, 'holding them at bay like a mighty boar with a pack of dogs', but in the end he too was overpowered and taken prisoner, having sustained a serious wound to his leg.[3]

The news of the attack reached Henry at the final peace conference with Louis, just before the deal was signed. That deal sketched out a future plan which was to be key to the events of the next few years. One feature was an agreement to marry Richard (whose previous betrothed appears to have died) to Louis' second daughter by Constance of Castile, Alys, then about six years old. But the most politically significant feature of the agreement was the division of Henry's lands between Young Henry (England, Normandy, Anjou, Maine in his own right and Brittany as overlord), Richard (Poitou and Aquitaine directly from Louis) and Geoffrey (Brittany as vassal of his eldest brother). Henry in the event had no leisure to finalise this deal, or even to deal with Eleanor's difficulties in Poitou, because on his way south he heard of a more serious uprising in Brittany, which required him to be on the spot there as soon as was possible. It was during the course of dealing with this uprising that Henry II took as a hostage the teenaged daughter of his rebellious cousin Eudes de Porhöet, and made her his mistress. It appears that the offspring of this liaison did not survive.[4]

How Eleanor dealt with the situation in Poitou following the attack on her is not particularly clear, but we know that she purchased the freedom of the hostages and gave young William Marshal 'horses and arms and money and plenty of fine robes'. That her generosity was perhaps seen as excessive by some appears to be indicated by the *Histoire*'s reference to her doing this 'cui qu'il en peise' (whoever might cavil at it) and the Marshal's own recognition of her as a 'brave and courteous lady'. Certainly Eleanor would have been very grateful for William's actions, but the events also offered her an opportunity to display her personal power of patronage at a key point. As Evelyn Mullaly notes in her study of the relationship between Eleanor and the Marshal, this episode resonated with the Arthurian paradigm outlined by Geoffrey of Monmouth, which required the great lord to be a generous gift-giver.[5]

Harmonising with this display of power and patronage, we also know that Eleanor arranged the lavish funeral of Earl Patrick in the Abbey of Saint-Hilaire in Poitiers. One of the first charters surviving after her return to Poitou is an endowment to the church for an anniversary Mass, supported by a generous donation of land, to be said annually 'for the soul of Earl Patrick who died in our service'. Prudently, the same gift covered maintaining the anniversary of Eleanor's own death in the future. It is interesting to note that, anticipating or affirming Richard's role in the duchy, Eleanor associated both Henry and Richard with her in this donation: 'by the will and command of my lord the king and my son'.[6] The document also evidences her having about her a considerable court, including the Bishop of Poitiers, Raoul de Faye, her cousin the Viscount of Châtellerault, Saldebreuil de Sanzay, and numerous members of her household and clerics.

Infuriatingly, there are no equivalent sources to the Pipe Roll materials for Eleanor's activities in Aquitaine. What we do know is that there seems to be no further trouble for that year, though matters were still sufficiently tense that Henry arranged to come into the province in the New Year. The surviving charters, predominantly made at Poitiers, suggest that Eleanor established herself here for the majority of the time.

Some biographers suggest[7] that Eleanor spent the rest of the year taking homage at Niort, Limoges and Bayonne, dismissing unpopular seneschals and reviving ancient customs – but the source for this is not given and it does not fully reflect the charter evidence, which cannot be dated so precisely. Nonetheless, there are a number of charters which probably date from the late 1160s which show Eleanor exercising her power at different locations in a variety of ways. So, for example, she issued a charter at St Jean D'Angely confirming a grant by Guillot Boardus to Fontevraud and the priory of Soussis of the land of Belleville near Niort, and also granting rights to take timber in the wood of Chizé; this can be dated to sometime after 1169 only because of the date of promotion of Peter, the Bishop of Perigueux. However, we do know that Eleanor held her Christmas court in Poitiers, while Henry held his in Argentan.[8]

The other place which comes to the fore in the charter evidence is Fontevraud. Eleanor's charters do not disclose her as a major patron of religious houses; her religious patronage seems to have been predominantly personal to the clerks in her household. The main exception is Fontevraud, and dates from this period. Prior to this, Fontevraud had received only one of the surviving grants – less than the Abbey aux Dames in Saintes, and no better than a number of other notable establishments. But from 1168, when it seems Eleanor's younger children were in residence there, it becomes an object of her patronage and disproportionately so compared to other abbeys. Not only this, Eleanor is noted on the witness lists of others who made charters at Fontevraud; so in 1172 she witnessed a gift by her steward Manasser Biset and his wife to the abbey, providing for the purchase of herrings during Lent. On another occasion she is recorded as witnessing the religious profession of a widow, and the gift given by the novice's parents to the abbey. She also figures, in her role as Queen of England and Duchess of Aquitaine, as one of the main witnesses to grants in this period by Henry in favour of Fontevraud.[9]

All of this suggests that Eleanor based herself at Poitiers for ease of access to her younger children and often visited them at the abbey, becoming, as she did so, increasingly bound to the place.

It was very probably during this year that Eleanor commissioned the famous stained-glass crucifixion window above the high altar in the cathedral of St-Pierre in Poitiers. The rebuilding of the cathedral had been a joint project of Henry and Eleanor in the early days of their marriage, and while Eleanor was doubtless pleased to see the investment in her home cathedral, the style of the work, in particular the fortress-inspired massive rear wall, suggests that Henry's was the dominant opinion in the building phase. But by the time of Eleanor's return to Poitou, the work was nearing completion, with the choir being finished just before her arrival.

The work on the window can be timed with some precision since it includes depictions of all Eleanor's sons, as well as herself and Henry; it must consequently date to after John's 1166 birth and before the events of 1173. It is thus about as clear as it can be that this item is genuinely a result of Eleanor's own patronage. This conclusion is reinforced when the figures of Henry and Eleanor at the foot of the window offering their window to God are examined, for one can see that Eleanor is on the right hand of God (the position of power) and in the portrayal of the pair proffering a model of the window, her hand is more evident. This can very probably be taken as a deliberate sign that it was she who commissioned and oversaw the design of the window.[10]

This subtle message is echoed in the charters which Eleanor was issuing from this period. As is apparent from the charter to St Hilaire quoted above, Henry no longer features as 'dearest' husband, but simply 'my lord the King'. Henry during this period seems to issue no charters at all pertaining to Aquitaine. The impression is given of Eleanor ruling her lands by herself.

As for those who surrounded her at this time, the picture is very partial. While Eleanor kept a number of the domestic staff who had surrounded her, such as her chaplain Peter and her butler Philip, there was a considerable change in administrative staff. No replacement for Earl Patrick arrived, and otherwise her Norman advisers seem to have been confined to a few lower-level staff such as Simon de Tournebu and Richard de Camville. Indeed, Simon was hardly a Norman adviser. He had previously been the Bishop of Bayeux's seneschal, and had been in Poitou serving as Henry's constable of Thouars Castle since the showdown with Eleanor's cousin in 1164. Richard de Camville was more properly a Norman. He had been a supporter of Stephen throughout his reign, but was plainly a useful man, since he was swiftly made Sheriff of Oxfordshire under Henry. One suspects that he was brought to Poitiers at Eleanor's behest, she having spent much time at Oxford while acting as regent.[11] Otherwise, we find two Anglo-Normans: Manasser Biset, the steward and previously steward to the entre royal household; and on just one occasion, coinciding with Henry's presence, Joscelin de Balliol. But coming to the fore are more Poitevins. Most of these are men with a family history of service to the count-dukes but also a recent track record for serving Henry. They include William Maingot II, custodian of the lordship of Surgères, and son of Eleanor's father's seneschal; Fulk de Matha, whose father had in turn served Eleanor's father, Louis and Henry as seneschal; Maingot de Melle; and Porteclie de Mauzé. Also rejoining Eleanor's household was Harvey le Panetier, who had been appointed Prévôt of Poitiers in 1157.[12]

There is a question mark over the size of Eleanor's court during this period. We know that Eleanor already had one female relative, Marchisa, with her, for money was spent on saddlery for her. Judging by her name, this lady was probably a daughter of the Count of La Marche and appears to have joined Eleanor's household before her return to Poitou. Her adoption as a foster daughter seems to have resulted from her father's repudiation of her mother for infidelity, leaving the daughter with no female carer. There would have been some complement of ladies, probably noble young women such as Marchisa. It seems likely that more Poitevin ladies were included, although Henry's half-sister Emma may well also have formed part of Eleanor's household.[13]

However, assertions that Eleanor kept a household of up to sixty ladies, including Marguerite of France and the affianced wives of her younger sons, do not find support in the records. Furthermore, placing such valuable female bargaining chips in such a relatively unstable location as Aquitaine seems unlikely, particularly if the decision to leave John and Joanna at Fontevraud was indeed down to security considerations. And certainly after 1170 we can trace Marguerite in her husband's household and with her own retinue; this is also one possible location for Alys and Constance (aged between seven and eleven at this time). We can in fact find Constance at other locations during this period; and, in truth, given that both her parents were still alive and her father was loyal to Henry, there would be no reason for her to be brought up away from her own home.[14]

So, too, would there have been knights. We know that Eleanor was able to offer William Marshal a position following his ransom, and the designation 'miles' (soldier/knight) is far from uncommon in Eleanor's witness lists.

On balance, though, it seems unlikely that Eleanor kept great state or a formal court; most of the surviving charters are witnessed by lower-ranking nobles or household members; aside from Raoul de la Faye and his brother the Lord of Châtellerault, few great names appear. Marchisa's putative father, Audebert of La Marche, is noted once and Theobald Chabot, Lord of Vouvant, who was Constable of Aquitaine, appears twice. It is likely that in many respects her court was not dissimilar to the comital court of her childhood, lacking nothing in terms of material needs but a long way from the huge court that surrounded Louis or Henry. This is consistent with the poetic description later given by Richard le Poitevin, which refers back to her life in Poitou. He speaks of her surrounded by her ladies, attended by the young men of her household and advised by her councillors. He also conjures up a picture of more leisure than business, and again emphasises Eleanor's taste for music, speaking of her enjoying the melodies of the flute and the drum or listening to songs sung to the accompaniment of the tambourine and the cithara.[15]

One aspect which is not reflected in Richard Le Poitevin's account can be deduced from the fact that Eleanor's charters again contain an unusually high ratio of clerical witnesses. This suggests that Eleanor was, as earlier, maintaining a considerable number of chaplains and clerics acting outside of clerical roles – for example providing Eleanor with her own chancery or secretariat and also maintaining regular contacts with the wider community of abbots, bishops and other churchmen. In the predominance of clerics, Eleanor's court seems to have been different both from the comital court and that of Henry.[16]

Consistently with all of this, when we look at the portrait of Eleanor in the cathedral window at Poitiers (which we can safely assume to be a representation authorised by Eleanor) we do not see the famed beauty or dangerous seductress of the poets' and chroniclers' accounts. The Eleanor in the picture is, like the real Eleanor, a woman in late middle age. The artist has placed lines on her neck, on her brow and around her eyes. The eyes are fine, but the emphasis of the portrait is on her decisive brow line and the experience inherent in her marks of age. She is a serious and commanding woman.

Shortly after New Year 1169, Henry, Louis, Young Henry and Richard met at Montmirail. This meeting is perhaps best known for being the occasion of another failed attempt at mediation by Louis between Henry and Becket. But it was also the occasion for the conclusion of the key treaty recording the division in Henry's lands that was to occur on his death, and consequently the finalisation of Richard's betrothal to Alys. It confirmed the structure agreed in principle, but not finally settled, the previous year: Young Henry was to receive England, Normandy, Anjou and Maine along with the overlordship of Brittany; Geoffrey, meanwhile, would be Duke of Brittany under him; finally, Richard would be Count of Poitou and Duke of Aquitaine, paying homage only to Louis. This was a key division of power not just for the recipients but also for Louis, as it protected him from the spectre of a united Plantagenet empire.

To confirm the structure put in place, Young Henry and Richard paid homage to Louis then and there: for Anjou and Brittany on Young Henry's part, and for Poitou on that of Richard. Henry himself reaffirmed the homage he had given for Normandy in 1151 by a handshake and a kiss of peace. Significantly, Young Henry's homage was unqualified; the agreement stated that he would 'owe nothing to his father or brothers save what they may deserve, or what natural affection dictates'. He therefore owed no prior loyalty to Henry above that owed to Louis. Louis will certainly have perceived this as a victory won because of the threat of interdiction; however, as would become clear, Henry perceived it as a provision which could work to his advantage. At the same time, Henry promised to arrange for the coronation of Young Henry and Marguerite as soon as possible – thereby putting pressure on Louis to get Becket to capitulate, since without him the coronation would not be perceived as valid.[17]

This meeting also saw the formal betrothal of Richard and Alys, with the county of Berry being stipulated as Alys's dowry. It was also agreed that Alys should be handed over to Henry's wardship. This provision indicates that it was unlikely that Alys went into Eleanor's household; of course, it is possible that she was sent to join the younger children at Fontevraud, and Louis' reluctance to have Alys directly in Eleanor's custody may be another factor leading to the younger children spending time there. He had, after all, had his daughters by Eleanor raised in a convent, so an upbringing at Fontevraud would not be inimical to him. Other provisions of the treaty, which hint that its terms were effectively wrung out of Henry against a threat of excommunication/interdiction and may not represent his own wishes, include the provisions (later ignored) that Henry should go on Crusade, and should permit Richard to be raised at the French court.[18]

The Treaty of Montmirail also had a significant element which pertained to Eleanor's lands and their troubled recent past, deriving from Louis' role as nominal overlord of at least parts of her lands. Henry was to restore the lands and castles he had taken from Eleanor's rebellious vassals, and Louis was to try to reconcile Henry with these vassals, some of whom had sought sanctuary with him.

In purported pursuance of this agenda, Henry moved from Montmirail into Aquitaine in early March, rapidly securing the submission of the Count of Angoulême and the Count of La Marche. Eleanor's cousin Geoffrey of Thouars was permitted to re-enter the duchy and resume residence at his castle. However, Henry's approach was not generally peaceable; one Robert de Sillé is recorded as dying in Henry's custody after Henry refused him food and water. By May, Henry had moved into Gascony proper, being at St Macaire near Bordeaux, and during this period it seems that his approach was quite as violent as before the peace, with seizures and destruction of rebels' castles. This was a development which led Louis, initially frustrated by Becket's refusal to compromise in February, to draw closer to him again.[19]

However, 1169 also marked more peaceful progress. Although the date of Leonor's betrothal is somewhat hard to pin down, with various dates from 1167 to 1170 being given in different accounts, it seems probable that during Henry's unusually long sojourn in Gascony – a part of Eleanor's duchy not normally given much attention by him or previous dukes – he met or corresponded with young Alfonso VIII of Castile, who would later that year take the rulership of his lands into his own hands aged fourteen, and reached an agreement in principle for his betrothal to Leonor. Leonor's betrothal to the son of Frederick Barbarossa seems to have been dropped, possibly on account of the young man's illness, which was to prove fatal in the very near future, or because of the difficulties which an alliance directly with the schismatic Empire would create for Henry in his current debates with the Church. In any event, an alliance with Castile had huge advantages for Henry's rule in Aquitaine, as it would give a peaceful border and indeed possible support to the south. It was far more advantageous than a match which John of Salisbury reports that Henry had previously contemplated with Navarre. For Eleanor it was as good a match for Leonor as could have been wished, giving her a crown, a husband close to her own age and a home close to Eleanor, assuming Eleanor stayed resident in Aquitaine for the rest of her life.[20]

The timeline suggests that the final arrangements, including those as to dower (financial provision for Leonor by her new husband) and dowry (bridegift from her family to her husband) and the conclusion of the formal betrothal, were left in Eleanor's hands when Henry moved north in August 1169 to resume dealing with northern affairs – including a resurgence of support for Becket. The agreements would not have been formally concluded until after Alfonso declared his majority in a grand assembly at Burgos on 11 November of that year. It seems likely that while negotiations were carried on Eleanor based herself somewhere convenient to deal with messengers from Castile. Her very active involvement in finalising the arrangements is reflected in the version of the marriage negotiations in the Castilian chronicles, which suggest that the marriage was arranged entirely by Eleanor. By the end of 1169, Eleanor had done as much as she could reasonably do to prepare for the seven-year-old Leonor's wedding.[21]

The interesting point in relation to the Castilian discussions is that it seems implausible that the dowry arrangements for Leonor were made without Eleanor's assent. This is significant because it is often stated that Leonor was given as her dowry or a part of her dowry the reversion to Gascony following Eleanor's death; and it has been suggested that this component of the deal was contrary to Eleanor's wishes and formed a not inconsiderable component of her reason for rebellion a few years later (and also that of Richard).[22]

The position on this issue is regrettably unclear; too unclear for firm conclusions to be drawn.

In the first place, it is by no means certain that Gascony did form a component of Leonor's dowry. No document survives which sets it out (although her dower assignment from Alfonso does survive).[23] What we know is that after Eleanor's death Alfonso VIII would assert a claim to Gascony as part of Leonor's dowry, and be prepared to back it with force; and that that claim would be reasserted fifty years later by Alfonso X and be compromised as part of the marriage settlement of Eleanor of Castile to the future Edward I. Part of the deal then struck was that all documents supporting the claim would be destroyed – and this undertaking sadly appears to have been thoroughly performed. The evidence therefore suggests that there was some claim to Gascony, but the indicators thereafter point in both directions. The fact of the requirement to destroy the documents indicates that there was some substance to the claim, but the fact that it was surrendered suggests that it was not considered a very strong claim by the extremely able Alfonso (known as 'the Wise').[24]

Taking all this into account, it is probably a fair inference that some grant in relation to Gascony was made. Some accounts suggest that the claim to Gascony derived from the fact that it was effectively a guarantee for the full payment of a financial or jewel-based dowry and that some small portion of that dowry was not paid or not paid promptly. This would make sense, because Henry was only to give cash dowries with his other daughters. Moreover, it seems implausible that Eleanor would consent to Richard's inheritance being diminished by an actual grant of Gascony; while Aquitaine's control over Gascony was extremely limited,[25] the struggles they had undergone to win it show that it held value for them, and this value can only have increased with the growth in trade in the region in the middle to latter period of this century. In this light a full grant seems implausible, and the better view is that Gascony (or those parts of it to which Eleanor's family had title) was included in the deal only as a pledge against the non-payment of dowry sums. We can imagine Eleanor agreeing in principle to a deal like this without rancour.

Thereafter, Eleanor's attention seems to have moved to making plans towards establishing Richard as her co-ruler in line with the provisions of Montmirail. Meanwhile, Henry was doing much the same for Geoffrey – from Poitou he had moved into Brittany, where he held Christmas court with Geoffrey and his eight-year-old fiancée, Constance. We can also note from this that there seems room to doubt the theory that Constance was in Eleanor's household, since she self-evidently was not with Eleanor at the time. It has been suggested that this Christmas court – and the young couple – inspired Chretien de Troyes' romance Érec *and* Énide, written about this time and set in Brittany. The romance depicts King Arthur sitting upon a throne emblazoned with a leopard – the symbol of the Plantagenets. However, the ages of Geoffrey and Constance (eleven and eight respectively) really preclude their being the inspiration for the work. The work is better seen as another reflection of the way in which Henry and Eleanor were perceived and depicted at this time – close to the apogee of Henry's success – 'never was there so rich a court'. The play gives another vivid description of court celebrations, sketching the singing and the dancing and the wide variety of instruments deployed to create the lively atmosphere. In more concrete terms, Henry is the great, all-powerful king presiding over a sophisticated and gallant court, working as a team with his beautiful queen; but one may note alongside the tone of admiration the essentially feminine and submissive role which the queen plays in Érec *and* Énide – at best she is described as 'kind and sensible'.[26]

This continuing synergy in the projects of Eleanor and Henry, as well as Eleanor's subordinate role within the synergy, is also reflected in their joint plans for Young Henry, now nearly fifteen years old. Sometime early in 1170, Henry left Brittany for Caen and Eleanor moved north to meet him with a view to arranging Young Henry's coronation. It is likely that, with her marriage soon to take place, Leonor travelled with her mother to see the rest of her family, and her godfather Robert of Torigny, possibly for the last time.

As regards the coronation, it will be recalled that this event had been planned for years – Henry had bought the gold for Young Henry's crown and regalia early in the 1160s, but arrangements had hung fire because of Henry's estrangement from Thomas Becket, and the man's subsequent exile; as Archbishop of Canterbury, he was expected to perform the coronation rite.

By this stage, the row had escalated to such a degree that Becket had excommunicated a number of bishops and threatened to put Henry and his lands under an interdict (a threat which the not entirely devout Henry had mocked as 'not being worth an egg'). For all his mockery, however, Henry recognised the real political power of the threat, which would release all his vassals from their oaths of loyalty to him and technically render him incapable of exercising power. He had responded with a decree in which it was declared that anyone carrying an interdict was a traitor and that anyone willing to obey an interdict would be sentenced to deportation along with their relatives and dependents. No priest or monk was to leave the country without special leave. A last-ditch attempt at peacemaking between the former friends had foundered in November 1169 when Becket had insisted on being given a kiss of peace by Henry and the king had refused. This was regarded as extremely unhelpful by the Pope, particularly when Henry also refused to allow the kiss of peace to be given by Young Henry in his place. Thus, early in 1170, Pope Alexander (now safely out of Plantagenet territory and back in Rome) was in the process of considering an interdict.[27]

Henry was therefore determined to get his son crowned before any interdict could be declared. Further impetus was given to the plans by the fact that Emperor Frederick Barbarossa had seen to it that his own son Henry was crowned King of the Romans in the summer of 1169, and Young Henry had now reached the age at which Henry's own father had been invested with power in Anjou. Henry's statements at this time evincing an intention to go on Crusade may even have been genuine – this is a subject on which the academic jury remains out.[28] And so Henry determined to side-step the issue caused by the absence of reconciliation with Becket and arranged for the coronation to be performed by the Archbishop of York and papal legate Roger de Pont-l'Évêque, under the authority gained from the papal envoys for the planned coronation in 1161. It seems doubtful whether Eleanor was fully on-side with this piece of cleverness. The author of the Histoire tells us that Eleanor endorsed this decision, but a degree of hesitation may be inferred from the rider which is then added: 'for such was her duty'.[29]

What Eleanor almost certainly did not appreciate was that the extremely acute and well-educated Henry was probably doing this, and making simultaneous arrangements to apparently divest himself of power in Brittany and Aquitaine, for a clever reason of his own. With the threat of interdiction now very much in play, Henry had spotted a cunning legal loophole. If he crowned Young Henry and had Geoffrey invested with ducal power, the proper title to those lands passed to them, and the correlate was that technically Henry retained only a life interest in them. The position as regards Aquitaine, which was officially held by Eleanor with Henry only holding it through her, was, of course, subtly different. If he divested himself of power over his other lands, any interdict targeted at him could not properly and legally be laid on the lands, whose legal possessors would then be his sons and not himself. Essentially, if Henry could manage to get legal title transferred to his sons, the papacy's nuclear option against him became useless.[30] The implication of this plan was that Henry, despite his undertakings at Montmirail, perhaps did not intend any genuine divestment of power to his sons; but if so, this aspect he kept to himself.

It was at this point, with the family reunited and apparently making preparations for the coronation in harmony, that Eleanor recommended William Marshal to Henry as a suitable military trainer for the Young King, and William left Eleanor's service after only just over a year in her household. The fact of the specific recommendation suggests that he had been acting in a similar role for Richard in Eleanor's own household since his recovery. It also appears to reinforce the impression that Eleanor did not maintain a large household of knights, and that she perceived Marshal's advancement would be better served in a bigger household. One point should be noted here: the idea, often expressed, that Marshal owed a strong loyalty to Eleanor based on long service with her is thus simply wrong. He was only in formal service with Eleanor for just over a year. However, it appears perfectly clear that a strong bond of loyalty had indeed been forged between the pair during that period. Doubtless Marshal did consider Eleanor to have saved his life; doubtless too he was grateful for the advancement that she had arranged for him. While he was never to be formally in service to Eleanor again, he would act as one pledged to her for the rest of her life. Further, the Histoire has only fulsome praise for her, reflecting the tradition of respect for Eleanor which he inculcated in his own household.[31]

On 3 March 1170, despite violent storms in the Channel, Henry left for England to make arrangements for the coronation. Eleanor was left behind in joint control with the Justiciar of Normandy, Richard de Humez, and charged with a key job: to ensure that the Channel ports remained closed so that no awkward interdictions could reach England before the coronation was performed. Whether she was really needed on-site at the expense of her presence at the coronation, whether she was excluded by Henry, or whether, in line with her attempts to promote a reconciliation with Becket, she chose not to participate in this highly provocative affair is open to question. Perhaps a number of motivations intersected; one powerful one may have been that if Henry wanted to keep Marguerite away from this coronation he effectively also had to keep away Eleanor, in whose household Marguerite probably was until this time. Some degree of ambivalence about this question is indicated by the fact that Henry appears to have spent very considerable sums on clothes for both Marguerite and Eleanor for the event, which it is unlikely he would have done if it had always been his intent to exclude them both.

Whatever the reason, it must have been some sort of a wrench for Eleanor not to witness this hugely important moment in the life of her eldest son, who had apparently grown into a startlingly handsome young man – the Histoire calls him 'the handsomest prince in the whole world' and the normally level-headed Robert of Torigny writes that 'he was of the most handsome countenance, of the most pleasing manners and the most free handed in his liberality of all the individuals with whom we have been acquainted'. Young Henry also exhibited an unusual degree of personal charm and courtesy – in all at this stage a son of whom to be very proud.[32]

Interestingly (and consistently with the real subtext of Henry's plan), Young Henry, although about to receive coronation, and just turned fifteen, was not left with any formal responsibilities while awaiting his departure for England. He left for his coronation in England on 5 June 1170 – and did so without his thirteen-year-old wife, although accompanied by the bishops of Sees and Bayonne. His coronation, by the Archbishop of York and six assisting bishops, took place on 14 June 1170.

Meanwhile, back in April the Pope had despatched Henry's cousin Roger, Bishop of Worcester, with a stern injunction to the English clergy not to participate in the proposed coronation. Roger reached Caen sometime before Henry's council, but, according to the story which reached Becket's biographer, was intercepted by Eleanor and Richard de Humez on 5 June and forbidden by her from proceeding further.[33]

There is an interesting sequel to this which raises further questions about the relationship of Eleanor and Henry. Henry later (somewhat disingenuously) suggested surprise and disappointment that his cousin Roger had not attended the coronation. In response, the bishop refused to place the blame on Eleanor – and his words are intriguing: 'I will not blame the Queen, for either her respect of or fear of you will make her conceal the truth, and then your anger with me will be increased; or else if she told the truth your indignation would fall upon that noble lady. I would rather lose a leg than that she should hear a single harsh word from you.'

On one level this is simply a subtle dig at Henry: it is likely that both men well knew the reality – that the order was Henry's and Eleanor was obeying it. But the mention of Eleanor's fear of Henry and the bishop's wishing to avoid ire being brought down on her perhaps raises a question as to whether Henry's anger was confined to public displays, and whether in fact Henry had behaved violently towards Eleanor in temper in the past. Here we might also look back to Eleanor's apparently constrained refusal to assist Becket and John of Salisbury and her unlikely assistance to Henry in the matter of Mary of Boulogne. There is also a sniff, consistent with William Marshal's hint, that Eleanor did not obey the injunction happily. One cannot draw too much from this story, but it does provide some grounds for a suspicion of Eleanor having become very wary of being on the receiving end of Henry's temper – a point which has a significance in the next few years.

Amusingly, the order barring transmission of the interdict was in fact subverted by Mary of Boulogne herself. Mary had just succeeded in bearing a 'spare', to complement the heiress she had already borne; she had promptly obtained an annulment of her unwanted marriage and was en route back to her freedom as a nun in England. It is perhaps unsurprising that Eleanor, unhappily associated with Mary's earlier abduction, was not prepared to stop her, and equally that no one imagined that Mary was the bearer of the key documents.

On the face of it, this account of Eleanor in Normandy at the time of the June coronation conflicts with others. Vigeois (who is usually reliable) places her back in Aquitaine in May, together with Richard in performing one of his first roles as Count of Poitou, laying the foundation stone for the new monastery of St Augustine at Limoges. This dating is, however, very controversial. Different historians place Richard's investiture in Aquitaine in 1170, 1171 and 1172,[34] and the modern consensus has tended to favour 1172. Taken with FitzStephen's clear story placing Eleanor in northern France and the charter evidence, which seems to show Richard not acting independently yet for some time, it appears most likely that 1172 is indeed the correct date.

By July the coronation had reaped its result and interdictions authorised by the Pope had been declared on Henry's lands, ironically starting with Aquitaine. Henry was threatened with personal excommunication if he did not put the peace terms agreed earlier in the year into effect within forty days.[35] The result was a conference at Freteval at which a peace of some sort was patched up between Henry and Becket – setting the stage for the final chapter in their relationship.

Another factor suggesting that Eleanor distanced herself from the coronation row is the fact that she appears to have been absent from Henry's side at this conference and when, shortly after, in August 1170, he was taken seriously ill at Domfront, with his life being briefly despaired of. His will was made in accordance with the provisions of Montmirail and he made other arrangements for the event of his death, including that John should join the household of Young Henry. But he recovered and thereafter returned south to visit the shrine of the Virgin at Rocamadour in thanks for his recovery; a visit where Eleanor is again not recorded at Henry's side.[36]

But Eleanor had plenty to do on her own account in the months after June 1170, for in early September, having belatedly despatched Marguerite and her household to hold court in England with her husband, Eleanor (again without Henry) brought Leonor south to Bordeaux, where a council was convened to ratify the terms of the marriage negotiated with the Castilian commissioners. In attendance were the Archbishop of Bordeaux and the bishops of Agen, Angoulême, Poitiers, Saintes and Perigeux, along with Raoul de la Faye, the Count of Périgord, Theobald Chabot and William Maingot. Once the terms were signed, Eleanor handed over the not-quite-eight-year-old Leonor to the Castilian bishops and other nobles and notables who would take her to her new home.[37] Doubtless Leonor was accompanied by the usual lavish provision of domestic goods – such as had accompanied Matilda – and the preparations for this (as well as the considerable journey south) will have occupied a good deal of Eleanor's attention in the preceding months.

It is possible that Eleanor travelled a few miles down the road towards the Pyrenees with her daughter, whom she would not see again for thirty years. But she is not noted in the party as Leonor travelled via Jaca and Somport in Aragon (to avoid trouble from the hostile King of Navarre). Leonor arrived safely in Taragona in mid-September 1170, where she met Alfonso and within days was married to him. Their first joint act is recorded in Burgos – part of Leonor's splendid dower – on 17 September 1170.[38]

Nor does the timeline seem to allow Eleanor much opportunity for a prolonged farewell to her daughter, for by Christmas 1170 she was back with the remaining family (apart from Young Henry), which was together once again for Christmas at the hunting lodge of Bures-le-Roi near Bayeux. It was to be a fateful holiday, for it was on this occasion, with Eleanor present, that the bishops from England arrived to report on their excommunication by Becket, who had recently returned to the country following the 'peace' of Freteval.

On Boxing Day, or perhaps the day after, Henry convened a council of clergy and laity. Henry spoke bitterly and at some length against Becket, accusing him of treason and betrayal of trust. His accusations were strongly supported by key barons, and the decision was taken to send a force of knights under Richard de Humez to capture Becket. But at some point in the tirade four knights had slipped out, eager to prove they were not the useless drones Henry had just accused his knights of being. By the evening of 29 December 1170, Becket lay dead at their hands on the floor of Canterbury Cathedral. John of Salisbury had escaped part way through the attack, preferring discretion to valour.[39]

Whether Eleanor was with Henry three days later at Argentan when the news of Becket's murder reached him is unclear, but it seems unlikely for she is not mentioned either by Arnulf of Lisieux in his detailed and circumstantial account of Henry's reaction or as one of those Henry refused to see in the days which succeeded the arrival of the news.[40] However, she cannot have been far ahead of the story, and it will not have taken long both for her to hear the news and become apprised of the facts that Henry was being widely blamed and that his excommunication and the interdiction of his lands would inevitably follow. How she viewed his decision that summer to decamp to Ireland before engaging with the Pope's envoys, leaving the storm behind him, can only be a matter of speculation; his apparent insouciance will presumably have horrified her, but his disappearance offered her a guaranteed free hand in Aquitaine.

Interestingly, three documents from 1171 evidence some further movement by Eleanor away from Henry, at least in the terms of her charter wordings. Where previously she would have referred to the king's faithful followers and her own, she now starts to address just her faithful followers.[41] What interpretation to put on this is more problematic. On the one hand they may indeed, as Hivergneaux suggests, show a rift between the couple; but equally it may be seen simply as a measure to protect Eleanor's interests in the light of Henry's current unpopularity – insulating herself from the husband who was currently at odds with the Church. Certainly she seems to have taken no concrete steps. One way in which she could have done so – as she did after her divorce from Louis – would have been to change her seal, but what slender evidence remains suggests she did not. Another way in which she could have asserted her independence would have been to issue her own coinage; and yet, unlike other female rulers of the time (such as Ermengarde of Narbonne, Urraca of Castile or even the Empress Matilda or her future daughter-in-law Isabella of Angoulême), she issued no coinage in her own name. Such coinage as was issued bore the names of her husbands – until Richard was installed as count, at which point coins began to be issued in his name.[42] It seems an inescapable inference that Eleanor was still wedded to the concept of a united Plantagenet empire, even if she did not see eye to eye with Henry on methods.

Meanwhile, she continued to plan for Richard's recognition as Count of Poitou. In fact, it may have been at Easter 1171 that Eleanor arranged for Richard to hold his first plenary court at Niort as a prelude to his full emancipation in 1172.[43]

Nonetheless, through 1171 it appears to have been Eleanor who was in control; charters of this period do not record Richard's participation but are given by Eleanor alone, and witnessed by her inner circle, including Raoul de Faye and their kinsman the Viscount of Châtellerault.

Such information as we can glean from the charters suggests that Eleanor spent this period travelling through her duchy and showing herself exercising power. It seems quite likely that this was in part a tour to introduce Richard to the wider regions of the duchy and to prepare the people for his accession in the new year. The picture which emerges, albeit not with any great clarity, is of Eleanor and Richard fairly constantly on the move with a small mobile court, introducing him to as many people he would need to know as was possible. This period will probably have offered the longest stretch of close company that the two had experienced since Richard was a very small boy. The real closeness evident between the two in later years can probably be attributed to this time. So too can this period – when talk of Crusade remained in the air – be seen as a very likely time for Eleanor to have told Richard the full story of her crusading adventures, and fill him with the enthusiasm for Crusade which was to be such a hallmark of his adult life.[44]

The variety of the scenes and issues with which Eleanor was dealing come through from a consideration of the charters. So we find Eleanor at Argenson in the Charente, at the Priory of St-Bibien-du-Bois granting a right to take firewood from the forest of Chizé, or at the Abbey of Fontaine-le-Comte near Poitiers granting it protection, or at the Abbey of Fontmorigny on the borders with Louis' territory granting its abbot and monks a customs exemption, or in the Oléron making a grant to cover restoring vines. We can also infer that she had to contend with the various responsibilities pertaining to her household at this time; for example, the marriage of Marchisa, dating to this period, will probably have been held under Eleanor's aegis.[45]

However, she had to tread carefully for she was (since the death of Patrick of Salisbury) governing without apparent significant military support. This can be seen in spring 1171 when there was an uprising in the region of Limoges by the people of Souterraine against the Abbot of St Martial. The abbot did not call on Eleanor or Richard for aid, but appealed directly to Henry's military hierarchy, who came at speed and put the uprising down with the Angevins' customary force.[46]

As 1172 came around, however, moves began to be made for Richard to take independent steps. So, after mother and son celebrated Christmas together in 1171, early in 1172 Richard is to be found making a journey alone to Bayonne supported by the bishops of Bayonne and Dax and various nobles of the region. While there he made a grant of tax revenues to the town, saying that he did so for his parents and his siblings also.[47]

By spring 1172, it was time for Richard's installation as Count of Poitiers. This was a very interesting dual ceremony; the first part of it took place at Poitiers, and there was then a whole second portion given to a ceremony at Limoges. The location of Limoges for part of Richard's debut was highly significant, given Henry's intransigent approach to the town, its history and its traditions – as well as the recent unrest between the town and the abbey. Eleanor's decision to exercise patronage here, and associate Richard with it in his first act as count, speaks volumes about the message which she was giving to her vassals – that her intent was to rule with the carrot, not the stick. This message was also reinforced by the formal investiture which took place at the end of the month.

We have a good account of the ceremony from the pen of Geoffrey le Vigeois, the abbot of an abbey some distance south of Limoges and a former monk of the Abbey of Saint-Martial. He tells us that on the Sunday after Pentecost in the church of Saint-Hilaire-le Grand in Poitiers Richard was 'according to custom' raised onto the seat of the abbot and presented by the Bishop of Poitiers and the Archbishop of Bordeaux with a lance and banner, as the symbols of his authority as Count of Poitou. Even the title Richard took had a redolence of restoration of tradition to the locals. While Henry retained the title Duke of Aquitaine and allowed Richard only to call himself Count of Poitou, this of course reflected the mode which Eleanor's ancestors had followed, and which had only been disturbed by her 'foreign' husbands. It also, of course, avoided complications when it came to performing homage.

Thereafter the party proceeded to Limoges, and on 11 June 1172, in the abbey church of Saint-Martial, the apostle who was reputed to have converted Aquitaine, Richard was presented with the reputed ring of Saint Valerie. The saint was said to be a convert of Saint Martial who, after being beheaded for her faith, miraculously carried her severed head to present to Saint Martial. Her grave had (reputedly) been rediscovered after a fire, and the ring was that said to have been found on her finger. The wearing of the ring therefore symbolised Richard's union with his people, and particularly those of Limoges. Richard was also crowned with a golden circlet and handed a rod and sword – a ceremony which had been devised by the local clerics in imitation of a royal coronation, and borrowing elements from the records of the coronation of the last King of Aquitaine in 855.[48]

The purpose of all this was dual – benefitting both Plantagenets and abbey. For Richard, it evoked both the long links of his family to Limoges, where a number of the early Carolingian dukes of Aquitaine were buried, and an intention to be less Poitiers-centred than his immediate predecessors had been. This, it was surely hoped, would assist in bringing a more peaceful relationship not just with the citizens of Limoges but more generally with the nominal vassals in the Limousin. For the abbey, the benefit was publicity and the promotion of pilgrim tourism, as well as probably representing a bid to be established as the Plantagenet necropolis – the equivalent of Saint-Denis. All of this would help to maintain expensive buildings commissioned off the back of earlier tourism, and to enable the commencement of new projects. Indeed, the following years saw the building of an infirmary which the chronicler of Saint-Martial described as comparable to a royal palace in its magnificence.[49]

The extent of Eleanor's own role in this mythmaking for her son and her own lordship is an interesting question. While the initiative may indeed have come from the clerics of Saint-Martial, looking to enhance the prestige of their house, the idea of raising the status of the ruling house of Poitou to equivalent with that of the French Crown is a much more likely initiative of someone on the Plantagenet side of the fence. Henry's initiatives in this regard – for example in encouraging the Arthurian associations of his crown and 'rediscovering' the tomb of Arthur at Glastonbury – might be said to make him the prime candidate. However, Eleanor's own knowledge of the history of her house and the useful resonances which could be brought into play, as well as the desire to elevate this part of Henry's empire to quasi-regal status, suggest that she may well have had a significant input into this byplay. Further weight is given to this possibility by the fact that it appears that Eleanor commissioned a new biography of St Valerie during this period, and that biography, as well as promoting the cult of St Valerie and flattering the people of Limoges as to the historical primacy of their city over Poitiers, has obvious resonances vis-à-vis Eleanor and her position. In particular, Valerie's role moves from being that of a mere supporter of Saint Martial to being the heiress to Limoges, to whose rights her husbands owe their power. It also contained a subtle message diminishing the importance of Bourges, that city upon which the kings of France so much relied for their power in central France.[50] All in all, this sophisticated piece of PR suggests that in some respects at least Eleanor and Henry were still working together, but that Eleanor was also pursuing her own agenda.

Eleanor's other actions also suggest an intent to rule differently from Henry, and less confrontationally than him; for example, her association in a 1172 grant by Robert de Sillé's widow to Fontevraud provides a strong suggestion of sympathy with a family whose head had died as a result of the harsh imprisonment he faced at Henry's hands.[51]

Immediately following the investiture, Eleanor and Richard appear to have made a larger and more official tour of the duchy in which they issued a large number of charters together to the Abbey of le Chatelliers, Dalon Abbey, the Abbey of Maillezais, Merci-Dieu Abbey and the abbey church of St-Hilaire in Poitiers. More personal charters were also made, for example to Petita of La Rochelle memorialising a settlement she reached with Raoul de Faye and his mother.[52]

Following Henry's return and official reconciliation with the Church, which took place early in 1172, sometime in August Eleanor crossed to England to attend the second coronation of the Young King, and the official coronation of Queen Marguerite.[53] This took place on 27 August 1172 at Winchester Cathedral and (there being no new Archbishop of Canterbury as yet) was performed by Archbishop Rotrou of Rouen, assisted by Giles of Evreux and Henry's cousin Roger, Bishop of Worcester, so contentiously absent from the original event. After this, Young Henry proceeded to Windsor where he presided over the council designed to elect a new Archbishop of Canterbury.

Eleanor's movements after summer 1172 are unclear, and this hiatus provides a good space for considering Eleanor's reputed role in fostering a vibrant troubadour culture or convening 'courts of love' in this period of her residence.

As for the first, as previously noted, neither Eleanor's marriage to Louis nor the early years of her marriage to Henry support the view that Eleanor patronised troubadours or promoted troubadour culture. If there were to be such evidence, it is this period of her rule in her own lands which would be expected to yield best evidence of such activity.[54] However, the evidence for any meaningful patronage remains, as Ruth Harvey has tellingly demonstrated, non-existent. The scholars who have posited such patronage have been vaulting from wishes to facts – elevating 'must have been' into assertion.[55] Nor can it be said in their defence that such a form of argument is permissible because evidence would not survive, for at the same point detailed evidence of patronage of troubadours – including name or nickname references to patrons – survives in other regions. There is evidence at the courts of Castile and Aragon, and the comital courts of Limoges and Ventadour, and also by the counts of Toulouse, one of whom was actually credited as a troubadour himself. Troubadour activity was also vibrant in Catalonia, and was beginning to find its feet in Provence.

But perhaps most clearly there is extensive evidence of the patronage of Ermengarde of Narbonne – with her being mentioned by name by at least five troubadours: Bernart de Ventadorn, Peire d'Alvernhe, Azailais de Porcairages, Giraut de Bornelh and Pierre Rogier. Indeed, the last of these spent so long at her court that rumours arose that they were lovers. Furthermore, Raimon de Miraval, though not mentioning Ermengarde by name, speaks of the richness of rewards which a talented troubadour could expect at her court. Even on the Orkney Islands the Norsemen sang of the clever golden-haired ruler of 'Nerbon' at whose court visiting dignitaries competed to gain her favour with poetry.[56]

By contrast, references to Eleanor or her court in surviving troubadour lyrics are unflattering – and as such plainly composed for opponents, not for her. So at least two troubadours refer negatively to Eleanor's reputed exploits on Crusade, while

Peire D'Alvernhe, in praising Raymond V of Toulouse, contrasts him to 'those betailed English' (referring to a popular myth that St Augustine bestowed tails on the English when they initially scorned his preaching). To the extent that troubadour linkage can be established at all in Aquitaine at around this time, it is not with Eleanor but with Richard, who was (albeit later) named as a patron by Bertran de Born. The one troubadour located in Aquitaine at this time, Arnaut Guilhem de Marsan, appears only in his political role as Lord of Roquefort and Montagillard, witnessing Leonor's marriage settlement.[57]

However, having said this, it is necessary also to resist the tendency in recent scholarship to swing the pendulum too far in the other direction. If Richard was to become a patron of troubadours and a poet and musician in his own right, at his mother's court there is likely to have been opportunity to learn in the company of those whose business it was. Richard the Poitevin's picture also associates Eleanor's court with secular music-making, as do all the accounts of her joint court with Henry. Accordingly, the true answer probably lies somewhere between the two extremes. Eleanor was probably not a noted patron of the famed troubadours in this period; but her comital court, as a gracious and sophisticated place, will have benefitted from the presence of music and poetry, albeit possibly not by the most prominent practitioners whose names have come down to us.

As for Eleanor and the courts of love, the answer is much clearer. The reputed story goes something like this: having returned from her years in bleak England, Eleanor established a 'court of love' at her court in Poitiers. The purpose of the court was to instruct men in ways of chivalry – long since championed, of course, by her grandfather. This court heard 'cases' brought forward by knights and noblemen, who presented their romantic dilemmas to a women-only jury. The ladies, sometimes sixty strong, then passed judgement on how the men were to dress, speak, and act while in the presence of women. Principal among those who were said to have assisted Eleanor in this noble work were Eleanor's daughter Marie of Champagne, Ermengarde of Narbonne and Isabelle of Vermandois, Countess of Flanders.

The evidence for this charming idea lies in a book by one Andreas Capellanus (Andrew the Chaplain) known as '*Tractatus De Amore et de Amoris Remedio*' (A tract about love and the remedy for love). The premise of the work is that the author is informing his pupil,

Walter, 'a new recruit to love', of the dangers that await him. The work consisted of three books: the first discussed the origins of the concept of love and how it should be defined; the second consisted of a series of dialogues or conversations, showing how the process of romance should take place; the third comprised twenty-one cases from the supposedly 'real-life' courts of love, presided over by Eleanor and her associates. In one famous ruling the court is said to have been asked to settle whether true love can exist between man and wife, concluding that it is actually impossible. In another Eleanor is said to have ruled that between an older man of good character and a worthless but handsome young man, the woman should favour virtue rather than youth and virility. She is also to be found ruling against consanguineous marriages. Their rulings also included the ideas that 'moral integrity alone makes one worthy of love' and that 'the true lover believes only that which he thinks will please his beloved'.

Charming as the concept is, it is now generally accepted that no such courts of love took place. There is absolutely no evidence that Eleanor and Marie of Champagne ever met after Eleanor abandoned the French court.[58] Indeed, by this time Marie, now a married woman, was largely resident in Champagne, producing the four children she was to bear her husband. The Isabelle of Flanders referenced is probably the daughter of Eleanor's sister Aelis, for whose contact with Eleanor there is again no evidence. Nor is there any evidence for a meeting between Eleanor and Ermengarde, and if one did occur it is far more credibly placed well after the book was written.

Modern scholarship places Andreas Capellanus not at Eleanor's court, but either at Marie's or even that of Philip II sometime in the mid to late 1180s – and almost certainly during Eleanor's captivity.[59] On close reading, his book is replete with contradictions designed to point a joke or raise a laugh to a knowledgeable courtly audience. Among those 'in jokes' is one about Eleanor ruling on consanguineous marriages – in the light of her two technically incestuous marriages. Equally amusing is her ruling on the merits of the worthy older man over the virile young one in the light of her abandonment of the worthy Louis for the youthful but intractable Henry – and the path their marriage was to take. Panning out from Eleanor and looking at the set-up of the 'courts' generally, there is the obvious joke of a group of women, all of whom were subjected to fully arranged marriages, pontificating on women's rights in the matter of marriages.

But the mention of Ermengarde at this point is salient. Returning to the real political world from the fantasies of romantically minded writers, it is at this very point that Eleanor began to face trouble that overlapped with the problems nagging Ermengarde. Following the murder of her old ally Raymond Trencavel, Ermengarde had been forced into an uneasy alliance with Raymond V of Toulouse (the son of her first, involuntary, husband), and as Eleanor settled her children's destinies Ermengarde could be found trying desperately to ensure peace in the region in order to shore up her own unsupported position, her own marriage having been childless. Specifically, in November 1171 she arbitrated a peace between Count Raymond and Robert of Beziers, to be sealed by a marriage to Raymond's daughter Adalais. In spring 1172, Raymond brought off another coup of significance both to Ermengarde and to Eleanor's and Henry's lands and ambitions, being made Count of Maugio, technically as trustee for his future daughter-in-law and her mother but in reality as absolute ruler. By the start of 1173, then, Raymond V had assembled a power base which ran from west of Toulouse to the Alps. Ermengarde of Narbonne was effectively surrounded by him and an enforced ally, and Henry and Eleanor had to consider how best to deal with this burgeoning threat to their southern empire.

At the end of 1172, after returning from Ireland and meeting with the papal envoys in order to procure absolution for the death of Becket, Henry assembled his family, including Eleanor, around him again for a Christmas court at Chinon. This appears to have been a grand set-piece, with Eleanor and Richard together issuing charters relevant to the affairs of the duchy.[60]

This occasion provides a useful vantage point from which to review Eleanor's actual position – since within months Eleanor would be associated with her sons in rebellion. This fact presents a considerable puzzle to Eleanor's biographers. As one notes,[61] it is actually hard to find any sign of friction between Eleanor and Henry prior to Becket's death; and yet within a short period Eleanor was either party to her sons' rebellion against Henry or acting sufficiently transgressively to ensure that she was kept prisoner for the next fifteen years. The reasons for the fracture in the relationship have to be picked apart from the small indications to this point and from the events of the intervening months. This is by no means an easy task since the various groups who would come together in the rebellion seem to have had a variety of motivations. The rebellion would be not a single-issue event, but an alliance of the disaffected.

First to be considered is the person who was the real figurehead of the rebellion: Young Henry. He had been holding court in England since his first coronation, but was doing so with very limited means and power. Henry the elder had granted him no lands, even in England, and while he financed his son's court everything was at his discretion. This lack of power is reflected in the records of Young Henry's time in England, where his acts show him predominantly confirming charters already granted by Henry – much as Eleanor had done during her disempowered marriage to Louis. What is more, such charters as he did issue were witnessed by the tutors whom Henry had appointed to complete his son's education. In the last stages of the dispute with Becket, the responses to be made by him to advances on behalf of Becket were apparently dictated to Young Henry by his tutors. When Becket returned to England, the steps which Young Henry was to take to restore him to the king's peace were set out in detail by Henry senior, with no scope for independent action. Such evidence as there is of Young Henry's own wishes appears to indicate that he may well have wished to take a more welcoming line towards his former mentor than he was instructed to do – for Herbert of Bosham notes that when Young Henry met Becket's envoys unsupervised on the road he was much more affable than he had been in formal meetings.[62]

This discontent with his powerlessness almost certainly lay behind Young Henry's failure to join his father's Christmas court as early as 1170; he and Queen Marguerite held the feast in England, and it was there that the news of Becket's murder reached them. Young Henry can hardly have welcomed being associated with his father in the ensuing odium, which included an interdict against all of Henry's northern French lands declared by William, Archbishop of Sens. Young Henry also doubtless felt the insult when, on Henry II's departure for Ireland, he was still not entrusted with the true governance of any part of his nominal inheritance. His notional government of Normandy in this period, while marked by splendid courts like his Christmas court of 1171 at Bures-le-Roi, is in substance akin to Eleanor's in the early days of her marriage – hedged about by older trusted advisors.

The absence of Henry also exposed the younger king to the discontent of the nobles left behind. While Ralph of Diss identifies this as a time when Eleanor began to subvert young Henry's loyalty, his account must be doubted here. He was not at this time in any position to obtain reliable news. Furthermore, there appears to have been no grounds or opportunity for her to do so yet; as has been seen, her time in his company over the last few years had been extremely limited and there is no sign of their meeting, apart from briefly at the second coronation, since 1170. On the other hand, the nobles of England and Normandy were extremely unhappy about King Henry's declaration of an investigation into the extent of royal lands and rights – an investigation which was likely to impact negatively on many of them, as Henry's doubled revenue from Normandy following this would seem to attest. Adam de Port of Kington in Herefordshire was during this period charged with plotting Henry II's death, and he would later join the Young King's rebellion. William of Newburgh reported, consistently with concerns expressed by other chroniclers, that 'there were only a few barons in England who were not ... ready to defect'.[63]

Nor did Henry's return mend matters. Young Henry was forced to be party to his father's undertakings to restore his relationship with the Church and then to be the power-free figurehead who presided over the council to elect Becket's successor. At the same time, Henry's promise of Crusade, given at Montmirail and repeated as part of his reconciliation with the Church in 1172 – and which would leave the field free for Young Henry to exercise real power – was plainly not being actioned. Further, it appears that Young Henry felt a genuine sense of sorrow and guilt over the death of Becket, for in autumn of 1172, while his father was blithely considering his troubles with Becket over, Young Henry was publicly associating himself with the burgeoning cult of Becket, and making a well-publicised pilgrimage to the grave, which was fast becoming a shrine.[64]

It was perhaps in part these signs of independence which caused Henry to summon the young couple from England late in 1172, although it must be kept in mind that they were the obvious people to act as an embassy to Louis VII. What Henry neglected to take into account was that Louis would be keen to use them against Henry, and that Young Henry's discontent at being kept at his father's beck and call, insufficiently senior to hold any power or lands, would be an obvious weak point which Louis would not hesitate to exploit. And exploit it he did, suggesting that Henry be given an ultimatum that lands be properly ceded to the younger king, failing which they would take up their residence with the other royal father in Paris. Young Henry was hardly likely to take issue with this, and although he returned to Normandy at Henry's command, the couple again refused to spend Christmas with Henry, holding their own court at Bonneville.[65]

For young Geoffrey, similar issues were likely to be in his mind; after being invested with ducal power, Henry had despatched him back to England where he held household in Northampton while his father exercised actual power in Brittany via trusted administrators.

Richard would have had little grounds of disquiet at this point, although it is very possible that it was at around this time that the question of any non-payment of Leonor's cash dowry (over a year after her marriage) began to translate into an assertion of a right on the part of the Castilian Crown to Gascony – including, critically, Bordeaux. This would obviously be a concern for Eleanor too, and would in her case add to all the reasons for alienation from Henry which had lain behind their separation in 1168.

Following the Christmas court of 1172, Henry summoned Young Henry to join him to journey to a meeting with the Count of Maurienne at Montferrand (now a district of Clermont Ferrand) in the Auvergne. The result of this meeting – which was hugely distinguished, being attended by the kings of Aragon and Navarre and the Count of Savoy – was that the marriage of John to the count's daughter Alicia, floated originally in 1171, was agreed in principle. Her dowry was to be a chain of castles from the Rhone Valley to the valley of Aosta, and controlling the principal passes into Lombardy. Eleanor's presence at this meeting is suggested by the witness list, which includes a number of Poitevins, including Raoul de Faye.[66] Further separate reports of Eleanor meeting with the kings suggests that she rendezvoused with them in Aquitaine and escorted them to the meeting. That is more credible than some unsupported reports of a separate meeting with them in June 1172. It appears also that Raymond of Toulouse, whose interests would be seriously affected by having Henry's empire controlling not just Aquitaine to his east and north but also the key Alpine passes to his north and west, was also present.[67]

After the meeting Henry turned into Gascony, being recorded making a grant to the Knights Templar at the Abbey of Saint-Macaire just outside Bordeaux. The occasion for this was probably the appointment of William the Templar, Abbot of Reading, to the position of Archbishop of Bordeaux, which is recorded as having been performed in the presence of Henry. It is tempting to suppose that Eleanor was not happy with Henry's interference in such a key appointment within her duchy; and while Reading Abbey was a foundation close to her heart, William was not the abbot she knew from her own time in England, and it is therefore unlikely that he was her choice. His closeness to Henry, though, is well established – he had been a prominent supporter of Henry over Becket (against his own prior and most of the rest of the monks) and had forbidden pilgrimages to Becket's tomb. Thereafter, Eleanor, Henry and the children journeyed to Limoges for a formal court at which the marriage of John would be formally settled.[68]

In the event, the proceedings in Limoges may best be looked to as the immediate trigger of the rebellion which was to follow. On its face it was the high-water mark of Henry's international status. A constellation of kings and nobles had followed him from Montferrand. His youngest (landless) son was sought as a desirable match for a rich marriage which would position him to seek to be King of Italy. He was looked to as an arbitrator between princes, negotiating a peace between Raymond V and Alphonso of Aragon.[69] But during the course of this meeting, Henry managed to alienate not just his entire family but also Louis of France.

For Young Henry, the principal cause of offence was the announcement – which seems to have come upon him without warning – that John was to be granted the castles of Chinon, Mirabeau and Loudon. As these fell within the lands which were notionally Young Henry's, and as he still had not a single castle to call his own, it is perhaps unsurprising that, though these were castles which had previously served as a younger son's portion, Young Henry took grave offence. It is hard not to see this as a deliberate act by Henry, perhaps seen as a rap across the knuckles in response to Young Henry's demands via Louis and petulance in refusing to join the main Christmas court. If so, Henry miscalculated. The message sent to all his sons, including Geoffrey and Richard (whose lands these castles also bordered), was that Henry retained the intention to deal with all his lands as he saw fit and without consulting the sons who nominally ruled them.[70]

Further concern was raised by the incident which primarily alienated Eleanor and Richard, as well as Louis of France. Henry had persuaded Raymond of Toulouse transfer his homage from Louis VII. Raymond had fallen out with Louis VII after repudiating Louis' sister Constance, and was immediately threatened by the Maurienne match, which had the potential to encircle him. There were two aspects to Eleanor's and Richard's concern. First of all, Eleanor's family had always regarded Toulouse as rightfully part of Aquitaine, and therefore, respecting this, they would (slightly optimistically) think that any homage should have been paid to Eleanor and Richard. However, Raymond performed his homage to Henry, then to Young Henry and then to Richard – giving no homage to Eleanor at all. Secondly, by accepting the homage Henry implicitly abandoned Eleanor's own claim to Toulouse. The implications of this act of homage were multiple and inflammatory. To Eleanor, the refusal of homage to her by the count and Henry's acceptance of it and abandonment of her own rights was an insult, pure and simple. However, there was also a concern both on her and Richard's part that homage via Henry and Young Henry indicated an intention, contrary to Montmirail, to render Aquitaine part of Young Henry's inheritance, with Richard ruling as his agent only; this effectively denied Richard's status as count, holding the lands directly from the King of France. Louis, meanwhile, interpreted these actions as an indication that Henry intended to bequeath everything to Young Henry – leaving him surrounded by a Plantagenet empire.[71]

Lest it be thought that this point is overemphasised, it is instructive to see how Ermengarde of Narbonne regarded the new pact – and in particular the submission of Toulouse. She wrote to Louis VII, in answer to a somewhat panicked letter from Louis asking her to detach herself from her current alliance with Raymond:

About what you charged me, truly, that I flee the company of your enemies and persevere in love of you as I began, I want your nobility to know without doubt that I have made no pact with the enemies of your crown, nor shall I be closely associated with them. Vowing to love you with sincere affection, I shall strive to deliver up me and mine to your commands and service at the appropriate time and place. I desire to defend the affairs of Toulouse and as necessary, I shall not resist your prayers. But if your right arm should take up the shield of your protection and rise in aid of Toulouse, I would more willingly and constantly follow behind your arms. I do not grieve alone, but all our compatriots are consumed by ineffable sadness that we see our region, ... coming under the rule of another, to which they are little inclined, by your, shall I say, failure, or guilt. Let it not offend your highness, dearest lord, that I presume to speak so boldly with you. The more I am a special woman of your crown, the more I suffer when I see it sink from its height. For it is not Toulouse alone but all our region from the Garonne to the Rhone, as our adversaries boast, that I feel them hastening to seize, so that, with the members reduced to servitude, the head may more easily be overthrown.[72]

Ermengarde therefore also saw this move as momentous and highly threatening to her own interests as well as to those of the throne of France.

This was not the end of Raymond V's troublemaking on this occasion. Geoffrey le Vigeois says that at the close of the Limoges meeting Raymond warned Henry to beware because there was a plot involving Eleanor and their sons.[73] Whether this is true or not is open to doubt. Vigeois claims to have been on the spot, though it is thought that he wrote his chronicle somewhat later, in the 1180s – when the fact of the revolt was well known and Eleanor's name was in the dirt. Having said this, Vigeois is fairly reliable and not very hostile to Eleanor – indeed, he has been suggested by one historian to be Eleanor's semi-official chronicler. Secondly, if Raymond of Toulouse did say this, it does not mean it was true. Indeed, it would appear that Henry did not entirely believe it, for he did nothing to stop Eleanor, Richard and Geoffrey from leaving Limoges. And Raymond, forced into this homage by Henry's dominance, had good reason to try to keep his new overlord busy elsewhere, allowing him free rein to improve his position.

However, while any suggestion of an actual plot was probably premature, it must be likely that the corridors of the palace were awash with furious mutterings from the younger royals and Eleanor. And this fury came on top of a situation which had enabled them all to see and share their own local notes that discontent with Henry's approach to government was fairly widespread among the nobles of the various regions. Among the concerns were issues of stronger administration, unprecedented enquiries into legal rights, and imposition of strict feudal structures in southern areas where such an approach had never before been adopted; the result was that, wherever one looked, nobles were looking for a figurehead to lead an expression of their discontent.

Furthermore, however much Henry had reconciled with the Church, he remained the man who had provoked if not ordered the murder of Becket (now canonised, even as the Limoges meeting was taking place) and who was personally in default of his undertaking to make a penitential Crusade. It is interesting that Young Henry's letter to the Pope after the commencement of the revolt paints his motivations in very much a reforming mode, and by reference to Becket's legacy.

Henry must in part have been alive to the discontent, for when he left Limoges he effectively compelled Young Henry to join him. But Young Henry had made up his mind. On 7 March, he decamped under cover of darkness from Chinon for Paris, where he was reunited with his new mentor Louis VII, who had grown considerably in subtlety since the days of his youthful marriage to Eleanor.

Meanwhile, Eleanor and Richard returned to Poitiers, accompanied by Geoffrey. Eleanor's part in the rebellion which followed is not at all clear. That she had a role is substantially assumed by chroniclers writing after the event. The actual evidence, however, is very thin, and one must take account of each writer and the context in which they wrote. Torigny, perhaps closest to the royal household and closest in time, points the finger at Eleanor and Raoul de Faye, but makes it plain he is only repeating rumours. Ralph Niger, who wrote later but is a scrupulous source and knew Eleanor personally – witnessing one of her charters – speaks rather of Eleanor following as opposed to leading her sons into revolt. Gervase of Canterbury takes a similar line to Torigny, again referring to Eleanor's role as one which was rumoured – 'dicebatur'.

Roger of Howden, an habitué of Henry's court and a primary source for Richard's reign, gives two versions. The first, in his *Gestae*, written during Eleanor's imprisonment, places the blame at her door. But later, after Eleanor's political rehabilitation, he amended his account to remove blame from her and Richard and point the finger at Young Henry and Geoffrey.

William of Newburgh, writing at a similar time to Howden's second account, puts the blame primarily on Young Henry, whom he has sneaking back from Paris after his escape to visit his mother and brothers in Poitiers. He then also casts Eleanor's complicity in 'it is rumoured' ('*ut dicetur*') terms.

Finally, Ralph of Diss (again writing later, and very much Henry's man) faces both ways. On the one hand he speaks in terms only of rumoured involvement ('*sicut dicitur*'), but on the other he speculates that Eleanor used Henry's Irish absence to poison the Young King's mind.[74]

What are we to make of this? The reality is that the sources are sufficiently distant and sufficiently mixed to require treating with great caution. The only thing that can be done is to weigh them against the evidence of who was definitely involved and how the revolt had to work. So, to start with Ralph of Diss's suggestion that Eleanor poisoned Young Henry's mind during Henry's absence in Ireland; the problem is that this ignores the very limited direct contact Eleanor had with Young Henry from the late 1160s – and indeed the limited contact she had had with him since he had moved to Becket's household. Corruption by letter writing and messenger is of course possible, but it seems less plausible.

Then one comes to the realities of the revolt. The alliance which Henry soon faced, comprising the Scottish king, the earls of Leicester, Chester, Derby and Norfolk and their affinities in England, William de Tancarville in Normandy, the Lusignans and the St Maures in Aquitaine and the families of Acenis and Fougeres in Anjou and Brittany, as well as his neighbours and former close allies the counts of Boulogne and Flanders, with assistance from Henri of Champagne, was plainly not one which Eleanor alone could have conjured. Her exposure to the English and northern French barons in the previous years was too limited – unlike that of Young Henry, who was perfectly placed for picking up on discord among others. One should also consider the very limited evidence there is of Eleanor having influence over the Norman and English nobles – as her difficult regency had demonstrated.

Even in Aquitaine the evidence is very marginal. The chronicler of Tours, albeit writing with hindsight, appears to think (with Torigny and others) that Raoul de Faye and Hugh of St Maure were instrumental in turning Eleanor away from her marriage. But there is no sign of a rally of Eleanor's intimates – at least at an early stage in the revolt. In reality, the roll call of those in Aquitaine who did rebel in the early stage looks more like a list of the habitually discontent who would be likely to take any opportunity for rebellion: the count of Angoulême, the Lusignans, their cousin Geoffrey de Rancon and two other lords of the Saintonge region, the lords of Blaye and Mauléon in Gascony. The only real Poitevin noble named is the Lord of Chauvigny, who was reputed to hate every Englishman.[75] Furthermore, it seems unlikely that Eleanor should ally herself with the Lusignans. The flavour of the revolt at this stage is far more that conveyed in the verse of Richard le Poitevin (albeit probably written during the 1168 rebellion): 'Rejoice O Aquitaine! Be jubilant O Poitou! For the sceptre of the King of the North Wind, Is drawing away from you ...'.

Most often and most compellingly, Eleanor is accused of arranging the flight of Richard and Geoffrey to Paris – an escape which occurred soon after that of Henry. There the boys (sixteen and fourteen) renewed their homage for their lands to Louis and promised to be counselled by him. Ralph of Diss specifically says that they did this 'by the counsel of their mother that they should choose their brother over their father', while the usually well-informed Robert de Torigny speaks of Eleanor's separation from Henry as coterminous with that of Richard and Geoffrey.[76] It is therefore likely that Eleanor was at least involved in their decision to decamp to Paris. What seems credible is that if Young Henry did not visit he at least sent messengers, and that Eleanor (on the advice of Raoul de Faye and Hugh of St Maure) encouraged the younger boys to join their brother.

What in fact seems quite likely is that there was no advance plan at all; while Young Henry had probably spread his discontents widely and learned of the extent of others' unhappiness with his father's rule, nothing was in place at the time of Limoges. This, interestingly, is the version which is most consistent with the account of Jordan Fantosme – who actually wrote at the time of the revolt and from the perspective of one supportive of Henry II, and who was yet very well placed to know Eleanor's own account. He mentions no other instigators of the revolt. It also coheres with what we can infer is William Marshal's version; the Histoire speaks only of traitors who turned the two kings against each other, inferentially looking to those surrounding the two main protagonists. This version is also lent probability by the fact that it was only after he had arrived in Paris that Young Henry began to put alliances in place, that he travelled without his seal and that he had even neglected to ensure his wife was safely in his supporters' power; Queen Marguerite was soon a state prisoner in Henry's hands.[77]

This left both Eleanor and the younger boys with a choice. With their own antipathy toward Henry, loyalty to him cannot have seemed very attractive, and Eleanor would rightly be apprehensive of Henry's plans for the boys if they were not secured elsewhere. Here one should perhaps bear in mind the evidence as to Henry's violent temper and Eleanor's possible fear of it; indeed, there is also the possibility that the placement of the younger children at Fontevraud was a deliberate move on Henry's part to separate Eleanor from the children. It is far from unrealistic to suppose that, with Young Henry in rebellion and nobles rising across Henry's empire, Eleanor feared the steps Henry would take regarding her and her sons. This would make sense of what we do know to be the case – namely that they were sent to Paris, though she did not as yet formally separate herself from Henry or join them. This despatch to Paris appears to have taken place sometime in spring 1173, and so not very long after Young Henry's escape.

As will be apparent, Eleanor's role in the rebellion is a highly controversial topic. The view taken here, that her involvement was peripheral and reactive rather than central, is a minority view. Flori reviews the same chronicle materials which are examined above and reaches a different conclusion, seeing the hesitation to place blame on Eleanor as the product of her return to power in the 1190s.[78] However, what he does not do, and what really tips the balance in the opposite direction, is to consider the roll call of those involved at an early stage, and the timeline of the rebellion. These are subjects on which more recent scholarship has brought forward much relevant material.

As for Eleanor's own decision to flee, once the younger boys had gone, remaining in place and notionally allied to a Henry who was determined to rule her lands his way, and who would be enraged by her decision to send her children beyond his power, would have been extremely unappealing – particularly after July, when Richard and Geoffrey took part in an attack on eastern Normandy under the command of Philip of Flanders.[79] It must have become even less palatable after the arrival of Henry's message to Eleanor under the name of Rotrou of Rouen. The letter was in fact penned by the scholar Peter of Blois, a relative of the bishop and a former tutor to the young King of Sicily. An accomplished lawyer and theologian, his passionate love of words and writing was to make him one of Henry's foremost propagandists – and the letter is a good example of his work.

This letter made it clear that Henry would not leave Eleanor in peace in Poitou, but expected her to return to his side as a hostage for the good behaviour of her sons and her vassals:

To the queen of England from the archbishop of Rouen seeking for peace ... greetings.

It is publicly known and no Christian may ignore it, that the conjugal bond is firm and indissoluble. Truth, which cannot lie, decreed that matrimony once begun cannot be separated: whom God, it said, joined, let no man put separate. Just as he made him a transgressor of the divine mandate who separates a married couple, so a married person is guilty who separates herself from her husband and does not observe the faith of the social bond. Since married people are made one flesh, it is necessary that unity of spirits be joined to union of bodies. That woman who is not subject to her husband voids the condition of nature, the mandate of the apostle, and the law of the gospel. For man is the head of woman; woman is taken from man, united to man, subject to the power of man.

We all deplore with common and lamentable complaint that, though you are a most prudent woman, you turn away from your husband, side recedes from side, the member does not serve the head. And what is far worse, you suffer the flesh of your lord king and yourself to rise against their father, as the prophet might say: 'I have nourished and exalted my sons and they have spurned me.' Would that, as another prophet calls to mind, our last hour ended our days and the earth covered our face before we saw such evils! For we know that unless you return to your husband, you will be the cause of general ruin and what you now abandon singly will be turned to common expense. Return, therefore, illustrious queen, to your husband and our lord, so that by your reconciliation rest may be restored to those who labour and by your return, happiness may return to all. If our prayers do not move you to this, may the affliction of peoples, the threatened oppression of the church, the desolation of the kingdom stir you. For unless truth lies, 'every kingdom divided against itself will be desolate.'

Truly this desolation can not fall on the lord king but on his sons and their successors. You provoke the displeasure of the lord king ... a king to whom even the strongest kings bend their necks. Before the situation gets worse, return with your sons to your husband, whom you are bound to obey and live with; turn yourself around and let him not be anxious about you or your sons. We are certain that he will show you every kind of love and the fullest firmness of security. Admonish your sons, I beg you, to be subject and devoted to their father, who has suffered such anguish, so many crimes and travails from them. Let casual carelessness not squander and disperse what was acquired with such sweat. We say these things to you, most pious queen with the zeal of God and the affection of sincere love. ... Either you will return to your husband or we will be constrained by canon law and bound to exercise ecclesiastical censure against you, which indeed we say reluctantly and which, unless you return to your senses, we will do with sorrow and tears. Farewell.[80]

In the light of this letter, Eleanor plainly had a choice of effectively surrendering herself to her husband or joining her sons and her ex-husband in Paris. It says much about her lack of trust in Henry that she chose to put herself in the power of Louis. The timing of this letter and of Eleanor's decision to attempt to reach her sons is very uncertain – only one English chronicler, Gervase of Canterbury, mentions it. He tells how Eleanor and a small escort left Poitiers to try to reach Paris, with Eleanor disguised in male dress and riding astride. However, before she could reach safety she was apprehended – according to some by traitors among her companions – and taken prisoner by Henry's forces. Richard le Poitevin names William Maingot, Portclie de Mauze, Fulk de Matha and Harvey le Panetier as those involved, all of whom were later rewarded by Henry. If so, the betrayals of those she had long supported and promoted (particularly Harvey) must have been a bitter blow to Eleanor.

The location of the incident is unclear, though some have suggested the vicinity of Chartres.[81] So too is the date; its position in Gervase's account suggests it was in spring 1173, while others favour autumn, probably November, and still other accounts have it coincide with Henry's own move against Aquitaine, framing it so that Eleanor is fleeing the imminent arrival of her husband. Although the latter version is preferred by Turner, it appears the less likely: there is no record of Eleanor being met by Henry on her capture, and more significantly Henry is not actually recorded in Aquitaine until May 1174, by which time we know Eleanor was in captivity.[82] On balance, the November 1173 date, when Henry was just north of Poitou but not yet in Aquitaine, best suits the facts, although it is not possible to be confident about it.

But this much is clear: from some time in 1173, Eleanor would disappear into real captivity for over ten years.

8

The Lost Years

The matron was rapt away, with streaming hair, bound fast
  Without even a sad farewell to the household gods.
  Nor could the captive press a kiss on the threshold
  Nor cast one backward glance toward what was lost.
                    Radegund of Thuringia (St Radegonde)

Oh captive, return to your own people if you can. If you
cannot, call out like the King of Jerusalem and say: 'Alas, Alas
how long drawn out has been my exile!' I have lived with an
            ignorant and uncivilised tribe.
                                Richard le Poitevin

From the time of her capture, Eleanor disappears almost entirely
from the record for years. Indeed, as will appear below, very
little is known for sure about Eleanor's life over the next decade.
All that can be done is to set out the small traces which remain
and recreate as best one can the conditions in which she was
held – as well as to consider the effect her captivity had on her
reputation.

Just as the circumstances and location of her capture are obscure,
Eleanor's itinerary after her initial apprehension is completely
unclear. Henry understandably did not want to advertise her
defection, and her sons did not want to advertise her loss. However,
we can be sure that Henry will have moved her as quickly as
possible to a location where she could be securely held. Chinon is
often posited as a venue for her initial captivity, but if Eleanor was
ever at Chinon she will have been removed from a place so close

to combat as quickly as possible.[1] Rouen, which held strongly for Henry, and which was his own base, has to be considered a prime candidate; other prisoners were held at Falaise.

Perhaps appropriately, given the mystery over the circumstances of Eleanor's captivity, there is a famously puzzling fresco on the wall of the chapel of St Radegonde at Chinon which dates to sometime around this period and which is commonly associated with Eleanor. What remains is probably a survivor of a larger work – it sits to one side of an arch in a long wall, and it would make sense if the picture continued at least on the other side of the arch, and along the rest of the wall. The surviving fragment shows five riders. On the left, one of a pair of riders in caps holds a falcon. In the centre are two riders, one crowned and reaching a hand back towards the falcon and one with long, uncovered hair. On the right is another crowned figure, this time bearded. The picture is highly controversial; though it is often said to be associated with the Plantagenet family, we cannot be confident even of this much. One popular view is that it is actually a representation of Eleanor's capture or of her transport into captivity, and that Eleanor (dressed in men's clothing, as in one version of the account of her capture) is the central figure, handing over the falcon as a sign of the safe custody of Aquitaine as she is carried away by Henry.[2] This reading is made tempting to many by the location of the fresco, as St Radegonde was not only a saint associated with Eleanor's home town but also the patron saint of prisoners – and, significantly, she was a woman who escaped the oppressive power of her husband to become a nun.

However, this reading is much criticised: the fresco is equally frequently said to depict Eleanor with a range of other people at a range of other dates. Another view – and the most convincing intellectually, if one accepts the initial premise that the scene shows Henry II's family – is that it indeed references Eleanor's capture, but is actually of Henry and his sons riding happily into an Eleanor-free future. This view has much to commend it, not least in that it is consistent with what, judged against other contemporaneous depictions, does appear to be the male dress of all the figures shown. Yet even this hypothesis has a significant problem: it fails to account for its location in the chapel of St Radegonde. Other views as to its meaning and genesis will therefore be considered later.[3]

Whatever Eleanor's initial itinerary, it was only in July 1174 that Eleanor and the other state prisoners (notably the Earl of Chester) were moved to England. Eleanor was initially imprisoned in Salisbury while the others were held at Devizes Castle, where captives from the English campaign, including the Earl of Leicester and his wife Petronilla – who had, true to her formidable reputation, taken the field with him[4] – were already established. Also transported to England at this time were Joanna and John, plus Constance of Brittany and Alys of France;[5] for most of these a nursery establishment was probably set up, though its location is not clear from the Pipe Rolls. As for Alicia of Maurienne, it is unclear whether she was alive to make the journey, because she died at about this time.

It is often supposed that Eleanor's time in captivity was one of strict confinement, with her effectively in jail; moreover, it is assumed that she hated England generally and Salisbury in particular, so her confinement there was intended to be as unpleasant as possible. In fact, we can be sure that this is quite far from the truth. While England would probably never be as dear to Eleanor as Poitou, we have seen that Eleanor had spent fulfilling and probably happy years in England towards the start of her marriage. It was the location of the birth of most of her children. And Salisbury had been a repeated stop on her itinerary, even when she was alone, with more of her surviving letters and charters from her regencies being dated there than any other place; a real fondness for it on her part may therefore be inferred. It was also one of the earliest centres of the cult of St Radegonde in England, boasting a lock of the saint's hair. With all this taken into account, Salisbury might credibly be posited as Eleanor's favourite place in England.[6]

The Salisbury of Eleanor's day was what is now known as Old Sarum, with roots going back to at least the Iron Age and development from the Roman era. It had a substantial keep, originally built in the previous century, and a vibrant cathedral which had been extended and improved as recently as 1130. Her residence there was in what was known as the Courtyard House – a modern building dating from the early years of the twelfth century and contributed by the then Bishop of Salisbury. Furthermore, the palace compound was the subject of renovations throughout her period of residence. Thus, a sum of £24 was spent on the bridge and the castle in 1170–71; £17 on the walls in 1172–73; and £47 on the houses, the wall and the gates in 1173–74. So, all in all, Salisbury probably offered a comfortable and well-appointed residence.[7]

To add to the amenity of her situation, the Bishop of Salisbury, Joscelin de Bohun, will have been well known to her as he had been the incumbent since her first arrival in England. He was also the brother of the Bishop of Coutances, who had often acted as Chancellor of Normandy for Henry. She will therefore have been able to pursue her devotions there easily and under the supervision of a long-time acquaintance. Also likely to be there on occasion was Godfrey de Lucy, the son of the justiciar and long-term partner of John's nurse Agatha; he held a prebend in Salisbury, although for some of the period he was studying abroad.[8]

The picture is similar for Winchester, where Eleanor also had considerable spells. While we do not know exactly where she stayed within the luxurious palace, we do know that it was a major palace with a garden, both of which were subject to regular upgrades. Again, it was a major clerical and administrative centre – as to the latter it was still contending with London for primacy, as its location for Young Henry's second coronation shows. It also had a thriving cathedral – and a chapel to St Radegond, complete with relics. While the bishop, Richard of Ilchester, was probably largely absent, being one of Henry's closest confidants on administrative and legal matters (he was later Seneschal of Normandy), the spiritual chancellor of the diocese during Eleanor's captivity was one Jordan Fantosme, a former pupil of Gilbert of Poitiers, and a poet whose work was influenced by the troubadour poems he encountered in his time in Poitiers. Here, therefore, Eleanor would have had access to a cleric who was likely to be sympathetic and with whom she could converse on topics of mutual interest. And, as noted earlier, he is one source for the revolt who does not point the finger at Eleanor.

We know that Eleanor ended her captivity in robust good health, which suggests adequate nutrition and freedom to exercise. While riding out may have been forbidden during the early stages of her detention, when the outcome of the rebellion was still in the balance, it was certainly not so later, and she was then fit enough to avail herself of that opportunity, suggesting even the earlier confinement left her in reasonable health. Properly, therefore,

Eleanor should be regarded as being kept under a form of house arrest that was somewhat strict at the start of her captivity and gradually eased over the years.

That is not to say that she had anything like her full liberty. Because of the nature of her offences, her correspondence was almost certainly extremely limited; correspondence with her sons directly was prohibited, and it is likely that her letters in and out were all read by Henry's agents to prevent this being worked around. She may well also have been deprived of a good deal of news, at least during the currency of the Young King's rebellion – and indeed while Richard later continued to hold out in Aquitaine, which he did until September 1174.[9] How successful this sort of censorship could be over the longer term, however, when Eleanor was held for long periods in large, heavily staffed palaces such as Salisbury and Winchester, is doubtful.

It may seem obvious that this captivity was the worst that could be done to Eleanor, but this is a false assumption. Queen Ingeborg of Denmark would, just a few years later, be held in very dubious conditions, with insufficient food, by Philip II Augustus of France. It is likely that Eleanor will have at least initially been unsure what Henry intended for her. While it would probably have been imprudent to despatch her given the Poitevins' loyalty to her and Henry's own battered reputation after Becket's murder, a slightly delayed death in captivity could perfectly well have been explained away as natural. After all, the fifty-year-old Eleanor was now entering the age band where death was not so unexpected in medieval times. Indeed, her younger cousin Petronilla of Aragon died just as Eleanor was commencing her captivity. And it was certainly not beyond Henry to arrange such a convenient death; the story of Robert de Sillé demonstrates Henry's willingness to allow a captive to die as a result of inadequate care and nutrition. Furthermore, at about this time Henry secured the surrender of Robert of Leicester's garrisons at Leicester, Mountsorrel and Groby by threatening (obviously with a degree of conviction) that the earl would not taste food or drink until they did so. Henry must have appreciated that whether he despatched Eleanor or merely allowed her to die, her death would be laid at his door and would provide his enemies (at a time when he was never short of such things) with a glorious public relations bonus which they would use against him. Effectively, Eleanor had to remain alive, and demonstrably so. This will have ensured that her health was very well cared for.[10]

This necessity may well partially explain the relative lavishness of the arrangements for her detention; descriptions by biographers of the amounts paid on her behalf as a 'pittance' are wide of the mark. While Eleanor was deprived of her revenues, including from her dower lands, considerable sums were expended on her behalf. In the first full year of Eleanor's captivity, payments made on her behalf totalled £161 – the income of a lesser nobleman. With limited obligations to others (unlike when she was heading up a court), these sorts of sums permitted a very comfortable lifestyle.[11] Further, the significant sums paid to Eleanor's hospital in Surrey did not cease – even if she was captive, her charities appear to have been respected.

But if Eleanor's physical and charitable welfare was properly cared for, the same could not be said of her reputation. This period, with Eleanor off the stage for years, effectively marked the start of the 'Black Myth'. Eleanor's transgression of marital duty was duly noted by the chroniclers and, as was remarked earlier, the version of the story which appears to have been current during her imprisonment placed the lion's share of the blame on her when assigning fault for the origins of the rebellion. Even the sympathetic Richard le Poitevin's lament reinforces the story of Eleanor's involvement:

Of the Eagle of the Broken Covenant: Tell me Eagle with two heads, tell me: where were you when your eaglets, flying from their nest, raised their talons against the King of the Eagles/North Wind [footnote: The Latin for the north wind is Aquila – the same word as is used for eagle]? As we heard it, it was you who urged them to attack their father. That is why you have been ravished from your own country and carried away to a strange land...[12]

This created the climate in which others, such as William of Tyre, came to evaluate her earlier actions on Crusade. In his case, the link is clear because in writing of the Crusade he explicitly says that 'her conduct before and after this time showed her to be ... far from circumspect.' The reference to 'after this time' is plainly a cross reference to her association in her sons' revolt. It is a similar case with William of Newburgh, who tacitly places on Eleanor's shoulders much of the blame for the failure of the Crusade once one takes into account his focus on the deleterious effects of women among the Crusaders as an occasion to sin, his disapproval of Louis' insistence on her presence and his disapproval of her repudiation of Louis, which he unfairly ascribed to a desire to marry Henry. That approach is obviously informed by what has happened since.

But one can also see how the coincidence between the timing of the writings on the Second Crusade and Eleanor's imprisonment created a climate in which discussion of her as transgressive was easy – and doubtless encouraged by those close to Henry. Thus the re-emergence and magnification of the rumours as to Eleanor's behaviour on Crusade noted earlier, in the works even of broadly sympathetic later writers such as Richard of Devizes and Gervase of Canterbury. In the latter, indeed, when talking of Eleanor's capture we see the emergence of the theme of Eleanor as transgressive in her dress. The idea of a woman dressing as a man was seen as an attempt to annex the higher status of a man, to which she, as a lesser being, was not entitled; this chimed with the picture of Eleanor emerging as the moving force behind the rebellion, which itself tied into the stories about her demand for a divorce from Louis.[13]

Feeding into this – probably to Eleanor's discredit – was the Arthurian dimension. Just as Henry and Eleanor had been depicted as Arthur and Guinevere in their time of success and prosperity, now the chroniclers and poets reached for their Arthurian lexicons – after all, was Guinevere not herself a betrayer of Arthur? It is from Geoffrey of Monmouth's account of Merlin's prophecies that Eleanor's characterisation as the Eagle comes: 'Queen Eleanor, described by Merlin as the Eagle of the Broken Covenant'. So too is the reference to Henry as 'King of the North Wind' a nod to Geoffrey. Surely that pre-existing parallel between Eleanor and Guinevere facilitated a state of mind where Guinevere's faults could be attributed to Eleanor and she could be seen as iconically transgressive and outrageous.

And yet although the chroniclers rushed to call her actions unprecedented, the truth is that Eleanor was judged harshly in this regard – and this itself perhaps demonstrates the hand of Henry in acting to diminish Eleanor's reputation.[14] Her actions were not unprecedented at all, and those who said so demonstrated an interesting ignorance, wilful or otherwise, of relatively recent history.

After all, in the early twelfth century Urraca of Castile spent two years of her reign in open warfare against her estranged husband, Alfonso the Battler of Aragon, supported by the lovers who fathered her later children. At a slightly earlier date, Matilda of Flanders, wife of William the Conqueror, had provided money and materiel to her son in his rebellion against his father in the late 1070s. Both women's actions seem more extreme than what is actually proven against Eleanor. So Eleanor, imprisoned and unable to mount her own defence through her own chroniclers, became the victim of character assassination.

For the first part of her captivity Eleanor may well have had Marguerite and Alys for company, since they were unlikely to have been held in the high security of Devizes. But by early 1175, Young Henry had reconciled with his father and Marguerite had travelled to France to join him; when she came back with him, she stayed with him at Winchester and elsewhere. It is unlikely that Alys was entrusted to her sister's household; she was probably transferred to the location where Henry's wards were resident, perhaps the Tower of London, under custody of the justiciars. Emma of Anjou may have remained with Eleanor for some time but was married to Dafydd, Prince of Gwynedd early on in Eleanor's captivity.[15]

How much and how often Eleanor was moved we do not know. Only one chronicler, Roger of Howden, mentions her at different locations, and we cannot know to what extent even he provides a full list. It seems likely that at first Henry was minded to hold Eleanor at Salisbury pending taking steps to put her aside by placing her in a convent. Certainly the theme of the first year or so after Eleanor's confinement is that Henry was seriously contemplating divorce, and this seems to have been no secret. Gerald of Wales writes of Eleanor's rebellion as a punishment on Henry for his incestuous marriage, and this surely reflects the widespread gossip about the future of the marriage, given its shaky legal foundations and obvious breakdown. But matters could not be so simple for Henry; he was no doubt aware of the risk that on divorce Eleanor's lands would revert to her, as had happened with Louis. However, it is likely that he felt that the investiture of Richard was sufficient to keep the lands of Poitou within his power – at least so long as he also held Eleanor.

Gervase of Canterbury, writing closer to the time and with access to better sources of information than Gerald, says that in autumn 1175 a papal legate, Cardinal Uguccione Pierleone of Saint Angelo, arrived in England to deal with the latest in a long succession of disputes between the archbishops of Canterbury and York and was received exceedingly graciously by the king, who after plying him with gifts and soft words then sought his agreement to obtain a divorce for Henry from Eleanor on the grounds of consanguinity. The cardinal, however, was unreceptive to this suggestion. Since the marriage was indubitably consanguineous, the relatively low esteem in which Henry was held by the Church may have had something to do with this. So too might Eleanor's own harmonious relationship with those in the papal corridors of power. There certainly doesn't seem to be any contemporaneous ground for the suggestion of some biographers that this visit was a 'put-up job' or that the legate's visit resulted from a request from Henry in relation to his desire for a divorce. What is more, if that were the case, the sending of the cardinal would indicate a more favourable view of the request than the evidence suggests was given. In fact, Henry had to petition the Pope formally to pursue the matter, which he did shortly afterwards.[16]

It is often suggested that the reasoning behind Henry's attempt to put Eleanor aside was so that he could marry his now long-term mistress Rosamund Clifford. Gerald of Wales says that Henry ceased to hide his infidelity following Eleanor's imprisonment, displaying Rosamund at his side openly, 'not a rose of the world* but an unclean rose'.[17] It is simply based on this speculation that he infers that Henry proposed to marry Rosamund. But of course, Gerald was not writing this until some twenty years later; in 1174 he was either still studying in Paris or just moved to distant Brecon as assistant to the archdeacon there.

The truth is that while a divorce was certainly sought, there is no reason to assume that Henry was looking to marry Rosamund. He had no need of further heirs, and Rosamund brought no advantageous connection which would make it worthwhile marrying her. Indeed, there is some reason to think that Rosamund's reign as Henry's mistress was now close to over, if not actually at an end. We know, for example, that Rosamund died late in 1176 or in early 1177 and that Henry gave generously to the convent where she was buried. But there are some indications in the chronicles that Rosamund may have entered the convent before her death.

---

*   *rosa mundi*, a play on Rosamund's name contrasted with *immundi*, unclean

This may have coincided with the gift made by Henry to Rosamund's father in 1174 of a manor 'for the love of his daughter, Rosamund'.[18]

And there is certainly incontrovertible evidence that at least during 1175 Henry had turned his attentions elsewhere: in 1176 one of Henry's wards, Ida de Tosny, herself a cousin of Rosamund Clifford, gave birth to Henry's son, the future William Longsword. Ida was probably the daughter of one Ralph de Tosny and Margaret Beaumont, daughter of the late Earl of Leicester, and may well have been daughter or niece to the mother of Henry's son Geoffroy. Once her father died in 1162, she became a royal ward until her marriage. Her parents having married sometime after 1155, Ida was at most nineteen in 1175, and very probably younger, since she was one of seven children and was also still deemed young enough for marriage to Roger Bigod in 1181. Again, however, it seems unlikely that Henry wished to marry her, since no substantial advantage could accrue to him from such a match.[19]

Most likely, therefore, Henry did indeed seek a divorce, but not initially with any particular candidate in mind for a second wife. Nor did the idea of divorce go away. Henry broached the subject directly with Eleanor in early 1176, offering her access to the revenues of her lands if she took the veil at Fontevraud. He is also said to have offered her the position of abbess, although this may well have been aspirational on his part since Audeburge of Haut Bruyeres had been occupying the position since 1155 and would hold it until her death in 1180. More likely he intended to place her at the head of the abbey of Amesbury, where a recent investigation had found considerable misbehaviour and mismanagement. This of course gels with Eleanor's rather tart letter to Amesbury some years before. But the investigation had also found more – with the nuns coyly described as 'lacking in continence' – a designation apparently covering the birth of three illegitimate children to the abbess herself. As part of his deal with the Church after Becket's death, Henry had vowed to make a pilgrimage to Jerusalem; now he had sent to Rome to ask for absolution from it on the basis that he would instead found three monasteries. The Pope having assented to the compromise, Henry had it in mind to re-found Amesbury as a daughter house of Fontevraud, and as such he would have influence over its choice of abbess.[20]

That Henry's request for Eleanor to take the veil was made sincerely and somewhat forcefully seems beyond doubt, for at

Easter 1176 Eleanor was appealing to Archbishop Rotrou of Rouen to protect her from being forced to become a nun. That the Church had firmly turned its face against such an approach is evident from the fact that even Henry's most intimate ecclesiastical ally supported her in her protests. But again Henry's determination is marked by the fact that in the face of such consistent discouragement he nonetheless appealed to the Pope directly. It may be by way of revenge on Eleanor that he appears to have used some of Eleanor's dower, now in his hands, to re-found Amesbury.[21]

Both Henrys were in England for the second half of 1175 and into early 1176, holding Christmas at Windsor but there is no record of whether Eleanor was allowed to join them, or whether either they or William Marshal, part of the Young King's household, paid her a visit at Salisbury. One fact which does suggest that she would have seen Young Henry is that the Pipe Rolls disclose that he had ordered a new mews constructed there, and substantial sums were paid to a royal falconer for the keep of his hawks there.[22]

However, we know that at Easter 1176 Eleanor was summoned to join them, and her other sons who had recently crossed from the continent, at Winchester. £3 of expenses were paid to Eleanor's custodian Robert Mauduit for this period. Richard was able to report on his progress in Aquitaine, where he had conducted his first successful siege at Castillon, but was now facing a dangerous alliance of the families of Angoulême, Limoges and Turenne which required him to seek further support from Henry. This would be the last time that Eleanor saw all her sons together. Richard and Geoffrey returned to France in April and Young Henry and his queen also left after Easter.[23]

Aside from being a time when Henry pressed Eleanor hard to agree to enter Fontevraud, Easter 1176 was also when he revealed to her that a deal for the marriage of her remaining daughter, Joanna, which had been raised in 1170 and recently revived at the Pope's instance, was almost done, and that emissaries from William, King of Sicily, would be arriving in the near future to meet her and finalise the arrangements.[24]

Joanna and Eleanor therefore remained in Winchester after Easter when Henry departed for London. This raises the question of where Joanna had been for the previous months, and one real possibility is that she had in fact remained with her mother, pending arrangements being made for her marriage. She is not accounted for elsewhere, and the fact that Eleanor was then left in charge of her for the visit does suggest that she was, despite detention, trusted at least this far. Certainly it would have been very helpful to Joanna to be with her mother in this period, for of course Eleanor had actually spent time in Sicily on her return from Crusade. She could describe some of the places which would form Joanna's new home and prepare her for the very different feel of the Sicilian court.

The Sicilian envoys (two bishops and a certain Florius, Count of Camerota, the royal justiciar) arrived in May with Archbishop Rotrou of Rouen, who was related to King William's mother. After visiting Henry, they made their way to Winchester and were entertained there by Eleanor and Joanna. Norwich states that the visit was insisted upon by William, who wanted to be assured of the attractiveness of his prospective bride; this appears to echo Roger of Howden's words that the emissaries were 'satisfied with Joanna's beauty'. Whatever the reason for the visit, they returned to London, where Henry appointed his own emissaries to travel to Sicily and negotiate terms for the marriage.[25] He himself returned to Winchester in August, which would have constituted his farewell to his youngest daughter, and enabled him to ensure that arrangements for her wedding were progressing well.

Meanwhile, the emissaries arrived in Sicily in August and terms were quickly agreed, for Joanna left Winchester en route for Palermo on 27 August, accompanied by the Archbishop of Canterbury, her uncle Hamelin de Warenne and a number of bishops including, of course, Rotrou of Rouen. The accounts of her departure indicate that she and Eleanor had made good use of the four months since the visit, for she was provided with a trousseau of clothing including a wedding dress costing over £114, gold and silver plate and many costly gifts. Her suite involved the hire and equipping of seven ships at a cost of nearly £20. On the first stage of her continental journey she would be escorted by her brothers Henry and Richard, before she was handed over the Henry's emissary the Bishop of Norwich who awaited her at Saint Gilles.[26]

Eleanor remained behind at Winchester, technically under the guardianship of Ranulf de Glanville, a former High Sheriff of

Westmoreland who had recommended himself to Henry both in the field and in the council chamber and had recently been made a king's justice (judge). However, at this stage he seems not to have been active in supervising Eleanor and her needs, for after Henry's departure we find a payment for her maintenance being made to Robert Mauduit, indicating that her primary residence and accounting centre remained Salisbury. Meanwhile at Windsor Eleanor's youngest son John, who appears to have been attached to his father's household after Eleanor's capture, was engaged to his distant cousin Avise of Gloucester, who was probably even younger than her ten-year-old fiancé. John's earlier betrothal to Alicia of Maurienne, the trigger for the rebellion, had come to nothing upon her death. John and Geoffrey would then go on to spend Christmas with Henry at Nottingham, while Young Henry and his queen held court at Argentan and Richard at Bordeaux.[27] Eleanor, we must assume, had again been returned to Salisbury.

It was probably also in 1176 that Rosamund Clifford died, still in her mid to late twenties. Eleanor may not have been aware of this event, and the only reason for mentioning it here is to point up the inaccuracy of the later tradition which had Eleanor murdering Rosamund. Two almost equally dramatic tales were long told about her death. The first, and these days the better known, had Eleanor offering Rosamund poison at the heart of a labyrinth in which Henry kept his lover. The fourteenth-century Chronicle of London had an even better version: Eleanor, having tortured Rosamund with vicious toads, killed her by part roasting her and then leaving her to bleed to death in a hot bath. It will be apparent that Eleanor herself could have played no part in any such murder, since she was securely imprisoned at the time. Further, while we do not know for a fact that (as is sometimes asserted) Eleanor had no contact with the outside world so as to hire assassins, we do know that Eleanor had borne Henry's frequent infidelities with no such resort to violence for years. Besides, by 1176 her marriage was over in all but name; disposing of Rosamund could do no good. The obvious target for a 1176 disposal would be Ida de Tosny, who had just borne Henry a son – or Ida's successor in his favour.[28]

Quite what did dispose of young Rosamund is unclear. She may have died in childbirth, taking her baby with her. The tradition which has her retiring to Godstow before her death suggests the possibility of a longer illness. But all we know for sure is that she was buried at Godstow and that Henry erected a beautiful tomb there in her memory and gave gifts to the convent in her honour.[29]

One possibility as to who had by now succeeded Rosamund in Henry's 'affections' is Alys of France, Richard's fiancée. She was now sixteen years old, a good age for marriage, as was Richard at twenty. It was in 1177 that questions began to be asked about why Henry had not arranged for this marriage to take place, and Roger of Howden also speaks of a threat to place England under an interdict if Richard and Alys were not married. The most salacious version of the story comes (again) from Gerald of Wales, who says that from around this time Henry took Alys as his mistress and intended to make her queen.[30]

Were the matter only mentioned in this source it could be easily discounted, but a number of other sources also suggest that Henry took Alys as his mistress, though without giving a date. They include Roger of Howden's probable first-hand report of Richard's later reason for refusing to marry Alys as being that 'it is impossible for me to marry her because my father slept with her and had a son by her'. Howden's evidence on this has to be taken seriously because he was a cleric who had direct contact with Henry II and later Richard I as a senior clerical negotiator and Crusader with Richard. He is also a chronicler not given to scandal, and one who tends to be favourable to Henry II. While his chronicle was not written until the 1190s, he was active in royal circles from 1175, and was writing a history of Henry at that time; so contemporaneous notes likely form the basis of his later work. Later sources, including the fourteenth century-chronicle of Meaux, also suggest that Alys bore Henry a child who did not survive.[31]

Is this story credible? It has long been conventional to reject it as mere scandal, but recent consideration has tended to incline towards accepting it. In particular Richard's statement, reported in very clear terms, seems incredible if not true. While Richard was at the time looking for a reason to reject Alys, it was unnecessary and even damaging to involve Henry in the story unless it was true; an accusation that Alys had betrayed him with an unnamed knight would have been sufficient. By making the specific accusation he did, Richard accused his father of a serious breach of trust, for Alys was his ward. He stood *in loco parentis* to her, and had done since she was a small child. Again, why would Richard do this if it was not true?

What is more, the seduction of Alys fits Henry's established *modus operandi*. If we look at Henry's other attested relationships, we can see a pattern of attraction to much younger women who were in his power and, as such, should have been forbidden fruit. In the 1160s there was Alix de Porhöet, the teenaged daughter of the Vicomte of Porhöet, a vassal of Henry whose seduction was decried by her father as 'treachery, adultery and incest' because of the fact that she was in his safekeeping and because of the blood relationship between them. There was Nest Bloet, whose 1224 death date suggests she too was very young at the time of her affair with Henry.[32] There was Rosamund herself, likely seduced in her teens while present under her father's roof – and Annabel de Balliol may well fall into the same category. Most similarly of all there was Ida de Tosny, Henry's teenaged ward, again made pregnant in contravention of the relationship of trust between them.

None of this justifies Flori's sensationalist conclusion that Henry was a paedophile who had seduced Alys as a child, which appears to be a deduction too far. However, the facts do suggest that a seduction of teenaged Alys would have been consistent with Henry's previous form. This, taken with Roger of Howden's credible evidence, does indicate that there was truth in the seduction story – and this view is now accepted by such highly reputable historians as Ralph Turner and John Gillingham.[33]

Whether Henry intended to marry Alys is much more dubious. If that was his intention, there would be no difficulty in raising this as a possibility with Louis. A marriage to a reigning king was a better match for her than one with a second son. Louis' influence in favour of such a match could also potentially help to facilitate the divorce from Eleanor. But there are no records of such discussions – just gossip from courtiers that Henry had it in mind to disinherit his sons and start a new family.[34] So far as diplomatic records are concerned, what we see is that, on the contrary, Louis was pressing for the marriage to Richard to take place.

How soon would any of these stories have come to Eleanor's ears? It is impossible to say. However, we know that Eleanor was typically imprisoned in large castles with many people employed about them. All appear to have been significant centres of the administration of English business, and therefore centres for visitors from other locations, for example seeking passes to travel out of the jurisdiction, or to do business with senior administrators such as Robert Mauduit. At Salisbury, too, significant repairs and upgrades were ongoing throughout the period, with workmen doubtless on site continuously. As such, gossip would have been rife and relatively well informed. It was also in 1177 that the records suggest that Eleanor started to gain more independence, and therefore would be likely to have greater access to the news circulating around the town. Eleanor would surely have heard of this scandal within a relatively short time.

As for this greater liberty, it seems to have come more or less in tandem with Henry feeling secure enough to release the earls of Chester and Leicester, which occurred at a great council held in Northampton in January 1177, although their lands were only gradually restored to them, with a third of the Earl of Leicester's revenues still being paid to the ling in 1179–80. This left Eleanor as the only rebel still imprisoned; but from here we can see that her conditions of detention were improved. It is to this period that records of the ordering of luxurious clothing date, with Henry recorded providing Eleanor and her maid with cloaks and capes of scarlet, matching grey furs, and an embroidered coverlet at Michaelmas 1178. Later come further orders for another scarlet cloak, for furs and leather goods. It is also in this period that we see Eleanor being provided with a gilt saddle for her own horse and a more workaday one for the maid who accompanied her on her rides in the neighbourhood.[35]

However, Henry, who spent the early part of 1177 in England, seems to have gone out of his way to avoid Salisbury, instead visiting Winchester and Marlborough when he headed west. The nearest Eleanor will have come to direct information on her children was when the bishop who had accompanied Joanna to her wedding in Sicily in February returned in late spring to report on the event. This of course raises questions about the extent to which Eleanor was able to correspond with her children. Correspondence with her sons was almost certainly forbidden, or at least scrutinised. But there is some reason to suppose that Eleanor managed to maintain some form of correspondence with her daughters before, during and after her captivity. Colette Bowie has traced the lives of Matilda, Leonor and Joanna, and has marked a considerable amount of maternal influence in the activities of the three young women. And while sadly no letters to prove the hypothesis survive, the later actions of Matilda and Joanna in seeking out their mother in times of crisis are surely only sensibly compatible with some continued correspondence in the interim. Eleanor certainly had the opportunity – and plenty of time – to correspond with her daughters. She may even have had an opportunity to speak with a clerk of Leonor's who came to England in 1175, sent by her to perfect his education.

Through her daughters, Eleanor was now a grandmother many times over. Matilda, married in 1165, had already produced four children: Mathilde (christened Richenza), Heinrich, Lothar and Otto. To date, Matilda was the only one of Eleanor's daughters by Henry to produce children; it appears that Leonor did not take up residence with her husband until near her fifteenth birthday in the autumn of 1177, and Joanna was still only twelve years old and was never to produce a surviving child. But by Eleanor's firstborn, Marie, she was also a grandmother three times over – to the future Henry, King of Jerusalem, and two girls named Marie and Scholastica. By her second born, Alice, she already had a further three grandsons and a granddaughter to her credit. But now Eleanor had the prospect of a grandchild she might actually see, for in summer 1177 Marguerite gave birth to what would be the Young King's only child, William. Yet Eleanor was never to meet this child, who was born in Paris, under the eyes of his grandfather Louis; little William was dead within three days.

One question which hangs over these years is whether Eleanor's sons visited her at all. John, for example, had been in England with his father for most of 1176. The next year saw Henry and Geoffrey in the country for a considerable period and Geoffrey, now nearly eighteen years old, was knighted on 6 August. As for Christmases, in 1176 Geoffrey and John spent Christmas with their father at Nottingham and in 1178 they were with him at Winchester. Young Henry was in the country for the spring of 1179, with enough time for hunting and a mini-progress. It is therefore tempting to suppose that at least some visiting was permitted during these periods. During Lent 1179, Young Henry, Geoffrey and John were all with Henry in Winchester. Again, however, it is unclear whether Eleanor was brought to meet them, or whether any of them met her. Two things suggest that they did. The first is the likelihood of visits by Young Henry to Sarum, where he had based his mews. The second is that William Marshal later alluded to having met with Eleanor during the course of her captivity, which would suggest that some visits were indeed paid to her.[36]

There also seems good evidence that Eleanor met Richard later this year, when he crossed briefly to England. Richard was having a tough time subduing Aquitaine, but had recently managed to take the supposedly impregnable fortress of Taillebourg, an event which had persuaded the Count of Angoulême to surrender his own castles and the heads of the Limoges and La Marche families to depart on pilgrimage to Jerusalem. Henry received him with great applause and the pair made a pilgrimage to the shrine of Becket. But the main purpose of his visit appears to have been to bring him and Eleanor together before a formal council to witness her ceding all her rights in Poitou to him, to facilitate his campaigning there. It has been speculated that this renunciation was a blow to her affection for him, but there is no evidence for this.[37] Nothing in her later relationship with Richard indicates that this caused friction. One might rather more credibly infer that Eleanor would have been delighted to see her twenty-one-year-old prodigy of a son, whose successes had now driven many of the most difficult of her vassals into passivity or exile.

Eleanor generally seems to be placed in Wiltshire during this period, and therefore probably at Salisbury. That means that she will certainly have missed a final meeting with her former husband Louis, who crossed to England to make a pilgrimage to Becket's tomb in August 1179, seeking the saint's intercession for the life of his only son, Philip, who had fallen into a coma following a hunting accident. Her two husbands proceeded together to the cathedral from Dover and there spent three days in vigil, prayer and fasting.[38]

The saint was efficacious and Philip recovered, with his coronation scheduled for November; but in an ironic twist of fate, Louis himself was struck down by paralysis, from which he was never to recover, just before the ceremony and was unable to attend the event. He died in September of the same year. Plantagenet interests at the coronation were represented by Young Henry, who was Seneschal of France, as well as Richard and Geoffrey, who paid homage for their lands to young Philip, who would henceforth be the true ruler of France. The display put on by Young Henry appears to have been a worthy forerunner to the Field of the Cloth of Gold.[39]

Change was also afoot for Eleanor. From 1180, Robert Mauduit disappears from the accounts for Eleanor and her custody passes more obviously into the hands of Ranulf de Glanville, now Chief Justiciar of England. Because of Glanville's other responsibilities, her needs were increasingly overseen by Ralph FitzStephen, another of the king's justices and formerly one of Young Henry's tutors. This change appears to have seen Eleanor moved about somewhat more, with records of her in Hampshire – probably at Winchester – in 1180, Dorset and Somerset in 1181 and 1182, and Berkshire (perhaps Windsor) also in 1182. During much of this period, Eleanor, though technically a prisoner, was the only representative of the royal house in England – apart from John, who was by now probably in Ranulf de Glanville's household. This would have offered opportunities for Eleanor to see John, though no evidence of such meetings remains. Of the rest of the family, Henry himself remained in England until April 1180, and returned in July 1181, staying until March 1182, and Young Henry joined him briefly in April 1180 before returning to Normandy. For considerable portions of Henry's visits he was at Winchester. It may have been this use of one of Eleanor's primary residences that prompted her removal to Dorset and Somerset – or it may truly reveal a greater liberty being afforded to her.[40]

With 1182 came a rush of bad news for Eleanor's family. Joanna, who had borne a son, Bohemond, reported his early demise. Eleanor's niece Isabelle of Flanders (daughter of Aelis) died, aged just under forty. Her death would provoke a war between her widower and Philip of France, who supported the claim of Aelis' surviving daughter, Elenor. Matilda and her husband and children had to flee to Henry's court in summer 1182 in consequence of Henry the Lion's disagreements with Emperor Frederick Barbarossa.[41] On what appeared to be a more cheerful note, Geoffrey finally married the now twenty-year-old Constance of Brittany, probably in about October 1181, but in fact this simply prompted him to use armed force to press his claims to the Duchy of Richmond.[42]

Meanwhile, in late 1182, at his massive Christmas court at Caen, Henry revived his plans for all his younger sons to do homage to Young Henry.[43] Richard, who continued to rule actively and mostly alone in Aquitaine, generating complaints of his violence and brutality, as well as his tendency to violent abduction of his subjects' womenfolk, refused to agree to this approach unless it was made clear that Aquitaine would be his, and transmissible to his heirs – a condition which Young Henry (who had already been in talks with the disaffected Poitevin nobles) in turn rejected.[44] It was to be the turning point for six months of violence and upheaval, news of which Eleanor will only have received staccato instalments as the months progressed – perhaps also with news of the huge sums which Henry was having shipped from England to keep his armies in the field.

In the early months of 1183, Young Henry and Geoffrey, backed by Aimar of Limoges and hired mercenaries, invaded Poitou, encouraging barons disaffected at Richard's treatment to rise again. Supported but not financed by Philip of France, they looted their way across the county, seizing not just money but also Church goods. Among them were golden crosses, altar frontals and a reliquary casket from the Abbey of Saint-Martial at Limoges – where Eleanor had organised Richard's theatrical installation as Duke of Aquitaine and where, scant weeks before, Young Henry himself had pledged to take the Cross. Further news of the uprising will have travelled to England when Henry, who took the field in support of Richard, sent orders for the Earl of Leicester and his wife Petronilla (and at least one of their daughters), as well as a number of other barons whose loyalty was suspect, to be taken into custody as a precautionary measure. By late May, Young Henry, already probably sickening, visited the famous shrine to the Virgin at Rocamadour. But his men, habituated by now to plunder, stripped the church of treasures and took the precious metals and jewels from the shrine of St Amator. It is unsurprising that later tellings of the story credit them also with seizing further items, including the reputed sword of Roland.[45]

The next news to come across the Channel was catastrophic. Young Henry had contracted dysentery, and on 11 June 1183 he had died, unforgiven by his father. Sceptical of its veracity, Henry had ignored his son's deathbed message begging his father to come to him. Young Henry – not yet twenty-nine years old – managed an excellent death in publicity terms, prostrating himself naked on the floor before the cross, then assuming penitential rags and taking to a bed strewn with ashes wearing a hairshirt and a noose; as if that were not enough, he took up again the crusading vow he had not yet fulfilled, pledging William Marshal to complete his Crusader's vow for him after his death. He also, in token of contrition, commanded that his eyes, brain and intestines were to be buried before the shrine at St Martial.[46]

There are two views about the Young King. The more prevalent is that he was incompetent as well as being irresponsible, arrogant and a spendthrift. The other is that he was the next best thing to a genuine chivalric hero. But whatever the chroniclers say, at the time his glamour, charm and public visibility as a tournament aficionado across France had won for him a considerable following which his recent actions had not dissipated. His death unleashed an outpouring of public mourning similar to that seen on the death of Diana, Princess of Wales – to which was added the campaign for sainthood which was the natural aim of such a wave of feeling in a highly religious era. So fervid was the atmosphere that the cortege on its way to Rouen was ambushed by his fans and forced to divert to Le Mans and bury him there. Rouen later had to take legal steps to get the body exhumed and transferred to Young Henry's chosen burial place near his grandmother.[47] Henry, however, did not break off the business of his siege of Limoges to visit his son's body when it was prepared for burial at Grandmont, though that was just a few miles away from his camp. Nor did he attend Young Henry's reburial on 22 July, even though by then he had reduced the walls of Limoges to rubble.

So it was that in July 1183, Thomas of Earley, Archdeacon of Wells and one of Young Henry's chaplains, arrived in Salisbury and sought an interview with Eleanor. Given Thomas' position, and the absence of contact between Henry and his son's household in the aftermath of the tragedy, one may perhaps doubt the usual account that he was the messenger sent with the news by Henry II. But the significance of the visit is that Thomas gave a detailed report of his interview with Eleanor in a sermon which he later preached and had published.

Contrary to some accounts, it is clear from his text that Thomas did not actually bring the news to Eleanor – by the time of his arrival she had already heard reports of the death of Young Henry. It also seems likely that she had heard of the beginnings of the campaign for his canonisation, for the archdeacon records that she met him with a serene face and took his official confirmation of her bereavement calmly. Her lack of surprise was explained by her to him; she had, she said, already understood Young Henry to be dead from a dream she had had, in which he appeared to her wearing two crowns, one brighter and clearer than the other. She had interpreted the less shining crown as the sign of earthly power, and the brighter one as signifying eternal bliss beyond what mortals can see, sense or understand.[48]

Tempting though it is for Eleanor's sake to take this account at face value – as a number of her biographers do – a considerable degree of caution is called for. One reason is that this story appears at the tail end of a sermon which was plainly designed specifically to support the campaign for the canonisation of Young Henry; it details cures and miracles allegedly wrought by his relics and the wonder of his apparently incorrupt body. The sermon is a manifest piece of special pleading and Eleanor's reaction is deliberately deployed as a valuable piece of evidence in favour of the expressed object of the sermon. And if Eleanor truly saw the visions which Earley says she reported, it sits rather ill with the fact that she is later reported by one close to her in 1193 to have said that she was tortured by the death of Young Henry. It is also inconsistent with her later gifts involving intercessory commemoration of Young Henry, which would be unnecessary if she believed him to have been received into paradise already.

The two versions can be reconciled, though not with perfect credit to Eleanor. It seems most likely that Eleanor knew of Young Henry's death before Earley's visit. Some rumours of the outpouring of grief for him will have reached her too. Though stricken by her eldest son's death in his prime, she was herself keen to see him sanctified – both for his eternal benefit and also that of the family upon whom he would then shed such lustre. Let us not forget that Eleanor's family already had one saint: St William of Gellone. She therefore said something which the willing Earley was able to turn into the comforting vision which he reported in his sermon. She may indeed have actively promoted or commissioned the preaching of the sermon. However, the campaign was not to bear fruit; and Earley, its advocate, seems to have risen no further in his career.[49]

So the story that Eleanor's loss was taken away by an inspired vision should be rejected, and we should conclude that the death of her beautiful and talented son in his prime was every bit as much a blow to her as one would expect. Indeed, it would be hard to imagine any mother not being tortured by the thought of the death of her promising son from dysentery, aged only twenty-eight. Eleanor, at least, was spared the guilt which would have fallen so heavily on Henry; she was never alienated from Young Henry. She remained in captivity precisely because she had supported him. Yet Henry had to face that his heir had died in arms against him; and that Young Henry had begged him to come and be reconciled but Henry had not trusted his message, sending only a sapphire ring in his place.

Awful as the news was, however, the death of Young Henry had immediate benefits for Eleanor. One of his last wishes, communicated to Henry after his death, was that his father should treat Eleanor mercifully – perhaps a sign of the relationship maintained through her captivity.[50] Henry could not now reconcile with his son, but shortly after the news of the death came to Eleanor it was followed by instructions from Henry that she should be set at liberty. She had been captive for nearly ten years.

9

False Freedom

assensu et voluntate domini mei Henrici regis Anglie
[with the assent and at the wish of her lord Henry,
King of England]
Charter in favour of Fontevraud, 1185

Of course, Eleanor was not truly freed, and the accounts of the extent of her liberty and even how she came to that greater liberty are conflicting. The usually reliable Geoffrey of Vigeois has Eleanor crossing to France in the summer of 1183. However, none of the English chroniclers record this and there is no record of her passage, so this suggestion should probably be doubted. Equally dubious is Gervase of Canterbury's assertion that Eleanor was freed for a short time at around this period by reason of a petition by the Archbishop of Canterbury.[1]

More likely to be correct is Roger of Howden's account that Henry ordered Eleanor to be freed in late 1183, and also ordered that she make a progress around her dowerlands. Howden's account is supported by an entry in the Pipe Rolls 'for carrying the saddles of the queen and her maidens to Waltham'. It is also consistent with the sudden reappearance in the Pipe Rolls of dower payments to Eleanor from her Queenhithe property in London and her Devon estates.[2]

Eleanor will have found her dowerlands somewhat diminished. Henry had of course taken manors from her dower to provide for the endowment of Amesbury, but this was not a one-off. At Waltham itself, for example, she would have found that in 1177 Henry had taken a church of secular canons and converted it into an abbey of Augustinian canons. Given that at least two out of the three new religious houses Henry had sworn to found were funded by taking lands from Eleanor's dower, there must also be a presumption that when Eleanor toured her Wiltshire dowerlands she found that they too had been diminished to found the third, the Carthusian priory at Witham, where the future St Hugh of Lincoln was now labouring to bring the priory into being.[3]

It is true that Eleanor had greater liberty and renewed access to considerable, if diminished, financial resources following Young Henry's death. But the story is not so simple or so sentimental as it might seem. The evidence suggests that Eleanor was not immediately freed, as might be the case if Young Henry's plea was truly the motive force; nor is there any sign of a real rehabilitation. The brutal truth is political: from here on in, Eleanor became a very useful pawn for Henry to utilise to his best advantage. The immediate need to deploy her was both financial and political. Young Henry's death had widowed Marguerite of France, and her half-brother Philip was insistently pressing for the return of her Vexin dowry and the provision to her of English dowerlands. It is likely these two points that Vigeois has conflated in his suggestion that Eleanor was summoned to make a progress through Norman dowerlands. Henry's response to Philip was that the English dowerlands simply could not be given, because they were under Eleanor's control. Having made that statement, he had to give it a patina of verisimilitude, which was not easy if Eleanor was kept in detention with no access to those lands and if the accounting records could not be made to show receipt of their revenues; hence the partial release of Eleanor and her English tour. In a similarly slippery fashion, Henry settled Marguerite's claim to the Vexin by a cash settlement, taking the Vexin as Alys's dowry for her marriage to 'whichever of his sons married her'– which he promised would now be actioned.[4]

The mention of Eleanor's maidens noted in the passage from the Pipe Rolls above brings up another sign of her increasing status. In 1177, the accounts show purchases for Eleanor and her handmaid (singular). By 1183, Eleanor is travelling with 'maidens' to Waltham; this is echoed in the records of 1186–87, with a sum noted to cover the maintenance of the 'maidens who live with the Queen at Salisbury Castle'. At some point in the intervening period, Eleanor seems to have acquired something closer to a personal household. That her relationships with these girls, probably young women of noble blood, were very close is evidenced by the charter later issued by one of them, Amiria Pantulf, sister of the Baron of Wem in Shropshire, which describes her as Eleanor's former handmaid and foster-child ('*domicella et nutrita*'); the designation of her as a foster child shows a real bond of care, above that of an employer. This echoes the earlier case of Marchisa, who appears to have been taken under Eleanor's wing after her mother was cast off, so Eleanor stood to her in place of a mother.

The case for Eleanor's maidens being of noble blood is also supported by the fact that in 1177 and again at around this time the materials supplied for Eleanor and her maiden or maidens were identical and of the highest quality (scarlet, fur, samite – a rich silk fabric). This would of course be unthinkable if they were serving girls. What this suggests is that Eleanor's earlier lifestyle as head of a household including a group of noble young people whom she was raising and educating had revived at some point during her years of detention – if indeed it had ever fully ceased. On this point it is interesting to note that, judging by the date of her father's death and the fact of his having had a second family, the chances are that Amiria, if indeed with Eleanor from her childhood, would seem to have been with her from early in her captivity.[5]

To this period we can also trace one of the most controversial references in the records. The Pipe Rolls speak of payments 'for clothes and hoods and cloaks and for the trimming for two capes of samite and for clothes of the queen and of Bellebelle, for the king's use, £55 17s, by the king's writ'. Biographers of both Henry and Eleanor have speculated that Bellebelle was a mistress of Henry, being kept in similar style to Eleanor. Certainly this was intriguing, even if this form of accounting for mistress and wife together seemed odd, and the only plausible Bellebelle (Annabel de Balliol) was long since married off. But recent scholarship suggests a far more sensible, if prosaic, explanation. It suggests that 'Bellebelle' is not a name, but a notation denoting the purchase of baubles (i.e. small items of jewellery to be given as gifts). And indeed, with Eleanor's clothing being mentioned in close proximity, it does conjure up the possibility that Henry may even have gifted some items of 'bellebelle' to Eleanor, as part of a gradual rapprochement.[6]

Turner suggests that Eleanor attended Henry's court at Windsor in 1183 in order for him to convince her to align herself with his new plans for dividing their empire. However, Henry's itinerary appears to demonstrate that he was not in England at all in 1183 after Young Henry's death. It was therefore in France and almost certainly in Eleanor's absence that Henry, late in 1183, demanded that his sons make peace with each other and first indicated that his intention was for John to take Richard's place as ruler of Aquitaine. Richard responded to this suggestion with contempt, and proceeded to hold a lavish Christmas court at Talmont, near La Rochelle, where he distributed the kinds of generous gifts likely to encourage loyalty in his vassals.[7] Eleanor therefore did not see her sons in the first winter after Young Henry's death.

But other close ties were soon to be revived, bringing a short period of pleasant domesticity to Eleanor's life. In June 1184, Eleanor's eldest daughter, Matilda, who had sought refuge for herself and her family with her father in 1182 and had since been living in Normandy, arrived in England. Matilda had apparently developed into quite a beauty; Bertran de Born, writing of her in late 1182, sighs, 'Her breast makes night seem like day; and if you could glimpse further down, the whole world would glow.' In another poem he compares her to Helen of Troy.[8]

She and her family went to Winchester, where Eleanor was then residing, and they appear to have stayed in England for nearly a year, presumably largely with Eleanor. On arrival, Matilda, who had lost a child in 1183, was heavily pregnant. She would give birth to her final son, William, at Winchester in July 1184, with Eleanor's presence to support her. Their arrival also made it possible for Eleanor finally to get to know at least some of her grandchildren: twelve-year-old Mathilde, who was betrothed to William the Lion of Scotland over the summer; eleven-year-old Heinrich; and eight-year-old Otto. Ten-year-old Lothar was the only child left in Germany, a hostage for his father's good behaviour. After the birth of William, it appears from the Pipe Rolls that Matilda and her family moved with Eleanor to her recently regained dower manor of Berkhamsted, where they spent the rest of the summer.[9]

Nor were Matilda's children the only grandchildren in Eleanor's mind; at about the same time news arrived of her second grandchild by Geoffrey – his wife Constance of Brittany gave birth to a second daughter in 1184, and the baby was named Eleanora, presumably in Eleanor's honour. This decision – a rare one so far amongst Eleanor's children – may be seen as a sign of her partial rehabilitation, or equally as a coded message of support from Geoffrey and from Constance, who had herself been Henry's effective prisoner since childhood. Given the fact that Geoffrey had been stripped of control of Brittany in the wake of the Young King's death and spent the summer of 1184 in rebellion against his father's peace by raiding into Poitou in company with sixteen-year-old John, the latter may be the more likely scenario.[10]

This period shows further evidence of Eleanor being maintained in fairly luxurious style. A considerable sum was spent for maintenance of Eleanor and Matilda when they travelled from Windsor to London. This journey may have been in November 1184, when Henry summoned a council to London to decide on a nomination to the archbishopric of York. Attendees included all three of Eleanor's surviving sons, whom Henry had summoned to London to make their peace with each other. Eleanor had probably not seen Geoffrey (now twenty-five) since Easter 1176, nor Richard since summer 1179. Also in attendance were the Count of Flanders and Matilda and her husband, as well as the expected array of churchmen. While the overt business of the meeting progressed, with Baldwin of Worcester being elected as the new archbishop, the likelihood is that Henry had another agenda: addressing the right to Aquitaine was a key issue both between Henry and his sons, and between the sons *inter se*. This made Eleanor's attendance not just polite but essential. However, her presence at the assembly meant that Eleanor was effectively back at court, and with the majority of her family. And there she remained through Christmas, with the court moving to Windsor for the event. Geoffrey apparently missed this Christmas court, being sent back to take charge of Normandy shortly before the festival, and Richard departed for Aquitaine on the cusp of the New Year.[11] Within weeks, the brothers were at war with each other again.

Henry moved on himself shortly after Christmas to Winchester, leaving Eleanor and Matilda's family in residence at Windsor. It seems likely, however, that the whole family was again expected to be present in February when Henry formally received the Patriarch of Jerusalem, Heraclius, at Reading Abbey. Heraclius, who had travelled in great state, was trying still to persuade Henry to take up the mantle of Crusader, and in an attempt to move him he went so far as to present Henry with the keys to the Holy Sepulchre. He was probably also able to bring the news to Henry and Eleanor that William Marshal had completed the crusading vow which he had undertaken to perform as Young Henry's proxy, and for his soul. It seems likely that the whole court party, including Eleanor and her daughter, as well as Henry and John, then proceeded to London to witness Heraclius' consecration of the new church of the Knights Templar, which had been modelled on the Church of the Holy Sepulchre. After the consecration, a council was held on 18 March at Clerkenwell to consider the feasibility of Henry's taking the Cross in the near future, at the premises of the Knights Hospitaller, which Heraclius also consecrated. The eventual decision was that this was not possible.[12]

However, some more positive news was emerging: Matilda's husband Henry had been pardoned, and work was afoot to enable their return to Saxony. Thereafter, the court progressed to Windsor where on 31 March Henry knighted John, now at least eighteen years old, in preparation for his first solo venture – an expedition to pacify the Irish lands which he had been assigned. Henry, Heraclius and a large suite of nobles and churchmen then moved to Dover to cross to France. They were probably here when the largest earthquake in memory convulsed England and caused severe damage to Lincoln Cathedral. Once in France, Henry moved to confront the still recalcitrant Richard, who had recently met and allied with Alphonso of Aragon, with a view to making common cause against Raymond of Toulouse – a part of a reworking of alliances in Occitania which was to leave Eleanor's contemporary Ermengarde of Narbonne cruelly isolated.[13] For now, Eleanor, away from the political manoeuvrings of the Plantagenet empire, was left behind with Matilda and her family, probably in London.

Within a month they were all on the move again, having been sent for by Henry, this time to France. The Pipe Rolls record expenses for Eleanor and Matilda and her husband at Portchester and Portsmouth as well as the expenses of the royal *esnecca* and seven other ships to carry the party and their attendants and baggage. It was Eleanor's first trip across the Channel in more than ten years. The reasons for the summons were twofold. Henry had plans both to forward Henry of Saxony's return to his lands and to use Eleanor in his continuing dispute with Richard. His scheme was to restore Eleanor to the rule of Aquitaine in her own right, meanwhile recalling Richard to be under his own eye. Howden reports that Henry threatened Richard that if he did not hand the lands over to Eleanor she would come with an army to seize the land. Richard did so, and came to court 'like a tamed son' – but then returned to Poitou technically as his mother's delegate. In fact, Eleanor had no direct input into the course of events there, and Henry was in effective control. She did not actually visit Poitou at this time, but remained in Henry's court in Normandy.[14]

Eleanor's positive acts at this point appear to have been limited to making two grants in favour of Fontevraud, probably during May when Henry was based at Chinon. One, made 'with the assent and at the will of her lord Henry King of England and of Richard, Geoffrey and John, her sons', granted £100 per year from her Poitevin revenues, invoking as its reason a desire for the salvation of Henry's soul and those of Eleanor and her children. The second grant, which no longer survives, was a foundation – £50 was given for the founding of a priory affiliated with the abbey at La Rochelle – a town which had remained resolutely loyal to Henry in the upheavals of the previous years. On their face, these show Eleanor acting as the ruler of Aquitaine; but the evidence suggests these were, like her tour of her dower lands, publicity exercises orchestrated by Henry. He could tell the world that Eleanor was ruling Aquitaine, but the reality was recorded by Eleanor in coded terms; she acted 'at his will', a form of words never previously used by her. Furthermore, reinforcing the point, Henry specifically confirmed these grants himself. With Richard also occasionally making the point that he was Count of Poitou by confirming grants, some applicants found themselves with three effectively identical grants from the three notional rulers of the area. One scholar describes Eleanor's role in these documents as being 'only a plaything in Henry's hands'; that description cannot well be contradicted.[15]

Nonetheless, for the first time in years Eleanor was apparently meeting with her vassals: eight of her Poitevin nobles feature in the witness list. Among them are her cousin the Viscount of Châtellerault, Geoffrey, Lord of Tonnay-Charente; Ralph, lord of Tonney-Boutonne; and the seneschal of Poitou, Robert de Montmirail, her son Richard's chief deputy. Another Poitevin witness was Chalon de Rochefort, who would become a notable member of Eleanor's military household during her last years. It also seems possible that her visit to France offered the opportunity for her old clerk, Jordan, to return to her service, since after her return he appears on the Pipe Rolls once more, being paid £24 for her expenses.[16]

Eleanor's locations between this point and her return to England in late April 1186 are unclear. Turner infers that Eleanor visited the tomb of Young Henry at Rouen, and this seems credible; indeed, Eleanor would almost certainly have wished to visit her son's grave. Until recently it has not been possible to fill in the remaining gaps at all. However, recent scholarship has given a new aspect to these days. For in 2016 a psalter in the National Library of the Netherlands, then known as the Fécamp Psalter, was posited by a researcher, Jesus Viejo, as a commission by Eleanor. It is now known as 'the Eleanor Psalter'.[17]

The reasons for the ascription are essentially as follows. Firstly the book, which is a beautiful production of the highest quality, was commissioned by a noble lady who is pictured on the page opposite the Beatus page. That commission was undertaken by the abbey at Fécamp in Normandy. Therefore, logically the commissioner must be a lady of the highest status in Normandy. Secondly, the document has visual parallels to the St Radegonde depiction often said to be Eleanor. In particular, both the commissioner of the psalter and the nobleman pictured as the illustration to April wear garments with the exact same blue-and-white geometric motif as is sported by the St Radegonde depiction – and which is also depicted on the enamel memorial on the tomb of Geoffrey le Bel. Thirdly, the saints mentioned, which include St Thomas Becket, St Hilaire (patron saint of Poitiers) and St Radegonde herself, point towards Eleanor. Finally, there is just one very similar psalter in existence. It is known as the Helmershausen Psalter, and was verifiably produced for Eleanor's daughter Matilda, probably after her return to Saxony. There are other, more subtle points arising out of the depictions which can be found to resonate with the Angevin position – for example the depiction of King David, which can be said to reference both his struggles and the death of his beloved son.

The attribution is not perfectly safe – in particular the parts which are dependent on the St Radegonde mural and the cape lining are (for reasons detailed later) very weak – but it should still be considered a reasonable one. There are other problems with it – for example the absence in the surviving charter evidence of any donation to Fécamp by Eleanor, and the absence of any reference in the psalter to St Valerie, whom one might well expect Eleanor to include. But the material is fairly compelling, and excuses can be found for these absences. A charter may well have been lost, or this may have been a cash transaction from Eleanor's revived dower funds, or the commission may have been a present from Matilda, knowing that her departure was imminent. As for St Valerie, this could reflect real doubts as to the veracity of the story, or a political move, given Limoges' recent intransigence in its dealings with the Plantagenets.

But there are points in favour of the identification which may be added to those which Viejo has marshalled. As far as the roster of saints is concerned, the feast days of Saint Martial and Bordeaux's Saint André are also marked, as is that of Saint Laurence – celebrated at Poitiers, and a saint to whom Eleanor was later to show a particular devotion. There is also another feast day (that of St Marie ad Mures on 13 May), which is only celebrated at Poitiers. But in particular, as will be described below, the document's provenance also appears to point a link with Eleanor, which is as close to definitive as can well be.

It therefore appears that Eleanor and Matilda spent many happy hours over summer 1185 collaborating with the scriptorium at Fécamp in the design of this beautiful book, which so inspired Matilda that she would commission her own version on her return to her husband's lands.

That return probably occurred at some point late in 1185. It was, however, only a partial return. Matilda and Henry the Lion returned to Germany; but they left behind all of the children who had travelled with them, except the baby William. The boys, being of an age to be trained for war, were absorbed into Henry's household; but Eleanor will have had numerous opportunities to see them. Mathilde, rapidly approaching marriageable age, remained with Eleanor. There was little opportunity for Eleanor to see her sons: John was still in England, awaiting a good moment to depart again for Ireland; Richard was busy in Aquitaine, where he claimed to be driving off Raymond of Toulouse; and Geoffrey was cementing good relations with the King of France and intriguing against his brothers and father.[18]

Henry spent most of the time in Normandy, with Christmas at Domfront and further negotiations with Philip of France regarding Alys's marriage (now again said to be with Richard) and Marguerite's dowry at Gisors in February and March. At some point early in 1186 William Marshal seems to have reappeared; he had been absent since Young Henry's death, having undertaken to go on Crusade in his master's place. Frustratingly, there is no detail of his reunion with Eleanor in the Histoire, which tends to focus on action. But we know that Henry – possibly with a foreboding of trouble to come and the need for good men – welcomed Marshal back and began to give him some concrete preferment, including the wardship of a minor heiress, Heloise of Kendal, and lands abutting hers.[19]

The reason for Eleanor's return to England in April 1186 seems plain; however much her relations with Henry were improved, he would not be minded to leave her and Richard on the continent when she and Henry appear to have been at odds regarding the future of her lands. Despite the terms of his agreement with Philip in April, which postulated Richard and Alys as rulers of Aquitaine, Henry seems to have revived his plan to remove Eleanor's lands from Richard's hands and give them to John (and perhaps understandably, in the face of the death of Young Henry without heirs). While this plan did not surface in the records at this point, it seems that Henry had this in his eye. Perhaps he also had in mind that Eleanor was more than a pawn – she was also potentially an excellent hostage for Philip and Geoffrey if they chose to make mischief. Eleanor was therefore deemed safer in England.

On her return in company with Henry in April, Eleanor took with her Matilda's thirteen-year-old daughter Mathilde; the adoption of this name in place of her birth name, Richenza, came at this point, suggesting that a French marriage was already planned for her, the Scottish one having failed for lack of a papal dispensation.

Where Eleanor was located on her return is not clear, but it seems unlikely that she initially travelled with Henry beyond Winchester. He set off on one of his peregrinations, taking in Oxford, Kent, Nottinghamshire, Shropshire, Carlisle, Worcestershire and Staffordshire before his return to Woodstock. Eleanor's absence from this tour and this stay can be inferred from the fact that she is not mentioned as being present at the marriage of Mathilde's previous fiancé, William the Lion, King of Scots, to the daughter of the Viscount of Beaumont le Roger – a major event at which her presence would have been expected.[20] It was at Woodstock that Henry learned of the death of Geoffrey, who on 19 August 1186 was fatally wounded in a tournament at Paris; interestingly, by this stage he had plainly forged a relationship with his half-sister Marie of Champagne, with whom he had attended an anniversary service for Young Henry in 1183, and who now in turn attended his funeral and endowed a memorial service for 'my brother'. He left behind the babies Matilde and Eleanora, and a pregnant wife. The next March she would give birth to an heir, who would be named Arthur. Eleanor's reaction to the death of a second adult son is not recorded in any of the chronicles, and Geoffrey's death attracted none of the outpouring of public grief which had accompanied that of Young Henry.

It seems likely that Eleanor was throughout this period in residence at Winchester – certainly she is noted as present there when the king visited early in October 1186. However, while Eleanor and Henry did not reside together, it is not unlikely that in the middle of that month Eleanor accompanied Henry to Reading, the burial site thirty years before of their first son, William, and thence to Amesbury where, late in November 1186, he introduced the nuns sent from the mother house of Fontevraud to populate the revived abbey which had benefitted from her dower revenues during the period of her formal incarceration. This would suggest that they spent the best part of two months in the same household, something that is perhaps reflected in the reference in the Waverley Chronicle (written from an abbey in Surrey) to a reconciliation between Henry and Eleanor.[21]

As Eleanor confronted the mortality of another son, and spent a prolonged period with Henry, she must surely have also begun to anticipate that she was likely to outlive her second husband. Eleanor was now in her sixties, whereas Henry was not yet fifty-five. But Eleanor's years of relative tranquillity as a captive and her more moderate habits now began to tell. Henry had lived at full stretch since his teens; and this period was plainly one of high stress as he was forced to contend with his maturing sons, as well as the emergence of a truly formidable opponent in Philip of France. Accounts of Henry from this period make it clear that his health was failing. He had battled his weight for years, and was losing the battle. That made it more difficult for him to maintain his habitual level of exercise. He was also haunted by the legacies of old injuries, including a sore leg, which again kept him from his wonted levels of activity. It was sometime in this period that he developed the agonising and debilitating anal fistula which was to be the bane of his final months.[22]

Henry's Christmas was spent at Guildford, with John being the only son present. However, the party included (apparently for the first time since his pardon) the Earl of Leicester – and inferentially his formidable wife Petronilla. Very possibly this was intended to be an opportunity to test their loyalty as Henry planned to return to confront his problems in France. Eleanor's presence is not documented, but is not unlikely.[23]

However, when Henry and John moved to France in February 1187, Eleanor was left behind. Following Geoffrey's death, Henry had made clear his intention to move John into place in Aquitaine, something both Eleanor and Richard opposed. Because of this, she could not be brought to France but must remain incommunicado in England. While Henry and her sons met in February and then later in spring with Philip of France, Eleanor disappears again from the record. However, we at least know from the records that her clerk, Jordan, was still with her, which indicates that her household was no longer skeletal – though it must be assumed that her correspondence was monitored to preclude further encouragement to Richard.[24]

During this period, with Henry just about holding his sons on his side but failing to agree with Philip, and both sides preparing for the war which briefly flared and fizzled out in summer of 1187, Eleanor was not entirely at Winchester – the Pipe Rolls record her presence in Dorset and Somerset, probably inspecting her dower lands. She is also noted in London. This latter visit may have been made in preparation for the dispatch of young Mathilde, who was sent to France late in 1187, presumably in preparation for her engagement to the Count of Perche, a close associate of Philip. It is possible that Eleanor may have seen William Marshal again during 1187, for in this year, following his award of lands and a wardship in Cumbria, he visited both and confirmed a charter.[25] However, Marshal's stay in England was brief; he was to return to Henry's service by the next year.

From the records of Eleanor's household, this period looks quiet and fairly optimistic. Not only had she regained her dower properties, but her queen's gold revenues were restored. Furthermore, a regular pension amounting to around £20 per month was paid to her for her expenses. She also received a generous clothing allowance for herself and 'her maidens'. But summer and autumn 1187 was actually a highly charged time that would have a profound influence on Eleanor's future. As in the early part of her captivity, she must have awaited the arrival of news from the continent with considerable trepidation. Following the peace reached between Henry and Philip in June, Richard, up until then siding with his father, decamped to Paris where he and Philip forged what appeared to be a close friendship; it was some weeks before he would return and re-pledge his fealty to Henry, and the seeds of their final alienation had been sown.[26]

Later in the year came news of huge significance to Eleanor. For while all of this was happening in France, the fate of the Kingdom of Jerusalem hung in the balance. On 3 July, Guy de Lusignan – Eleanor's attacker of 1168, a thorn in the flesh of Angevin rule and now husband to Queen Sybilla, granddaughter of Queen Melisende – decided to advance to the relief of his city of Tiberias. His experience was even worse than that of Eleanor so many years before. Exhausted by the blazing heat of the summer and the constant attacks of Muslim archers, his army was forced to a halt on the plain of Hattin, with no water available. The next day, the sun rose to show them surrounded by the enemy. The army was annihilated, and Guy de Lusignan captured. The sequel was inevitable: on 2 October 1187, Jerusalem fell to troops led by the experienced and skilful ruler of Egypt and Syria, one Al-Malik al-Nasir Salah ed-Din Yusuf – perhaps better known as Saladin.

The news reached France by autumn, and the very first prince to commit himself to Crusade was Richard, son of a Crusader and great-grandson of a King of Jerusalem, who took the Cross from the Archbishop of Tours immediately on hearing of this catastrophe, vowing that he would dedicate his life to liberating the Holy Sepulchre. So great was his haste to do so that he neglected to seek Henry's permission – though it is hard to imagine that Henry, in default of his own crusading vow and the subject of Heraclius' pleas for help, could well have refused permission. Henry was stunned upon hearing Richard's decision, refusing to see anyone for days.[27]

What Eleanor felt can hardly have been less acute, given her own knowledge of the dangers of crusading. Yet Henry was reconciled to the idea; he and Philip both took the Cross in early 1188, in response to an impassioned sermon delivered by the Archbishop of Tyre – one of the remaining Christian cities clinging to its independence. When Henry and Richard met again late in January, the talk was all of the Crusade and raising taxes for it. Notably, it was agreed that the only women to accompany the Crusade would be washerwomen of good character.[28] It would seem that there was no role for Eleanor or her successors.

Nor is there much sign of Eleanor rendezvousing with Henry on his return in early 1188. Throughout the period Henry travelled in areas well away from Eleanor's usual residences – arriving at Winchelsea, and then heading north for Geddington before returning to Clarendon, Woodstock and London. The only possible meetings between them were in February, when he appears to have stopped in Winchester, or in early July 1188, when he may have stopped briefly at Salisbury before his return to France. The ambiguity of the evidence concerning whether there was a meeting echoes the general lack of clarity about the extent to which there was reconciliation, at least to the point of a restoration of civility. It seems likely that at least one such meeting did take place and that Henry, following a gradual thaw in the past couple of years, would not leave the country without at least speaking with Eleanor. Given his failing health, it seems both would be aware that it might be their last meeting, as indeed it was to prove. Having narrowly escaped death in a Channel storm in his crossing, Henry would commit himself to a final disastrous campaign in July 1188.[29]

The initial purpose of Henry's return was to deal with the war which Richard was pursuing – with less than perfect success – against the Count of Toulouse, who had upped the stakes by persuading Philip of France to support him. Henry had gathered a substantial force to take with him to deal with the military stalemate which had developed. Over the summer Henry and Richard campaigned against Philip, but were steadily driven apart by Philip's negotiating strategy, which was to offer much to Henry in exchange for the cession of Richard's gains in Toulouse. By autumn, Richard was negotiating directly with Philip and seeking recognition as heir to the throne in exchange for his promise to marry Alys, who was now twenty-eight years old and still unmarried. Meeting at Bonsmoulins in November 1188, Henry failed to accept this stacked deck, upon which Richard swore fealty for his lands and conquests as well as Normandy and Anjou to Philip. Eleanor is highly unlikely to have known of this in advance, but news will have reached her by Christmas, which she spent in England while Henry, deserted by much of his court, held the season in Saumur. By early 1189, Henry had fallen ill and was unable to attend the next peace conference scheduled for January.[30]

Although Eleanor's year was not marked by great events, or much movement, there is a likelihood that at some point in 1188 she was joined at Winchester by her grandson William, Matilda's youngest son and the only one of her grandchildren whose birth Eleanor had attended. We know of his presence because records survive for his maintenance. It is therefore likely that Eleanor was at this time heading up not merely a household of her young ladies but also some sort of nursery establishment including boys of William's age. This likelihood is reinforced by slightly later evidence of the presence of Eleanora of Brittany (born in 1184) in Eleanor's household. Eleanora probably joined the household at about this time, when her mother, Constance, was married against her will to the eighteen-year-old Earl of Chester. Her sister Matilde had died shortly before.[31]

In early 1189, Eleanor was probably joined by Matilda's husband, Henry. He had declined to follow the Emperor Frederick on Crusade, choosing exile instead. He will have been able to bring Eleanor the latest news from the continent, both as to Richard's alliance with Philip and his refusal to hear from his sick father.[32] It is unlikely that Matilda joined her husband on his journey. She was to die in Germany in late June, aged just thirty-three. It seems likely that she was left behind because of a pregnancy and died in childbirth, though the sources are not explicit. She became the fourth of Eleanor's children to predecease her.

Matilda's death barely preceded that of Henry himself. It was not until after Easter that Henry's health permitted him to attend a conference. By Whitsun the Church had convened an arbitration panel near Le Mans under the leadership of John of Agnani. Philip and Richard proposed three pre-conditions – Richard's marriage to Alys, his recognition as heir and the committing of John to Crusade – but Henry rejected them and withdrew to Le Mans. There, in mid-June, he was pursued by Richard and Philip and escaped them only thanks to the heroics of William Marshal (according to William, at any rate), who cut back to attack Richard directly but chose to kill his horse from under him rather than attack the man bodily when he perceived that Richard wore no armour.

Henry, sick again, fell back on Chinon, where from his sickbed he could do nothing to stop Richard and Philip overrunning his lands. On 3 July 1189, with Tours having fallen, he was forced to accept the pair's terms, dragging himself to a conference at Ballon though he could barely sit a horse – indeed he had to leave the meeting in a litter. On 6 July, just hours after he heard that Richard had been joined by John, for whose rights Henry had so often fought, Henry II died at Chinon.[33]

Eleanor was finally free. It was just over fifteen years since she had sailed to captivity in England.

10

The Queen

Igitur ex mandato regine Alianor, quae tunc temporis regebat Angliam...

[This was done by the command of Queen Eleanor, who at that time ruled England.]

Gervase of Canterbury, i 515

Although Henry died after Matilda, the importance of the news in England probably ensured that it reached Eleanor within days, and therefore before the news of her beloved daughter's death. The upheaval caused by Henry's demise may at least have proved some distraction from what must have been a great grief to Eleanor, as well as to Matilda's husband and son, probably still in residence with Eleanor.

Quick though it was, news of Henry's death did not come fast enough for Eleanor to travel to France for the funeral – or even to have a say in where Henry was interred. The Histoire recounts how the old king died in the middle of a heatwave – in which circumstances no delay could be contemplated – and recounts the considerations which were run through in the funeral arrangements, decided by William Marshal and the others who were with the king. Henry's own wish had been to be buried at Grandmont in the Limousin, that abbey whose austerities he much admired. Since 1170 he had been making plans for his burial there, sending workmen to put in place the structural changes to accommodate the tomb he planned, and sending a new lead roof to cover the extension. His will of 1182 reiterated his desire to be buried there.

But Grandmont was near Limoges, and that was over 120 miles away – much too far in the summer heat. The same went both for Reading – Henry I's intended royal necropolis and the burial site of Henry's own first child with Eleanor – and Rouen – resting place of his mother and second son. Le Mans, in the heart of Anjou and the site of Geoffrey le Bel's tomb, was also over 80 miles away, and the territory was currently overrun by Richard's and Philip's men. Fontevraud, by contrast, was only 12 miles away, and since 1187 it had been under the direction of Henry's own cousin Mathildis of Flanders. But Fontevraud was a controversial choice. It was, of course, very much a female-dominated organisation; it was effectively Eleanor's preferred institution; it was technically within the diocese of Poitiers; and it was a remote, unconventional place. Gerald of Wales specifically noted the irony of Henry, who had attempted to immure Eleanor in Fontevraud, being 'left to return to dust in that same out of the way place, unworthy of his royal majesty'.[1]

This may account for the fact that, while the obsequies were performed in style, with the coffin being borne to the abbey by a retinue of noblemen headed by William Marshal and Henry's illegitimate son Geoffroy, the arrangements for Henry's interment were somewhat basic. It seems likely that it was intended for the location of the burial to be reviewed, and for Henry to later be moved to his preferred home, as had happened with Young Henry. That this never happened was almost certainly Eleanor's decision. Thus, though Eleanor played no part in the decision to bury her estranged husband in Fontevraud, the fact that he lies there today is the result of a positive decision on Eleanor's part. So too is the way that he is portrayed there, as will become apparent.

These facts are significant, and also indicative of the huge change in Eleanor's life brought about by Henry's death. At the time of Henry's death, she was, if not formally a prisoner, very much a pawn. From July 1189, she emerges as a queen on the chessboard. She becomes a major force in politics and a decisionmaker of considerable power within the Plantagenet empire as a whole. References to Eleanor have thus far been few and far between, inconsistently placed between the chronicles; from here on in, Eleanor's actions are covered by multiple chroniclers. This accession to real power is reflected in the charter evidence. Before 1189, there are sixty-six recorded acts and charters of Eleanor covering the whole period since she succeeded as Duchess of Aquitaine. After 1189, there are more than sixty charters issued for Aquitaine alone and a total of over ninety.[2]

It is important to remember that in one sense Eleanor's new role was not as controversial or contrary to convention as is often suggested. As already noted, it was not uncommon for women to exercise power even during their married years in the southern territories of France in Iberia – and of course in Jerusalem.[3] But even in England and Normandy, where female power had been tailing off, the emergence of women as greater forces in family and property issues after widowhood was not unique to Eleanor. The comparison with Adela of Blois, the mother of Theobald the Great and Stephen, who ruled Blois as regent until her sons' majority, may be a little unfair, since she inhabits a period where female power was somewhat better tolerated, but there are more valid ones. In England, other notable widows were in operation at the same time: RaGena de Aragon has analysed the careers of some of the foremost, including Petronilla of Leicester, her daughter-in-law Loretta of Leicester, Isabel of Oxford and Beatrice de Say. Similarly, Maud of Chester had ruled her dower lands for many years; and in northern France, Eleanor's own daughter Marie was the ruler of Champagne for her absent son for many years. In this sense Eleanor was simply *primus inter pares* – the most elevated example of a fairly standard situation; or, as Michael Evans puts it, Eleanor represented 'one end of a continuum, not an outlier'. This oft-overlooked fact is actually reflected in the lack of negative treatment of her actions as a widow; as a married woman, Eleanor's fairly rare independent actions attracted a firestorm of criticism. But from this point on, her treatment by the contemporaneous chronicles is much more sympathetic than it had hitherto been. The chroniclers saw nothing strange about an aristocratic widow exercising power in support of her sons.[4]

The relative normalcy of her position is also reflected by William Marshal's record that long before he arrived with direct messages from King Richard (with whom he had reconciled) those wielding power on behalf of Henry had moved to release Eleanor from whatever constraints she had previously been under, and she had assumed the position of regent de facto. A real flavour of this is seen in Howden's description: 'Circulating with a queenly court, she set out from city to city and castle to castle just as it pleased her.'[5]

But Eleanor's position should really be regarded as one better than that of regent. In fact, she would never formally hold the regency for her son – unlike Philip of France's mother, Adela of Champagne. Eleanor's position was actually extraordinary in that she appears to have been regarded as a regnant queen, with no further authority needed. This is reflected in charters of Ranulf de Glanville from this period, which state that they are made with the agreement of Eleanor ('by the Queen's precept'), as if, justiciar though he was, her authority was superior to his.[6] It is seen also in the fact that Eleanor continued to use her regnal seal, in which she appears as 'Eleanor, by the Grace of God Queen of England, Duchess of the Angevins'. The imagery of that seal reinforces the message that Eleanor was presenting herself not as queen mother or queen regent but as a queen in her own right: she is depicted crowned and deploying the orb capped with cross and bird which was part of the seals of Henry I, Stephen and Henry II – but not, it will be recalled, of earlier queens.

The authority which was naturally accorded to Eleanor was to be fully reinforced by Richard. Ralph of Diss reports how she was entrusted with full power: 'indeed he issued instructions to the princes of the realm, almost in the style of a general edict, that the Queen's word should be law in all matters'.[7]

Perhaps what is most striking about Eleanor's role from this point on is not the fact that she exercised power but that she did so with such notable success while facing so many difficulties. After years in the shadows, Eleanor did not merely embrace the challenge – she excelled.

As for what Eleanor was actually doing, there is little contemporaneous primary record, but the reliable Roger of Howden states that she traversed the kingdom and despatched royal representatives to the counties to release those imprisoned by those acts of Henry where he was governing according to his will and not by the accepted law of the realm, while those accused of a crime under English law were to be released on bail if they could find sureties for their appearance at trial. She also despatched agents to take oaths of fidelity to the new king.[8]

This freeing of prisoners is often said to be simply a symbolic act on Eleanor's part, based on her own delight in once more being at liberty, and indeed Roger's claim that 'she had learned from her own experience how painful captivity is for humankind and how sweet it is to emerge from prison with a joyful heart' sounds like it may even have been borrowed from Eleanor's own proclamation; but the distinction drawn between those imprisoned under the proper laws of the realm and those incarcerated as a result of Henry's excessive acts is interesting. It reflects an understanding of the issues which were concerning people in England, one of which was Henry's excessive use of power and punishment in his later years. Furthermore, the freeing of prisoners was calculated to increase both Richard's popularity and Eleanor's own, as well as her mystique. This deftness in capturing the public mood should not surprise us, for Eleanor had, as we have seen, spent some twenty of the last thirty years in England and for the last decade and more she had been in a situation which insulated her from the sycophants who normally surround a monarch or an heir. The result was that Eleanor was probably better placed to understand the national feeling across classes than any monarch preceding her.[9]

This feel for current issues can also be seen in her moves to relieve abbeys of the obligation to provide free fodder for the king's horses, and to curb the excessive punishments being imposed for forest law infringements, which had been carried out with Henry's tacit approval. Eleanor is also credited with the restoration of the Earl of Leicester's lands, but this is a mistake; the restoration of the remainder of his lands was an act of Richard prior to his return to England.[10]

It was probably also in this period, and with the same motives, that plans to standardise weights, measures and coinage across the country were announced by Eleanor; this was a subject whose advantages Eleanor, as a long-term resident of two prominent market towns, would have had ample opportunity to consider. The yardstick for foods was to be 'one good horse-load'; measures for wine, ale and other drinks were likewise to be identical, albeit 'according to the diversity of liquors'; and woollen cloth was to be of similar quantity across the piece. The formal legislation encapsulating this decision, the Assize of Measures, was introduced in 1196.[11]

The result, as was doubtless intended, was an upswing of enthusiasm for the rule of Richard, who was commonly known in England as 'the Poitevin', reflecting his lack of contact with the place of his birth. As Roger of Howden says, in cadences anticipating St Francis's famous prayer, 'Whom Henry had dispossessed, Richard had restored; whom Henry had banished, Richard had recalled; whom Henry had imprisoned, Richard had set free; whom Henry had afflicted with penalties, Richard had sent away rejoicing.'[12] But the reality is that these were Eleanor's works, done to promote her son's future popularity.

Something we can infer, though not entirely confirm, is that Eleanor immediately put in hand preparations for Richard's coronation, for such an event would require months of preparation. The fact that she is the person who issued the relevant summonses for nobles to attend indicates her involvement in the planning. That it was ready to take place on 3 September is testament to Eleanor's hard work and organisational skills. It also seems likely that Eleanor was the person responsible for commissioning and approving the music composed for the occasion, which announced 'the age of gold's return' and triumphed that 'God has ordained a King greatly desired by us'.[13]

It is important to note that throughout all this, Eleanor did not forget Henry. Among her first acts were ones making provision for alms to be distributed on Henry's behalf, and money to be given to the nuns of Amesbury and the Carthusian brothers whom he had installed on her lands, to ensure that prayers were said for his soul; a further grant was then made, apparently at her instance, by Richard to Amesbury in late November 1189.[14]

One of the first visitors to reach Eleanor was William Marshal, who shortly after reconciling with Richard was despatched by him to England with a dual mission: convey to Eleanor Richard's formal authority and take possession of his bride. Richard had awarded him the right to marry Isabelle of Pembroke – one of the richest heiresses in the kingdom, probably only fifteen years old, and therefore a generous reward even for Marshal's years of loyalty to the family. Again, Marshal was the man able to give an account of the death of a member of Eleanor's family and was able to tell Eleanor not just how Henry died but how and why the decision had been made to bury him at Fontevraud. It appears from Ralph of Diss that Marshal was also the person charged with conveying the formal edict to all the barons of the kingdom that they must obey Eleanor's commands. Following his meeting with Eleanor in Winchester, he went to claim Isabelle from her residence at the Tower of London, where she was in the custody of Ranulf de Glanville. This fact implies that Eleanor had not yet absorbed this particular household – which probably also included John's intended, Hawise of Gloucester; Denise de Deols, the heiress of Berry; and the ever controversial Alys – into her own. This absorption nonetheless took place before Richard returned, arriving at Portsmouth on 13 August 1189 – interestingly the feast day of St Radegonde – with John.[15]

It is therefore likely that Eleanor met Richard at Winchester in mid-August.[16] This meeting is regularly depicted as a huge emotional reunion, with much made of Richard as Eleanor's favourite child. Some caution should be exercised here. The arguments advanced by some, including Pernoud, that Eleanor never referred to any other child as '*dilectissimus*' or '*carissimus*' (dearest or most beloved) has now been comprehensively debunked. Eleanor referred to all her children by these appellations – and most often after their deaths.[17] There is simply nothing in the record which justifies a conclusion that Richard was Eleanor's favourite child. If Eleanor had a favourite we should more probably look to her daughters, who spent more of their youth with her; Richard, like Young Henry, Geoffrey and John, was moved into a separate household for education in knightly skills around the age of seven. The girls, however, remained with Eleanor largely until their marriages, and there is compelling evidence that close bonds existed between them. As we have seen, Matilda had plainly been keen to spend time with her mother when fate allowed – and the coming years would offer parallel evidence for Leonor and Joanna. However, the combination of liberation and reunion with the son she probably knew best, courtesy of their joint rule in Poitou between 1168 and 1173, will no doubt have been a real joy to Eleanor.

Ralph of Diss has perhaps most memorably captured the imagination of subsequent writers on Eleanor when he described this reunion as one which revealed the truth of one of the so-called prophecies of Merlin: 'The eagle of the broken covenant shall rejoice in her third nesting.' He says that it was in fulfilment of that prophecy that Eleanor, the eagle whose wings stretched out over England and France, was restored to her freedom and power by her third son. Again, caution is needed; this interpretation involves

entirely ignoring Eleanor's daughters and her first son by Henry –
Richard was actually Eleanor's sixth child.[18]

Aside from preparations for the coronation, the immediate
order of the day was marriage. Shortly after Richard's arrival, the
wedding of the sixteen-year-old Denise de Deols took place under
Eleanor's auspices at Salisbury. Denise, like Isabelle of Pembroke,
was married to a loyal supporter of the Plantagenets. In her case
the lucky man was Andrew de Chauvigny, a relation of the Bernard
de Chauvigny who had served first Eleanor as chamberlain and
brother to Richard's chamberlain Geoffrey de Chauvigny. Andrew
had suffered a broken arm in the face-off between Marshal and
Richard in Henry's last days.[19] At about the same time, William
Marshal was married to Isabelle de Clare; however, its separate
reference in Roger of Howden's chronicle suggests that this was
not a double wedding, and the evidence points to it taking place
in London – possibly even before Richard's return. Following
this celebration it seems likely that Eleanor moved with Richard
to Marlborough – for it was there, on 29 August 1189, that
John was married to Hawise, in defiance of a veto interposed by
Archbishop Baldwin of Canterbury on the grounds of the couple's
consanguinity.[20]

The next stop in Richard's itinerary was Windsor, where
Eleanor is recorded joining with Hubert Walter (bishop-designate
of Salisbury) and Ranulf de Glanville in opposing the promotion
of his half-brother Geoffroy to the archbishopric of York. This
dispute reflects one of Richard's priorities, namely to ensure
that this half-brother – unwillingly destined for the Church but
more inclined to politics and war, and ultimately the closest
of Henry's sons to him – was forced to be ordained. Geoffroy
had been appointed Bishop of Lincoln as early as 1173, but
had refused ordination, and had served as Henry's chancellor
in the 1180s. One of Richard's first acts had been to ensure
Geoffroy's election as Archbishop of York, but still Geoffroy
had resisted ordination. Richard was, despite this resistance and
the representations made to him by Eleanor and the authorities
spiritual and temporal, determined to take Geoffroy out of the
running for any usurpation of his throne, and hence Geoffroy
was ordained.[21]

The coronation on 3 September is the first for which a
detailed record exists, so we know that Richard and Eleanor

processed together through London to St Paul's and thence to Westminster. We also know that Richard entered the abbey church in a procession behind Godfrey de Lucy, who carried the cap; John 'the Marshal' (older brother of William) with the gold spurs; William Marshal with the sceptre with cross; the Earl of Salisbury with the sceptre with dove; and John and the earls of Huntingdon and Leicester carrying the three ceremonial swords. We even know the words to some of the music which serenaded Richard as he was crowned, lauding him as the flower of chivalry and a new-day star who would herald a time of prosperity. However, the coronation is controversial for the significance that commentators have attached to the exclusion of Jews and women from the event.

So far as the exclusion of women is concerned, some have looked to make this a signifier of Richard's sexual preferences; but the absence of any comment on it at the time makes this unlikely. Richard's biographer John Gillingham argues that there was nothing unusual about this, and that the chronicler Matthew Paris was correct in his later explanation that the exclusion of women from the coronation as a feast day was traditional and in the Trojan tradition. He suggests that women were never included in coronations.[22] With all respect, this seems unconvincing – not least when the record of items purchased for Eleanor suggests she did have a role in the three days of celebration which surrounded the coronation. The Pipe Rolls show robes for Eleanor and her attendants, including Alys and Isabelle Marshal, at a cost of over £7, of which the majority went on a beautiful cape of silk trimmed with squirrel and sable for Eleanor's use. Indeed, there is some dispute as to whether Eleanor attended the coronation, with two reliable sources in conflict. Roger of Howden says no women attended, whereas Ralph of Diss maintains that Eleanor attended at the request of the earls and the barons. Normally one would simply prefer Roger of Howden, as a particularly reliable source; however, we know (from Howden) that Ralph of Diss was actually present, standing in for the Bishop of London, so he really should be correct.[23]

However, there are some factors relating to Richard's female dependants which might well have militated strongly in favour of a decision to exclude all women from the coronation itself. The first was the status of Alys. At the time of the coronation,

Richard was again pledged to marry Alys; this had been agreed as recently as 22 July directly between Richard and Philip. If women were involved, some status would have to be given to Alys – and indeed the question of why the marriage and her coronation should not all be wrapped up together would present themselves. And yet it is likely that by now the issue of Alys's relations with Richard's father had surfaced, and the marriage was therefore unwelcome. Alys was in Eleanor's household by this stage, and Eleanor will have had ample opportunity to question those who had had custody of her – and indeed to arrange for a physical examination of Alys. By excluding women Richard avoided the Alys issue, which would be extremely useful if he was not minded to marry her.

Secondly, there was Eleanor herself. Richard had taken Aquitaine as Eleanor's deputy and under her aegis. Only a few years before, he had been made to surrender it to her – at Henry's instigation, but again reinforcing his subordinate role. Eleanor remained a consecrated Queen of England. If she attended, the coronation would risk looking like another subordinate event. Indeed, the evidence for Henry's coronation suggests that the correct mode would have required Eleanor to process to the abbey already crowned. Moreover, Eleanor had a long track record with the people of England which Richard utterly lacked; this is alluded to by Ralph of Diss's comment that the baronage sought Eleanor's involvement, suggesting that she was highly regarded by the English barons. Only with Eleanor absent could Richard – a relative stranger to the English people – be truly centre stage. And that is what he was. The bare-chested Richard was anointed with holy oil before being dressed in his coronation garments, and when the decisive moment came he was the prime mover. Anticipating Napoleon, he took the crown from the altar and then gave it to the archbishop, making the Church's role accessory and subordinate.[24] However, Eleanor will have come into her own in the subsequent feasting and celebrations, and it is probably this which is reflected in Ralph of Diss's comment as to Eleanor's attendance.

As for the exclusion of the Jews, this was probably a sign of political, if not actual, anti-Semitism. Financial times were hard – Henry had already obtained what was known as 'the Saladin tithe' in aid of the proposed Crusade, but Richard, himself deeply committed to Crusade, will have been aware by the time of the coronation that it was not enough and that he would have to get people on-side for further taxation. As Flori notes by reference to the passive approach of the contemporaneous chroniclers, hostility to the Jewish population always played well at such times – all the more so when what was in view was a holy war against the infidel.[25] So in London, as the coronation proceeded, mobs hunted down the Jewish population, stole their possessions, torched their houses and made attempts at forcible conversion; and similar outrages took place in Norwich, Lincoln Stamford and Bishop's Lynn.[26] The perpetrators may well have been encouraged by a rumour – never effectively denied, although the identified perpetrators were later punished – that the king himself favoured such action.[27] Nor did Richard's response, although condemnatory, prevent the later persecution of York's Jews, which led to a mass suicide on 16 March 1190.[28]

Before he departed again for the continent, Richard took care to place Eleanor's finances on a suitable footing. Even as Henry's queen, Eleanor had not been fully dowered – possibly because it was assumed that she could draw on her own revenues of Aquitaine. During captivity this resource was denied her, and her limited dower was also effectively withdrawn from her for much of the time. Now, any constraint on her accessing Aquitaine's wealth was removed. Furthermore, not only was Eleanor's original dower restored to her but Richard ensured she was awarded the full dower which Henry I and Stephen had given to their queens.[29] This gave her a very lordly estate and income, even before Aquitaine and French revenues were considered, since it added to her previous dower the baronies of Arundel and Berkeley.

Eleanor was given further lands in France to add to the lands in Normandy, Touraine and Maine which she had previously held.[30] And revenues for queen's gold seem to have been on the upturn, in that they began to justify keeping a clerk to deal with the accounting on this revenue. A charter reveals that the Abbot of Waltham supplied this clerk 'to serve with her other clerks' to collect the queen's gold. Amounts received are hard to pin down, but this fact indicates that they were considerable. So too the story, which Turner cites, of Eleanor receiving a great golden chalice valued at 100 marks in lieu of cash for her share in the price of a land purchase made by the monks. Eleanor's response – to return the vessel to the monks for the sake of (i.e. in return for prayers for) the soul of her late husband – also illustrates the elegance and finesse with which she was managing her affairs.[31]

Similarly, we can see Eleanor immediately making grants in relation to her new lands – on 30 October 1189 at Henry II's hunting lodge of Freemantle in Hampshire she made a grant to Maurice de Berkeley, confirming a grant already made by Richard.[32] But Eleanor was not above taking some advantage of her restored eminence, asking Archbishop Walter of Coutances of Rouen to keep a prebend in a new chapel at Tickhill in Nottinghamshire for her old chaplain Peter, who had come with her to England in 1154 and returned to her service in 1168.[33]

At the same time as he made provision for Eleanor, however, Richard set in train a process of fundraising in aid of his Crusade. While the suggestion that he said he would sell London if he could find a buyer is one which we owe to later commentators, and is probably not accurate, it encapsulates a truth about Richard's priorities – and those he set for Eleanor and his new chancellor.

This priority is reflected in the tour which Richard took following his coronation through many of the heartlands of the country, including St Albans, Northampton, Geddington, Warwick, Woodstock, Guildford, Arundel, Winchester and others. At each stop there are grants to abbeys; it is overwhelmingly likely that they were more than counterbalanced by payments extracted from them. Eleanor's presence on this tour is not certain, as she is not recorded in the witness lists of the charters; however, the fact that she gave a charter at Freemantle on the same day Richard was staying there on 30 October indicates that she did join him for some, if not all, of the tour. One may also wonder if Eleanor's hand can be traced in two key pieces of ecclesiastical promotion made on 15 September at Geddington. On that date, Godfrey de Lucy, whom she will have come to know well although Richard did not, was appointed to the plum see of Winchester. On the same day, Hubert Walter, currently Dean of York but known to Eleanor from his time in his uncle Ranulf de Glanville's household, was made Bishop of Salisbury.[34]

Shortly thereafter, Richard and, by inference, Eleanor were joined by Mathilde, now Countess of Perche, coming ahead of her husband to see her brother William, who of course was still in Eleanor's household, and Eleanor herself. On 12 November she was joined by her husband, Geffrey of Perche, who arrived in London as an envoy from Philip of France to finalise the rendezvous date for the Crusade – and perhaps also to survey the extensive dower given to Mathilde in England.[35]

After this, Eleanor and Richard seem to have progressed in different directions; Richard went to Bury St Edmunds, while Eleanor went to Canterbury where Richard joined her on 25 November.[36] However, Eleanor did make a grant to Bury St Edmunds while in London, which Richard doubtless conveyed to the abbey when he made his visit.[37]

Richard did little more in England before his departure on 11 December 1189. One move was to dismiss Ranulf de Glanville and impose a heavy fine on him. Glanville responded by pledging to join Richard on Crusade – this being his best opportunity to prove his worth to the new king. Richard in the meantime resigned his powers as Duke of Aquitaine to Eleanor, although arrangements were made for Matilda's son Otto to be her deputy on the ground.

On Richard's departure, Eleanor was given a council of advisers that included Hugh de Puiset, Bishop of Durham, and William Longchamp, Bishop of Ely, who was made chancellor in Glanville's place. But Eleanor would still rule as if she were *de jure* monarch. An example of this occurred shortly before Richard's departure when, in relation to a dispute between the Archbishop of Canterbury and the monks of the city in relation to a plan for the archbishop to found a new college of canons, the Pope attempted to send a legate to rule on the matter. It had already been agreed that Richard would sit with a council of clergy to determine the matter, so when Cardinal John Agnani came as far as Dover but had no permit to visit, Eleanor sent from Canterbury to forbid his entry to the country. 'That,' says the chronicler, 'settled the matter.' Eleanor's power was on further display later in the month when she sat with Richard and a panoply of bishops and abbots to determine that the college should be sited elsewhere than Canterbury and that a contentious prior should be moved to Evesham. Only after this was Cardinal Agnani admitted to admire the result.[38]

If more evidence of Richard's affection for his mother and promotion of her authority were needed, one of his first acts on arrival in France was to grant a charter to the cathedral at Rouen (burial place of Empress Matilda and Young Henry) 'at the petition of my dear mother Eleanor, Queen of the English'. Again, Eleanor, through Richard, sought intercession for the good of Henry's soul, this time joined with her own and that of Richard.

Meanwhile, back in England there is little to show what Eleanor was doing. We know that she spent a few months in the south of England visiting Winchester and Salisbury (against neither of which her long confinement seems to have prejudiced her), as well as Windsor and Canterbury.

A few vignettes remain, however. It is to this period that we can date the story of Bury St Edmunds referred to earlier – they were driven to send the gold cup gifted to them by Henry in lieu of a fine of ten marks of gold, although Eleanor excused them this contribution in return for their offering prayers for the blessed martyrs and 'this especially, however, for the health of our dearest son Richard'. She also required them to confirm their gratitude by sending a charter promising never to let the cup out of their possession again. Her charter was witnessed by the chronicler Ralph Niger, who can therefore be seen to have been operating in proximity to Eleanor and with a degree of her trust.

Another affair in which Eleanor's hand can probably be indirectly detected at around this time is the foundation of an abbey dedicated to St Radegonde near Dover. Richard donated 100 acres of land adjoining the main abbey lands, which were themselves lands ultimately held by the Count of Perche as part of Mathilde's dowry.[39]

But Eleanor was not to remain long in England. She was summoned to Richard's side in France in early February 1190 following Richard's meeting with Philip of France to thrash out the agreement which would permit them both to depart on Crusade. Eleanor was accompanied on this journey by John and Geoffroy as well as Alys, and Eleanor's five-year-old granddaughter Eleanora of Brittany. Also part of the party were two marital prizes destined for disposal. The first was Hawise, Countess of Aumale, who had just (late in November) lost her husband, the Earl of Essex. This formidable lady, described by Richard of Devizes as 'a woman almost a man, who was deficient in nothing masculine except manhood', was, like Eleanor in her younger years, too valuable to be allowed to remain single for any period of time. She travelled to be married, against her wish, to another of Richard's Poitevin warrior companions, William de Forz. He would leave her pregnant before he departed on Crusade. Also accompanying

Eleanor was the daughter of the Count of Eu, granddaughter of the Earl of Arundel and Henry I's relict Adeliza of Louvain; she may at this stage simply have formed part of Eleanor's household, but as her male relatives died, and she acceded as Countess of Eu, she too became destined to be married to one of Richard's adherents, in her case Ralph de Lusignan.[40]

Eleanor and her retinue rendezvoused with Richard at Nonancourt. Four themes can be traced there – with Eleanor involved in each one. First, Richard made generous provision for John, including the county of Mortain and three shires in England, but indicated that he wanted a promise from John not to return to England for three years. This promise was extracted, but interestingly was soon released. At some point before Richard's departure, someone persuaded him to allow John to return to England subject to the chancellor's approval – Howden in one chronicle points the finger at Eleanor, but in another he does not.[41] If Eleanor did so, her reasoning cannot be faulted – except with hindsight. With his presence England would provide less access to intriguing with Philip of France, plus John had lands to manage there and should, given his training in Glanville's household, have been well placed to be actually useful, as well as being the Plantagenet figurehead whom Henry had always liked to have present in England. Geoffroy, too, despite his new role as Archbishop of York, was made to promise to remain outside England. No one interceded for him.

Secondly, it was probably at this meeting that a final decision was taken between Richard and Eleanor as to whether the marriage to Alys should take place; bringing her to France made little sense if the marriage was not still a possibility. The decision was against Alys; she would be kept effectively a prisoner at Rouen while Richard and Eleanor departed for the south. Inferentially, at more or less the same time a decision was also taken to pursue another marriage, to ensure Richard had a chance of siring an heir as soon as possible. The candidate settled on was Berengaria of Navarre. Traditionally, following William of Newburgh, this decision has been painted as one made by Eleanor. However, there is no evidence for this and most scholars now accept that, as Gillingham argues, the initiative came from Richard. He was best placed to judge the considerable strategic advantages of the match in maintaining peace on the Gascon borders while he was away on Crusade. Moreover, Richard knew both Berengaria's father and brother; indeed, he may well have campaigned with them in the early 1180s.

It is unlikely that, as suggested by the *History of the Counts of Poitou*, Richard had met Berengaria and loved her since a visit to Pamplona in 1177 – Berengaria was probably only twelve at the time, to Richard's twenty. While it is possible that he retained a positive impression of her from that meeting, it is more likely that he met her again during his 1180s campaigns or in the context of his meeting with the King of Aragon at Najac in April 1185. One very real possibility is that a marriage alliance was discussed at the time of Najac, and maybe even agreed in principle – for in a song which has been dated to 1188 Bertran de Born accused Richard of faithlessness for promising to go ahead with the marriage to Alys when the King of Navarre had agreed to Richard's marriage with his daughter. Certainly, the convening of a council at La Réole in February seems consistent with a marriage to Navarre being under discussion in advance of the decision to renounce Alys which was to follow.[42] Rather than being an advocate for the marriage, it is far more likely that Eleanor indicated the importance of a marriage being concluded and consummated as soon as possible, and Richard, with the political utility of the Navarrese connection in mind quite as much as his recollections of Berengaria, preferred to take Sancho's daughter. Ascribing this role to Eleanor – pushing Richard to a decision at this point – gives sensible context to the fact that Eleanor was charged with the job of finalising arrangements and bringing Berengaria to Richard in Sicily.

Thirdly, it appears to have been only at this point, when the decision had been made that Eleanor would not return to England, that Longchamp and de Puiset were formally appointed justiciars (Eleanor no longer being in the country to outrank them). The appointment of Longchamp appears to have been an unwise decision. Longchamp was a Norman with no real network of supporters in England. He was extremely loyal to Richard, but was plainly not the kind of emollient character who could redress the disadvantage of his outsider status with personal charm.

Fourthly, a likely subject for discussion between mother and son was the fate of Eleanor's daughter Joanna, who had been left a childless widow by the death of her husband in late November 1189, and who was being held by her husband's nephew Tancred, who had assumed the throne on his death.

But first Richard and Eleanor moved to settle their southern lands. After a period of travelling together – for example they are noted in the same place at Argentan on 6 April 1190[43] – the pair separated. Playing to their strengths, Richard conducted focussed punitive raids against Gascon lords who had turned brigand against pilgrims en route to Compostela, compelling them to destroy their own fortifications.[44] At the same time, since his route took him close to Navarre, he may well have concluded a deal in principle with Sancho of Navarre for the marriage with Berengaria. It is also likely that he consulted on it with his Gascon nobles at the council which he convened at La Réole.[45]

Meanwhile, Eleanor launched a charm offensive, journeying through Anjou and Poitou confirming grants to abbeys before settling at Chinon, where she met Richard in June. It would appear that they visited Fontevraud together, and there made a gift to the abbey. To this period can probably also be traced a gift by Eleanor to the Knights Hospitaller, of a tract of land near La Rochelle called Le Perrot, which grant was confirmed by Richard. This journey also gave her an opportunity to say a final farewell to her uncle Raoul de Faye, who died later in the year.

It was also during this period that Hawise d'Aumale was married to William de Forz, who was to be Richard's admiral for the journey; Richard, possibly with Eleanor's tales of her own journey in mind, had opted for a maritime approach to the Holy Land. Richard departed from Chinon in June, journeying via Tours, where he was given his pilgrim's staff and scrip by the archbishop.[46]

This visit to Chinon calls back to mind the fresco at St Radegonde, briefly discussed earlier in the context of it as a possible representation of Eleanor's captivity. Another hypothesis as to its story sees Eleanor at this time commissioning the piece, perhaps jointly with Richard, to reflect their current position. On this reading, Eleanor is apparently centre stage, in a fresco located in the chapel devoted to one of her early patron saints, memorialized in her recent psalter, and who herself escaped captivity at the hands of her husband. What can be said for this view is that a commission by Eleanor for this chapel makes sense in a way that a commission by any other person does not.

Proponents of this theory say that, in addition, the symbolism works: Eleanor is wearing a male style of cape, logically to emphasise her power – now that of a queen regnant – lined in the same way as that of Geoffrey le Bel on his tomb. Richard, also displaying a cape with 'Angevin' lining, and also crowned, is on the far right, riding away, indicating his departure on

Crusade. With Eleanor, and obviously under her protection, is an uncrowned woman – Berengaria. Eleanor reaches back to the two smaller, uncrowned figures. She seems to pass the falcon to the first, who can be argued to be Otto, trusted with Aquitaine. The final figure also apparently wears an 'Angevin' cape: this would make sense as John, acting as figurehead in England by Eleanor's intercession but not trusted with power. The picture can therefore be said to speak tellingly to the circumstances of 1190; and we can find both Eleanor and Richard at Chinon to commission the work. One problem with this reading is the strong argument that all the figures in the painting are male. The style of cape being worn is never worn in surviving depictions by adult women. And even if one might stretch a point for Eleanor (queen regent/regnant) in a male cape, the clothes beneath the capes are also male. Because of this, the hypothesis really has to be abandoned.

However, this does not mean that association between Eleanor and the mural needs to be lost as well. One reading which has received very little consideration is that which does not involve depictions of the Plantagenet family at all. Logically, there are two more obvious subjects for a mural here: St Radegonde herself and her mentor St John of Chinon, whose grotto lies through the arch flanked by the mural. The chapel essentially honours both. To date, any association with St Radegonde has been rejected both on the basis that the clothing is contemporary to the mural and on the basis that the scene does not match anything from the best-known life of St Radegonde by Fortunatus. Both are weak bases. Though the style of clothing depicted is of the late twelfth century, it would be natural for an artist of the period to depict historical figures in contemporary clothes. As for the content, this fails to bear in mind both that what we now see is probably part of a larger set of pictures and therefore need not represent any of the major points in Fortunatus and secondly that there were several other Lives of St Radegonde which deal with her early life more fully. The scene actually works credibly in the context of an episode from the early life of St Radegonde, although in fact the lives of either saint might provide the context for this depiction as part of a larger work.

This reading is novel, and can only be offered as a real possibility. However, as noted above, the commissioning of a mural for this chapel is something which is most credibly done by Eleanor, and a mural honouring St Radegonde also fits into a discernible pattern of her devotion to the saint.[47]

Richard reached the agreed departure point of Vézelay on 2 July 1990. There each king departed separately, to rendezvous again in Sicily. Philip arrived in mid-September, and Richard followed on 22 September 1190. Doubtless the breathlessly admiring account given by Howden (an eyewitness) reflects the bulletins which were carefully sent back home, in the manner of Caesar. So Eleanor will in due course have received a description of how the populace rushed to see his arrival, the oars of his ships making the water appear as if it was boiling; and finally, to the sound of trumpets, a magnificently dressed Richard could now be seen standing on a raised platform (for maximum visibility). She will also have heard how their party was joined six days later by the widowed Joanna, prudently released by Tancred; and how she quickly attracted the attention of Philip Augustus, himself widowed earlier in the year. What appeared a suitable match was not promoted by Richard, however – possibly because of the news which he was about to spring regarding his own matrimonial intentions.[48]

For from Chinon, Eleanor (now, it must be recalled, in her sixty-seventh year) set off to Navarre. She first conducted some business at Saumur, sitting on a tribunal alongside the Seneschal of Anjou to settle a dispute between the Abbess of Fontevraud (Henry II's cousin Mathildis) and the Mayor of Saumur.[49] She also stopped for a while at Bordeaux, which she had probably not visited for over twenty years. From there, with a retinue of Poitevins, she set off in autumn for Navarre.

No records survive of her journey. All we know is that she proceeded from Bordeaux in September 1190 and that, once arrived, she finalised the agreement for the marriage and set off for Sicily with Berengaria. This journey probably provides the date for Eleanor's charter to the Abbey of Le Valasse, confirming a grant made by Henry of land and moor in the forest of Lillebonne. In it, Eleanor makes the grant for the soul of Henry, the health of King Richard, and her soul and those of all her ancestors and successors – perhaps a suggestion of trepidation at the journey which she faced. But this charter, dealing with property in Normandy, indicates that Eleanor was dealing with business from throughout Richard's lands.

No records survive of the journey until the Alps were passed, but intriguingly Eleanor's route would logically have taken her either to or near Narbonne. There is no record of whether the two heiresses finally met at this time, after years of their stories running in parallel; if they did, despite her many troubles in her marriages and with her children Eleanor can only have rejoiced in her fate. She was now at the height of her power, and respected across the continent. Ermengarde, without children to support her, was clinging on to power by her fingernails as her Aragonese nephew and heir gradually sidelined her.

The journey to Italy was one which might have discomposed a fit young woman – though Eleanor's Crusade experience doubtless stood her in good stead as they journeyed that winter through Provence, travelled across the Alps by Mont Genevre over the Christmas of 1190, and then headed down the Italian peninsula.

It is in connection with this journey that Richard of Devizes gives the description of Eleanor as 'a matchless woman, beautiful yet chaste, powerful and modest, meek yet eloquent, qualities which are most rarely found in a woman, advanced in years enough to have had two husbands and two sons crowned king, still indefatigable in every undertaking, whose power was the admiration of her age'. Tempting as it is to regard this description as pure admiration, readers should bear in mind two facts. The first is that Richard of Devizes then goes on to rehash the story of Eleanor's supposed misdeeds on Crusade. The second is that modern scholarship tends to the view that the work is an elaborate satire; the passage may be intended to be at least partly tongue in cheek. But even William of Newburgh has by this stage conceded a grudging admiration for Eleanor, praising her for the extent of her motherly love in making this difficult journey despite her great age. Eleanor was, at last, admired by all.[50]

As for the vicissitudes of the journey, we have no information, though Berengaria's biographer paints a picture of the windswept and forbidding Pyrenees only giving place to the wilderness of ice and sleet which would be the Alps. The journey could not be fast – a good pace for a horseman would be some 30 miles a day; with baggage and hilly territory, progress would naturally have been painfully slow. Following their arrival in Italy, the two women and their retinue travelled for sixty-eight days, rendezvousing with Richard at Reggio in March.[51]

During this period, we glimpse them only briefly: we know that they travelled with Philip of Flanders, who was on his way to join the Crusade. Like Eleanor's eldest daughter, Marie, Philip had a keen interest in Arthurian romance – Marie had supplied the theme for Chretien de Troyes' *Lancelot, or the Knight of the Cart* in around 1181, and on his death in 1190 the poet had left unfinished a commission for Philip: *Percival, or the Story of the Holy Grail.* The two had indeed toyed with the possibility of marriage after their respective widowhoods, though ultimately nothing had come of it. Through this contact, Eleanor may not simply have had the opportunity to enliven the journey with talk on a popular literary theme, as Owen has speculated; she will also have had the chance to learn more of the daughter she had been forced to abandon on her divorce from Louis.[52]

We do know that on 20 January 1191 Eleanor and Berengaria met up with the Emperor-elect, Henry VI of Germany, who was en route for his coronation in Rome. Henry was twenty-five years old and had been King of Germany since his fifth year. In 1186 he had married Constance of Sicily, the legal heir to Joanna's husband William. Eleanor witnessed a charter which the Emperor-elect issued in favour of the Bishop of Trent, which indicates that also in the party at that time were the bishops of Milan, Asti and Vercelli, the Marquis of Montferrat and two German counts. Also listed is a mysterious person known as Elizabeth, Queen of Variet.[53] Richard of Devizes suggests that after this they went to Pisa to await Richard's instructions, but his sources of information on the Crusade are doubtful. Howden says that Eleanor and Berengaria went to Naples to take a ship for Sicily, accompanied by Philip of Flanders, but that when they reached Messina the ladies' ship was denied entry by Tancred's officials and had to go on to Brindisi. The reason appears to have been that Tancred was egged on to this, in part by Philip of France and in part by his own concerns about the number of soldiers who accompanied Eleanor, not least in light of contacts between Eleanor and the new Emperor, Tancred's rival for the throne.[54]

Philip's involvement was due to the fact that, as Eleanor and Berengaria neared Sicily, he could see the overwhelming likelihood was that the marriage to Alys was not going to take place. Once Philip's involvement in the delay to Eleanor's arrival was in the open, Richard finally called off the engagement to Alys, telling Philip that it was impossible for him to marry her because she had been Henry II's mistress. As indicated above, this account is powerful evidence of the veracity of the rumours reported elsewhere. So too are three other things. The first is that Howden reports that Richard was able to tender witnesses who could vouch for the truth of the allegations against Alys. The second is that there is no account of a denial by Philip – rather, following advice from friends, he acquiesced and an accord was reached in fairly short order, with Richard being released from his promise for a substantial cash payment. The third is Alys's fate; she was only married in 1195 to the very much younger Count William of Ponthieu. This was no match for a daughter of France and granddaughter of the King of Castile; it is surely only consistent with Alys being known to be 'damaged goods'.[55]

However, Philip was not prepared to wait and greet Eleanor and his sister's replacement; he sailed for Acre the same day. Richard saw him off and then made straight for Reggio, where Eleanor and Berengaria had just arrived. He conducted them to Messina, and was apparently noticeably glad to see Eleanor – the Crusade's official chronicler records no conversation with the bride-to-be, but says that Eleanor and Richard talked freely together, saying whatever they would, while Richard of Devizes speaks of him embracing Eleanor warmly.[56]

In Messina, Eleanor was reunited with Joanna, last seen on her departure for Sicily in 1176. Joanna was now twenty-five years of age, and the accounts suggest that she was a beautiful woman. But there was no possibility of her returning home with her mother; she would be needed as a chaperone for Berengaria until Richard was married, and after the marriage it was only kind to have a young woman of Richard's family around to ease the strangeness of the bride's new life. Moreover, Joanna was a matrimonial prize; she was probably not regarded as safe to be sent with Eleanor and her fairly limited retinue.[57]

It may be surprising that Eleanor did not accompany Berengaria to her marriage, but we know that news of the difficulties pertaining in England made their way to Sicily by the time of her arrival. The details are clouded, but it appears that William de Longchamp had stirred up a great deal of resentment, and friction with John was also a problem. Roger of Howden suggests that Richard had sent back a number of envoys, including William Marshal and Walter de Coutances, Archbishop of Rouen, both of whom were promoted to the council of justiciars. He suggests that they failed to deliver their messages; however, given the timeline it is more likely that Richard doubted whether their authority would be sufficient. It was evidently important that Eleanor was back in the vicinity to superintend – which had always been her intended role. Accordingly, she departed, probably by sea to Salerno and then overland to Rome just three days later, arriving on 2 April. This puts paid to suggestions that Eleanor had time to be inspired by the mausoleum established by King William at Monreale, on the other side of the island.[58]

Richard of Devizes tells how Richard saw Eleanor to her ship in a magnificent procession, accompanied by Walter of Coutances, who was being charged with smoothing affairs over directly in England.[59] Eleanor's precipitous departure can therefore be rationally accounted for. However, one may permissibly speculate whether she might have accompanied the couple at least for so long as the marriage had she and Berengaria bonded closely during the course of the voyage. There is no sign that they did so. In later years neither was to make any effort to see the other, and Eleanor's references to Berengaria always refer to her simply as 'Queen Berengaria', without the addition of the '*carissima*' or '*dilectissima*' regularly applied to her own daughters.[60]

Also accompanying Eleanor on her return journey was Peter of Blois, the author of the famous letter of reproof to Eleanor after Young Henry's initial revolt. In recent years he had been in the employ of Archbishop Baldwin of Canterbury, in particular arguing the case which Richard and Eleanor had resolved before his departure on Crusade. Peter had accompanied the king and the archbishop on Crusade as far as Sicily, where Baldwin died. Peter was therefore in need of a new patron. It would appear that at some point on the journey he made his peace with Eleanor, and though there is no evidence he formally entered her employment he appears to have done some work for her, featuring as a witness to two of her charters.[61]

The timing was fortuitous, for Pope Clement III died at Rome just as Eleanor completed her journey. On the very day of Eleanor's arrival at Messina, the Sacred College elected as his replacement Eleanor's friend and correspondent Hyacinth Bobone, who would take the name Celestine III. Like Eleanor, Hyacinth was enjoying a later-life triumph – he would be eighty-five or eighty-six when he assumed the role of Pope and would do so at a time when, despite his age, he was preparing to voyage into Iberia for the third time. By leaving on 2 April, taking the sea route to Salerno and then onwards by road, Eleanor was able to reach Rome in time for his installation, and for his coronation of Henry VI the next day; clearly such an opportunity was not to be missed, both in terms of relations with the papacy and also with the new Emperor.[62]

The accounts of the investiture and coronation are regrettably thin, and in the fuller versions coloured by the hostility which was to arise between Richard and Henry. Thus Roger of Howden, though normally a reliable source for this period, cannot be trusted in his account of events, which is tainted by his absence (he was with Richard) and his partisanship. What we can probably accept is that Celestine, despite being a cardinal deacon for many years, was still not in priestly orders; his role had been essentially that of an international diplomat. Indeed, his elevation may well have come about because of the key role he had recently played in negotiating the return of papal lands from the Emperor – and his reputation as 'the most able of procrastinators', as well as his uncontroversial views, which Ralph of Diss says prevented a schism in the Church. He was therefore ordained shortly after his election, probably on 13 April 1191, and installed immediately thereafter on Easter Sunday, 14 April 1191; and on the next day he enthroned Henry as Emperor together with his wife, Constance, as Empress. It is probably also the case that Celestine warned Henry that he would find his claim to Sicily hard to pursue. What we (regrettably) cannot accept is the story that Celestine kicked the imperial crown away from the kneeling Henry. This would be quite incompatible with the other evidence, and also inconsistent with the description of him which says that 'to see him and hear him was to learn a sense of honour'.[63]

During her stay in Rome, Eleanor had an opportunity to renew her acquaintance with the Pope – who had also been friendly with Leonor during his visits to Castile. Her friendship with him doubtless made it easier for her to obtain the two main objects which she had on her list: to ensure that Geoffroy was approved for formal consecration as Archbishop of York, and to obtain a legateship for Walter de Coutances to counterbalance the authority of Longchamp, who had already been appointed a papal legate. Both of these were attained. Eleanor also obtained 800 marks from moneylenders in Rome, presumably to cover expenses for crossing the Alps back to France.[64]

It is sometimes suggested that by the time Eleanor arrived back at Rouen via Bourges on 24 June, Walter de Coutances had been in England for about three months. However, that depends on a misreading of Ralph of Diss's chronicle. Coutances was with Eleanor in Rome and simply could not have been back by the date in April often given. It appears that he travelled back with Eleanor, both arriving in northern France sometime around the end of June 1191.[65]

In that time, John had commenced an active rebellion against the chancellor, possibly in part prompted by his discovery that, as part of a peace treaty with Tancred of Sicily, Richard had designated Geoffrey's baby son Arthur of Brittany (who was to marry Tancred's daughter) as his heir. John's position in England was assisted by his readiness to travel the breadth of the country and meet people, and above all by his actual knowledge of and interest in things English, fuelled by the amount of time he had spent in the former justiciar's household. For the present, Eleanor appears to have remained in France, keeping an eye on whether the steps taken by Richard would prove sufficient. Coutances commenced sensibly by convening a council in Winchester in July. Although John and Longchamp both attended with armed supporters, a tentative peace was imposed, in no small measure because Coutances' authority was bolstered not just by Richard's instructions but also by the papal legateship which Eleanor had obtained.[66]

In August, Eleanor acted on the second string which she had obtained from Celestine. On the 18th, Geoffroy was consecrated as Archbishop of York by the Archbishop of Tours at Tours Cathedral, apparently under her watchful eye.[67] Although it is often said that his subsequent return to England was made against Richard's orders, it looks far more as if he was despatched to England by Eleanor, presumably to act as another counterweight to Longchamp. If her intention was to force Longchamps to overstep, the plan worked to perfection. In September, attempting to prevent Geoffroi from returning to England, Longchamp had his dynamic sister Richent, wife of the Castellan of Dover, seize Geoffroi in the very act of celebrating Mass. His subsequent imprisonment resulted in further unrest, which was carefully tended by John, and Coutances was able to use it to force Longchamp to surrender the justiciarship and leave the country.

The appearance that Eleanor was the *eminence grise* behind this manoeuvring is only reinforced by the records, which state that Coutances was 'advised and supported' in these steps by Eleanor, as well as by key barons such as William Marshal, now Earl of Pembroke in right of his wife. Eleanor's influence is also apparent in smaller issues at this time – indicating that she was kept thoroughly up to date and consulted extensively on many aspects of decision-making; thus Gerald of Wales (not generally prone to praising Eleanor) credits her with the primary authority for his appointment as an envoy to Wales in this year – during the course of which he was offered the bishopric of Llandaff.[68]

However, at more or less the time that a tentative peace was being put into place, Philip of France decided to abandon the Crusade and return to France. In part this was to take up his inheritance on the death of Philip of Flanders, who had died at Acre in July 1191, but in large part it was because he and Richard had fallen out comprehensively in the months which had succeeded Richard's repudiation of Alys, in particular in relation to the succession to the kingdom of Jerusalem (in relation to which Richard had supported his and Eleanor's vassal Guy de Lusignan), as well as their various contributions to the fighting. Given the level of hostility between the pair, Richard was naïve if he believed the oath given by Philip not to take any action against Richard's lands and men while Richard was absent on Crusade.[69]

Philip also passed through Rome on his way back to his lands, and, according to Howden at least, he too sought useful orders from the Pope. Howden says that he sought to be released from his oath not to attack Richard's lands but that this application was indignantly refused by Celestine, who said that 'like every Christian prince you should observe a peace agreement without an oath' and approved and endorsed the oath with his own authority.[70] Whether this is true or not is uncertain; there is no other account of this request and reaction, and again, in relation to this, Howden's absence as well as his outrage at Philip's later actions renders him unreliable.

In any event, by autumn Philip was back in France and demanding the return of Alys while Eleanor, who had custody of her, stalled for time. However, Philip's next move was to begin to lay out lures for the ever-discontented John, suggesting he could be recognised as ruler of all Richard's French lands – if he would marry Alys.[71]

Meanwhile, Longchamp also now began to create problems for Eleanor. Arriving in Normandy, he sought assistance from the cardinals Jordan and Octavian, who had been despatched by Celestine to try to facilitate a peace. They were sympathetic to his complaints and approached Gisors, presumably en route to remonstrate with Eleanor. Eleanor, acting through the Seneschal of Normandy, refused them safe conduct, which resulted in the seneschal's excommunication and an interdict on Normandy. This, however, was speedily discharged when Eleanor herself interceded directly with Celestine. The reality of Eleanor's beneficial connection with Celestine is clear, and is also evidenced by the fact that, even though the orders had come from her, she herself had apparently been excluded from the excommunication.[72]

Eleanor spent the Christmas of 1191 at her dower property of Bonneville-sur-Touques. But Philip had appeared within days, calling a meeting of the seneschal and barons of Normandy between Gisors and Trie, and openly seeking the return of Alys – with a supplemental threat to come in arms to take her if the request was not fulfilled. Eleanor, determined to hold Philip to the letter of his agreement with Richard, moved to fortify castles in Normandy, and then, despite the season, sailed for England.[73]

She arrived on 11 February 1192 at Portsmouth, and the catalogue of her activities in the following months testifies to a hugely busy period for her.[74] Her primary concern was to ensure that John did not leave England and make common cause with Philip – and to ensure that he knew that the majority of the English nobility were supporting her. To this end, Eleanor staged a series of meetings attended by local nobles – one at Windsor, one at Oxford, a third in London at the Temple Church and the fourth at Winchester.[75] Roger of Howden tells how Eleanor, backed by Walter of Coutances and the justiciars, refused him permission to leave the kingdom, informing him that a breach of their order would come at the cost of seizure of all of his lands and castles. Following this intervention, Eleanor called the meetings and ensured that as many nobles as possible renewed their oaths of loyalty to Richard against all comers. At the same time, she dealt with the return of Longchamp, who had arrived at Dover at the start of March. After what seems to have been a spirited debate, she and the barons wrote to him to advise him to leave the country unless he wished to face imprisonment. Longchamp duly left.[76]

Eleanor also dealt with the row which had sprung up between justiciar Hugh de Puiset, Bishop of Durham, and Geoffroy, Archbishop of York, summoning them to appear before her at the Temple Church in London. Howden indicates that Geoffroy was initially uncooperative, very possibly reflecting a personal hostility based on Eleanor's role in his removal from the political world, and reports that Eleanor dealt with him briskly, threatening to sequestrate his assets. Once again, it appears 'that settled the matter' – at least on the surface, though the row was still alive in essence when Richard returned.[77]

Eleanor found time amid all this high politics to conduct personal business, claiming her share of queen's gold on the tax levied following Richard's marriage. It also appears to be at about this point that she made provision for three former members of her household. Amiria Pantulf, formerly Eleanor's 'damsel', was granted the manor of Wintreslewe as a reward for her faithful service. Part of that donation was passed on by Amiria to Amesbury Abbey for 'the weal of my lady, Eleanor, Queen of England' when Amiria entered the abbey herself.[78] Hamo de Passelewe was also made a grant at this time, as was 'Robert Le Saucier' – evidently a member of Eleanor's kitchen team (and one of three cooks to whom grants by Eleanor can be traced).[79] It is also possible that one of two grants made to Agatha, 'the Queen's nurse' – the morganatic wife of Godfrey de Lucy, Bishop of Winchester – dates from this period. It appears likely that the bishop separated from her at around this period and that Eleanor made sure that Agatha had adequate means for her support.[80]

It would also appear that she travelled more widely, including to some of her dower lands. Richard of Devizes tells how during this year Eleanor was visiting dower lands in Ely, when the consequences of the quarrel between Longchamp and Coutances were brought vividly home to her. The two men had placed reciprocal interdicts on each other's dioceses – one of which was Ely.[81] To them the consequences were probably not too serious, consisting largely of a cash flow difficulty, but the people of Ely were left unable to christen their babies, marry or even buy their dead. Corpses rotted in the street. When Eleanor rode by, the people ran up to her to seek her aid. Eleanor, speaking no English, could not understand their words 'but they needed no interpreter for they could be read like an open book'. When Eleanor returned to London, she 'requested – or rather demanded' that Coutances revoke the interdict. 'And what steely heart,' asks the chronicler, 'could have been so fierce as not to yield to the will of such a woman?'[82]

But Eleanor was clear that the steps she had taken were no more than a temporary fix, and that John remained in correspondence with Philip. Her travels will also have enabled her to ascertain the extent to which John had made contingent alliances with influential barons – for example John Marshal, the brother of William and custodian of the important castle at Wallingford, which John began to use as a base. She therefore wrote in no uncertain terms to Richard telling him that he should come home as soon as possible because John was allying himself with Philip. One of Richard's Crusade chroniclers, Ambroise, reports how the impression conveyed to Richard was that if he did not go home at once he would find that he had lost his country.[83] This period therefore demonstrates clearly both the reality of Eleanor's authority and its limits. She exercised more overt authority than she had ever done before, and her actions were more effective. However, in one sense the position remained ultimately that which had bedevilled her position throughout her life; as long as she had no powerful military leader to back her up, her power was vulnerable to challenge from those who did.

It is perhaps ironic that at exactly this point in Eleanor's life this very dynamic was being tested with less success by Ermengarde of Narbonne. Sometime between April and September 1193, Ermengarde was expelled from Narbonne by her heir apparent, her formerly beloved nephew Pedro de Lara. Without sons, and reliant on an 'old guard' of supporters who were now either dead or waning in power, her attempts to retake Narbonne were in vain. By 1195, Pedro was secure enough in his usurped lordship to go on Crusade in Spain.[84] Ermengarde herself, once the second-greatest heiress in France, now disappears from the record, to surface again only at the time of her death.

Eleanor, by contrast, had a loyal son who could enforce her decisions; and Richard, in turn, heeded her advice. Having won a strategic victory at Jaffa in September, he concluded a truce with Saladin and was on his way home by 9 October 1992. Berengaria and Joanna were despatched first, on 29 September, and arrived at Brindisi in November.[85] Letters announcing Richard's imminent return will have been with Eleanor before Christmas. She will have known that he was safe, which was by no means a given.

It was not just Maria of Champagne who had lost her husband; Mathilde's father-in-law the Count of Perche died at Acre, as did Eleanor's daughter Alice's husband Thibaut of Blois and the Duke of Burgundy. But with Richard safe, one must assume that Eleanor will have been looking forward to a peaceful retirement from frontline politics. In fact, she was to be forced to assert herself to unprecedented levels.

It was at the turn of the years 1192 to 1193 that news reached Eleanor at Westminster, where she held her Christmas court, that Richard had been taken prisoner by the Duke of Austria; the news reached Henry VI on 28 December, when he wrote to Philip of France to share the good news,[86] and must have reached Eleanor at the very end of the old year or soon after the start of the new. By this time, Richard had been transferred into the custody of Henry himself. One point must be made at the outset: the news must have been a complete surprise. This is because Henry's detention of Richard was effectively illegal according to accepted norms of the time. It was against the laws of chivalry, against the civil laws of the Empire and against the laws of the Church – which provided specific protection to the person and property of Crusaders. Even Philip of France's own tame historian, Rigord, acknowledged that the detention was immoral and against all custom.[88]

When the news reached Eleanor via Coutances, who had obtained a copy of the letter, she at first had no information as to where Richard was being held. Her first act was to send messengers to Germany to find out the facts and start negotiations for his immediate release. These representatives were two abbots and the Bishop of Bath – a relation of the Emperor.[88] Richard suggests that Eleanor was tormented by the notion that Richard's fate was somehow her own fault and that she was wasting away from anxiety and despatching grants to Fontevraud to secure prayers for him. While a grant to Fontevraud may well have been made,[89] there is no contemporaneous support for such a negative picture of Eleanor's reaction. Indeed, her response appears to have been extremely practical and to the point.

She was also rapidly alert to the fact that Richard's detention had upset the delicate balance of power which she had been maintaining. John was informed of the situation by Philip, and immediately crossed the Channel to try to gain support from the Norman barons and seal a deal to marry Alys and gain Philip's support. John proclaimed himself Richard's heir and met Philip in Paris, doing homage for the Angevin lands.[90] Once apprised of this, Eleanor moved swiftly to ensure that the Channel coast was strongly fortified – Gervase of Canterbury, well placed to know the facts pertaining to Channel defences, reports specifically that the orders were given 'by command of Queen Eleanor, who at that time ruled England'. This is clearly verified by letters in the Canterbury Cathedral archive. One letter patent refers to the fact that she had been obliged by urgent necessity to call on the prior's men to execute defences at Canterbury and that no derogation from the liberties of the abbey was intended. The second refers to similar works at Dover which also impinged on the abbey's lands.[91]

The result of the works which Eleanor commanded and superintended was that John did not feel strong enough to launch the full-scale invasion which he and Philip had been planning (with a fleet being mustered at Wissant). He instead returned to England with a force of mercenaries which he used to capture certain strategic castles.[92]

Meanwhile, Ralph of Diss reports that Eleanor, with Walter of Coutances and key loyal barons (including William Marshal), 'did their utmost to conserve the peace of the kingdom'. With her support, Marshal and other loyalists rapidly recaptured some of the castles taken – including Windsor.[93] In Normandy, Philip launched a spirited attempt to take Rouen – where Alys apparently remained – but was thwarted by the new Earl of Leicester. Ultimately, John was forced to a truce under whose terms he was to deliver the royal castles of Windsor, Wallingford and the Peak 'into the hand of Queen Eleanor'.[94]

The response of the papacy is more unclear. Roger of Howden suggests that Celestine excommunicated Leopold of Austria and threatened Philip of France with an interdict if he trespassed on Richard's lands. He also reports that Henry VI himself was excommunicated. This is one area where recent scholarship suggests that Howden (a Crusader with and strong partisan of Richard's) is not to be fully relied upon. There is a record of the excommunication of Leopold of Austria, but there is none of interdict or excommunication, or threats thereof, against either Philip or Henry.[95] So far as Philip is concerned, the reasons for this are obscure; it appears that Celestine appreciated that antagonizing Philip was unlikely to help his long-term plans to bring about accord and future Crusades. As regards Henry, the evidence is clear; Celestine had been elected a short while before precisely to maintain the good relations with the new Emperor which his diplomatic skills had been key in bringing about – he simply could not afford to antagonise the empire. In essence, Celestine went as far as he could by enforcing strict punishment for Leopold and the men involved in the detention of Richard on his behalf – they were to release and compensate all the hostages taken, and were to perform a penitential Crusade to last the same period as Richard's captivity.[96]

This reaction obviously provides the link to the well-known letters to Celestine often attributed to Eleanor – the most famous of which, characterising her as 'Eleanor, by the wrath of God, Queen of England', gives the title to Alison Weir's biography and to various chapters in other authors' works on Eleanor. The key tone of these letters is anger at the Pope, tinged with not a little derision and contempt; but they also demonstrate a lyrical, deft use of language which takes the breath away. They purport to lay bare Eleanor's innermost feelings: 'a mother so wretched', 'pitiable and hoping in vain to be pitied'.

The letters are fascinating, but they should not be relied on as forming any part of Eleanor's story. For one thing, they were certainly written by and almost certainly actually composed by Peter of Blois, that famous 'pen for hire' whose work has already been seen. For another, there is considerable doubt over whether they were ever sent – they may have been intended by Peter as part of a portfolio for publication. This possibility is strongly suggested by the fact that they were found in Peter's files and nowhere in the Vatican's records. The argument against their having much, if any, relation to Eleanor's words was first advanced by Lees in 1906 by reference to detailed textual analysis of the letters. Her arguments were accepted and expanded by Owen in his biography of Eleanor and are now endorsed by Peter's own biographer.[97]

Most modern biographers of Eleanor, including both Weir and Turner, tend to suggest a middle line – that they should be seen as conveying Eleanor's feelings if not her words. But the basis for this appears to be wish fulfilment – the idea of Eleanor speaking to us so eloquently is almost too tempting to resist. Flori sums up this view: 'There is no reason why we should not accept these letters as expressions of Eleanor's deepest thoughts.'[98]

But the sceptics' view is compelling. There is no evidence for Peter even forming part of Eleanor's household, still less acting as Eleanor's confidential secretary, so as to be entrusted with such a delicate piece of work, even if it is true that he can be traced to her entourage at some point by dint of having witnessed two charters for her. The letters are exactly the kind of showy piece of work which would make sense as a demonstration piece for publication. On any analysis they look like a very poor piece of diplomacy, in circumstances where Eleanor would want to make sure that no false steps were taken. The absence of any response is also telling; three such letters from any queen regent would call for some response. Furthermore, one may doubt whether Eleanor – who had thus far in her life manifested no such signs of plaintiveness, self-pity or a tendency to 'emotional sharing' – would have written or approved such letters. Viewed with detachment, on any view they sit far better with the style of Peter of Blois, in love with words and less than charitable in his wit.

However, to this can be added the perspective gained by the consideration of Eleanor's relationship with Celestine – which has not been considered by previous writers. In this context, the idea that these are genuine letters from Eleanor to Celestine becomes practically unarguable. As has been explained above, Eleanor and Celestine were old friends, known to each other for fifty years and long in the habit of direct communication. Were Eleanor to write to Celestine, it is unthinkable that her letters would not invoke this history – as her surviving letter to him as a cardinal does – or that they would partake of none of the tone to be expected from such a long correspondence.[99] The letters, striking and interesting as they are, must be dismissed as speaking for Eleanor or as letters which were ever sent.

What we do know about Eleanor's actions is far more consistent with the picture of her built up thus far than it is with the self-pitying howls of the letters. She was in fact very busy doing everything she could to get news of the potential ransom and making arrangements to find the genuine 'king's ransom' which was now needed. In a letter sent at the end of March 1193, Richard thanks his mother for the devotion she has shown in defence of the kingdom.[100] She was central to the effort to obtain the ransom monies once news was received in April 1193 that it had been set at an eye-watering 150,000 marks, although Richard was to be released on a down payment of 70,000 and the surrender of hostages from the sons of the English and Norman baronage for his payment of the balance. Eleanor and Walter of Coutances approved a tax of a quarter of the value of all moveable goods, 20*s* on each knight's fee and the surrender of all the gold and silver in English churches. The Cistercians and Carthusians, who had no precious metals, were to give the value of their wool crop for the year. Nor did Richard's continental lands escape: Caen was a major contributor, and collections were also made in Anjou and Aquitaine, with the Abbey of Saint-Martial providing 100 marks.[101] The involvement of Berengaria, who had returned with Joanna to Aquitaine, in collecting the ransom is not clear, though it is reported that she was active in this regard. John, of course, was charged with assisting in the collection of the ransom from his own lands – and swiftly diverted the sums raised to his own uses.[102]

In June, Eleanor attended the council at St Albans which put in place arrangements for the custody of the ransom as it was assembled. Five officers were in charge of its collection: Coutances, the Bishop of London, the earls of Arundel and Warenne and the Mayor of London. But Eleanor was once again at the heart of the arrangements – the ransom was to be tallied and deposited at St Paul's, with each chest, once valued, sealed with Eleanor's seal and that of Walter of Coutances. While Eleanor's movements in this period are not documented, it seems likely that she was moving about the country to some extent assisting in the fundraising effort – Ralph Niger speaks feelingly of the pressure exerted ('no church, no order, no rank or sex could escape the obligation to contribute to the King's ransom')[103] and William of Newburgh testifies to the difficulties in getting the money to flow inwards, which is hardly surprising given Henry II's abortive Crusade tax and Richard's more recent one. It appears that there was a certain amount of *quid pro quo* involved; the charters which Eleanor executed in favour of Waltham Abbey at this time – confirming specific grants and charters made by Henry, Young Henry and Richard, and in particular tidying up an issue surrounding a grant of the manor of Waltham and the village of Nasinges – are strongly suggestive of the greater abbeys seeking something in return for their doubtless significant contributions.[104]

The fact that the Pope threatened to place England under an interdict if the ransom was not forthcoming reinforces the picture of the difficulties which Eleanor encountered in collecting the ransom. But it also suggests a more credible and practical correspondence between Eleanor and Celestine than that of the Blois letters.[105]

Meanwhile, Eleanor also became involved in the election of the new Archbishop of Canterbury when Richard, from his captivity, nominated Hubert Walter, the Bishop of Salisbury. Richard wrote directly to Eleanor in terms which bear repeating in that they show his affection and his understanding of her efforts:

> to his revered lady and dearest mother Eleanor, by that same grace queen of England, greeting and all the happiness that a devoted son can desire for his mother. First to God and then to your serenity, sweetest mother, we give thanks as we can, though we cannot suffice to actions so worthy of thanks, for your loyalty to us and the faithful care and diligence you give to our lands for peace and defence so devotedly and effectively. Indeed ... we also know that through the mercy of God and your counsel and help the defence of our lands is and will be in great part provided. For your prudence and discretion is the greatest cause of our land remaining in a peaceful state until our arrival. Now, however, dearest mother, we transmit to your benevolence our dearest one, the venerable man Hubert bishop of Salisbury. ... we wish to promote him to the church of Canterbury. Our will is for him and against any other. Dearest mother, with all possible entreaty of devotion, we beg you that as you love us you take care to hasten his promotion in the Canterbury church with all speed. This is the only business, after the business of our liberation, that we commit to you to press for.[106]

Richard also addressed the royal officials and the monks of Canterbury in separate letters. That to the monks advises them to seek the opinion of Eleanor; they obviously did so, for not only was Hubert Walter elected in May but Eleanor's hand can be discerned at this time in dealing with another row between the Canterbury and Christchurch monks.[107]

Matters were further complicated by additional demands made by Henry VI in mid-1193; by July that year the ransom was 150,000 with a down payment of 100,000, and the number of hostages increased to two hundred. Among those who were to act as hostages for the payment of the full ransom were two of Eleanor's grandchildren by Matilda, Otto and William, plus Berengaria's brother Fernando and Coutances and Longchamp. However, this agreement, declared publicly by Henry at Worms, seemed firm – sufficiently for Philip of France to warn John (somewhat prematurely) that 'the devil is loosed', leading John to flee for sanctuary at Philip's court.[108]

By October 1193, the first instalment of the ransom was in place. Once Henry's envoys confirmed it had been safely received, he announced that Richard would be released on 17 January 1194 if the remaining payment arrived. So Eleanor (now just months shy of her seventieth birthday) again set out for a winter journey, this time in company with Coutances and the hostages as well as a retinue including some of her own vassals. Hubert Walter remained in England as justiciar. The route the party took is not recorded. Some writers speculate that it may have run through Champagne, permitting Eleanor to meet her eldest daughter, Marie, now ruling Champagne for her absent son Henri, who had married Isabelle of Jerusalem at the conclusion of the Crusade. However, there is no evidence of any such meeting and none is to be necessarily inferred; Eleanor could reach Speyer without travelling via Champagne. Further, the assembly of a fleet at the Suffolk ports of Orford, Dunwich and Ipswich suggests that the route was direct to a German port, not a short crossing to France.[109]

By Epiphany, Eleanor had arrived at Speyer and was presumably able to see Richard. But Henry VI predictably delayed, pressing his advantage further. In early February, Eleanor attended an assembly at Mainz directed to settling the final details of Richard's release – in particular whether further terms should be imposed or further delay made by reason of offers received from Philip of France (with John's implicit support). Ultimately, the Emperor imposed only one further condition: that Richard do homage to him for England, surrendering it as an Imperial fief and paying an annual tribute of £5,000. It seems Richard was minded to refuse, but Eleanor counselled acceptance, and he agreed[110] – another example of Eleanor's very real influence.

On 4 February 1194, Eleanor watched Richard agree the final deal and do homage to Henry VI, offering him a leather cap and receiving it back from him as a token that he received his lands back at Henry's will and giving him a double cross of gold.[111] Henry then put his name to a letter to Philip and John, calling on them to restore those lands and castles of Richard's which they had taken and promising Imperial support if they did not.

Shortly thereafter, Eleanor and Richard plus their retinue, including William Longchamp, set off for home. Staying first at Cologne, they were entertained for three days as guests of the

Archbishop of Cologne. Thereafter they passed on swiftly to Louvain, Brussels and then Antwerp, where the fleet from England awaited them. Howden reports something like a pleasure cruise near Zwin for a few days exploring the islands on galleys. It is unclear whether this delay was due to the weather, as Ralph Niger suggests, or because an ambush by Philip was feared, or simply to allow time for celebrations at home to be prepared. But the party in due course sailed on 4 March.[112]

On 13 March 1194, Richard arrived with Eleanor safely at Sandwich. From here they proceeded to Canterbury, where they spent the night, allowing for prayer at the tomb of Becket. The next day they rendezvoused near Rochester with Hubert Walter and probably stayed the night in that city. On 16 March, Richard and Eleanor entered London to universal rejoicing, processing through the city to St Paul's.[113]

One might have expected Eleanor, after the exertions of the past months, to remain in London, but the next day she was off again with Richard, first to Bury St Edmunds and then to Huntingdon, where they were met by William Marshal – now 'the Marshal', having succeeded to his brother as hereditary Marshal of England. Together the party moved on to Nottingham,[114] one of only two locations still holding out for John. As Richard prepared to besiege Nottingham, news came of the surrender of Tickhill. This and the prospect of attack from a campaigner of Richard's repute quickly provoked a surrender of Nottingham too.

For the next few days, the royal party remained at Nottingham. From 30 March, Eleanor is reported at Richard's right hand during a four-day council whereby John's principal supporters were deprived of their positions and new trusted men installed – one of them being Geoffroy, Archbishop of York, who had presented himself at the council along with a large number of bishops and the earls of Huntingdon, Surrey, Ferrers, Chester and Salisbury. On the second day of the council, John was summoned to appear by 10 May; if he did not, he was to be banished from the kingdom. On the third day, a tax was levied to cover the redemption of the hostages and begin a fund for war against France.[115]

Although Eleanor does not appear in the record for the next couple of weeks, her next appearance by Richard's side in Winchester in mid-April suggests that she continued to journey with him, which would mean travelling to Clipstone and then Southwell to meet the King of Scots, and then moving to Melton

Mowbray and Geddington before spending Easter at Northampton and proceeding via Silverstone and Woodstock to Winchester.[116]

There, on 17 April 1194, Eleanor makes one of her most dramatic appearances in the record, when Richard was crowned by Hubert Walter. This was no mere crown-wearing but a second coronation, explicitly so called in one charter to the priory of St Swithun. Richard proceeded into the cathedral in his full regalia, and the canopy above his head was borne by four earls: Norfolk, Isle of Wight, Salisbury and Ferrers. This time, Eleanor was not absent from the coronation. She and her ladies witnessed it sitting on a platform in the chancel facing the king – to all appearances presiding over the ceremony. She plainly had no female competition; Berengaria, technically Queen of England, had not been summoned to meet her husband on his release, nor to join his progress and second coronation. She remained in Anjou.[117]

On the same day, as well as attending a banquet in St Swithun's priory, Richard dealt with matters clerical, issuing a letter to the clergy of England thanking them for their loyal response in the matter of the ransom. But also, perhaps on Eleanor's advice, he wrote to Celestine asking him to order the release of the hostages, the return of money paid to Leopold of Austria (now excommunicate) and that amends be made by Leopold for his injuries to Richard. Again reflecting the good accord which Eleanor had with the Pope, Celestine actioned this request, though Leopold was to die shortly thereafter.[118]

The party remained at Winchester for five days more, during which time Eleanor secured a grant (witnessed by her) for her cook Adam. A grant was also made to Eleanor's grandson Otto, and, perhaps reflecting Canterbury's support to Eleanor in Richard's absence, to the monks of Christchurch Canterbury of the wood of Blean.

On 24 April, Richard, Eleanor and their households arrived in Portsmouth to make the passage to France. The winds prevented a crossing until 12 May, but on that day the crossing was made to Barfleur.[119] Eleanor would never return to England.

Her first action on return to France was to secure a reconciliation between her sons. She and Richard proceeded via Caen to Lisieux, and it was there in mid-March that 'through the mediation' of Eleanor a reconciliation was brought about, with Richard nonetheless refusing to return any land or castles to John.[120] Accounts of Richard receiving John 'with good natured contempt' have the ring of truth.

With England now at peace and John returned to the fold, Richard could turn his attention to his favourite occupation: war. And Eleanor, released from the demands of the past few years, could return to her lands in Aquitaine. This she did not do. Instead, she retired to Fontevraud. This decision has attracted little attention; with the perspective of hindsight, and influenced by the burials at Fontevraud, it seems obvious and natural. However, it was not. That Eleanor should retire was not at all surprising, but there were far more obvious places for her to be: the Abbaye aux Dames at Saintes, for one, which had been headed by her own aunt in childhood. Other possibilities would have been Nieul-sur-l'Autise, which Eleanor had given royal status and which was the location of her mother's grave, or Montierneuf, which had been the focus of so much patronage by her family and which was actually in Poitiers.

The reason behind the decision in favour of Fontevraud can never be known. But we must at least accept the possibility that it reflects a less passionate attachment to the land of her birth than it has been traditional to attribute to Eleanor. Another strong possibility, combining with this, is that Eleanor had by this point decided not to have Henry II's grave moved, and had also decided on Fontevraud as the base for a dynastic memorial and celebration of Plantagenet power. There is also a third consideration: security. Even with Richard back, Eleanor might still be seen as a legitimate hostage or even marriage target for the disaffected. Eleanor's own great-grandson Edward I would not hesitate to send his minions to force a sale of key properties upon ninety-three-year-old Isabella de Forz on her deathbed in 1293.[121]

The most likely answer seems to be that Eleanor had at least tentatively decided to make Fontevraud the Plantagenet dynastic foundation, which made retirement there sensible. The damage to the joint vision of a Plantagenet empire which she and Henry had shared could in part be repaired by such a step. Moreover, a decision to do so would chime nicely with the work which her daughter Leonor had been doing in Castile. There, at least by 1187 (its formal foundation) but possibly as early as 1179, she had been planning a new foundation called Las Huelgas to be the funerary centre for the Castilian royal family.[122] While we do not know for sure that Leonor and her mother continued to correspond, it seems likely – not least from the fact that Eleanor would a few years later be invited to spend a considerable period of time with her daughter's family. So too does the donation to Fontevraud by Leonor and Alfonso of 100 gold coins a year in 1190,[123] a donation which, although technically within the letter of her marriage contract, seems likely to have been prompted by some notification that Henry would rest there for good. The benefits of a family necropolis would have been well known to Eleanor courtesy of Saint-Denis, and her appreciation may also have been heightened by a visit to the Navarrese mausoleum at Najera when she visited Navarre to collect Berengaria.

From Fontevraud Eleanor could superintend such works as she felt necessary to bring the abbey up to the level she wished for her family. What is more, as had been demonstrated with the schooling of Joan and John, its location was more convenient for keeping in touch with her family than a retreat into Aquitaine. On the borders of Poitou and Anjou, it permitted her to sally forth for family gatherings or to take action if needed.

However, it seems the final designation of Fontevraud as the dynastic home was not made until after 1199; it is not until that date that the image of Henry II which we see today was begun. Perhaps Eleanor's first retirement should therefore be regarded as a tentative step, which might have been revoked if she found the house uncongenial, or her wishes hard to bring about – a possibility with a change in abbess taking place in 1194 on the death of Henry's cousin Mathildis of Flanders.

One other possible attraction, which has not been previously remarked, is the presence at the abbey of her granddaughter Alix of Blois, daughter of Eleanor's second daughter Alice and her husband Thibaut of Blois. Alix was born after 1183 and does not appear in a donation of 1190, so she may have joined the abbey young as an oblate, and thus been present when Eleanor made it her home in 1194. Eleanor definitely built up a relationship with this granddaughter, for in 1199 she would make a gift to her. Another tantalising possibility is that this also provided an opportunity for Eleanor to finally know her daughter Alice, for she had been widowed in 1191 at Acre and it would be natural for her to make visits to the abbey where her youngest daughter was growing up. Any acquaintance with her daughter would not last long, however; Alice died in around 1196.[124]

Eleanor also had with her a fairly considerable household; hers was by no means a monastic retreat. We know her household at this time contained a number of priest-clerks. Traceable to her household are her almoner Richard, John the chaplain, another chaplain named Ranulph and two other clerks, Peter Morinus and William. The latter received four Angevin pounds annually from her dower estate of Bonneville-sur-Toques.[125] Again, this emphasizes the importance to Eleanor, even in a religious retreat, of her own religious household.

Eleanor is often described as retreating 'behind the walls' of Fontevraud. In fact, it would appear that there were no such walls, at least at the time of her first retirement; one of her donations to the abbey was precisely for the purpose of building them.[126] She also funded a new kitchen, and what was in effect a private chapel. Interestingly, this was devoted to St Laurence, the patron saint of students and librarians, who had also featured in the window donated by Eleanor to the cathedral at Poitiers. This can perhaps be taken as an indication of the pleasure which Eleanor took in books, in learning, and in the company of her learned clerks.

Nor did she remain in total retirement. The limited surviving charter evidence indicates that in 1196 alone Eleanor visited Chinon and Saumur.[127] This would suggest a rendezvous with Richard in February, since his itinerary places him in those locations then.[128] The charters she granted on these occasions give interesting snapshots of Eleanor's business. One Saumur charter confirms a gift to Fontevraud of part of the gift of Eaton Bray which she had made to her former butler Ingleram at Winchester before she left England. Another confirms a grant made by Richard to Grandselve Abbey for three measures of salt at Bordeaux each year, and free passage for one ship for the abbey down the Garonne. There is also in this period a charter in favour of the Abbey of Bourgueil made from Fontevraud which shows her mediating a dispute over wine supplies between the abbot and monks of Bourgueil on one part and her men of Jaunaium on the other.[129]

There is a question as to whether Eleanor spent Christmas 1195 with Richard at Poitiers. This is asserted as a likelihood by numerous of Eleanor's biographers (including Flori and Turner). The reality is that there is no solid evidence one way or the other; only the issues of proximity and Eleanor's apparently having ventured further afield to Christmas courts in other years provide any indications in favour of this conclusion.

Another charter indicates that Eleanor received guests, including her family, at Fontevraud. A charter of 1194 indicates that Eleanor and Joanna together determined a dispute between Fontevraud and one of its neighbours in that year. Indeed, it is possible that Joanna had joined Eleanor at Fontevraud, where she had spent some portion of her childhood, for there is no other record of her between her return to France with Berengaria and her second marriage in 1196.[130]

This marriage was to Raymond VI of Toulouse, son of Raymond V of Toulouse and Constance of France, and formed part of Richard's peace strategy. It took place at Rouen in October 1996, and it may well be that Eleanor accompanied Joanna to her marriage there. Although the marriage hardly promised well – Raymond had repudiated two wives in the previous five years – the evidence of Joan's fecundity following it suggests a tolerably happy match at the outset; she would give birth to a son just under ten months after the marriage, and a daughter who was given the same name as her mother in 1198. The pair spent Easter of 1198 with Richard in Le Mans – possibly with Eleanor in attendance.[131]

A further likely guest is her grandson Otto, who was created Count of Poitou by Richard in 1196 and who ruled there until mid-1197, when the death of Henry VI caused Richard to consider his political plans. He himself was solicited to put his name forward as a candidate for the Imperial throne, but sensibly declined. However, he threw his weight behind the candidacy of Otto, who was elected King of the Romans in July 1198. According to Ralph of Coggeshall, Otto resembled Richard closely in his tastes, in his bravery and in his host of admirers. Given his recent engagement to the daughter of the King of Scotland and his investment with the county of York, up until his departure for the Imperial election he had seemed a very possible contender for the throne of England in the absence of Berengaria providing Richard with heirs.[132]

Aside from such welcome guests, Eleanor also had guests on business. She apparently maintained some knights in her household at Fontevraud, and also received others who acted as her deputies in administering her various lands. Turner identifies three such: Henry de Berneval, her steward for her English lands; Geoffrey de Wancy, constable of the Berkhamsted estate; and Wandrill de Courcelles, probably her steward for her Norman dower lands. It is the first of these who witnesses another grant to John's nurse Agatha in 1198 or 1199 of part of a wood in Hemel Hempstead, perhaps to ensure that Agatha should have a dowry to bring on her marriage, which took place around this time. Henry himself received the village of Biddestone – perhaps on a significant birthday, as that charter is witnessed by two other Bernevals.[133]

Eleanor will also have received regular updates of the main items of news – of the progress of Richard's wars, of his illness in April 1195 and his subsequent reconciliation with Berengaria, who had not joined Eleanor at Fontevraud but appears to have been living alone near his base of operations. Other news to come her way would have been of the marriage in August 1195 of Alys of France to William of Ponthieu. Alys, now almost thirty-five years old, was probably not expected to provide an heir. However, in 1196 she was to provide a daughter who would secure the line – which would ultimately contribute brides for Eleanor's great-grandsons Ferdinand of Castile and Edward I. That year Eleanor will also have been apprised of the Bretons' refusal to deliver up Arthur of Brittany and the uneasy peace which was achieved with Constance following a show of force by Richard. She will have heard news of the death of her peer Ermengarde of Narbonne, who died at the end of 1196, an exile from her own lands, in a minor Templar house at Mas-Dieu. Her bequest to them being ignored by her heir and usurper, the second-greatest heiress of her generation would largely fade from memory. No image remains of her; she is not even mentioned in the cartulary of the house where she died.[134]

The year after Joanna's marriage, Eleanor seems to have made a more significant foray from Fontevraud. Howden records her visiting Rouen – probably around the time of Richard's Christmas court there in 1197 – and intervening on behalf of Philip of Dreux, Bishop of Beauvais, who had been instrumental both in souring Richard's relations with the Emperor and in delaying his release. He had been captured in May 1196, and was being held in prison in Rouen, despite an appeal from Celestine. Roger of Howden tells how Eleanor (perhaps looking to oblige Celestine) sought to have the bishop brought to her to talk with him – presumably to work out some deal by which he could be released. However, en route the bishop made a spirited attempt to escape and seek sanctuary in a church. This mishap prevented Eleanor from acting, and resulted in still harsher terms of captivity for the bishop.[135]

Although the bishop's custodians sought to blame Eleanor, it does not seem to have done her any real harm with Richard, for at about the same time we find Eleanor joining with Walter of Coutances in asking Richard to pardon a debt owed by long-time royal servant Hugh Bardolf to the Earl of Chester; a partial remission was granted. And the record also shows Eleanor being looked to for active help despite her 'retirement': in 1198 the monks of Canterbury wrote to her seeking her aid in the ongoing dispute with the archbishop in which she had earlier been involved.[136]

The death of Henry VI, apparently such sweet news, in fact proved something of a harbinger of death for Eleanor's own family. It was closely followed by that of Eleanor's old friend Celestine III, who died in January 1198. At roughly the same time, news will have emerged of the death of her grandson Henri of Champagne, King of Jerusalem. His mother, Eleanor's eldest daughter Marie, herself died in March 1198 having lived in retirement in a priory near Meaux after her son's death. Much has been written about the possible relationship between Eleanor and her daughter in their later years, but the historical record – which, as discussed, does not support to speculation around the 'courts of love' – does not even provide any support for the theory that the pair met in these years. The possibility of their meeting remains a tantalising speculation, far from impossible given Marie's contact with her brothers (Richard wrote a poem to her while in captivity and she had also developed relationship with Geoffrey), marriage ties between courtiers at the two courts and verifiable visits by her husband to Henry's court. In these years, for example on Eleanor's return from Italy, there would be no handicap to such a meeting. However, even if that direct contact did not occur Eleanor may well have had the opportunity to meet her second grandson by Marie, the new Count of Champagne, Theobald, who was engaged to Berengaria's sister Blanca at around this time.

In early 1199, Richard had gone to deal with trouble from Eleanor's habitually difficult vassals in Limoges and Angoulême. On 25 March, he was besieging the castle of Châlus in Limoges when he was hit by a crossbow bolt in the shoulder. What happened next is evidenced by Ralph of Coggeshall, who took a detailed statement from someone who was there – very possibly Richard's confessor. Richard neglected the wound and ignored his doctors, and gangrene set in. After several days, Richard realised that the wound was festering and that death was close. He at once sent for Eleanor – who was over 100 miles away.[137] Pausing here, one can see the clear evidence of genuine attachment and affection between Richard and Eleanor; approaching death, Richard wanted his mother at his side – regardless of the difficulties involved in getting a woman now into her seventies transported over a hundred miles.

Eleanor's reciprocal affection is evidenced by the fact that she immediately went to Richard's side, apparently by forced marches, since she arrived in time to be with the son who appears to have been closest to her, and of whom she was deservedly proud – referring to him as 'that mighty man'.[138] She was accompanied on the journey by the abbot Luke of Turpenay, whose abbey was a close neighbour to Fontevraud, being situated between Chinon and Langeais. The abbot was already well known to Eleanor – he is a frequent witness of her charters in her Fontevraud years, and appears to have been the latest in the line of churchmen upon whom Eleanor leaned for advice during her life.

The fact of Eleanor's presence at her son's deathbed is actually verified by her own words – in a grant shortly afterwards she says, 'Know that we were present at the death of our son the King.' That death came as evening fell on 6 April 1199. It was, almost to the day, forty-three years after the death of Eleanor's first son.

11

The Matriarch

> She graced the nobility of her birth with the honesty of her life, enriched it with her moral excellence, adorned it with the flowers of her virtue and by her reputation for unmatched goodness she surpassed almost all the Queens of the World.
>
> Eleanor's epitaph at Fontevraud

Richard reputedly asked on his deathbed to be buried with his father at Fontevraud, with his heart to go to Rouen to lie with his grandmother the Empress and his brother Henry. On his death, his body was accordingly eviscerated and the parts prepared for transport. His viscera were buried in the church of Châlus Castle – possibly as a mark of contempt for the locals who had defied him.

Eleanor was back on the road again soon after his death, this time in the company and at the pace of a funeral cortege. Again she was accompanied by the Abbot of Turpenay, but with them rode a number of Richard's intimates, including Eleanor's cousin the Viscount of Thouars and his brother Guy, the new husband of Constance of Brittany and hence stepfather to Arthur of Brittany. Also in the party were William des Roches and Peter Savaric, as well as Miles, Abbot of Le Pin, formerly Richard's almoner and the likely eyewitness source for Coggeshall's account of Richard's death. At Fontevraud the party found Bishop Hugh of Lincoln, who had been travelling to meet the king and settle a dispute which had arisen between them.

The funeral took place on Palm Sunday, 11 April 1199, and the crowd of mourners was joined by the bishops of Angers and Poitiers. The chief celebrant was Bishop Hugh, but Eleanor recorded in a grant to the Abbey of Turpenay two weeks later that Abbot Luke 'laboured above all others in the arrangement of his funeral'. It appears likely that Berengaria did not attend; she is not listed as a witness to a charter which Eleanor granted to Fontevraud that day, and one account refers to Bishop Hugh visiting Berengaria at her residence before the funeral, implying that he did not go to bring her to it. This reinforces the impression that Eleanor and Berengaria had formed no affectionate tie. Our knowledge of the attendees of the funeral derives from a charter which Eleanor executed making a grant to provide for the soul of her 'dearest' son. It reveals the presence of the bishops of Poitiers and Angers supplementing the funeral party.

This grant also refers to the complete confidence which Richard placed in her 'that we would provide for his salvation in accordance with our maternal solicitude'; and he did so rightly. He could justly be confident in this; even before his death Eleanor had made grants contingent on prayers for him, and after his death she was scrupulous about seeking intercession for him at every opportunity. Another grant a few weeks later was for Henry, Young Henry, Richard and Eleanor's sons and daughters, and her grant to Turpenay was specifically contingent on perpetual prayers for 'my dearest son Richard' and for annual memorial services for him. Another grant on the day of his funeral by William de Mauzé, at Eleanor's 'will and request' in order that Richard 'might swiftly obtain mercy from the Lord', provides tunics for the nuns who would be praying for him.[1]

But Eleanor was not mourning and memorialising in seclusion. By the time of the grant to Turpenay on 21 April 1199 she had been joined at Fontevraud by yet more distinguished guests, including John, Berengaria and the bishops of Capua and Agen. Berengaria acted as witness to this grant. Also recorded as present were Alix of Blois and Eleanor's granddaughter and former houseguest Mathilde, indicating that Eleanor's female relatives came to offer her support in what must have been the greatest tragedy of her long life.

While the cast of characters who assembled round Eleanor in late April 1199 doubtless came in part to pay their respects, there is also in the list a suggestion that it was at least as much in Eleanor's presence as in the more famous debate between William Marshal and Hubert Walter in Vaudreuil that the future of the English monarchy was hammered out. Richard notes accurately how in this interregnum period the only undoubted source of regal authority was Eleanor, 'who continued to qualify as Queen of England, Duchess of Normandy and Aquitaine and Countess of Anjou'.[2]

This reality is also apparent when picking apart the Histoire. It tells how the Marshal was notified of Richard's illness by the king himself, who told him to store his treasure in a keep in Rouen. It does not suggest that the letter gave instructions as to Richard's intentions for his successor. It then goes on to tell how William hurried to tell Hubert Walter once news of the death reached Vaudreuil, and they then had a discussion, the upshot of which was that Marshal countered Hubert Walter's lawyerly view that Arthur was the correct heir and advocated John's claim. According to the Histoire, Hubert Walter changed his view simply because Marshal advocated John – and despite his view that they would live to regret the decision. That a clever churchman and lawyer should meekly take the advice of William Marshal – a doughty warrior but no subtle counsellor – is inherently implausible. Still less so when one ponders the omissions in the tale. Whence came the Marshal's knowledge, and his certainty of view? It appears likely that the source of the Marshal's information as to Richard's death, and the line which should be taken on it, was Eleanor herself; who, let us recall, was well placed to send such information, and who trusted Marshal as Richard had.[3]

Why did Eleanor elect for John, as she certainly did? Traditionally, the story goes that Eleanor disliked (or according to Flori loathed[4]) Constance of Brittany and consequently distrusted her son Arthur. On this view, John was essentially her choice *faut de mieux*. This overstates the position as regards Constance, and understates it as regards John. There is no evidence of a loathing or history of distrust between Eleanor and Constance. That is a much later construct. There is in fact relatively little sign of their having much to do with each other. Constance was not as much based in the English court as a girl as was Marguerite of France, and consequently knew Eleanor less well. Constance was well enough inclined to Eleanor to name her eldest daughter after her. Constance certainly did resent Henry's forcing her to marry Ranulf of Chester, but the blame for this could hardly be placed at Eleanor's door; the marriage had occurred in 1188, when Eleanor was completely outside the circle of power, if no longer formally imprisoned. Since Henry's death, Constance and

Eleanor seem unlikely to have met. However, that very fact was one source of Eleanor's reluctance to favour Arthur.

Constance had sought protection from Philip, and although he had technically been at peace with Richard it was a peace brought about by hostilities and hostages.[5] Arthur's supporters had deliberately kept him from Angevin custody, and it was with French support and protection that he maintained his court in Brittany. And events were to demonstrate the veracity of this view – within days of Richard's death Constance and Arthur had sworn fealty to Philip Augustus. To promote Arthur as heir would be doing exactly what Philip wanted, effectively subjugating the Plantagenet empire to France. On this point, at least, Eleanor and Henry were as one; and Eleanor's actions following his death indicate strongly her commitment to promoting that empire.

Practicality also dictated John as the ruler of England at least; a good portion of his childhood and early adult years had been spent there. Of all her sons, he was probably best educated to take up the mantle of being English king. Moreover, as his actions against Richard showed, he had established networks and allies in England which would not be open to any other candidate. These two factors seem to have underpinned Richard's own tacit acknowledgement of John as his heir in the later years of his reign. This logic would not, of course, apply to Poitou and Aquitaine; John was more of a stranger in Eleanor's homelands than Richard had been in England. Nearly all of his childhood had been spent in England; his last visit to Poitou was as part of the internecine struggles of the mid-1180s.[6] But Otto, the natural alternative, could by no means claim the title with his hands far too full trying to convert his election as King of the Romans into full recognition as Emperor.

One should also not neglect the role played by genuine affection on Eleanor's part towards John. While Turner asserts that Eleanor had never been close to John, the evidence does not entirely bear him out. On two occasions, the records have shown Eleanor advocating John's cause to Richard, a course (given her acknowledged fondness for Richard) most consistent with affection for John. Again, just after the funeral Richard suggests that Eleanor assisted John to gain control of the castle of Chinon and its treasury by advocating his cause with the Seneschal of Anjou.[7] It is of course traditional to doubt Eleanor's bond with John; this forms the bedrock of a number of historians' approaches to John's failings. However, as noted above, John appears to have been with Eleanor until her move to Aquitaine in 1168, and within easy reach of her in the years thereafter, with the evidence suggesting strongly that she visited Fontevraud not infrequently. And while he was not in her household following her imprisonment, he was placed for some time in the household of Ranulf de Glanville, who was in overall charge of Eleanor, and must have encountered her at least periodically throughout the year. In truth, John might in fact have had more contact with his mother after the age of seven than her other sons, who had been moved into separate households, often in a different portion of the Angevin empire.

Whatever the combination of reasons, Eleanor plainly elected for John at an early stage, and may well have been the person responsible for alerting John to Richard's imminent death, causing him to slip away from Arthur's court in Brittany where he had been paying a visit at the time of Richard's injury. Eleanor is also slightly implausibly credited by Roger of Howden and the later Roger of Wendover in the days after the funeral with more extreme measures in support of her son. He has her actually taking to the field in the company of her cousin Aimery of Thouars and Mercadier, and marching on Angers – a story which would inspire a warlike elderly lady in the epic poem *Aliscans*.[8] However, it seems far more plausible that she personally remained at Fontevraud throughout the period between the funeral and her donation to Turpenay in late April – a donation, it is notable, in which she associated her 'very dear son' John, thereby bringing him into her circle of power. Having said that, the despatch of Mercadier to devastate the land around Angers, where Arthur had been already recognised as Duke of Brittany, and of Poitevin nobles to confront Arthur at Tours, forcing Arthur's withdrawal to Paris with Philip, will have been an exercise of Eleanor's power rather than that of John. It demonstrates decisiveness, a keen tactical appreciation and, at last, the confidence of the male military hierarchy in the commands of a woman. This is in itself remarkable, and represents an advance in the power previously exercised by Eleanor.

With initial steps taken on his behalf, John moved to be invested as Duke of Normandy by Walter of Coutances in Rouen Cathedral on 25 April 1199; Eleanor, however, did not join him. Instead, and doubtless the result of agreement between her and John when they met earlier in the month, she set off with a considerable household to her own domains, without an Angevin leader since the death of Richard and the return of Otto to stake his claim as Emperor.

So on 29 April – less than a month after the death of Richard – Eleanor is found in Loudun accepting in part the petition of Raoul de Mauléon, formerly Lord of La Rochelle and Talmont, to be restored to his lands. Talmont she granted, but La Rochelle was exchanged for the castle of Banaum. Raoul performed liege homage directly to Eleanor, swearing to defend her and all her lands and honours. So far the transaction seems simple, but it appears to show a rather nasty situation with which Eleanor had to deal urgently. For the charter speaks of Raoul's offer to prove his right to the lands sought by not just his own oath but the oath of one hundred of his knights; this rather suggests that he came to the meeting supported by a hundred knights, thereby indicating the size of the force he had to put in the field if his right was disputed. Further, Richard, knowledgeable about the affairs of Poitou, analyses the charter as granting unprecedented concessions. So too does the charter implicitly betray itself as a deal of necessity, for Eleanor records that she makes the grant because 'we wish to have his service, which is necessary to us and our son John'.[9]

Beneath the veneer of an easy transition, then, is the reality which had dogged Eleanor's sole exercise of power throughout her life: the need for an enforcer. In this period, that need was provided in part by Richard's mercenary captain Mercadier. He is glimpsed on occasions throughout Eleanor's tour, conducting punitive raids on those who were deemed to have misaligned themselves and also on one occasion in a charter being proffered as protection to the Abbey of Candeil. It appears that Eleanor and Mercadier formed a fairly close bond from the time of Richard's death and that he was content to pursue his career at her side rather than that of John. Other prominent military men seem to have formed part of her party, namely Chalon de Rochefort and Laon Ogier. Also at her side were other knights or magnates whose loyalty she could count on, among them her cousins Raoul II and William de Faye and Andrew de Chauvigny's brother Geoffrey, who had acted as Richard's chamberlain. Apparently one or both of the Lusignans were to be found travelling with Eleanor some of the time, inferentially with their own military retinues.[10]

Within days Eleanor was at Poitiers for the first time since 1173, holding court among her barons (including Geoffrey de Lusignan and her de Faye relatives) at the Abbey of Montierneuf, so long associated with her house. It was perhaps the first time she had been able to use the new hall, whose building she had initiated before her captivity. Her charters note her early return after the death of 'her dearest son King Richard' and re-grant the monastery of St John privileges granted by her forebears. She also made further grants to Fontevraud. A charter in favour of the recently orphaned Alix of Blois, described as Eleanor's 'dearest ward', suggests that her granddaughter was travelling with her. Eleanor was also accompanied at least as far as Poitiers by a considerable number of older women of high status. Principal among these was Matilda, Abbess of Fontevraud, but also mentioned are a Countess Matilda, which may signify her granddaughter Mathilde of Perche (though Matilda, Viscountess of Aunay is also mentioned), the Duchess of 'Borbonie' and the Countess of Tonnerre. Some of these may well have been affluent widows who had themselves retired to Fontevraud and had struck up a friendship with Eleanor, but the last named appears to have been an eleven-year-old heiress who was presumably being educated under Eleanor's aegis, perhaps with Alix.[11]

At this time, Eleanor also granted Poitiers the status of a commune – some sixty years after the move was so violently opposed by her first husband. However, she did not stay long – within a day she was moving south again, this time to Niort. Here she issued charters to Grace Dieu Abbey and Grandmont Priory, confirming grants of Richard and Otto. At Niort, too, Eleanor had a distinctly bittersweet encounter. Joanna, pregnant for the third time in as many years, had been attacked by her husband's vassals while he was (as was his wont) off making war against other vassals. The unfortunate Joanna, burnt and very possibly in distress owing to difficulties in her marriage as well as the ordeal she had undergone, had decided to seek out Richard – only to hear of his death. Eleanor thus saw her daughter again for only the second time since her departure for her marriage in 1176; but as with the previous encounter, it was vanishingly brief. The importance of Eleanor's job is evidenced by the fact that she despatched the injured Joanna to Fontevraud to be cared for by the nuns, but pressed on with her tour.

Eleanor appears to have been accompanied by a considerable court of leading men, for we find Raoul de Faye and Hubert de Forz at Poitiers and Bordeaux with her and also at Rouen at the end of the tour, implying that they were with her throughout. Others such as Hugh de Lusignan and Geoffrey de Chauvigny appear repeatedly in the witness lists also. And of course Eleanor was accompanied by a number of prominent churchmen – the bishops of Saintes and Poitiers seem to have accompanied much of the tour, and the Archbishop of Bordeaux's advice is specifically mentioned.[12] In addition, at each place the most prominent local citizens appear as witnesses, demonstrating that Eleanor effectively held local courts as she progressed.

Next she was at La Rochelle, where she issued a charter to the men of the port granting them a corporation – similar to the steps she had taken in Poitiers. Eleanor would grant similar charters in the other major cities of Poitou, including Oléron, Niort, Saintes and Bordeaux, confirming the liberties of the cities. Although Weir describes this as an initiative of Eleanor's, it should in fact be seen as a continuation of the policy of Henry II and Richard, both of whom had appreciated the economic arguments for such a course; nor was it likely that John, trained in Glanville's household, would have a different view. Indeed, in the case of Bordeaux he specifically confirmed the grant later in the year. Moreover, such charters operated as a necessary *quid pro quo* at this time. Eleanor's job was to obtain pledges of loyalty, and also of military aid if needed; the granting or confirming of a charter of liberties in each case resulted in reciprocal pledges of loyalty and assistance. The slightly enforced nature of the multiple grants is made clear again in Bordeaux, where the townspeople also petitioned for the removal of certain impositions put in place by Richard (in particular as regards taxes on wine) which they regarded as unjust; Eleanor's assent states in terms that she is expecting in support of her 'dearest son, John' all the fidelity and devotion which Bordeaux had always shown to her family. The argument that Eleanor innovated or supported economic development as a particular aim is therefore wide of the mark, but it is true that she took politically acute steps to shore up support for John.[13]

Hindsight creates the illusion that John's succession was inevitable. However, that is not so. That there were doubts throughout the higher ranks of Richard's followers is indicated by the exchange between William Marshal and Hubert Walter. It is reinforced by other vignettes. The family of Thouars was split down the middle; Aimery at least initially stayed loyal to John, while Guy (married to Constance of Brittany) espoused Arthur's cause. As noted above, the grant which Eleanor made to Raoul de Mauléon specifically states that his service is necessary to Eleanor and to John. Finally, a charter from Eleanor's time in Bordeaux speaks of the loss of her elder sons and says, 'God having left us still in the world, we have been obliged in order to provide for the needs of our people and the welfare of our lands, to visit Gascony.'[14]

The need for action to ensure support is also reflected in the extent of Eleanor's tour: from Poitiers she went to Niort, and then on to Andilly, La Rochelle and Oléron, Saint Jean D'Angely, Saintes and Bordeaux, which she reached by 1 July 1199. This amounted to a distance of over 180 miles from Fontevraud. At most of these places Eleanor issued charters in favour of the towns or local churches and abbeys, such as Saint-Eutrope de Saintes, or her long-supported Notre-Dame des Saintes. In Bordeaux, Eleanor presided over a large gathering of the lords of the more southerly parts of her lands: the Archbishop of Bordeaux, the bishops of Saintes and Lectoure, the Count of Bigorre and Bearn, the Count of Foix and the Viscount of Tartas.[15] While there she issued a number of charters, to the men of Bordeaux and to the cathedral. Often, we should note, the charters describe John as '*karissimi*' or dearest, giving the lie to suggestions that only Richard ever attracted this adjective – but also making plain to what extent Eleanor was attempting to associate John with her, and invest this stranger to her lands with some of her political capital. It is also usually the case with the charters to religious houses that Eleanor seeks prayers for herself and for Henry and Richard – confirming Eleanor's habit of seeking intercessory prayers for her family. Nearly always, ironically, despite the huge power she was now exercising, she described herself as 'humble Queen of England'.[16]

From Bordeaux Eleanor headed north, at first to Royan but then in the direction of Rouen – a further distance of over 400 miles. She appears, judging by the charter evidence, to have stopped off at Poitiers – a charter to Cadouin Abbey is dated from there on 15 July. She was accompanied on her journey by a substantial retinue including the Archbishop of Bordeaux, Geoffrey de Lusignan, the Count of Eu, William Maingot and the 'faithful' Raoul de Mauléon. She accomplished this journey in less than a month, being recorded with John in Rouen late in July.[17] On the way she also found time and opportunity, sometime around 20 July 1199 (not June as Weir asserts), to rendezvous at Tours with Philip of France – perhaps to meet her grandson Arthur, who was under Philip's guardianship, but certainly to perform homage to Philip for Poitou.[18]

This homage is a remarkable act in itself. As Martindale notes, it was not normal for a woman to perform homage in person. There is no previous record of Eleanor performing homage for her lands, for example on her divorce from Louis, and since then all acts of homage had been performed by her husband or her sons. Further, the legal text accredited to Ranulf de Glanville indicates that as a matter of English law homage should be performed by the nearest male relative, doubtless because of the military connotations of the act. Philip accepted Eleanor's homage and offered her the kiss of peace. The extent to which that homage also applied to the legally separate territories of Aquitaine and Gascony will likely have been a question on which the parties differed subjectively. However, the idea of Eleanor's performing homage was indubitably a clever one, binding Philip not to act against her in the lands for which she had given homage (and implicitly those for which he chose to believe she had given him).[19]

On the way to Rouen Eleanor also stopped at Le Vaudreuil, where she made two grants in favour of Andrew de Chauvigny, a long-time supporter of Richard's whom she attempts to bind closer to her, acknowledging him as her dear friend and relative.[20] The difficulties Eleanor faced are also well illustrated by this transaction, for Chauvigny, who had been close to Richard and rewarded by him with a highly valuable marriage to the heiress of Chateauroux, had still been minded to take Arthur's part. These grants, witnessed by such luminaries as Robert of Leicester and William Marshal, represent a significant intervention by Eleanor, who offered him further lands in exchange for his support.[21]

In Rouen, Eleanor and John then completed the legalities concerning Aquitaine. She acknowledged him as her rightful heir, ceding Poitou to him and transferring to him all the oaths of fealty which she had just extracted from her lay and ecclesiastical magnates. John then granted her a life interest in the province, indicating that she would rule as lady of both Poitou and all his other territories. The documents make clear that Eleanor is not simply a delegate but one with equal and co-extensive power, and that her landholding rights are joint with John. In some ways these documents look remarkable as emphasising Eleanor's power, but they are actually more remarkable in that it is John whose position is being protected. The trick of the documents was twofold. In the first place, John gained the benefit of the feudal protection which Eleanor had extracted from Philip. But secondly, on Eleanor's death there could be no question about the right to inheritance of her lands; as joint tenant of the rights and lands, John would seamlessly become their ruler, with no *scintilla temporis* at which Philip and Arthur could claim there to be an interregnum. By the homage and these documents, Eleanor sheltered John behind her skirts.[22]

Who was responsible for this genius idea, and the partner idea of the homage? The prime candidates are Eleanor and John. It may be said to be more likely that they are John's, for they are worthy of a man who had studied in the household of Glanville, where one of the leading medieval works on English law was authored. But Eleanor had herself spent much time in Glanville's company, and would have had much greater knowledge of the subtleties of her own lands' procedures for homage. It is therefore likely that at least some of the planning of this suite of actions was Eleanor's own work. There is also, as Martindale notes, a significant parallel here between the 'get out of jail card' which Eleanor advised Richard to deploy in giving homage to Henry VI and this shield for John via her homage to Philip. As Eleanor is convincingly accredited with the former, it is hardly unlikely that she had a real role in the latter.[23]

In the days which followed this settlement, Eleanor ensured that John endorsed various gifts to faithful servants and knights. So a gift of a second manor in England to Agatha was confirmed. Also confirmed was a gift to Geoffrey de Chauvigny, and the bestowal of the Ile D'Oléron on the Forz family. She restored to St Radegonde's Abbey of St Croix at Poitiers a moor taken from them by Richard during his life. Eleanor also ensured that John confirmed all past gifts to Fontevraud and made a donation to Amesbury Priory, Fontevraud's daughter house.[24]

At some point either on the tour or during August, Joanna, now heavily pregnant, joined her mother and brother at Rouen. Her estranged husband was not paying her any allowance, his view being that she should be with him; John, explicitly at his 'dearest lady and mother's' behest, therefore made some arrangements to cover her expenses. As soon as she had money at her disposal, Joanna made a gift of 1,000 shillings from her dowerlands in Agen for the maintenance of the nun's kitchen at Fontevraud – a subject about which she obviously felt keenly as she emphasised the grant was 'for no other purpose'.[25] The grant was also made subject to a provision that it was made for the welfare of her soul and that of her dearest brother King Richard and the rest of her family.

The grant for the welfare of her soul indicates plainly that Joanna's health was a concern, despite the fact that she was only thirty-three – perhaps not surprising after her sufferings and the lengthy journey north in the heat of summer while heavily pregnant. This concern is also apparent from the fact that John granted her 3,000 marks to allow her to make a will at this time, in which she left bequests to her servants and religious houses, including a further bequest to Fontevraud for annual memorial services and a bequest to the Abbey of Turpenay, as well as bequests to her maids Beatrice and Alice. Joanna's interest in food speaks through her will, with a specific bequest for fish for the nuns in Lent. Bequests were made to the nuns of Bonneville (Eleanor's dower property) as well as to the cathedral of Rouen and all the other religious houses of the city. Again, Eleanor's closeness to her daughter and her power are evident in this will, the bequests being stipulated to be paid 'by the hands of the most reverend Eleanor our mother' and at intervals which she would agree with the archbishops of Canterbury and Rouen.[26]

At the start of September, Joanna seemingly went into labour. It seems probable that the baby was a breech presentation and could not be delivered. In any event, it became apparent that she would not survive much longer. She begged to be veiled as a nun of Fontevraud – a request entirely contrary to convention since she was both married and pregnant. Eleanor and others tried to dissuade her, but Joanna was insistent. Abbess Matilda of Fontevraud was sent for, but with Joanna *in extremis* Hubert Walter was prevailed upon to consider the case. He too counselled patience, and the advent of the abbess, but as Joanna's condition worsened Eleanor persuaded him to convene a committee of nuns and clergy who agreed that Joanna's vocation must be inspired by heaven and authorised the exceptional move. With Eleanor at her side and many witnesses including the archbishop and Luke of Turpenay present, the dying countess was veiled. Within a very short period she was dead, and the baby was delivered and christened Richard before he, too, died.[27]

Joanna's body was despatched to Fontevraud to lie near her brother and father, as she had stipulated in her will. It seems likely that Eleanor accompanied her daughter there, to see her interred among the nuns, before taking another journey south to take the will to Joanna's estranged husband to ensure that he honoured the relevant portions of it. It also seems possible that she took with her on this journey the daughter of Isaac Komnenos, whom Richard had displaced as Emperor of Cyprus. This young lady had travelled back to Europe with Joanna, narrowly escaped marriage to the Duke of Austria as part of Richard's peace deal, and is tentatively identified as the Beatrice who was Joanna's companion in her last days, and who received a bequest under Joanna's will. Raymond of Toulouse was to go on to marry 'the damsel of Cyprus' in early 1200; however, as with his earlier marriages the match did not last, ending in divorce in 1202.

On her return, Eleanor settled down once more at Fontevraud. It was probably at this point that she began to have leisure to consider the memorials which would need to be raised to her husband and son – and in due course to herself. And it was now that the final decision as to whether to make Fontevraud an Angevin necropolis would have been taken – and the decision also taken as to its style. In this Eleanor had plenty of inspiration to draw on – from her visits to Constantinople, Jerusalem and Sicily on Crusade, from Reading and Saint-Denis, and probably via correspondence with Leonor, who was hard at work on Las Huelgas in Castile for a similar purpose.

The tombs erected to Henry and Richard were probably created at the same time and by the same artist. They are also stylistically self-evidently a pair; they are portrayed with all the references to the Angevin coronation rite, which was replicated in Angevin convention. Both therefore had a crown, a sword, and a sceptre, the spurs and gloves and the evidence of anointing. The figure traditionally identified as Henry is clean shaven, dressed with an undergown of green, over which is layered a red-and-gold gown and a blue robe. He reclines on a drapery of gold. Richard (bearded) is dressed in the same colours but slightly differently layered and arranged. One point to note is that while it is clear that the two representations are of Henry and Richard, there remains a question as to whether they have been correctly assigned. There is, in fact, a very credible case to be made for Richard's being the clean-shaven figure.[28]

Modern scholarship, particularly by Alain Erlande Brandenburg and Kathleen Nolan,[29] suggests that the images of Henry and Richard were executed at the same time, shortly after Richard's death. From our modern perspective it is tempting to regard them as charming but part of a continuum of similar depictions. This is a fundamental misconception. The images are novel in two ways.

Firstly, they are among the very first tombs to portray their subjects with fully sculptured life-sized effigies – a fashion which was to be much copied in the years to come. They were also ground-breaking in depicting the ruler lying in state in the glory of kingship and yet definitely recumbent.

This is best appreciated by comparing some of the other high-status monuments of the era. Empress Matilda was buried under a slab marked with an epitaph. Geoffrey le Bel had a beautiful but small enamel plaque depicting him ready for battle. Substantial monuments might not have been unusual in the East, but they were in the form of sarcophagi or funerary urns. In Castile there was some tradition of tomb chests carved with a frieze, not unlike more elaborate roman tombs, though there is a record of one statue – that to Queen Urraca.[30] But prior to Eleanor's commissioning of the Fontevraud tombs, only two full-size personal depictions are verifiably on record. The first of these was that of Eleanor's one-time mother-in-law Adelaide of Maurienne, whose tomb boasted a full-length image in something like mosaic form; it was therefore not unlike a scaled-up version of the Geoffrey le Bel monument. But the nearest parallel was the tomb of Louis VII, commissioned by Adela of Champagne, at the monastery of Fleury. Like the images which Eleanor commissioned, it was a fully fashioned sculptural depiction, with him clad as for his coronation with a crown and sceptre. The decision as to the nature of the monuments can only have been Eleanor's, and she should be seen as having considered and carefully selected every part of this set of images. Eleanor was deliberately both taking funerary art a step further forwards and asserting the status of her royal house as equal to or exceeding that of France.

But Eleanor's peaceful occupations were soon to be disturbed. Outside the new walls of Fontevraud, Philip and John moved closer to peace. In early 1200, Eleanor was notified that this peace was to be ratified by the marriage of Philip's heir, Louis, to one of the daughters of Leonor and Alfonso VIII of Castile. Eleanor was asked to make the journey to the court of her only surviving daughter, whom she had not seen since autumn of 1170, to select the appropriate bride and bring her back to France. Early in the new year, Eleanor once again set off for the Pyrenees in winter. This time she was accompanied by the Archbishop of Bordeaux and Mercadier.[31]

It is sometimes suggested that Eleanor was ambushed and taken captive by the Lusignans on this journey, being released only at the price of ceding to them the county of La Marche, long in contention between the Lusignans and the Count of Angoulême. In fact, this story seems unlikely; it is far more plausible that the grant of La Marche was part of Eleanor's tour the previous year, and unsurprising given that the rival claimant was supporting Arthur's claims and that the Lusignans had been very present in her support. Furthermore, this exciting event seems not to fit with the timeline, since Eleanor is recorded in Castile (either Toledo or Burgos) by the end of January 1200.[32]

Leonor and Alfonso had by this stage had eleven children. The eldest, a remarkable young woman called Berengaria, was now married to her cousin Alphonso IX of León. The four boys and a girl who came after her had died young, but there was still a good-sized nursery in 1200: Urraca was thirteen, Blanca eleven, Fernando ten, Mafalda eight and Constanza four. Eleanor stayed for two months, since the peace was not due to be signed until after Easter, and had ample opportunity to get to know these grandchildren and to renew her acquaintance with Leonor. That the visit was a happy one is probably reflected in the fact that Leonor's next baby was named for her mother. There is no contemporaneous record of how Blanca came to be the chosen bride, but a later Spanish chronicle places the decision at Eleanor's door, saying that she chose her on the grounds that her name would translate better to French. Other writers have deduced, with the benefit of hindsight, that Eleanor perceived in Blanca greater qualities of mind and temperament, and made the decision on that basis. Blanca, or Blanche as she henceforth became, was indeed to become a remarkable force in French politics.[33]

It was therefore late in March that Eleanor set off again with Blanche, travelling through the pass of Roncevalles into Gascony. By 9 April they had reached Bordeaux for Easter, and here Mercadier came to constitute an escort north. But Mercadier had enemies in the city, and on the second day in Easter week he was assassinated by a man in the service of a rival mercenary captain. The combination of the long journey and this shock appears to have hit Eleanor hard; Howden describes her as 'worn out by her long and tiring journey'. So she decided not to accompany little Blanche north to Normandy but to send her with the Archbishop of Bordeaux, while she returned to her retirement. Blanche married the future Louis VIII on 23 May 1200.[34]

Eleanor's final years at Fontevraud may have been placid, but they should not be suspected of being lonely or without intellectual stimulus. Aside from the female friendships which the events after Richard's death evidence, Eleanor continued to maintain a substantial household of clerks, usually men of religious training. 'Roger our chaplain' had followed Eleanor on her 1199 tour of her lands, acting as her secretary also. At Fontevraud he became a monk and had the conduct of what was in effect Eleanor's private chapel, devoted to St Laurence,[35] his needs being funded by donations Eleanor had made to the abbey. He was later supplemented by two other chaplains, Roger and Jocelin. Religious men also staffed Eleanor's private office. William of St-Maixent, hailing from the well-known abbey in Poitou, was Eleanor's clerk and notary, and later served John. Eleanor also had a clerk of the chamber called Richard of Gnosall. She also continued to receive her men of business and petitioners. In October 1200, we find her executing two charters in favour of St-Maixent Abbey.[36]

Nor did Eleanor remain at Fontevraud entirely; she appears to have visited Poitiers on numerous occasions, probably in part to supervise her building project renovating the great hall of the ducal palace in the modern style.

As with her first retirement, she remained in contact with the political currents of the day. In early 1201, although ill, she summoned (he said commanded) her cousin Aimery of Thouars to her bedside to pressure him into remaining loyal to John and indeed to take steps to deal with those who had not, despite John's decision to replace him as custodian of Chinon Castle. The encounter is recorded in a letter from Eleanor to John (again, it is worthy of note, accorded the greeting 'Dearest').[37] This letter may perhaps be regarded as the closest thing to Eleanor's authentic voice which we are likely to find: it is a letter to her son, rather than a letter of business or a letter to an eminent churchman. It is also signed *'teste me ipso'* which is thought to signify that the ruler has dictated or specifically approved the document.[38] And it is genuinely a 'speaking' letter; the flavour of a redoubtable old lady laying into a younger relative with little compunction comes across loud and clear.

Eleanor reports with glee that she is recovering better following the meeting – revelling in her success. She explains how she at once praised Aimery for not being disloyal like others and berated him for sitting on his hands while others were disloyal. She says that Aimery, wilting under her attack, promised to do everything in his power to bring back to John's command the lands seized by his disloyal friends, and pledged his own loyalty wholeheartedly. Eleanor rounded off the meeting by telling him to write to John and set John's mind at rest; and Aimery duly did so, writing a lengthy letter of his own, telling of the meeting and assuring John of his fidelity. Sadly, the effects of Eleanor's intervention were not long-lasting. By 1202, John had succeeded in alienating Aimery again.

The illness referred to in this letter was not Eleanor's only illness; she is reported ill in mid-1201, and was visited by John, who went on to tour parts of her Poitevin territories. It was during the course of this tour that he met and married Isabelle of Angoulême, daughter of the Count of Angoulême and intended bride of Hugh de Lusignan, an event which created a considerable amount of scandal, as well as alienating the Lusignans at a very unfortunate moment.[39] It is likely that on the return leg of the journey the newly married pair paid their respects to Eleanor, for at around this time Eleanor dowered Isabelle with the cities of Niort and Saintes, thereby effectively backing John in his refusal to convey the traditional dower of an English queen to Berengaria.[40] John and Eleanor probably felt more confident in maintaining this stance because Berengaria's sister Blanca had been widowed earlier in the year and so Berengaria had no male support in the region. Both sisters were effectively reliant on the support of their brother Sancho.

In September 1201, Constance of Brittany, aged forty, died giving birth to her second daughter by Guy de Thouars. Such influence as she had been able to exert over her teenaged son Arthur was thus removed and he fell completely under the influence of Philip of France. In spring 1202, Philip, whose summons to answer the Lusignans' complaints John had ignored, acknowledged Arthur as Duke of Brittany and Count of Anjou and Poitou 'if God grants that either we or he shall acquire it by any means whatsoever', and celebrated his engagement to Philip's daughter Marie. While Philip remained in the north to confront John directly, and did not directly breach his oath to Eleanor, he tacitly sent Arthur to assert his own claims in the south.[41]

It is thus that in summer 1202 Eleanor – and possibly the recently widowed Mathilde of Perche – is found besieged at Mirabeau.

The sources concentrate on John's reaction and do not explain whether Eleanor had taken the initiative following Philip's recognition of Arthur and gone to rally support, or whether she fled to Mirabeau to escape capture. Both aspects probably came into it. Authority in Aquitaine still legally lay with Eleanor. She still had the power to revoke her grants to John and remake them to Arthur. Just as at the time of her first and second marriages, a seizure of her person at this juncture would have been key to interested parties – in this case to John's enemies. And Fontevraud lay en route into Poitou for any troops making their way from Brittany.

Any sensible plan would therefore involve seizing Eleanor, 'persuading' her to recognise Arthur, and not being terribly bothered about how soon thereafter she died. This is the version inclined to by Ralph of Coggeshall, the Essex-based chronicler whose account of events is the most detailed. He says that Arthur, at Tours, heard that Eleanor was lodging at Mirebeau and set out to besiege the castle with a view to taking Eleanor hostage, and perhaps bartering her for Queen Isabella. However, mapping what we know suggests this is improbable and that Eleanor had been heading for Poitiers from Fontevraud and was cut off at Mirebeau. Arthur's homage had occurred at Gournay, close to the border with Poitou and on the road to Chauvigny and hence to Poitiers. He was charged by Philip with taking his own territories; it would therefore make sense for him to proceed to Poitiers rather than backwards and north to Tours.

The route also coheres with what we know of those who accompanied Arthur; aside from Hugh and Geoffrey de Lusignan, he was accompanied by Andrew de Chauvigny and William Maingot, both of whose lands lay in that direction. Mirebeau, on the other hand, is about 20 miles north of Poitiers, on the direct route between Fontevraud and Poitiers. What seems to have occurred is a race for Poitiers, which Arthur won, turning north and trapping Eleanor at Mirebeau. The good news for Eleanor was twofold. First, she had time to send two letters: one to William des Roches, Seneschal of Anjou, at Chinon Castle, and one to John, miles away – probably at Le Mans, from where he was superintending the rather messy proceedings in the north. The second piece of good news was that Mirebeau had been a fortress of Geoffrey Le Bel and was thus designed for defence, albeit those defences were in a state of disrepair after so many years of relative peace.[42]

With the limited military resources at her disposal, Eleanor could do no more than defend the keep for as long as possible. The town and the outer defences were soon overwhelmed by the attackers' forces. One source suggests that Arthur tried to persuade Eleanor to leave the castle, promising that she would be free to go in peace wherever she wished. If he did make any such promises, Eleanor was not naïve enough to believe them and she suggested that if he meant well his best course was to go elsewhere and take her faithless vassals with him. It was, she said, 'a great marvel to her that either he or those Poitevins who were supposed to be her vassals should besiege a castle where she was staying'.[43]

Whether the besiegers would have attempted to storm the keep or contented themselves with starving the inhabitants out was never put to the test, for John and William des Roches had both sprung into action. John made his way to close to Chinon, covering 80 miles in less than forty-eight hours, and met William des Roches en route. They arrived at Mirebeau in the early hours of the morning of 1 August to find that Arthur's army had failed to post adequate sentries to protect their rear. Hugh de Lusignan was enjoying a breakfast of pigeons; others were dressing and arming themselves for the day. The surprise was complete. William des Roches' troops in the vanguard easily defeated the disoriented army of Brittany. Even better, numerous prestigious prisoners were taken. First among them, of course, was Arthur himself. With him was his sister Eleanora. Hugh and Geoffrey de Lusignan were taken, as were Andrew de Chauvigny, the Viscount of Châtellerault (a descendant of Dangereuse and hence cousin to Eleanor and John), Raymond of Thouars, Savaric de Mauléon and (as John gloatingly reported in a letter to his barons) all the other faithless Poitevin leaders, and more than two hundred soldiers, 'with not one escaping'.[44]

The crisis over, Eleanor returned to Fontevraud and, according the annals of the abbey, was consecrated as a nun. It was apparently after this near-death experience that Eleanor made her will, which is recorded as having been finalised in 1202, though its contents are unknown.[45]

We do not know which, if any, of Eleanor's grandchildren came to visit her after her final retirement. She had Alix nearby, but Alix was to die that same year of 1202. It seems a safe bet that the widowed Mathilde and her sons Thomas and Thibaut would have come. But there is reason to believe that they were not the only granddaughters to pay their regards to Eleanor; the Eleanor Psalter has a further piece of evidence to offer. For at some point, we can see from the 'obit' notices marked in the psalter that this precious book came into the hands not of Mathilde, as one might expect, but of Maria of Champagne, the eldest daughter of Eleanor's first daughter. She passed it to her eldest daughter, Jeanne, Countess of Flanders and Hainault, who, her own eldest daughter being dead, passed it to her sister's eldest daughter, Joanne de Dampierre, who became the wife of the Count of Bar. From here it passed into the hands of a relative who became Bishop of Arras in the fourteenth century. It would therefore seem that towards the close of her life Eleanor did at some point have company from the next generations of her female relatives, including the descendants of her first daughter, Marie, and bonded with them enough to pass on this precious commission to them.

There were therefore some happy times for Eleanor in her final years. However, there were also times of great trial, so far as her surviving male relatives were concerned.

In Germany, Otto was conducting a desperate struggle for power with the help of his brothers. Even William, who had spent so much of his childhood in France and England, was firmly fixed in Germany, married to the daughter of the King of Denmark. As for John, and other relatives nearer to home, matters were even worse. The victory at Mirebeau was the high point of his military career to date – indeed, it was to be the high point of his entire military career. But he did not prove a graceful victor. The captive leaders were clapped into heavy chains and paraded in oxcarts for a long journey to secure prisons in Normandy and England. The Lusignans were imprisoned in Caen, and held in chains until they were ransomed. Many others were not so fortunate. Eleanor's cousin Hugh of Châtellerault died in 1202, inferentially in prison. So too did Richard's close friend and Eleanor's relative Andrew de Chauvigny, whose heiress wife remarried the next year. The causes of their deaths are not known, but it was reputed to be the case that, taking a leaf from Henry's book, John had simply deprived them of food. He certainly did so in relation to some other prisoners at a later stage, so the accusation cannot be counted as incredible. Savaric de Mauléon reputedly survived only by escaping from the supposedly secure Corfe Castle, though his later eminence under John as Seneschal of Poitou suggests that a deal may actually have been done. Raymond of Thouars, another of Eleanor's cousins, may have escaped by the good graces of his brother Aimery, who was still at this time – and following Eleanor's intervention – loyal to John.[46]

Her grandson Arthur, meanwhile, disappeared. Two later accounts suggest that Eleanor, before her return to Fontevraud, commanded John not to harm his nephew. Whether she did this or not, the securing of Arthur at Falaise, far from Breton and Poitevin lands, and in the hands of the Marcher lord William de Braose, caused concern among John's other key supporters, particularly Aimery de Thouars and William des Roches – and the freed Lusignans. That their concern may have been more about the share of ransom moneys than any more high-minded motives is suggested by the fact that in January of the new year Aimery of Thouars was besieging Queen Isabella at Chinon, in hopes of holding her to ransom. The threat was enough to provoke John into moving Arthur to safer territory; in March he was moved to Rouen and placed under the guardianship of Robert of Vieuxpost.[47]

In early April 1203 it appears that John killed Arthur, or had him killed. Shortly thereafter he was notifying Eleanor and the key Aquitanian authorities (the Archbishop of Bordeaux, his seneschals of Poitou and Gascony and Hubert de Burgh) of some unspecified piece of good news from the lips of a confidential messenger.[48] Debate rages as to whether the confidential messenger was notifying them of the death of Arthur or referred to some other subject – and as to whether, if it did refer to Arthur's death, it reflected an earlier agreement with those notified. Turner, following Richard and Powicke, accepts the letter as evidencing Eleanor's being made aware of Arthur's planned murder; Weir argues that the conclusion is unsafe by reference to Eleanor's reported intercession for Arthur the previous year and the repellent nature of the act of accepting the murder of a grandchild, however little known. Flori leaves the question hanging.[49]

On this question, and despite the eminent scholars lining up on the other side, Weir's view is surely to be preferred, certainly insofar as they argue for Eleanor's complicity in the murder ahead of time. Eleanor had demonstrated a serious view of religion throughout her life and was now resident within and very possibly admitted to a community of nuns. At very nearly eighty years of age, her own reckoning with God was surely not far off. Whether or not she actually besought John not to harm Arthur, which seems likely, it is almost inconceivable that she could have connived at or endorsed Arthur's death. If she had felt that to be the appropriate course, she would have advised it and seen it executed at the time of Mirabeau. At best, one might therefore credibly see this as John informing Eleanor of a death which she had not expected or advised.

But also the letter, when read carefully, seems very unlikely to be such a communication. First of all, there is the question of its limited addressees; why send such news only to this limited list dominated by those in Aquitaine? It was not only or even principally Aquitaine which was affected by Arthur's death. Why also would he send such news as good news to the Archbishop of Bordeaux, who would be bound to regard such an act as mortal sin? Secondly, the letter talks of the messenger (a monk) being someone who 'has seen what is going forward with us and who will be able to apprise you of our situation'. If the reference is to an extrajudicial killing, the monk is an odd person to have seen 'what is going forward'.

Further apprising of the situation suggests a general update, not a particular piece of news. Church has described the monk, John of Valerant, as a high-flying diplomat; if so, it is far more likely that he was involved with John's attempts to gain ground via papal diplomacy – something in which Eleanor (and the archbishop) would of course be interested. As for the following sentence, which refers to the grace of God being 'even more with us than the messenger can tell you', there is no reason why that should be associated with a reference to Arthur, particularly in the context of the next phrase, 'concerning the mission which we have made to you', which suggests a plan probably relating to Aquitaine in which all addressed are concerned. This reading is reinforced by the postscript, which refers to money sent (to be distributed only in Eleanor's presence), logically referring back to this same mission. And even if John did have the killing of Arthur in his mind, there is no reason to suppose that this phrase must have conveyed the truth to his readers.

Whatever this plan was, and however well it was faring in April 1203, Eleanor would soon have become aware that John's position was unravelling. By the end of 1203, the defence of Normandy had failed and John had returned to England. Philip had captured great swathes of Anjou along the Loire, and Eleanor was cut off from her son. In this context, a charter to Niort during the year smacks of a desperate attempt to secure support for John to aid in his defence. Similarly, a charter to Aimery de Rochefort granting him Saint-Amand or Saint-Aignant en Aunis appears to be a reward to one of the ever-dwindling group of faithful supporters.[50] Yet even with some remaining supporters, in March 1204 Richard's favourite project, Chateau Gaillard, would fall.

Meanwhile, Eleanor's supporting granddaughters were themselves dispersing. Alix had died in around 1202. Mathilde, widowed since 1202 and therefore able to spend much time with Eleanor in this period, was married again early in 1204 to Enguerrand de Coucy, a great-grandson of Louis VI. Enguerrand, one of the most able and ambitious nobles of his day, would later win himself the epithet, 'the Great', and it seems likely that this marriage was an attempt by John to bind him to his side. The marriage does not seem to have been happy – Mathilde never mentions him in her charters, as she did with her first husband,[51] and any alliance would not outlast her life. She was to die, probably in childbirth, in early 1209, aged around thirty-six.

At more or less the same time, Eleanor's granddaughter Maria, Countess of Flanders would leave France to join her husband Baldwin, who had been elected Emperor of Constantinople in the wake of the Fourth Crusade. She would die almost as soon as she reached Jerusalem, leaving her four-year-old daughter Jeanne, the recipient of the Eleanor Psalter, in the custody of her uncle.[52]

Less than a month after Chateau Gaillard fell, Eleanor's death is recorded by the Waverley Chronicle, which says that 'she passed from the world as a candle in the sconce goeth out when the wind striketh it'. Whether she was even aware of Chateau Gaillard's loss is unclear; the wording of the record suggests a gentle end after a long period of fading. But the words are ambivalent, and used by a chronicler hundreds of miles away. We have nothing akin to the eyewitness account of Richard's deathbed. Even the place of her death is unclear. The only chronicle to state a place clearly says Poitiers; other texts simply report her burial place as Fontevraud, from which many historians have inferred that she died there too.[53] This conforms with Eleanor's usual residence, made particularly likely by her now advanced age. But the possibility of a death at Poitiers cannot be discounted, particularly given the fact that Eleanor might have thought it imperative to rally support for the beleaguered John. Indeed, such an action would be consistent with her forays of recent years – to engage with the Bishop of Lisieux, to garner support for John, to race John's enemies to Poitiers and to secure the pledge of peace by fetching the King of France's bride.

We do know, however, that her death was marked with affectionate respect by John. The Annals of Saint Aubin describe him as 'most violently saddened' and indeed attribute his withdrawal from Normandy to his inability to cope without her.[54] Nor did he confine himself to personal grief: in an echo of Eleanor's own act on her liberation he ordered all prisoners to be set free, however serious their crime, 'for the love of God and for the salvation of the soul of our dearest mother'.[55] He also made a donation to the Abbey of St Radegonde near Dover, which Eleanor and Richard had supported.

Eleanor's death was also a matter of huge significance in Fontevraud, where an obituary was compiled by the nuns, honouring her as 'from her earliest years a patron of the church of Fontevraud ... who brightened the world with the splendour of her royal offspring. She graced the nobility of her birth with the honesty of her life, enriched it with her moral excellence, adorned it with the flowers of her virtue and by her reputation for unmatched goodness surpassed almost all the queens of the world.'[56]

Other churches noted her passing with regret. At Rouen Cathedral, plans were made for an annual commemoration of her death as they were in Canterbury, with which she had been so closely associated during Richard's reign.[57] Eleanor's good relationships with England's lawyers and administrators are perhaps also spoken to by the description of her by the author of *Leges Anglorum Londoniis collectae* as 'a noble queen indeed and a spirited and wealthy lady'. Even her former jailer Ralph Fitzstephen made a donation in her memory, suggesting that she had endeared herself to him in their years of contact.[58]

It is Eleanor's burial, however, which has gathered the most attention. Following her interment, an image of her was raised on the site to partner to the ones she had commissioned of Henry and Richard. It is overwhelmingly likely that this image was commissioned by Eleanor herself. Modern scholarship seems to be substantially agreed that her tomb was commissioned a short period after those of Richard and Henry.[59] It thus represents the image which Eleanor herself wanted to present to the world after her death.

The image can be easily described. It is of a mature but not old woman with elegant features wearing a crown over a wimple. She is clothed in a pale, flowing dress with a blue gown draped over it. She is lying on something like a sleigh bed, with her head supported on a blue pillow and her feet on the footboard of the bed. The bed itself is richly draped in red fabric. But the most eye-catching feature of the image is that she holds, a little below her line of vision, an open book. She is not actually reading; rather it is as if she has just taken a rest from reading from the book or is reflecting on what she has just read. Again, as with Henry's and Richard's images, the figure is ground-breaking in art history terms – it is the first medieval sculptural representation of a lay woman holding a book, though it may perhaps be seen as a nod to the representations of St Radegonde. The treatment of the clothing is also hailed as a new departure – a step forward in realism from the images of Henry and Richard.

As Flori notes,[60] the nature of the book has caused endless scholarly speculation. Bible, psalter, troubadour poetry and Arthurian romance have all been suggested. Is she asking us to see her as a penitent, or as a patron of the arts? Both views have their advocates. Given that a Bible is surely too big, and there is no convincing evidence linking Eleanor to patronage of troubadour poetry or courtly romances, these candidates can be put aside.

A possibility not previously canvassed is that the book is a work of theology. This would be a nod to the school of theology with which Eleanor would seem to have sympathised in life – the dialectic approach of Pierre Abelard, Gilbert of Poitiers and John of Salisbury. This possibility would fit well with the pose, which suggests a reflective engagement with the book and a more concentrated approach than any of the conventional choices. On this basis it would be tempting to posit the work as a commentary on the psalms, such as that of Gilbert of Poitiers.

But in the light of the knowledge which has recently emerged of Eleanor's commissioning of her own psalter, that psalter itself must be seen as the most likely candidate for the book. This respects the use which Eleanor actually made of the book, and would provide a recognisable portrait to those who knew her. The pose is perhaps not perfectly suited to this possibility, but given the links which the book contains to her family, her pose may be explained by her pausing to think of the member of the family brought to her mind by a particular page in the book.

But whether the book is a work of theology or the psalter, a degree of unconventionality remains. A purely conventional approach to theology at this time would discourage laymen, and still more so laywomen, grappling with the complexities of faith. In choosing to be portrayed with any book, Eleanor subtly defies convention – in a way she had already done by choosing to bury her 'alpha male' husband and son in an eccentric foundation headed by a woman.

In one other sense, too, the image is defiant of convention: it presents Eleanor as fully the equal of her husband and son, and yet in a different way. Henry and Richard each boast a sceptre and a sword – symbols of traditional authority – but Eleanor is depicted as equal in size and entitlement to them, yet she has eschewed the sceptre to which she was entitled and with which other queens had been depicted. Eleanor faces the judgment of eternity as every inch the equal of her great husband and son, but she does so relying only on her faith and her wit.

12

Mother of Empires

Eleanor's story does not, of course, end with her death. As noted in the introduction, her personal story has lived on, albeit in generally rather inaccurate form, for over eight hundred years. But there is also the story of how her personal influence manifested through later generations.

The simplest way to look at this is Eleanor's role as progenitress. Sometimes she is, like Queen Victoria, alluded to as 'the Grandmother of Europe' – and with some justification, for the territorial reach of her bloodline is truly astounding. Eleanor is of course best known in her role as one of the progenitors of what is loosely called 'the Angevin Empire'. While there is some debate as to whether it was ever truly regarded in those terms by those involved, she and Henry certainly by their marriage created a power base which was equivalent to an empire, and attracted the equivalent status and hostility for Henry and his sons. She has therefore been seen predominantly through the prism of the rulers of that empire: as queen to two kings and mother to two more kings, and thus by reference to her male relations. So for example Amy Kelly's biography was entitled *Eleanor of Aquitaine and the Four Kings*. That is certainly the natural headline story from an English perspective, since it is through the male line that the English and eventually the Scottish monarchs descend. It would probably have been what Eleanor and Henry primarily anticipated when they looked at their brood of sons.

Ultimately, of course, the lines from most of their sons led nowhere. Young Henry left no surviving offspring, nor did Richard; and with Arthur of Brittany dead, only Eleanora of Brittany remained from the male line. Although her marriage had been arranged in 1194 as part of the agreement surrounding Richard's release, it never came about, and she lived on, unmarried, in genteel captivity until her death without heirs in 1241.[1] From the male line, therefore, comes only the English royal family. This is itself not negligible, of course; aside from the kings and queens who followed, it produced a number of notable personages including among John's children a King of the Romans (Richard of Cornwall) and Eleanor de Montfort, a woman who held real political power. She would negotiate on her own behalf in relation to a major international treaty and would assist her husband to hold Henry III and the future Edward I in captivity, holding Dover Castle for some time after she was widowed.

But what is often neglected is the influence produced by the marriages of Eleanor's daughters.

Via Leonor, Eleanor's line was carried into Castile where it continued up to and beyond both the great queen Isabella of Castile and her husband Ferdinand of Aragon. They, of course, were responsible for reunification of Spain and the commencement of the Spanish Empire, via their support for Christopher Columbus. Similarly, via Leonor's least famous daughter, Urraca (and various intermarriages with Castile, Aragon and England), it continued in Portugal through and beyond the foundation of the Portuguese trading empire. Meanwhile, through the Spanish line came, albeit briefly, an Empress of Constantinople.

In France, Blanche's line of course produced a line of French kings which would return to England in the person of the original 'She-Wolf of France', Isabella, the queen of Edward II and mother of England's greatest high-medieval king, Edward III. But also through Blanche, via Charles of Anjou, it extended to kings of Sicily, Naples and Hungary. The last of these was 'King' Maria of Hungary, the reigning queen of that nation. Charles would also be the ancestor of England's other famous 'She-Wolf', Queen Margaret of Anjou, wife to Henry VI and de facto ruler of England periodically during the Wars of the Roses.

As for Matilda, her children's destinies add considerably to the range of influence enjoyed by Eleanor's descendants. Matilda's oldest son, Henry, was to become the father of the future Duchess of Bavaria and thus the ancestress of Isabeau of Bavaria, Queen of France to Charles VI 'the Mad', regent during his indispositions, and mother to Henry V's wife, Katherine of Valois (herself of course the progrenitress of the Tudor line). Matilda's youngest son, that William raised by Eleanor in his infancy, was to become the originator of the dukes of Brunswick, which was ultimately to produce George, Elector of Hanover – later King George I of England.

Still more neglected tends to be the descent via Eleanor's 'lost' family. Courtesy of Marie of France's line, Eleanor's blood also descended to the kings of Cyprus, via Marie's son Henri's marriage to Isabelle, Queen of Jerusalem, and their daughter's marriage to King Hugh (formerly Lusignan) of Cyprus. It also descended to the kings of Navarre, via Theobald of Champagne's marriage to Berengaria of Navarre's sister Blanca.

Alice's line was less fertile, but from her descended the counts of St Pol. This is a line which was to produce Jacquetta of Luxembourg, wife of John of Lancaster and mother of Elisabeth Woodville, Edward IV's queen. It is amusing to think that Elizabeth, often derided for her plebeian birth, was herself a descendant of Eleanor. From Alice's line too would come the Counts Palatine of Burgundy, and the queens of Philip V and Charles IV of France.

Simply in terms of her bloodline, then, Eleanor is ill-served by being called the Grandmother of Europe – she is better regarded as the mother of empires. But this too undersells her personal influence, and in particular her role as an influencer of her daughters and granddaughters.

It is strongly arguable, in fact, that Eleanor was far more influential as the mother of remarkable daughters than as the mother of sons. For, as the earlier chapters have explained, Eleanor cherished her role as a mother, and she was afforded greater opportunities to influence her daughters by Henry than she was the sons who were removed from her household at a relatively young age.

The daughter through whom Eleanor's influence over generations can be best seen is Leonor, though for all of Eleanor's daughters we can see evidence of very real affection. Both Matilda and Leonor spent much of their time until their marriages with their mother, and Matilda's later attentions to her mother and decision to place her own daughter and youngest son with her demonstrate clearly the affection and trust which resulted. Joanna probably spent less time with her mother at a very young age, but was effectively married from within her mother's household. Her own resort to her mother in times of difficulty again shows that Eleanor had forged a very meaningful bond even with this less closely reared daughter. Even with Eleanor's eldest daughters of her first marriage, the evidence of their later contact, which can be seen in Eleanor's last years, suggests that a bond of affection had existed and had not been broken entirely by their enforced separation on Eleanor's divorce.

With Matilda the evidence is very slight, owing to her early death. However, tantalising fragments survive. Matilda apparently taught her own children to read. Like Marie, she promoted romance poetry: two epics, the *Rolandslied* (the earliest German version of the *Chanson de Roland*) and *Tristant und Isalde*, are thought to have been composed as a direct result of her influence, with source material for one coming from England at Matilda's request. She introduced the cult of Becket into Germany, with her son Henry adopting Thomas as the patron saint of the duchy. And young William, Eleanor's late foster child, appears likely to be connected with the introduction of the veneration of St Radegonde into his territory of Brunswick: outside England and France, the only two churches devoted to her appear within the territory of the dukes of Brunswick and appear to have been founded in the early thirteenth century.[2]

But the single line which descends via Leonor provides by far the best evidence of Eleanor as an influencer of future generations. In this line we can see Leonor herself, her daughter Blanche, Blanche's sister Berengaria and Berengaria's own granddaughter Eleanor of Castile.

Leonor was sent into marriage at the youngest age of any of Eleanor's daughters, being just nine years old when she made the journey into her new country of Castile. Her resilience in coping with this appallingly difficult demand recalls Eleanor's own resilience in dealing with the demands of her life, from arranged marriage to battle, from imprisonment to loss of a child. In some respects, however, Leonor was luckier than her mother or her sisters in that she was married to a boy near her own age, and was enabled to finish growing up alongside him before the marriage was consummated, by which stage the two had become emotionally very close. Theirs was to be not just a fruitful but also a happy marriage; so much so that her death, which came just days after that of her husband, was deemed by the chroniclers generally to have been from a broken heart. Like Eleanor and Henry in the early days of their marriage, the Castilian royals worked together towards common goals; here the reconquest of Iberia from the Islamic invaders and the promotion of Castile as the *primus inter pares* country within Iberia.[3]

Leonor was not a secondary partner in this. The different political sensitivities of the peninsula, which not only ensured women entered into their dower on marriage but was also generally more accepting of female inheritance, offered Leonor a freer rein to collaborate politically in her husband's work than had been possible for Eleanor in either of her marriages. Leonor is more evident even than Adelaide of Maurienne in co-ruling with her husband. She appended her name to charters and grants and was credited with political direction. Like Eleanor in her final years, she should therefore be seen as a queen regnant. The Castilian charters speak repeatedly of her excellent education and her wisdom. The impetus to found the royal abbey and necropolis of Las Huelgas came from Leonor, not from Alfonso. So too did the introduction of the cult of St Thomas Becket, to whom Leonor dedicated a lavishly supported altar at Toledo Cathedral.[4]

Leonor's foundation for this role was an excellent education, remarked on by Castilian chroniclers. One describes her as 'very sensible and wise, knowledgeable, good, and eloquent', while another says that she was 'exquisitely educated, quiet and calm, very beautiful, greatly charitable, very kind to her husband, and honourable in all her dealings'. While a good amount of that education was received at the Castilian court after her marriage, it is plain that its foundations were laid before her marriage; that is, under Eleanor's aegis. We know this because when the time came to educate her own children Leonor sought English tutors for them, and also sent one of her clerks to England to receive an English education. This plainly indicates that she recalled the quality of teaching which she received.[5]

It seems likely that Leonor herself taught her children to read; certainly her sister Matilda is said to have taught her children to read the scriptures from an early age, and Leonor's daughter Blanche was to do so with her own children. As for affection, the testimony of the Castilian chroniclers is that Leonor was a loving mother who 'always showed her love' to her children. Indeed, there are heartrending descriptions of her grief on the loss of her son Fernando – eyewitnesses swore that they had never seen such pain as hers. This is reflected onwards in the devotion which her own daughter Blanche of Castile reciprocally demonstrated to her in later years, making her parents the principal focus of the prayers of the nuns at her foundation of Maubuisson and naming two sons after her father. All of this, and the absence of known female relatives at the court of Alfonso VIII from whom this paradigm might have been acquired, strongly suggests that the close attentions of a loving mother was something familiar to Leonor from her time with Eleanor.

A fine example of Leonor's political influence, which also intersected with the traditional territory of queens, was in the matter of the marriage of their eldest daughter, Berengaria, and the procuring of peace with Alfonso's nephew and enemy Alphonso IX of León. Considerable trouble was caused by Alphonso in the form of border raids, and following his marriage to his cousin Teresa of Portugal being declared consanguineous, the Castilian nobles suggested the marriage of Berengaria to Alphonso as the safest expedient to procure a lasting peace. Alfonso VIII was opposed to the match, which was also consanguineous. However, the sources are clear that he was brought to agree to the marriage by Leonor's influence; her 'wise counsel' persuaded him that because of the dividend of peace the match was 'more an act of mercy than a sin'. She also reconciled the reluctant Berengaria to the match. Leonor was therefore the prime political mover in this matter of high policy. The dower and dowry of Berengaria were the castles which each side had taken from the other in the clashes of the preceding years. Berengaria took active control of them, holding them to her father and mother's instructions, and effectively against her own husband, even as he attempted to sire an heir by her to ensure that the castles would in the long run end up in his own custody.[6]

Although the marriage was not long lasting – papal outrage ensured that it was annulled in 1204 – Berengaria's influence, like that of her mother, finds its way into the records of the Kingdom of León, where she is celebrated as 'very wise' and 'most prudent' and as having exercised a 'notable influence'. She encouraged her husband in prudent law-making, in construction projects and in religious benefactions. This is perhaps not surprising in that she had been raised, until the birth of a son to her parents, as the acknowledged heiress to the throne of Castile. Nor does her influence lapse once her marriage was annulled – even prior to her parents' death she can be seen intervening in acts, particularly relating to Las Huelgas, and acting on behalf of her young son Ferdinand. Both appeared routinely on official royal documents from 1207. She is also visible as an integral part of the court immediately surrounding her father, receiving the first news of the victory at Las Navas de Tolosa, and greeting him when he entered Alcaraz in state after his victory.

Following her parents' death she acted as regent for her young brother Henry II until his death, including arranging the marriage of her sister Leonora to the King of Aragon; and she then engineered the accession of her son Ferdinand to the thrones of both León and Castile, renouncing her own claim to Castile in his favour. After his accession she acted as one of his principal advisers, taking on a quartermaster's role in ensuring he had men and materiel available for his campaigns of reconquest. She also arranged both of Ferdinand's marriages. His second marriage was indeed arranged entirely between Berengaria and her sister Blanche, as one which dealt with a political problem for each of them. She also arranged a notable marriage for her daughter Berengaria of León; in order to prevent the marriage of a daughter of Alphonso IX to the famous knight John of Brienne, King of Jerusalem (who could have threatened Ferdinand's accession to León), she persuaded him – probably again acting in cahoots with Blanche – to marry Berengaria the younger, who thereby became Queen of Jerusalem; their daughter married the Emperor of Constantinople.[7]

Berengaria's influence over her son was incredibly strong, and her raising of him, which she undertook in the absence of his father but to some extent under the aegis of Leonor, was one which equipped him to be not just a soldier prince but a scholar, who endowed universities and whose eldest son was Castile's famous polymath king Alfonso X 'El Sabio'. What is more, for his work of reconquest and his religious efforts, Ferdinand was to become a saint. His daughter Eleanor of Castile would marry Edward I of England, and, using the first-class education which had become a Castilian tradition, she would acquire a property empire which kept future queens of England solvent.

As for Blanche, although the story of her marriage forms an integral part of Eleanor's own later story, it is her influence after marriage which is most celebrated – and offers fascinating parallels with that of her sister.

After her marriage to the future Louis VIII, she was considered a possible queen for England during the height of disaffection against John, and her husband actually launched an invasion to claim the English throne in her name. After her early widowhood, she acted as regent for the young Louis IX (later St Louis) for eight years. During his active rule she remained a powerful actor in French politics, sitting in judgment, organising major court events, acting in a diplomatic role and assuming the regency again during her son's illness in 1244–45. Even in this least active phase of her rule historians have concluded she is best characterised as a co-ruler with her son (much as Berengaria was in Castile). Then, from 1248, when Louis departed on Crusade, Blanche again assumed the full reins of power, ruling in his absence until her death in 1252. One of France's foremost medieval historians, Robert Fawtier, has argued that she should be counted among the kings of France. She was described by the English chronicler Matthew Paris as 'feminine in sex, but masculine in counsel'. One of her son's historians anticipated Elizabeth I's phraseology, describing her as having 'the courage of a man in the heart of a woman'.[8]

At the same time, like Eleanor, like Leonor and like Berengaria, Blanche was also far from being a distant mother. Her youngest son, Charles of Anjou, who would become the King of Sicily, attested to her closeness to her children, and the deep love which she evinced for them. This is reflected in the records which show her rushing from Melun to Vincennes to be with Charles when he was sick, the picture drawn by Matthew Paris of her nursing the sick Louis herself, and the fact that she twice allowed her daughter Isabella to refuse suitable marriages. After her husband's death she stayed for some time alone with her children, encouraging them to play outside, helping the builders of her new abbey of Royaumont. She herself taught the children to read, as an inscription in the Leiden Psalter attests, and ensured that they were well and strictly taught, laying a foundation for the saintliness which would result in her eldest son becoming St Louis, and a campaign for the canonisation of Isabella.

There is also, tantalisingly, scope for inferring some similar influence by Eleanor on her eldest daughter Marie of France, Countess of Champagne. Marie's well-documented taste for troubadour poetry is not well accounted for by her later childhood in an abbey; it is more suggestive of a treasured link with Eleanor. Unlike Eleanor, though, Marie would prove a noted patron of such works. De Troyes' *Lancelot* was composed at the 'wish' of Marie; Gace Brulé composed a poem, *Bien cuidai tout ma vie,* at her 'command'. Andrew the Chaplain was her chaplain and was in her employ, a frequent witness of her charters, when he wrote his famous work. Marie was also a patron of religious works, commissioning a translation and gloss on the book of Genesis to assist her own personal study in the scholastic tradition. She also confirmed a new chapter of canons devoted to copying key works and making books. Like Eleanor, she was known for liking beautifully appointed churches and for her gifts to beautify churches in her county.

Marie, too, would prove to be a capable ruler in her own right. As her biographer notes, she was Regent of Champagne effectively without interruption from 1179, when her husband went on pilgrimage, until her son Henry's death in the wake of Richard's campaign in 1197. She presided over the High Court of Champagne and acted without any limitations imposed on her by either the king or any kind of regency council. She initiated a reconciliation with the family of Hainaut, modernised her household and presided over court and mediation proceedings. Like Eleanor, she granted commune status to some locations. She also asserted her authority over tenants who were seeking to evade her jurisdiction. She hosted political gatherings, including those attended by royalty. A contemporary commented that 'well did she protect and govern the land', and another described her as 'having the heart of a man and the body of a woman'. As noted earlier, Marie would take as her seal an almost exact copy of Eleanor's own seal.[9]

Marie's daughter Maria was herself notable for the power she exercised. After her marriage she issued charters in her own right, taking an interest in the economic development of towns. She was then regent of her husband's territory of Flanders until she went to join him and assume the role of Empress of Constantinople in 1204.[10]

Maria's daughters, Eleanor's great-granddaughters Jeanne and Margaret of Flanders, then became successive rulers in their own right of a county which exerted an influence akin to that of a country. Jeanne in particular had to negotiate difficult times, first during her childhood as a de facto hostage at the French court and later after her husband Ferdinand of Portugal made common cause with King John and was captured on the field of battle at Bouvines. During this latter period, which lasted for some twelve years, she ruled her county in her own right, juggling the needs to withstand French power, promote economic development and somehow acquire sufficient cash to ransom her husband. Her contribution to the economic development of Flanders via targeted exemptions from taxation and judicial reorganisation was considerable. So too was her contribution to infrastructure works to promote the economic welfare of her lands – building, riverine maintenance, repairs to damaged buildings, all came to her attention and were dealt with at her instance. Jeanne was seen as one of the great comital figures of the age, meriting a gift from the Crown on the occasion of Louis IX's marriage to Margaret of Provence in 1234; her daughter Marie was married to Louis' own brother. She also was a noted patron of female Cistercian orders – a development from the model of Fontrevraud – and the founder of a hospital for the poor sick.

Margaret 'the Black', who succeeded her, continued Jeanne's policies (despite having often been at odds with her politically during her lifetime). She paid particular attention to river trade traffic, funding locks and canal building, which in turn facilitated trade and improved farming. But she was more famous for her marital history, having married (for love) Bouchard D'Avesnes against the King of France's will and later abandoned him apparently after her own sister had taken him prisoner. Her second marriage, to Guillaume de Dampierre, was approved of by the French monarchy. The result was two families who after her death would compete for power in Flanders and Hainault. Margaret founded the Abbey of Flines, in part as a necropolis for her family. She was buried there, and her daughter Jeanne de Dampierre, the last recorded family member in the Eleanor Psalter, was to be its abbess. Interestingly, the abbey was noted for its emphasis on the education of women.

All in all, Eleanor's great-granddaughters, the sister countesses of Flanders, were noted for the extent to which they wielded power – even in the face of challenge from the male establishment. So much so, indeed, that they are pictured in an illustrated version of Thomas of Cantimpré's *Liber de rerum natura* wielding arms in defence of their freedom, and successfully holding at bay two rather disconcerted-looking knights.

What is also interesting is that both Jeanne and Margaret were linked to significant production of illustrated manuscripts. As well as owning a very fine copy of Chretien de Troyes' *Perceval* (a wedding gift from Blanche of Castile), Jeanne can be demonstrated to have commissioned religious works including a life of St Marie of Egypt. Margaret was the commissioner of a psalter, a missal, a breviary and an antiphonary (used for choral services). But her household plainly delighted in such manuscripts, with both her second husband and children commissioning a wide range of manuscripts, including psalters, missals, breviaries, a tropaire (a collection of choral pieces) as well as Arthurian romances, chronicles and saints' lives. But despite these extensive personal commissions, it appears that it was in the Eleanor Psalter that the family chose to commemorate those closest to them. Surely from this we may infer that aside from her influence as an exemplar as a woman successfully wielding power in troubled times, Eleanor's memory was also treasured even by her 'forgotten' family.[11]

Eleanor's influence can be seen to be not merely breathtaking in terms of her bloodline and their achievements, but also key in raising her daughters to rule and to raise their own daughters to rule. Remarkable as she was personally, her ongoing influence on the ruling families of Europe should not be forgotten or underestimated.

APPENDIX

The Witnesses

The Key Witnesses
John of Salisbury, c. 1115–80

John takes his name from the place of his birth, because he was born in Old Sarum (Salisbury), England. He seems to have had family in the Church and entered on a clerical career as a young man. He studied in the schools of Paris from 1136 until the mid-1140s. There he studied under Abelard, Gilbert of Poitiers, Rebert of Melun, William of Conches and Thierry of Chartres. After his studies he entered the service of the Pope, during which time he met Eleanor and Louis on their return from Crusade. He attended the synod at Reims in 1148 where Gilbert of Poitiers was tried for heresy. He returned to England at about the time of Henry II's accession and entered the household of Theobald, Archbishop of Canterbury, to whom Eleanor became close in her early years in England. There he became very friendly with Thomas Becket, who was also in the archbishop's household. He remained close to Becket throughout the dispute with Henry II, shared his exile and is a key source for Becket's life – and indeed his death, having been present on the scene. He was to become one of the most distinguished philosophers of what was called the twelfth-century renaissance; his Metalogicon is a defence of the course of study known as the Trivium, and explains the world of the twelfth-century Parisian schools. This intellectual distinction was doubtless behind his promotion to the bishopric of Chartres in 1176. He died in 1180.

John is a key witness for a variety of reasons. The first is that the arc of his own story was to bring him close to Eleanor over an extended period. The second is that he wrote extensively, though not as a formal chronicle. He wrote a history of the papacy and his Polictraticus, which is a book combining political theory, a guide to good government and a critique of court life, is based on his observation of Henry II's court. He was also an inveterate and lively letter writer.

Robert of Torigny, 1110–86
Robert ranks as one of the first-class witnesses to Eleanor's life, combining good sources of information, near-contemporaneous writing and a commitment to accuracy, with no major political agenda. He is, however, distressingly terse, and avoids gossip.

He was born at Torigni-sur-Vire, Normandy, around 1110, most probably to an aristocratic family. He entered Bec Abbey in 1128 and in 1149 became its prior, replacing Roger de Bailleul, who had by that time become abbot. At Bec he was well placed to hear reliable news from the Empress, who was a major patron of the abbey and close to the abbot.

His own ability to learn about events at first hand was improved when in 1154 he became the Abbot of Mont Saint-Michel in Normandy. In November 1158, he hosted Louis VII of France and Henry II of England at Mont Saint-Michel. Three years later, he became godfather to Eleanor and Henry's second daughter, Leonor, with whom he seems to have maintained a correspondence even after her marriage. In June 1186, Robert died and was buried in the nave of the chapel at Mont Saint-Michel under a simple grave marker.

Ralph of Diss (Ralph of Diceto), 1150–1202
Ralph of Diss is one of the more reliable witnesses. He was born in around 1120, and by the time Eleanor came to England he was already Archdeacon of Middlesex and close to Gilbert Foliot, one of England's leading churchmen. He would go on to become the Dean of St Paul's Cathedral. As a distinguished churchman, he was an eyewitness to some events and well placed to gain information of a relatively reliable nature. He also wrote as a historian, and without an eye to promotion. His closeness to Foliot ensured that his view of the Becket dispute was not as pro-Becket as that of most churchmen. He actually conducted research for his chronicle, and reproduces some important texts which came into his possession.

Gervase of Canterbury, 1141–1210

Gervase was a monk at Christ Church Priory in Canterbury from 1163, and sacrist there from 1193. He was (naturally) an admirer of Becket, to whom he dedicated his chronicle. His chronicle is a fairly typical monastic chronicle, in that the affairs of his own priory tend to dominate. But as the priory was close to London and had direct dealings with and visits from the main players in the court, including Eleanor, it is well informed and usually reliable.

Roger of Howden, 1176–1201

Roger was probably a cleric, but more notable as a civil servant under Henry II and Richard. He was very close to the court from around 1175 until his death. He tends to be favourable to Henry, and even more so to Richard (with whom he went on Crusade). He can be taken as being very well informed and as a predominantly reliable and scrupulous source.

Geoffrey le Vigeois (du Breuil), 1140–84

Of noble Limousin birth, Geoffrey entered the abbey of Saint-Martial at an early age, becoming a monk in 1160 and priest in 1168. He was provost at the monastery of La Souterraine and was appointed Prior of Saint-Pierre du Vigeois (Corrèze) in 1178. His close proximity to Eleanor during her years in Poitou makes him a particularly useful source, and he is sometimes (though with no particular basis) described as Eleanor's court historian for that period.

The Other Witnesses
Gerald of Wales (Giraldus Cambrensis), 1146–1223

Gerald was half-Welsh through his mother, a Welsh noblewoman. He was educated in Paris and appointed Archdeacon of Brecon in 1172. He had ambitions to gain a bishopric and served Henry II as a chaplain between 1184 and 1189. Writing in 1188 and later in the early 1200s, he is overall one of the most negative witnesses. His own ambition and disappointment cloud his reliability. His desire for advancement by Henry leads to a fairly positive view of him, contrasted with relentlessly negative views of Eleanor and her sons. Following refusals to promote him to the bishopric of St David's, he became a Capetian supporter and is therefore relentlessly negative about the entire Plantagenet world.

Henry of Huntingdon, c. 1088–1157
Henry was the son of a canon of Lincoln, and became Archdeacon of Huntingdon. He had no direct knowledge of Eleanor in her first marriage, and is unlikely to have had any in her second. His history of England was written based on the materials available to him in England.

Jordan Fantosme, 1120–85
Jordan's background is obscure – he may well have been an Italian who found his way to England via the patronage of Henry of Blois. It appears that he may have studied in Poitiers under Gilbert of Poitiers. However, he became one of the foremost clerics in Winchester, rising to become the spiritual chancellor of the diocese. From this and from his exposure to his bishop, Richard of Ilchester, who was close to Henry, he had good access to accurate news. He wrote a verse history of the rebellion of Henry's sons, much influenced by the troubadour style. He died around 1185.

Ralph Niger, 1140–1217
Born in Bury St Edmunds, Ralph Niger was another graduate of the Paris schools, where he studied under John of Salisbury. He also seems to have studied at Poitiers later. He was a clerk to Young Henry. He was part of Becket's entourage in his exile, and only returned to England after Henry II's death. He was a monk at Bury St Edmunds in Suffolk and became a canon at Lincoln Cathedral and later Archdeacon of Gloucester. As a chronicler, his work is somewhat terse. He was very anti-Henry, both from his perspective as a Becket partisan and also as an opponent of increasing legislative control. He also had some reputation as a theologian and a composer of church music. He witnessed one of Eleanor's charters.

Ralph of Coggeshall, 1187–1227
Abbot of Coggeshall in Essex until forced by his brethren to resign for ill-health, Ralph of Coggeshall continued Niger's chronicle. Although he reproduces very few contemporaneous documents, the corrections and erasures of the autograph indicate that he went to some lengths to verify his details. He appears to have had some excellent sources of information close to Richard I.

Richard of Devizes, late 1100s
A monk at Winchester's St Swithun's Abbey, he wrote an almost contemporaneous account of Richard I's deeds. Although his view

is positive, it is often unreliable; he was generally writing at a great distance from the events he describes. We do not know whether he was at the abbey during Eleanor's captivity, though his accredited later works suggest he may not have been.

Walter Map, 1140–1209

A friend of Gerald of Wales, Walter Map also claimed Welsh descent. A student in Paris from 11501 to 1160, he was active as a courtier by the mid-1160s – apparently in succession to a relation whom Henry had prized from the days before his accession. He was sent on missions by Henry in 1173 and 1183. He held a succession of posts at Lincoln Cathedral, and also became a Canon of St Paul's and of Hereford and Archdeacon of Oxford 1186. He wrote *De Nugis Curialum* or 'Courtiers Trifles' between 1181 and 1193. Like Gerald, he was a noted wit and writer. His surviving work is not a chronicle so much as a lively book of gossip, stories and character sketches. A disappointed man by reason of his failure to obtain the bishopric he desired and thought his due, he is an amusing but unreliable source, more witty than kind or accurate. He was, however, familiar with the court, of which he gives vivid details, and also with the rumours which swirled about in it. Writing predominantly during Eleanor's captivity, he is predictably negative about Eleanor. His anti-Plantagenet agenda also means that he has to be treated with considerable caution.

William of Tyre, 1130–86

A native of Jerusalem, William of Tyre became Archbishop of Tyre in the late 1160s. At the time of Eleanor's Crusade and until the early 1160s, he was probably attending university in Europe. While he has traditionally been regarded as one of the greatest historians of his day (particularly as regards his account of the First Crusade, in relation to which he evaluated and used a variety of chronicles which have since been lost). recent scholarship has suggested that even he is not immune from biases.

William of Newburgh, 1136–98

William of Newburgh was an Augustinian canon based in Yorkshire. It is unlikely that he ever met Eleanor, though he may have encountered Henry II. His History of English Affairs was written in his later years, probably around 1195–98.

Notes

PPP	Nicholas Vincent 'Politics Patronage Piety' in Plantagenets et Capetiens
QRP	Queens Regents and Potentates ed Vann
RC	Ralph Coggeshall
RD	Ralph of Diss (Diceto)
RDev	Richard of Devizes
RH	Rotuli Hundredorum
RHG	Roger of Howden Gesta
RHC	Roger of Howden Chronica
RI RII	Richard Histoire des Comtes de Poitou Vols 1 and 2
RP	Richard le Poitevin
RT	Robert of Torigny (Torigni) Chronicles
S&P	Martindale Status, Authority and Regional Power (Oxford 1993)
SLVI	Suger Louis the Fat
SLVII	Suger Louis VII
VC	Vincent Charters (unpublished notes)
WM	Walter Map De Nugis Curialum
WMM	William of Malmesbury Gesta Regum Anglorum
WT	William of Tyre Historia rerum in partibus transmarinis gestarum

Main Biographies of Eleanor: Flori, Kelly, Meade, Owen, Pernoud, Turner, Weir

Preface

1. Power, in The World of Eleanor of Aquitaine 115–35, Evans 31–2
2. Flori 404–5, Evans 32–3
3. Evans 91–5, Parsons Court and Household 24, Cockerill 366
4. Evans 38–9
5. Evans 53–7

1 A Rich Heritage

1. Webster, D.R. (1912). St William of Gellone in The Catholic Encyclopedia, New York: Robert Appleton Company. Retrieved February 4, 2015 from New Advent: http://www.newadvent.org/cathen/15633a.htm
2. Cheyette 41–2
3. S&P 34–9, Cheyette 25
4. Owen 5
5. Abel, Emma of Blois, Carpentier 'un couple tumulteux', Flori 120
6. Richard ed Chartres de Saint-Maixent, 123.
7. Soulard-Berger, Penelope D. Johnson
8. R II 128, CSMP, 393.
9. Martindale Aimeri in SP, Paterson 2
10. RD I 293–4
11. Martindale EA 28–33
12. Paterson 6–7, 85, 153, Higournet Histoire dAquitaine, documents 109, Viellard Guide du pelerine de Saint-Jacques Turner 18
13. Cheyette 42
14. Barber, Knight and Chivalry 56–8, 62–3, 74–5

15. CSMP, 404, RHGF XII, 381, RI, Turner 12
16. Owen 6, FMG, Reddy 96
17. Harvey, 'The wives', Wolterbeek.
18. Turner 17, citing Flori 32–3. In fact, the evidence is clear that Philippa was not married to Sancho of Aragon: Szabolcs de Vajay, 'Ramire II le Moine, roi d'Aragon et Agnes de Poitou dans l'histoire et la légende', in Mélanges offerts à René Crozet, 2 vol, Poitiers, 1966, vol 2, 727–750; and Harvey, 'The wives' 315.
19. Reddy 95, Turner 18–19
20. Bloch 179
21. Bloch 179.
22. Reddy 85–9, Taylor Heresy 46
23. Laffont 61, Orderic Vitalis likened Isabelle to the Roman Camilla, or the Amazons. Owen 9
24. Paterson 244, Bloch 178–83, Paterson in The Court Reconvenes: Courtly Literature Across the Disciplines
25. Owen 8
26. RI 468–9, Martindale Cavalaria 99, Bisson C279–80
27. Reddy 97
28. Maratu 33, 76, Pope Innocent II, RI
29. OV 336–8
30. Reddy 95 quoting Bezzola Les Origines 2:274, See also works cited at Martindale Cavalaria 91, WMM 510
31. http://www.trobar.org/troubadours/coms_de_peiteu/guilhen_de_peiteu_11.php. Author translation
32. CSM 188–9, 192–4, Martindale CEO 103

2 Eleanor's Childhood

1. RI 478, Song 11
2. Mulally and Lewis in L&L
3. The source material for Aelis/Petronille is very unsatisfactory and it is even possible that there were two sisters, not one.
4. Champollion Figeac (1843), Tome II, VII, 13 RII 18
5. RI 480–492
6. RII 2, Martindale Calvaria 114, Turner 20–1, Owen 10–11, Flori 24
7. Masson 40–41, RII 5–11
8. RII 20–1, CT, Innocent 1
9. Norwich 122–3, RII 21–5
10. RII 25–35
11. RII 35–8
12. RII 38–42, Maratu 310–20
13. Masson 47–50, RII 37
14. Masson 49, RII 40–3
15. OV v 81, RII 51
16. Some sources suggest that he did marry her, but this seems unlikely. Ex Chronico Gaufredi Vosiensis, 41, RHGF XII, 425, RII 44–5, 51
17. Turner 24

18. Van Houts in P&C p 104, MP i/214–6, Turner 32.
19. Turner 40, Smalley 27, Dutton 37
20. Madigan, Masson 41–2
21. Evans 71, B&L 3
22. WT 618, 635
23. CSML, 411, 419. http://fmg.ac/Projects/MedLands/AQUITAINE.htm#_Toc
    359829953 suggests various ways in which this might have been done
24. Weir, Meade and Brown in L&L amongst others. http://the-history-girls.
    blogspot.co.uk/2013/03/eleanor-of-aquitaine-and-brother-who_24.html HIINI
    45
25. Saint-Jouin-de-Marnes, 34.
26. Turner 22–3
27. Recherches sur les chroniques du monastère de St-Maixent, 63
28. Venantius Fortunatus, Baudovinia
29. Taruskin 51–2
30. Paterson 100, Beech in L&L RP, Weir 15
31. Swabey 55, 58. There is also of course a credible link to the Provencal trobar
    meaning compose or find
32. Swabey 55–65, Paterson 88, 258–9, Turner 24–5
33. Paterson 271, Turner 35

3 Duchess of Aquitaine, Queen of France

1. Cheyette 15–19
2. Turner 37 quoting Baltzer in Kibler 65, Cercamon VII ll 31–6 in Harvey
   103–4, RI, 488.
3. Martindale S&P 39 says Raymond's absence was more by good luck than
   good management. I beg to differ.
4. SLVI 156, RHGF 12, 409–10, 431–5, CM 66–68, RII 51–2, Turner 40
5. OV vi 490–1
6. RII 56 and to similar effect La Chronique de Saint Maixent 194–5
7. Bouchard, Those of My Blood 40, 'Consanguinity' 269–70, Herlihy WFS 160
8. Flori Family trees, Bouchard in L&L 226, Clairvaux letters 371
9. Martindale S&P 39, Vigeois RHGF 12 436, Suger 139–41, Weir 25, CM 65
10. RII 57, Turner 44, Brown L&L 6, Vincent in 'In Our Time' Radio 4
11. RII 59
12. SLVI 150, Pacaut 31
13. CT 134, RII 59–60
14. CM 67, Suger 282
15. Suger Grant 139, S&P 39, RII 18–45
16. RII 60, CT 134
17. Duby iii 93–4, Brundage, Law, Sex, Turner 34–5, Weir 30
18. SLVII 147, RII 61–2, Brown Franks 34–8, 49–50
19. Sassier 61, Martindale EA 31
20. SLVI 158
21. CM 70, RII 61, Turner 49
22. Roux Paris in the Middle Ages 7
23. Hussey Paris the Secret History ch 5

24. Galignani. 139–149. Holmes Everyday living 57–77
25. LJS I 24
26. Roux 9
27. Flori 35–6, Turner 50
28. Benedict XVI General Audience 21 October 2009
29. Abelard Marenbon 20–27
30. Morris The Papal Monarchy 305
31. Classen, 278, Magdaliano 361, FitzGerald 52
32. Baldwin 'Image of the Jongleur in Northern France around 1200' Speculum 72 (1997) 639–40
33. Fitzgerald 56
34. Baltzer in Ed Kibler, Meade 45, Weir 29.
35. Grant Suger, 142–3
36. Facinger Study of Medieval Queenship 35–7, Turner 54
37. Crouch estimates around 40 people: Image of the Aristocracy 239–40
38. Marenbon Abelard 26, Les Templiers, des moines comptables au Moyen-âge
39. See Turner 53 citing Parsons L&L 275, Weir 33
40. RII, Weir 32, Parsons Mothers Daughters 67
41. OV vi 508, Flori 36, Sassier 56–7, Turner 53–4, https://epistolae.ctl.columbia.edu/letter/25293.html Opera ep.113
42. Hanley 99, SLVII, Pacaut 40, Sassier 86
43. Including Weir, Meade, Pernoud
44. Grant Suger 147
45. Grant Suger 148, BC Letter 186
46. Pacaut 41, 47, Sassier 154
47. RII 62–5, Sassier 90, Turner 60–1
48. Pernoud 36, Turner 60 hints in the same direction. See also Flori 58, Sassier 90
49. See for example: T. Grasilier Cartulaires inédits de la Saintonge (Niort 1871) ii 51 no. 29, 48, Chartes et Documents pour servir à l'histoire de l'Abbaye de Saint Maixent, ed. A. Richard, Archives Historiques du Poitou xviii (1886), 16–17, no.402.
50. Hivergneaux L&L 56–62, Turner 60
51. Marcabru 313
52. Parsons The Queen's Intercession in Power of the Weak 147–177, Earenfight 139, Evans 11
53. Cockerill especially at 216–8, 301, 306
54. Berners, Juliana (1486). The Boke of St. Albans. London: St. Albans Press Suger 148, RII 7, Turner 60
55. Sassier 90
56. Grant Suger 149, RII 71, Hivergneaux L&L 59, P&C 63
57. Sassier 99–101, Pacaut 68, CL 294
58. CL 293–8, Sassier 101–2, Turner 63
59. McCabe Peter Abelard, 298, Mews, The Council of Sens
60. Ciii 5, 113–6, CL 242–7
61. Anecdotes historiques, légendes et apologues tirés du receuil inédit d'Etienne de Bourbon 212, Flori 223, Evans 34
62. Kenaan-Kedar in ed Kibler, Meade

63. Sassier 102, Pernoud 37–8, Turner 61–2, Weir 38–40
64. Martindale S&P 34–7, EA 26–7, Warren HII 82–8
65. Cheyette 17
66. Turner 61–2
67. RII 74–8, Turner 61–2, Cheyette 14
68. RGHF XII 331, Appendix Sigebert – the source for Aelis's being called Petronille RII 78–9, Flori 39
69. Sassier 109–13, Pacaut 43–4. Pernoud 39, Flori 39, Turner 63. Evans in ed Bardot reaches a similar conclusion at 110. For the children: Continuatio Praemonst VI 452, Hist Eccles Sancti Martini. 408
70. Grant Suger 150
71. CL 293, Sassier 110, Turner 64
72. Flori 39
73. Sassier 112–15, RII 79
74. CL 300, Flori 40
75. Different dates are suggested by Vacandard and Grant. Auxerre iii 332
76. CL 297–8, Duggan in Innocent II, Weir 39, RHGF xiii 395. For surviving letters RHGF xv. Evans also takes this view.
77. Facinger 1968 7–8. Earenfight 2013 138, Evans 7–8
78. Poitiers, Bibliothèque Municipale ms. Fonteneau 25, 287–88, copy s.xviii, https://epistolae.ctl.columbia.edu/letter/891.html
79. Kelly 20–1, Weir 35–6
80. WN I 31, RGHF 12, 89
81. Turner 68, Pernoud 48, Brown L&L 20
82. Reynolds, 7, 140–1

4 Crusade

1. Haines, 223
2. Phillips 58–60, Maalouf quoting Abu' l'Faraj a Syrian bishop who was present in Edessa. 134–6
3. WT XIV, 4–5, l'Faraj
4. Norwich 132–3, CL 205
5. Phillips Second Crusade 61
6. Flori 42, Otto of Feising Grabois
7. Phillips 34
8. Phillips 64–5, Flori 43, Turner 72 cites Sassier 142–4 but the basis underpinning this passage is far from clear.
9. https://sourcebooks.fordham.edu/source/eugene3-2cde.asp
10. Phillips 53–9
11. Kostick 195–6, OF 65
12. WN 96
13. Suger 159, OD 4–5, Flori 43 LBC 247.2
14. Kostick 200–2, RHGF xii 126
15. Turner 73
16. On chastity for crusaders: Brundage 57, Holt thesis156. For detailed debunkings of the Amazons story see Flori 43–5, Evans 42–3

17. OD 57
18. Kostick 203, Flori asserts the presence of most of the ladies – without sources. Turner 74 asserts the presence of the countesses of Flanders and Toulouse by reference to Flori.
19. Kostick 203, Cheyette 19–22, Stalls in QRP 51
20. Kostick 200–1, quoting the Annals of St Giles of Brunswick as well as the Annals of Wurzburg
21. Letter 511 at https://epistolae.ctl.columbia.edu/letter/1294.html
22. PPP Appendix Turner 74, Hivergneaux in L&L 57–9
23. Flori 70–1. Turner 74
24. OD 18–20, Sassier 155–8, Flori 47
25. Turner 77
26. OD 26, WN, Turner 78, accepts the criticism of Eleanor without citing a source.
27. Runciman, Philips 188, Turner 79, Odo 45
28. Runciman 2 363, Sassier 60
29. Nicholson History of the Knights Templar suggests he did not become a full member until 1163
30. Turner 80, Odo 49
31. Choniates 1984 35, Kelly 35, Owen 149, Weir 51, Flori 43. For a definitive unpicking see Evans 40. For Choniates' easily provable mistakes see 'Exonerating Manuel Komnenos' Darryl Keith Gentry II
32. Cambridge, Trinity College, MS 903 (R.14.30) Van Houts in P&C 99–102
33. OD, Bowie 22, Kelly 42–3. See also Markale 35, Turner 45 and the normally sensible Labande 182–3
34. Phillips 192 OD
35. Phillips 198
36. Phillips 200
37. Phillips 200
38. Phillips 201, Sugar Epistolae 496, Maalouf 147–8
39. Turner 84–6, Evans 43–4
40. Phillips 202, JSHP 54, OD 126-7
41. Phillips 203, Flori 52
42. Phillips 205, OD 135, 143
43. Pernoud 90, accepted by Turner 87, Kelly 55–8, Owen 214
44. OD 128
45. WT II 80
46. Phillips 207–8, Turner 87
47. Phillips 209–10, Jones The Templars 96–7
48. B&L 21, WT II 79
49. Turner 89, Flori 297–8
50. McCracken 250–2
51. Flori Chapter 10, Turner 89–90, Vacandard, Papers by Parsons, Brugieres, Brooke, Bouchard and Brundage in L&L
52. Flori 224
53. Phillips 211, Brundage L&L 26
54. JSHP 52–3, B&L 24–5

55. B&L 22, McCracken in L&L 249
56. Dealt with at length by Flori Ch 10.
57. Owen 105, Turner 90, 92, https://www.poetrynook.com/poem/satiric-love-song-0
58. Duby iii 19–20
59. RGHF 15 510
60. WT II 182–3
61. WT II 184–5
62. Phillips 217, Riley-Smith 129, Sassier 191–2, Maalouf 147–8
63. Phillips 213–4 quoting Otto of Friesing
64. WT II 187–9, Maalouf 148–9, Turner 94.
65. Hamilton 144–50, Tranovich Chapter 1
66. Tranovich 119–23, LBC 354, Bowie 222
67. WT ii 195, Sassier 196, Turner 94, Phillips 227
68. Turner 95, Sassier 197
69. JSHP 60, Chalandon 330–1, Kugler 209
70. RGHF 513–4, Sassier 198, Turner 96
71. Phillips 227
72. WT II 198, Mallett, 'The Battle of Inab', Maalouf 150–1
73. CIII 113–6, JSHP62
74. Phillips 227
75. JSHP 61–2
76. McCracken L&L 257
77. JSHP 54
78. Brundage L&L 216–7
79. Gaunt Marcabru 441
80. Norwich 135–7, Collins 236–7 on BoC's supervision of the Pope.
81. JSHP 60–2. Louis letters 513.4
82. Phillips 270–1
83. Suger 279–80
84. Pernoud 102–3, Pacaut 63 and Turner 101
85. Sassier 217–20, Suger 284–5
86. Yoshikawa, 173, 244
87. Suger 286, Sassier 223–4
88. Sassier 224–5, Weir 88, Turner 103, Suger 286
89. Suger 286, Sassier 225
90. Hartnell 234
91. WN I 93, Turner 103, Flori 59, Pernoud 113, Kelly 77, Labande 193
92. Sassier 225–6, Turner 103, Flori 59
93. Chronicon Turonensis Magnum 135
94. See for example Weir 91
95. RII 103–4
96. Brundage 217, Sassier 237
97. Brundage 218 discussing Markale 'La vie, la legend'
98. Brundage 218–9
99. Saintes Notre-Dame, XXIX, 36, Flandria Generosa 32, MGH SS IX, 324

100. CUL Ii.VI.24, fol 98r and Paris Bib Arsenal 3516, fol 314r See Power Stripping of a Queen: Eleanor in C13 Norman tradition in Bull/Léglu at 122–5 text at 134–5

101. Power 74

5 Success Is the Best Revenge

1. Flori 83, Weir 93, CT
2. PPP 40–2
3. RT 165, HH 756–8, Turner Household.
4. Flori Family Trees, Bouchard in L&L 232
5. Turner 101–2, Weir 54–6, Pacaut 60–3, WM 474–7, GW iii 300–1
6. RT 515, Martindale EA 31–2, Weir 94, Flori 84, CT 135, Turner 109–10
7. GW, EHD 409–20, WM 471–501, Peter of Blois Epistolae 14, 1, 66, 75
8. des Documents relatifs a L'Abbaye de Montierneuf 135–36. Hivgerneaux L&L 63–4, Turner Household
9. VC, Bienvenu CCM 1986 17–19. 'Empire of the Poitevins and Angevins' occurs in Paris BN ms. Latin 5480 part 1
10. Turner 113–4, PPP 34–8, Nolan 80–82, Hivgerneaux L&L 20–2, Turner Household, Layettes du Trésor des Chartes I, 415, 176, Itinerary 1, Itinerary 2
11. RT 169–70, RII 113–4, Turner 115, Weir 101, RGHF xii, 438
12. GC, i, 151–2; RT, 171, Itinerary 1 and 2, Turner 114–7, Turner Household, Chibnall 158–9, Richard II 115, VC.
13. VC, RT 176–7, HH 770–1, Turner 117–9, RII 115, RT, 235
14. Turner Household, Turner 119, Chibnall 158–9, Itinerary 2
15. Itinerary 1 and 2, VC RT 179
16. ed Rayounard, Topsfield 112, Harvey 105–8. For accounts relying on Uc: Weir 101–3, Kelly 85–7, Flori 291–2
17. Itinerary, Turner 119–20, RT 179–80
18. RT 180–1, Turner 120–1, Weir 105–6, Flori 69–70
19. RT 181–2, HH 774–5, GC I 159, RD I 299, Crouch Image 293–4, RT 181–2, HH 774–5, GC I 159, Flori 99, Vincent HIINI 307
20. HH 202–3
21. RT 176, Guy 67–73, Weir 107, Turner 120–1
22. GC i 160
23. FitzStephen, 2–15, Turner 124–5
24. Turner 123, GC1 160, RN 189, RT 182, WN I 101, Weir 107–8, Wace, 1803
25. Fitzstephen, Itinerary 1 and 2. There are some doubts expressed by some writers as to whether FitzStephen was actually referring to the Tower; however the fact that Westminster was not used for the coronation suggests strongly that refurbishments were needed
26. PR, Turner Agatha 3
27. GC1, 161, RD 530, Turner Household 4–5, Turner 132, VC, Weir 126, Kelly 94
28. GC I 162, RT 182, Turner 131–2, Weir 150
29. RT 184–6, WN 105, GC I 162, Itinerary 1 and 2, VC
30. Nolan 83–6, Brown in L&L 22–4.

Notes

31. RT 189, Cheney, PR, B.R. Kemp, Reading Abbey Cartularies no.466 and Richardson, 195, Turner 132 quoting the Cartulary of Holy Trinity Aldgate
32. JSLI 52
33. RT 186, Aragon in L&L 99–100, Turner 153, Crouch The Beaumont Twins 86–8, 207, 210, PR
34. Chronicon Monasteri de Abingdon vol 2, 225, Turner 154, citing CCR 5 61, Richardson ed Memoranda Roll 1 John
35. JSP I 41–2, Lazar in Kibler, WM 478–9, 494–5, Lovatt
36. RGHF 12 417, 439, Weir 133, Itinerary 1 and 2, Turner 132–3, Hivgerneaux, Turner Household 6–7, Charters RHGF XII, 439, RII 122
37. Warren 65 citing Boussard Le Comte d'Anjou 74, RII 122, RHGF, XII, 417
38. Turner Household, PPP 43
39. Itinerary 2, RT 192, Battle Chronicle 175, JSL 31–2, 50–1. Guy 90, 122, Turner 133
40. Itinerary 1 and 2, Chronicle of St Albans, Orme, Guy 82, Turner Agatha 4
41. Itinerary 1 and 2, PR 3 Henry II 82
42. Turner 134
43. Itinerary 1 and 2, Van Houts 99, Haskins 160–9, WN ii 9, RD I 302, Bowie 31, Washington
44. Guy 91–2, Turner 135, Weir 154
45. Itinerary 1 and 2, Guy 93–4, Bowie 31
46. Danelaw Charters, no. 494. Abstract: Itinerary 1 and 2, Cloulas 90–1, Bowie 135, RII 126, Martene Durand Amplissima Collection cols 995–7
47. RT 200, 321–2, GC I 166, Cheyette 34, 260, S&P 34–7, Guy 108–9, Turner 134–6, Warren 84, Flori 77, RII 127–8
48. RT 322–3, RGHF 12 439, 417, 374, Guy 110–1, Turner 136–8, Hosler
49. Weir 157, Flori 78, Turner 138, Gesta Abbatum Sancti Albani 161
50. RT 206, Itinerary 1 and 2, JSL I 151–2, 189, Turner 153, Lindeman Mariner's Mirror vol 74 (1988)
51. PR, Bienvenu, Briand, Itinerary, Turner Household, Turner 165–6
52. Guy 130–1
53. JSL I 121, WN I 103
54. Turner 138–9, Flori 78–9, Guy 114, RGHF 16 24–5, Ciii 117–8
55. RH II 9, RHG II 80
56. Guy 136–8, Itinerary 1 and 2, RT 210–1, PR, Turner 139
57. Guy 140–2, Strickland 39–43, Turner 139
58. Strickland 34–8, Guy 142–6
59. Bowie 31, Guy 149, 153–4, Itinerary 1 and 2, Turner 140, RD I 308
60. Milland Bove 2004 158
61. Moulinier-Brogi 146, Flori 289–90
62. Evans 75, O'Callaghan in L&L 301–17., Broadhurst 1996, Mora-Lebrun 2008, Aurell 139, Baumgartner & Vielliard 1998, 18–9, Flori 290–1
63. Evans 75, Moulinier-Brogi 145, Pappano in L&L, Owen 166 citing Hatto Gottfried von Strausberg 355 ff
64. Van Houts Memory and Gender 71–4
65. Owen 167
66. Bowie 46 citing PR, Turner 149, Moulinier-Brogi 145, Lazar in Kibler
67. Wace ll 10539–10556, Lazar in Kibler, PPP 42 fn 169

6 Disillusionment

1. Bowie 32, PR (72 for the pork and eggs), Itinerary 1 and 2
2. Turner 140, RT 258, RD 1 311, GW vi, 137–8. On Nest Turner 236, Crouch Marshal 139
3. RII 134, RD I 325
4. PL 200 c.1362 and HGF 15, 767–8 at https://epistolae.ctl.columbia.edu/letter/137.html
5. GC, i, 174, AM ii 238, Guy 174–8, 180–2, Turner 140–1, Strickland 51–3
6. Strickland 63–4, WM 278–9, Guy 183, Turner 141, HKW
7. JSLII 3–15, Guy 184
8. Guy 188–92
9. Duggan Italian Network, Ciii 73–8
10. Guy 194
11. RT 221, AM ii 57, RD I 313, GC I 182–9, Guy 197–211
12. Kerrebrouck (2000) 541, Guy 226
13. Chronica Albrici Monachi Trium Fontium 1152
14. Itinerary 1
15. Bowie 32
16. Turner 141, Flori 81, Guy 230
17. Monasticon VII, 569, Guy 230, Turner 141–2, JSLII 52–3
18. Schofield, Laytime and Demurrage paragraph 1.9, doubted Twiss Black Book of the Admiralty Vol 1 ii
19. RII 137, Cheyette 263
20. RT 224, RII 139–40, Turner 141
21. Weir 173, GC i 198, PR; RD i, 318; RT 226
22. PR
23. Itinerary 1 and 2, Bowie 33
24. RII 138, Itinerary 1 and 2, RT 228, PR
25. Itinerary RII 138–9, RT 229
26. BC 112
27. GC I 287, BM Vol 6, 233, Warren 103, Turner 183
28. Bowie 33, Itinerary, Chroniques Anglo-Normandes 1001
29. RII 140, RT 229, Turner 183
30. Lewis L&L 160
31. RT 369, Lewis 163–5, Flori Chapter 4
32. RII 142
33. Cheney EHR 82 (1967) 759–60, Turner 146, HKW ii 708
34. Orme, 11–12
35. PR, Green 222, Weir 175, Bowie 33–4
36. See for example Turner Eleanor of Aquitaine and her Children
37. Howell, Eleanor of Provence 76, 99–101, Cockerill Eleanor of Castile 250–3
38. Aragon in L&L 102–3
39. Bowie 30–4
40. Bowie 34
41. RII 141–2, Strickland 62–3
42. Weir 179, FitzStephen quoting a letter from the Archbishop of Rouen in 1173
43. Cheyette 264–5.

44. Guy 246–9
45. https://epistolae.ctl.columbia.edu/letter/1187.html
46. Flori 89, Turner 195, Kelly 328, 354. RII 375 refers to John's being placed there. Lewis in L&L 166–8, Bowie 51. The obituary notices which form the only real evidence for the placement are in a seventeenth century manuscript, which drew from a necrology whose date is uncertain: Lewis fn 45.
47. Weir 181, Bowie 35

7 'The duchy ... in her power'

1. RII 143–5, Bowie 35
2. RII 145–7, HGM ll 1268 et seq. HGM gives the March date, Richard opts for 6–7 April
3. HGM ll 1620–1860
4. Given-Wilson & Curteis (1988), 98
5. HGM ll 1878–82, Mullally in L&L 241–2
6. Recueil Des Acte d'Henri II I 425–6, Turner 186–7, RII 148–9
7. Weir 179, RII 150
8. VC, Marchegay 'Chartes' 329; Bienvenu Aliénor 16, Itinerary 1 and 2
9. Bienvenu 19–21, Hivergneaux L&L 68–9
10. Lozinski CCM 37 (1994) 91–100, Perrot 30, 182, Turner 181
11. Turner Household 11
12. Turner Household, Chroniques de Saint-Martial de Limoges, Varia Chronicorum Fragmenta, 189
13. Ralph Niger is cited without detail at Weir 181
14. Turner Household 25, PPP 46, RHGF, XII, 446–7, 563, Annales de Burton, 209. Constance's mother died in 1201.
15. RHGF XII 420
16. PPP 41–2, Hivergernaux in L&L 69
17. Strickland 70–1, Guy 251–3, Gillingham in HIINI 7–4, JSL ii 288
18. RT 240, GC I 27–10, Weir 183, Liebenstein in P&C 79–80, Strickland 68–9
19. RII 146, 150, Itinerary 1 and 2, Boutoulle 70, 200–01, Guy 255–7
20. Cerda dot Gascon LJS ii 179
21. Cronica Latina 21, Mariana, Historia general de Espana bk 11 ch 4, PPP 57
22. See for example Bertrand Compaigne, Chronique de la ville et diocèse de Bayonne (Pau 1663) 24
23. Gonzalez, i, plate between 192–3
24. Vann in QRP 138, EHD, Cockerill 25–6
25. Gillingham The Angevin Empire 27, 29 and 70, Vann 129, Aurell Plantagenet Empire 194
26. Ll 1983–2000, 6330–33, Lazar in Kibler
27. Guy 273–6, Strickland 78–9
28. Strickland 74–7, Guy 284
29. Strickland 79, HGM ll 1933–4
30. Lebenstien P&C 79, 81–2
31. Mullally in L&L
32. RD, Guy 286, PR 16 for Marguerite 'and her household', and only £6 for Eleanor. HGM ll, RT 305

33. Fitzstephen 103, Itinerary 1, Strickland 81, 92, Kelly 111, BM STC iv 87
34. Itinerary 1, Vigeois RHF XII 442D, RII 150, Hivergnaux 67 advocate 1170. Gillingham 58, Flori 134, Turner 190, Callahan 29 and Laube Zehn Kapital 62, advocate 1172
35. Guy 287–8
36. RGHF Xiii 143, RHG i, 7, RHC, i, 6, RT, 248
37. Itinerary 1, Labande les filles 107, Turner 347, Bowie 89–90
38. Bowie 112
39. Guy 308–12
40. RHG, i, 14; BM, iii, 542; RD i, 345, Guy 324
41. Hivergneaux L&L 69
42. Brown, L&L 27, Stahl Coinage 328–33, Poey dAvant Monnaies feodales de France 2, 1–4, 22–3, 28. There is one 'ducissa' survival, but it is highly controversial and none of the experts in the area is confident about its treatment
43. Richard 150, Vigeois Xiii 312
44. Richard II 156
45. VC Chroniques de Saint-Martial de Limoges, Varia Chronicorum Fragmenta, 188, though cf. RHGF xii 446–7 which called Marchisa sterile in 1177
46. RII 158
47. RII 159
48. RHGF 12 442–3, Callahan 34, Turner 189
49. Callahan 35–6, CSML 14, Brown in L&L 1–54
50. GW viii 128–9, RII 151–2, Callahan 32–3
51. Turner 191
52. VC
53. PR 19 Henry II 154, 182 records the purchase of robes for the three
54. Harvey 108 agrees
55. Jeanroy and Lejeune are notable in this regard. Amy Kelly and Regine Pernoud accept their assertions too
56. Paterson 90–100, Harvey Eleanor 109, Cheyette 2–3
57. Harvey 110–11
58. McCash Marie and Eleanor
59. Bourgain, Flori 368–74, Evergates loc. 1285
60. RHG I 31–2, 35, RHC I 35–41, RT 254–5, Turner 190, VC
61. Weir 196
62. Strickland Chs 6–7, CTB 311, Guy 299–311
63. RT 251, RD I 371, WN I 181, Warren 124
64. Strickland 114, 116–8, Liebenstein 80, 82–4
65. RHG I 34, RHC I 32, Strickland 119–20
66. Liebenstein 84
67. RD i 353, RHG, i, 35, RHC, i, 36–41, Cheyette 267, Hivergneaux in L&L 68, RII 163–4
68. Turner 179, Koopmans, RHG i, 41, RHC i, 45, RGHF, xii, 443
69. RHG I 36, RT 255, Strickland 121, Cheyette 267–8
70. CT 136, RHG I 41, RHC II 41–5, GC I 24, Strickland 122
71. Gillingham 47, Martindale Eleanor 33, Strickland 137
72. https://epistolae.ctl.columbia.edu/letter/17.html

73. RHGF 12, 443
74. RT 521, RC 18, RDI 350, 355, GC I 242, WN II 170–1, RHG I 42, RHC II 46, Strickland 134–41, Gillingham 43
75. Warren 122, RII 167, Norgate II 137, Strickland 142–5, Gillingham 47
76. Gillingham 41–3, RHG I 63, RT 256
77. JF 4, HGM ll 2193–5
78. Flori 101–105
79. RHG I 49
80. Epistolae
81. GC I 242–3, WN I 170–2, RHG I 41–3, 62–3, RHC II 46, RD I 355, Weir 209, Turner 227 citing Richard le Poitevin
82. RD I 380, RHG I 71, RHC I 61, Strickland 178, 191

8 The Lost Years

1. Turner 230–1, Flori 109, Weir 209
2. Kenaan-Kedar CCM 1998 318–330, Flori 115–7
3. See for example Flori 115, Weir 314–5, Nielgen, Voyer in 303 197–9, Evans 152, Chadwick: http://the-history-girls.blogspot.com/2014/10/guess-who-or-debate-over-radegonde.html
4. Itinerary 1, RHG ii 61, Turner 227–8
5. RHG 2 61, RD I 380, Turner 231, Bowie 35, Weir 212
6. PPP 20, Brittain xi
7. https://www.british-history.ac.uk/rchme/salisbury/pp1-24, PPP 20, Weir 14, Turner 231
8. Agatha, Clerical Wife 6
9. Gillingham 50
10. RHG I 73. The Leicester story interestingly was omitted from the later Chronica. Strickland 198, Turner 233–4
11. Weir 218, Turner 237
12. RHGF XII 420
13. WT 180–1, WN I 128, 93, 97, 281, Evans 23–9, Turner 227
14. RD i 350, 355, Borman Ch 13–14, Reilly Ch 12
15. Brut y Tywysogion (Williams), 225.
16. GC 1 256–7, Weir 222
17. Flori 122, GW 165–6
18. RH ii 93–4
19. Lovatt, London, nos. 481 and 646. Contra, Turner 219.
20. Turner 234, Weir 222, RHG, i, 114–5; RHC, i, 93
21. RHG 1 135, 136, Turner 237, McCash 705Eileen Power, 455, Hallam cf PPP 26 noting that there is no clear proof that the land used was part of Eleanor's dower
22. PR, Strickland 97
23. RHG, i, 106, 114–5; RHC, i, 87, Turner 237, PR 22 171, 198, Gillingham 52–4, Itinerary 1 and 2, Turner 237
24. Bowie 83, Norwich KiS 308
25. RHG I 115–7, RHC ii 94–5, RT 271, Bowie 74, Itinerary 1 202, 204, 205, 206, Norwich KiS 309, Bowie 74

26. RD I 408, 414, Turner 238, PR22 12–15, 47, 152, 198–9, Bowie 91–2, Strickland 321–2

27. RHG, i, 124; RD i, 415, Itinerary 1 and 2, Gillingham 56

28. Evans 35–7, Weir 225, Chroniques de London 3

29. Turner 12, HKW I 90

30. RHG I, 168–9, 180, 190–4, GW 57, Turner 235–6, Weir 226

31. RHG ii, 160. RDev 26. GW viii: 232

32. JS II, no. 279

33. Turner 236 and Gillingham 142

34. GC I 256–7, GW 58

35. RHG i, 132, RHC, i, 118, Strickland 210, 234, PR, Turner 239

36. Itinerary 1 and 2, RHG I 131, 182, 221, 238, 240, RHC I 117, 170, RD I 417, 428, 436, Strickland 260–1, HGM 9510, Leonor

37. RD I 242, RHG I 432, RHC I 193, RT 282, GC I 293, Gillingham 62–3, Turner 240–1, Weir 228, Labande 213

38. Itinerary 1 and 2, PR, RHG, i, 241, RHC, i, 192, RT 282–3, RD I 433, Sassier 468, Strickland 262

39. RHG I 242–3

40. Itinerary 1, PR, Turner 237

41. Flandria Generosa (Continuatio Claromariscensis) 4, MGH SS IX, 327, RT 284, RHG 287–8, Strickland 269, 275

42. RT 303, RGHF xviii, 212, Strickland 269

43. HGM 5693–714, RT 304, RHG, i, 291, RHC, i, 273, RT, 304, 308, RD ii 18, Gillingham 69–70, Strickland 282 et seq

44. GC I 303, RD ii 19, RHG I 291–2, RD ii 18, Strickland 284–5

45. RHG I 298, RHC ii 278, Turner 242–4, Weir 231, Gillingham 74–5, Strickland 297, 299, 301–7

46. RHG I 300, RHC II 279, RHGF 337–40, RT 306, HGM ll 6884, Strickland 306–9

47. WM I 234, Strickland 310–13

48. RC 272–3 setting out Sermo de morte et sepultra Henrici regis junior Crouch, WM 51, 55, PPP 43, Strickland 313–4, Turner 244, Weir 235

49. Strickland 313–7, Turner 244–5, Weir 235–6

50. RT 306

9 False Freedom

1. Itinerary 1 (probably based on GV), GC 1, 326

2. GR 1 305, Turner 245, Weir 238, PR26 95 (1179–80), PR

3. Hallam 124–5, Turner 236–7, HKW 1 88, Le Couteulx, Ann. ii, 325

4. RHG I 304–6, RGHF·xx 220, Turner 245, Flori 127

5. PR 33 Hen. II (1186–87) 40, Turner Household VC, Bienvenu 23

6. Weir 242, Meade 291, Short 'BelleBelle A ghost mistress for Henry II' Notes and Queries 64(1) January 2018

7. Turner 248, Itinerary 1 and 2, Gillingham 78, RHG I 311, Vigeois RGHF 18 218

8. Born no 8 160–7 noted in Gillingham 70, see also Born no. 2 quoted Flori at 128

9. RHG, i, 316; GC, i, 311

10. Gillingham 79

11. Itinerary 1 and 2, RHG, i, 319–21, 333–4, 337, GC, i, 318, 324, RD, ii, 24, RHC, i, 287–8, RD ii, 22–3 PR

12. Itinerary 1 and 2, RHG, i, 334–6; RHC, i, 299–302; GC, i, 325, RD ii 32. I am indebted to Elizabeth Chadwick for the suggestion that Heraclius must have been able to report on Marshal's crusade.

13. RHG, i, 336; RHC, i, 303; RD, ii, 34, Gillingham 81, Cheyette 334

14. RHG I 337–8; RD 2, 40, Richard 2 232, Turner 249, Weir 244

15. Hivergneaux L&L 71, Aurell 246 VC, Turner 249, Weir 245, Flori 129–30, Gillingham 80

16. Hivergneaux in L&L 71, Turner 249, Turner Household, PR

17. The identification was originally made by Jesus Viejo, in: 'Royal manuscript patronage in late Ducal Normandy: A context for the female patron portrait of the Fécamp Psalter (c. 1180)', Cerae 3 (2016) 1–35. The psalter can be viewed online at: https://www.kb.nl/en/themes/medieval-manuscripts/psalter-of-eleanor-of-aquitaine-ca-1185. The author's full arguments reinforcing this ascription are at: https://www.saracockerill.com/extra-materials

18. WN iii 7, RHG 1 343–5, 347

19. RHG I 343, RHC I 308, RD ii 40, Itinerary 1 and 2, Crouch William Marshal 70

20. Itinerary 1 and 2, RHG, i, 345–50, RHC, i, 308–9, RD, ii, 40, Falla, 185, PR

21. Itinerary 1 and 2, RHG, i, 353–4, AM 2 241, Evergates, Turner 251, Weir 246

22. GW III ch 25, HGM ll 8000–10000 have repeated references to Henry's illness, Turner 253

23. Itinerary 1 and 2

24. Itinerary 1 and 2, RHG, ii, 4; RHC, i, 317; GC, i, 356; RD, ii, 47, Turner Household, Turner 250–1

25. Itinerary 1, PR, Turner 250, Crouch 59

26. PR Richardson Letters 209–10, Turner 250, Gillingham 84–5

27. Runciman ii 424, RD ii 50, WN iii 23, 25, RNC, 95, RHG ii 29, GC i 389

28. RHG ii 29–32, GC I 406, WN iii 23

29. Itinerary 1 and 2 (conflict on the Salisbury stop), RHG ii 32–6, RHC i 335–8, RD ii 55, GC I 406, 408, 418–42, RHG ii 45

30. RHG ii 48–50, 61, HGM 8065–175, GC I 435, 439–40, RD ii 58, RII 244–8, RHC i 362, HGM 8285–8320

31. RHGF xii 569

32. Itinerary 1, Runciman iii, 10, Annales Sancti Blasii Brunsvicenses 1173 and 1188, MGH SS XXIV, 824

33. RHG ii 66–70, 72, RHC ii 363–6, RD ii 63, GC I 439–40, HGM 8381–8788, GW 3 24–6, Turner 253, Weir 250–1

10 The Queen

1. RHG, ii 71, RHC i 366–7, GW 306, GC i 449, RD ii 64, HGM ll 9039–9112, https://epistolae.ctl.columbia.edu/letter/886.html, https://epistolae.ctl.columbia.edu/woman/24.html

2. PPP 19

3. Earenfight 3, Evans 12

4. Chapter 4 in L&L, For the Adela comparison LoPrete in ed Evergates 7–43, Evans 13

5. RHG ii, 74–5
6. Role 79, Turner 258
7. RD ii 67
8. RHG ii, 74–5
9. PR, Weir 256, Holt Magna Carta 81ff
10. RD ii 68, RHC iii, 5 Weir 256 Pernoud 199
11. RHGF 18 708, RHC iv 33–4, RII 261, Weir 256, Pernoud 190
12. RHC iii 6
13. Gillingham 107–8, Music for the Lion Hearted King https://www.hyperion-records.co.uk/notes/55292-B.pdf
14. Turner 260, Landon 18
15. RD ii 67
16. GC I 457. RD ii, 67
17. Pernoud 332, Flori 137 debunks
18. RD ii 67, Flori 113
19. Turner 260
20. GC i 458, RHG ii, 73, 76–8, RHC iii, 6, RHGF, XII, 456, Turner 260
21. Landon 3, Gillingham 109
22. Gillingham 266
23. RHG ii 76, 79, Landon 4, Weir 260, Turner 260
24. RHG ii 80–3, Gillingham 106–7
25. RHG ii 79, 83, Flori 142
26. RHG ii 88
27. WN 295, RHG ii 84
28. Dobson
29. RHC iii 27
30. Cloulas Douaire 90–1, Power 118. The doubt over the Poitevin Castles is because the lands are identified by reference to Berengaria's dower, which was based on that of Eleanor. It may be that no specific Poitevin provision was made for Eleanor
31. Turner 261, Joscelin of Brakelond
32. VC, PPP 56
33. Turner 276
34. RHG ii 85, RHC iii 15, Landon 6
35. RHG ii 87, Rymer i, 63, RHC iii 19
36. Landon 16–7
37. PPP 56
38. RHC iii, 33, RHG ii 97, GC I, 477, RD ii 72
39. VC RHC iii 208–11, Turner 272 wrongly dates this to the time of the ransom; but the witness list includes William de Longchamp. Leland, Collectanea, i, 88
40. HGR 2 101, RHC iii 28, RDev 10, Landon 26, Turner 261, Flori 144
41. RHG ii 106, RHC iii 32, RD 6, Turner 261–2, Flori 140
42. Gillingham 123–5, Trinidade 68–9, Turner 263–4, Flori 144, Landon 32, Born no 35: http://www.trobar.org/troubadours/bertran_de_born/poem35.php
43. Landon 30
44. RD ii 11, Landon 32–4
45. Turner 264, RII 262–3

46. Flori 144, Turner 264, VC, RII 263–4, 268, Arch Hist de la Saintonge I 32, Seward 157, Pernoud 208
47. The likely content and genesis of the mural is considered by the author at: https://www.saracockerill.com/extra-materials
48. RHG ii 350, RII 267–8, GW ii 176, Flori 144–5
49. Turner 264, RII 268–9
50. RDev 24–5, WN iv 19, Bale, VC
51. Landon 47
52. Flori 150–1, Owen, 83, Trinidade 76, Evergates Preface
53. Landon 45 citing Cartellari ii 159
54. RHG II 157, RDev 25
55. RHG II 195–6, RHGF xii, 383
56. Ambroise ll 1135ff
57. RD 27, Flori 153
58. RHG ii 158, RHC iii 96, Landon 46
59. Bowie 222, RD 27
60. Trinidade 119
61. See Southern, ODNB. There is no evidence that he was her Latin secretary and chancellor as Weir 358 suggests
62. Duggan Ciii 1–2
63. Duggan, 1–2, 17–8, 11, Bolgia (271)
64. RHG ii, RHC iii 101RD, PR Landon 48
65. See Landon Appendix C at 192 for dating.
66. Turner 267
67. RHGF 17 516, RII 276
68. RHC 100, RDev 53–4, 58–64, HGM ll 9876–82, Turner 266–8, Bartlett, GW 15
69. RHG ii 181–4, 218, Gillingham 160–5
70. RHG ii 229
71. RHG ii 236–7
72. RHG ii 223–5, 247, RD 419–20, RDev 55, Montaubin in CIII 122
73. RHG ii 236, GC I 515
74. GC I 515
75. RHG ii 236–8, RD 58–64, RDev 56
76. GW 413, RHC iii 188, RDev 56
77. RHG ii 237–8
78. PPP 59, Weir 282
79. PPP 59–60
80. Turner Agatha 15
81. RD ii 58
82. RD ii 59–60
83. Ambroise 434
84. Cheyette 329–41
85. Landon 69
86. RH iii 187, 195
87. Flori 161 quoting Rigord 120
88. RH
89. VC
90. RH

91. Library of the D&C Canterbury Register E Folio 404, Landon 204–5, GC i 515
92. GC i 515, RHC iii 196, Turner 270
93. RD ii 67–9, HGM 9883ff, Flori 162
94. RHC iii 204–8, RHG ii 232–4
95. RHC iii 208, iv 31, Brundage CIII 17–19, Montaubin 122, Edbury 132
96. RD ii 119, Brundage 20
97. For the consensus as to their composition: Turner 272, For the sceptics: Lees EHR 21 (1906) 73–93, Owen 87–8
98. Turner 273–4, Weir 291, Flori 164, Pernoud 230–1, Kelly 311–2
99. See Turner 271–2, Owen 87–8, Cotts 41–2, 58
100. Ep Cant 362, Landon74, 205
101. RH iii 208–10, 228, WN 390, Chroniques de Saint-Martial 192, Flori 167
102. RH 3 208–10, Turner 273
103. RC 60
104. Waltham Charters 297 and 288
105. RHC iv 31
106. https://epistolae.ctl.columbia.edu/letter/148.html
107. RD ii 108, GC 517, Turner 271
108. Histoire RHC iii 216–7, 228, 231–3, Gillingham 248, Trindade 112
109. RHC iii 226, Turner 273, McCash 170
110. RHC iii 202–3
111. RHC iii 202, RD ii 113, 118
112. RHC iii 235, RC 62, GC I 524, Gillingham 250
113. Landon 85, WN I 406, GC I 524, RD ii 114, HGM 10012–16, Gillingham 251
114. WN I 406, GC I 524, HGM 10018–80
115. RHC iii 239–42, WN II 416, Landon 85–6
116. Landon 85–6, RHC 244, 246–8
117. RHC iii 247–8
118. RH iii 244, Landon 89
119. VC RHC iii 250–1, Landon 91–2
120. HGM iii 136–7, RH iii 252, WN 424
121. Morris Great and Terrible 367
122. Queens Choice 387–8
123. Bowie 213
124. Runciman Vol. 3, 32, Necrology of Chartres Cathedral
125. Turner 276, Bienvenu 23
126. Brown L&L 15, 43, Marchegay Chartes 339–40
127. Bienvenu 23, PPP 56–60
128. Landon 110–11
129. VC [BN ms 5480 415]
130. VC [BN 5480 121]
131. Landon 115, RC 70, Annales de Margan, 23
132. RHGF 17 578–9, RC 82, RII 299–315, Gillingham 311–2
133. Turner 276–7, Selden Soc 83 160–1
134. Trinidade 126–30, Cheyette 340–2
135. RH IV 40, 45

136. Turner 278, PR, Epistolae cantuariensis 437–8
137. RC 94–5, RH IV 82–4, RD II 166, Gillingham 323–4
138. CDF 1101

11 The Matriarch

1. VC
2. RII 331
3. HGM 11836–11903
4. Flori 187, Turner 280
5. Everard 162
6. Martindale LY 138–9
7. RII 334
8. RHC iv 88, Flores I 286, Turner 282
9. RII 335–6, VC, Turner 283, Hivergneaux Cour Plantagenet 81, LY 161–2
10. RII 337 VC
11. VC, Bienvenu, 'Aliénor d'Aquitaine et Fontevraud', 26
12. VC, AM 2 64, RII 341, Turner 285–6 VC
13. VC, Hivergneaux 81, Turner 283, Weir 327
14. Cirot de la Ville Histoire de Sauve Majeure 2, 141–2, Turner 284–5, LY 162–3
15. Turner 285 citing Cirot de la Ville, Histoire de Sauve Majeure 2, 141–2
16. VC, PPP 56, Weir 327
17. RII 347, VC Weir 14
18. Chaplais Essays in Medieval Diplomacy and Administration (London 1981), Martindale ELY 154–5, Rigord 50, RII 353, Weir 329, Turner 283, Flori 189
19. Rigord I 146, RII 353, Martindale LY 154–5
20. PPP 48, 57
21. HivCP 85, Turner 284–5, VC
22. Holt CCM 113–4, 1986 95–100, Flori 189–90
23. LY 158
24. PPP, 56–8, VC
25. Round 392. Bowie 213. The dating to Rouen is indicated by the witness list.
26. Bienvenu 24, Bowie 214
27. RHC iv 96, Turner 286, Bienvenu 24, Flori 190
28. Bowie 217, 222, Parks in Billado Feud, Violence and Practice: 288, Weir 33, http://the-history-girls.blogspot.com/2018/07/more-questions-than-answers-identity-of.html
29. Nolan L&L 377–406, Brandenburg 303 174–8
30. Bowie 227, Walker Royal and aristocratic burial in Spain 151
31. RHC iv 106–7, RC 100–1, Labande 106–8, Turner 288–289, Bowie 124, LY 140–1, 145–6
32. See for example Weir 333, relying on Richard 366
33. Flori 191–2, Kelly 358–9, Collecion de las cronicas de Castilla iii pt 1
34. RHC iv 114, RII 369, Turner 289
35. Turner 287–8, Marchegay Chartes de Fontevraud 339–40
36. PPP 37, Richardson Letters 206–8, Turner 288
37. Rot Chart 102–3, https://epistolae.ctl.columbia.edu/letter/900.html, Turner 291–2, Flori 195–6

38. Chaplais English Royal Documents: King John–Henry VI 15–16, LY 152. Letter Rot Chart 102
39. RHC iv 119–20, Rigord 153, HGM 11983ff, Flori 194–5
40. Cloulas Douaire 91, Trinidade 150–1, Foedera I 141
41. Rigord 138, RD ii 174, Martindale, LY 160
42. RC 137, Flori 199, Turner 291–2, RII 403–6
43. Histoire des Ducs de Normanie 93–4, Flori 198
44. RC 137–8, Turner 292, Flori 199
45. Rot Lit Pat 14b–15.
46. HGM ll 12096–12116
47. RC 139–41
48. Annals of Margam I 27, Rigord 197, Rot Lit Pat p 28B, Turner 292, Kelly 380
49. RII 42, Kelly 380, Owen 100, Weir 348, Turner 293, Flori 201
50. Layettes de Charters i 247
51. Thompson, 147
52. Runciman iii, 136
53. RC 144, Annals of Margam I 27, Waverley ii 1204, Flori 202–3 analyses the evidence
54. quoted Turner 295
55. Rot Lit Pat 54
56. Bienvenu 26 n.98
57. Vincent Alienor 61–66
58. Manchester Rylands Lat 155 f125. See Turner 297
59. Nolan in L&L 377
60. Flori 203

12 Mother of Empires

1. Florentii Wigornensis Monachi Chronicon, Continuatio, 178
2. Bowie 128, 180–4, Grant 164. In relation to Leonor I am indebted to Collette Bowie for sight of the English version of her biography of Leonor (forthcoming in Spain).
3. Bowie Leonor Ch 6
4. Bowie 115–6, 119, 188–90, Leonor Ch 2, 3
5. Chapter 1, 3
6. Bowie 121–3, Chapter 4
7. Bowie 126, Bianchini 238 et seq, Grant 164–6, Cockerill 30–32
8. Grant, Introduction
9. Evergates Preface
10. Nicholas in ed Evergates 128
11. Grant 8, Dessaux

Bibliography

Primary Sources

Andreas Capellanus, The Art of Courtly Love, ed. and trans. John Jay Parry (New York, 1990)

Annales monastici, ed. H. R. Luard (London, 1864–69)

Bernard of Clairvaux, The Letters of St. Bernard of Clairvaux, trans. Bruno Scott James (London, 1953)

Bernard Itier, Chroniques de Saint-Martial de Limoges, ed. H. Duplès-Agier (Paris, 1876)

Bernart de Ventadorn, The Songs of Bernart de Ventadorn, ed. and trans. Stephen G. Nichols, Jr, John A. Galm, and A. Bartlett Giamatti (Chapel Hill, NC, 1965)

Bertran de Born, The Poems of the Troubadour Bertran de Born, ed. W. D. Paden, Jr, T. Senkovitch, and P. H. Stäblen (Berkeley, CA, 1986)

Blyth Priory Cartulary, ed. R. T. Timson (London, 1973)

Calendar of Charter Rolls, 5, Public Record Office (London, 1916)

Calendar of Documents Preserved in France, 1, 918–1206, ed. J. H. Round (London, 1899)

Calendar of Patent Rolls Henry III, 3, 1232–47, Public Record Office (London, 1906)

Cartae Antiquae rolls 1–10, ed. Lionel Landon, Pipe Roll Society, new ser., 17 (1939)

Cartae Antiquae rolls 11–20, ed. J. Conway Davies, Pipe Roll Society, new ser., 33 (1960)

Cartulaire saintongeais de la Trinité-de-Vendôme, ed. Charles Métais (1893)

Cartulary of Holy Trinity, Aldgate, ed. Gerald A. J. Hodgett, London Record Society (1971)

Chartes de Fontevraud concernant l'Aunis et La Rochelle, ed. Paul Marchegay, 19 (1858)

Chartes du XIIIe siècle relatives à Saint-Martial de Limoges, ed. Henri Omont, 90 (1929)

Chartes et documents pour servir à l'histoire de l'abbeye de Saint-Maixent, ed. Alfred Richard, 2 vols (1886)

423

Chrétien de Troyes, Arthurian Romances, trans. William Kibler and Carleton W. Carroll (London, 1991; revised 2004)

Chronicon Monasterii de Abingdon, ed. J. Stevenson, 2 vols, RS (London, 1858)

Chronicon Turonensis magnum in A. Salmon, ed., Recueil des chroniques de Touraine (Tours, 1854)

Chronique de Morigny (1095–1152), ed. L. Mirot (Paris, 1909)

Chronique de Saint-Aubin d'Angers, ed. Paul Marchegay and E. Mabille in Chroniques des églises d'Anjou (Paris, 1869)

Chronique de Saint-Maixent, ed. Jean Verdon (Paris, 1979)

Chroniques des comtes d'Anjou et des seigneurs d'Amboise, ed. Louis Halphen and R. Poupardin (Paris, 1913)

Crawford, Anne, ed., Letters of the Queens of England 1100–1547 (Stroud, 1994)

Dugdale, William, Monasticon Anglicanum, ed. John Calley, new edn (London, 1846)

English Historical Documents, gen. ed. David Douglas, 12 vols, 2, 1042–1189, ed. David Douglas and George W. Greenaway (London, 1968)

English Lawsuits from William I to Richard I, ed. R. C. Van Caenegem (London, 1990–91)

Epistolae Cantuarensis, 1187–1199 in William Stubbs, ed., Chronicles and Memorials, Richard I, 2 vols, RS (London, 1864–65)

FitzStephen, Liber Custumarum. Rolls Series, no. 12, vol. 2 (1860)

Foedera, Conventiones, Literae, etc.; or Rymer's Foedera, 1066–1383, new edn (London, 1816–69)

Gerald of Wales, De principis instructione, ed. G. F. Warner in Giraldi Cambrensis Opera, 8 vols, RS (London, 1861–91), 8; trans. Joseph Stevenson, Concerning the instruction of princes (London, 1858; reprint Felinfach, Dyfed, 1994); Expugnatio hibernica, ed. and trans. A. B. Scott and F. X. Martin (Dublin, 1978)

Gervase of Canterbury: Historical Works, ed. William Stubbs, 2 vols, RS (London, 1879–80)

Gervase of Tilbury, Otia Imperialia, ed. and trans. S. E. Banks and J. W. Binns (Oxford, 2002)

Gesta Stephani, ed. and trans. K. R. Potter and R. H. C. Davis (Oxford, 1976)

Grand Cartulaire de Fontevraud, 1, ed. Jean-Marc Bienvenu with Robert Favreau and Georges Pon, AHP (Poitiers, 2000)

Great Rolls of the Pipe for the First Year of Richard the First, ed. Joseph Hunter (London, 1844) Great Rolls of the Pipe for the Reign of King Henry the Second, A.D. 1155, 1156, 1157, 1158, ed. Joseph Hunter (London, 1844)

John of Salisbury, Historia Pontificalis of John of Salisbury, ed. Marjorie Chibnall (Edinburgh, 1956); The Letters of John of Salisbury, ed. W. J. Miller and C. N. L. Brooke, 1. The Early Letters (1153–1166); 2. The Later Letters (1163–1180) (Oxford, 1979; 1986)

Jordan Fantosme's Chronicle, ed. P. Johnston (Oxford, 1981)

Layettes du trésor des chartes, ed. Alexandre Teulet, Henri-François Delaborde, and Élie Berger, 5 vols (Paris, 1863–1909)

Marcabru, a critical edition: Marcabru, Simon Gaunt, Ruth Harvey, Linda M. Paterson (Woodbridge 2000)

Materials for the History of Thomas Becket, ed. J. C. Robertson, 7 vols, RS (London, 1875–85)

Matthew Paris, Historia Anglorum in Historia Minor, ed. F. Madden, 3 vols, RS (1866–69); Chronica Majori, ed. H. R. Luard, 7 vols, RS (1872–83)

Memoranda Roll 1 John, ed. H. G. Richardson, Pipe Roll Society, new ser. 21 (1943)

Odo of Deuil, De profectione Ludovici VII, ed. and trans. Virginia Gingerick Berry (New York, 1948)

Orderic Vitalis, The Ecclesiastical History of Orderic Vitalis, ed. and trans. Marjorie Chibnall, 6 vols (Oxford, 1969–80)

Peter of Blois, Epistolae, in Migne, Patrologia, 207 (Paris, 1855)

Ralph of Coggeshall, Radulphi de Coggeshall Chronicon Anglicanum, ed. J. Stevenson (London, 1875)

Ralph Diceto, Radulphi de Diceto, Opera Historica, ed. William Stubbs (London, 1876)

Regesta Regum Anglo-Normannorum 1066–1154. eds H. W. C. Davis, C. Johnson, H. A. Cronne, and R. H. C. Davis (Oxford, 1913–69)

Richard le Poitevin, Ex Chronico Richardi Pictaviensis, RHGF, 12 (new edn, 1877)

Richard of Devizes, The Chronicle of Richard of Devizes, ed. and trans J. T. Appleby (London, 1963)

Roger of Howden, Gesta Regis Henrici secundi Benedicti Abbatis, ed. William Stubbs, 2 vols, RS (London, 1867); Chronica Rogeri de Hovedene, ed. William Stubbs (London, 1868–71)

Robert of Torigni, Chronicles, Stephen, Henry II and Richard I, ed. R. Howlett, 4, The Chronicle of Robert of Torigni (London, 1890)

Roger of Wendover, Flores Historiarum, ed. H. G. Hewlett, 3 vols (1886–89); trans. J. A. Giles, 2 vols (London, 1849)

Rotuli Chartarum, 1199–1216, ed. T. Duffus Hardy (London, 1837)

Rotuli Litterarum Clausarum, ed. T. Duffus Hardy (London, 1833–34)

Rotuli Litterarum Patentium, ed. T. Duffus Hardy (London, 1835)

Rotuli Normanniae in Turri Londinensi asservati, ed. T. Duffus Hardy (London, 1835)

Royal Writs in England from the Conquest to Glanvill, ed. R. C. Van Caenegem (London, 1958–59)

Sancti Bernardi Opera, ed. J. LeClercq and H. Rochais (Rome, 1979)

Suger, Lettres de Suger, Chartes de Suger, Vie de Suger par le moine Guillaume, ed. and trans. F. Gasparri, Suger, Oeuvres, 2 (Paris, 2001); The Deeds of Louis the Fat, eds and trans. Richard Cusimano and John Moorhead (Washington, DC, 1992); Histoire de Louis VII, ed. and trans. Françoise Gasparri, Suger, Oeuvres, 1 (Paris, 1996)

Thomas Becket, The Correspondence of Thomas Becket Archbishop of Canterbury, 1162–1170, ed. Alan Keith Bate (Turnhout, 1993)

Venantius Fortunatus, The Life of the Holy Radegund; translation by J. McNamara and J. Halborg (Durham, NC, 1992)

William fitzStephen, 'A Description of London,' in F. M. Stenton, Norman London (New York, 1990); reprint of Historical Association leaflets 93 and 94 (London, 1934)

William IX of Aquitaine, The Poetry of William VII, Count of Poitiers, IX Duke of Aquitaine, ed. and trans. Gerald A. Bond (New York, 1982)

William of Malmesbury, Willelmi Malmesbiriensis de Gestis regum, ed. William Stubbs (London, 1887–89)

William of Newburgh, Historia Rerum Anglicarum of William of Newburgh, in Chronicles, Stephen, Henry II and Richard I, ed. R. Howlett, 4 vols, RS (London 1885–90); trans. as History of English Affairs Book I, ed. and trans. P. G. Walsh and M. J. Kennedy (Warminster, 1988)

William of Tyre, A History of Deeds Done Beyond the Sea, ed. and trans. Emily Atwater Babcock and A. C. Krey, 2 vols (New York, 1943)

Secondary Sources

Abel, Mickey, Emma of Blois as an Arbiter of Peace, in ed. Martin Reassessing the Roles of Women as Makers of Medieval Art (Leiden, 2012)

Andrault-Schmitt, Claude, 'L'Architecture 'Angevine' à l'époque d'Aliénor,' in 303

Arts Council of Great Britain, English Romanesque Art 1066-1200 (London, 1984)

Asbridge, Thomas, The Crusades (London, 2012); The Greatest Knight (London, 2014)

Aurell, Martin, The Plantagenet Empire (Abingdon, 2014); Alienor d'Aquitaine (Association 303); 'Les Plantagenêts, la propagande et la relecture du passé', in Harper-Bill and Vincent, ed., Henry II: New Interpretations; Aurell, Martin and Noël-Yves Tonnerre, eds, Plantagenêts et Capétiens: Confrontations et héritage (Turnhout, 2006); Aurell, Martin, Catalina Girbea, and Marie-Aline de Mascureau, 'A Propos d'un livre récent sur Aliénor d'Aquitaine: portée et limites du genre biographique,' CCM (2005)

Auxerre, The First Life of St Bernard (Athens, OH, 2015)

Aziza, Margaret, 'Marie de France, Aliénor d'Aquitaine, and the Alien Queen' in L&L; 'La Regina Bisperta: Aliénor d'Aquitaine et ses relations littéraires au XIe siècle' in 303

Bachrach, Bernard, 'The Idea of the Angevin Empire', Albion, 10 (1978); 'Toward a Reappraisal of William the Great, Duke of Aquitaine (995–1030)', JMH, 4 (1979)

Bale, Anthony P., 'Richard of Devizes and Fictions of Judaism', Jewish Culture and History, 3(2) (2000), 55–72

Baltzer, Rebecca A., 'Music in the Life and Times of Eleanor of Aquitaine' in Kibler, ed.

Barber, Richard, 'Eleanor of Aquitaine and the Media', in Léglu and Bull, The Knight and Chivalry (Woodbridge, 1995)

Bardot, Marvin and Laurence Marvin, Louis VII and His World (Leiden, 2018)

Bartlett, Robert, Gerald of Wales, 1146–1223 (Oxford, 1982); England under the Norman and Angevin Kings 1075–1225 (Oxford, 2000); 'L'Attribution des poèmes du comte de Poitiers à Guillaume IX d'Aquitaine', CCM, 31 (1988); 'The Ventures of the Dukes of Aquitaine into Spain and the Crusader East in the Early Twelfth Century', HSJ, 5 (1993); 'The Eleanor of Aquitaine Vase, William IX of Aquitaine, and Muslim Spain', Gesta, 32 (1993); 'The Eleanor of Aquitaine Vase', in L&L

Benton, John F., 'The Court of Champagne as a Literary Centre', Speculum, 36 (1961), 551–91

Benz St John, Lisa, Three Medieval Queens (New York, 2012)

Bibliography

Bienvenu, Jean-Marie, 'Aliénor d'Aquitaine et Fontevraud', CCM, 29 (1986); 'Henri II Plantagenêt et Fontevraud', CCM, 37 (1994)

Bisson, Cultures of Power: Lordship, Status, and Process in Twelfth-Century Europe (Pennsylvania, 1995)

Bloch, Medieval Misogyny and the Invention of Western Romantic Love (Chicago, 1991)

Boase, Roger, The Origin and Meaning of Courtly Love: A Critical Study of European Scholarship (Manchester, 1977)

Bom, M., Women in the Military Orders of the Crusades (New York, 2012)

Borman, Tracy, Matilda, Wife of the Conqueror (London, 2012)

Bouchard Constance, Those of My Blood: Creating Noble Families in Medieval Francia (Philadelphia, 2001), 40; 'Consanguinity and Noble Marriages in the Tenth and Eleventh Centuries', Speculum, 56 (1981); 'Eleanor's Divorce from Louis VII' in L&L

Bullough, Vern and James Brundage (eds), A Handbook of Medieval Sexuality (New York, 2010)

Boureau, Julien, Richard Levesque, and Isabelle Sachot, 'Sur les Pas d'Aliénor, l'abbaye de Nieul-sur-l'Autise', in Aurell, ed.

Bourgain, Pascal, 'Aliénor d'Aquitaine et Marie de Champagne mises en cause par André le Chapelain', CCM, 29 (1986)

Bournazel, Eric, 'Suger and the Capetians', ed. Paula Lieber Gerson, in Suger and Saint-Denis: A Symposium (New York, 1986)

Boutoulle, Frédéric, 'La Gascogne sous les premiers Plantagenêts (1154–1199)' in P&C

Bowie, Colette, The Daughters of Henry II and Eleanor of Aquitaine: A Comparative Study of Twelfth-Century Royal Women (PhD, Glasgow, 2011); Leonor Reina de Castilla (unpublished)

Bozoky, Edina, 'Le culte des saints et des reliques dans la politique des premiers rois Plantagenêts', in Aurell, La Cour Plantagenêt

Bradbury, Jim, Philip Augustus King of France, 1180–1223 (Harlow, 1998)

Briand, Emile, Histoire de Sainte Radegonde, Reine de France, et des Sanctuaires et Pèlerinages et son honneur (Paris, 1898)

Broadhurst, Karen M., 'Henry II of England and Eleanor of Aquitaine: Patrons of Literature in French?', Viator, 27 (1996)

Brooke, Christopher, 'The Marriage of Henry II and Eleanor of Aquitaine', The Historian, 20 (1988) 3–8

Brooks, Polly Schoyer, Queen Eleanor, Independent Spirit of the Medieval World (New York, 1983)

Brown, Elizabeth A. R., 'Eleanor of Aquitaine: Parent, Queen, Duchess' in Kibler, ed.; 'The Prince is Father of the King: The Character and Childhood of Philip IV' in Brown; The Monarchy of Capetian France and Royal Ceremonial (Aldershot, 1991); 'Eleanor of Aquitaine Reconsidered: The Woman and her Seasons' in L&L; Franks, Burgundians and Aquitanians (American Philosophical Society, 2002)

Brown, R. Allen, H. M. Colvin, and A. J. Taylor, eds, The History of the King's Works, 1, The Middle Ages (London, 1963)

Brundage, James A., 'The Canon Law of Divorce in the Mid-twelfth Century: Louis VII c. Eleanor of Aquitaine', in Parsons and Wheeler; Law, Sex and Christian

Society in Medieval Europe (Chicago, 2009); 'Prostitution, Miscegenation, and Sexual Purity in the First Crusade', in Crusade and Settlement ed. Peter W. Edbury (Cardiff, 1985)

Bull, Marcus and Catherine Léglu, eds, The World of Eleanor of Aquitaine: Literature and Society in Southern France between the Eleventh and Thirteenth Centuries (Woodbridge, 2005)

Callahan, Daniel, 'The Coronation Right', in B&L

Calmel, Mireille, Les mots d'Aliénor (Paris, 2001)

Carpenter, David, 'Abbot Ralph of Coggeshall's Account of the Last Years of King Richard and the First Years of King John', EHR, 113 (1998)

Carpentier, 'Un couple tumulteux' in ed. Rouche, Mariage et Sexualite au Moyen Age (Paris, 2000)

Chambers, Frank McMinn, 'Some Legends concerning Eleanor of Aquitaine', Speculum, 16 (1941)

Chaplais, Pierre, 'Le Traité de Paris de 1259 et l'inféodation de la Gascogne allodiale', Essays in Medieval Diplomacy and Administration (London, 1981)

Cheney, Christopher R., 'A Monastic Letter of Fraternity to Eleanor of Aquitaine', EHR, 51 (1936), 88-93; Hubert Walter (Walton-on-Thames, 1967)

Cheney, Mary G., 'Master Geoffrey de Lucy, an Early Chancellor of the University of Oxford', EHR, 82 (1967)

Cheyette, Frederic L., 'Women, Poets, and Politics in Occitania', in Theodore Evergates, ed., Aristocratic Women in Medieval France, Ermengarde of Narbonne and the World of the Troubadours (New York, 2002)

Chibnall, Marjorie, 'Women in Orderic Vitalis', HSJ, 2 (1990), 105–21; The Empress Matilda: Queen Consort, Queen Mother, and Lady of the English (Oxford, 1991); 'The Empress Matilda and her Sons', in Parsons and Wheeler, Medieval Mothering

Chalandon, F., Manuel Comnene (Paris, 1912)

Chenu, M.-D., Nature, Man and Society in the Twelfth Century (Chicago, 1997)

Church, Stephen D., ed., King John: New Interpretations (Woodbridge, 1999)

Clanchy, Michael T., From Memory to Written Record: England 1066–1307 (Oxford, 1993)

Classen Albert, East Meets West in the Middle Ages and Early Modern Times (Berlin, 2013)

Cockerill, Sara, Eleanor of Castile: The Shadow Queen (Stroud, 2014)

Collins, Keepers of the Keys of Heaven (New York, 2009)

Constable, Giles, 'The Alleged Disgrace of John of Salisbury', EHR, 69 (1954)

Cotts, John, The Clerical Dilemma Peter of Blois and Literate Culture (Washington DC, 2009)

Cox, J. C., 'Mary, Abbess of Shaftesbury', EHR, 25 (1910); 26 (1911)

Crouch, David, The Beaumont Twins: The Roots and Branches of Power in the Twelfth Century (Cambridge, 1986); William Marshal (Abingdon, 2016); The Image of Aristocracy in Britain, 1000–1300 (London, 1992)

Damian-Grint, Peter, 'Benoît de Saint-Maure et l'idéologie des Plantagenêts', in P&C

Damon, Géraldine, 'Dames du Poitou au temps d'Aliénor', in 303; 'La Place et le pouvoir des dames dans la société au temps d'Aliénor d'Aquitaine' in P&C

Dessaux Nicolas, ed., Jeanne de Constantinople, Comtesse de Flandre et de Hainaut (Somogy, 2009)

Dobson, The Jews of Medieval York and the Massacre of March 1190, Borthwick Papers, 45 (York, 1974)

Doran, J. and D. Smith, Pope Celestine III: Diplomat and Pastor (Ashgate, 2008); Pope Innocent II: The Word and the City (London, 2016)

Duby, Georges, Women of the Twelfth Century, 1, Eleanor of Aquitaine and Six Others; 2, Remembering the Dead (Chicago, 1997), 3, Eve and the Church

Duggan, A., ed. Queens and Queenship in Medieval Europe (Woodbridge, 2002); 'Thomas Becket's Italian Network', in Pope, Church and City: Essays in Honour of Brenda M. Bolton (Oxford, 2004)

Dutton, 'Angevin Comital Children', in Anglo Norman Studies, XXXII (Woodbridge, 2010)

Earenfight, T., Queenship in Medieval Europe (New York, 2013)

Edgington, S. and S. Lambert, eds, Gendering the Crusades (Cardiff, 2001)

Evans Michael, Inventing Eleanor (London, 2014); The Missing Queen of France' in ed Bardot

Everard, Judith, Brittany and the Angevins: Province and Empire 1158–1203 (Cambridge, 2008)

Evergates, Marie of France, Countess of Champagne (Pennsylvania, 2018); Aristocratic Women of Medieval France (Pennsylvania, 2003)

Eyton, R. W., Court, Household, and Itinerary of King Henry II (London, 1878)

Facinger, Marion, 'A Study of Medieval Queenship: Capetian France 987–1237', Studies in Medieval and Renaissance History, 5 (1968)

Farmer, Sharon, 'Persuasive Voices: Clerical Images of Medieval Wives', Speculum, 61 (1986)

Favreau, Robert, 'Les Écoles et la culture à Saint-Hilaire-le-Grand de Poitiers des origines au début du XIIe siècle', CCM, 3 (1960), 473–78; 'Le Palais de Poitiers au moyen âge', BSAO, 4th ser., 11 (1971); Histoire de Poitiers (Toulouse, 1981); Histoire des Dioceses de France (Paris, 1988); 'Les Débuts de la ville de La Rochelle', CCM, 30 (1987)

Fawtier, Robert, The Capetian Kings of France, trans. L. Butler and R. J. Adam (London, 1960)

Ferrante, Joan M., 'Correspondent: "Blessed is the Speech of Your Mouth"', in Barbara Newman, ed., Voice of the Living Light: Hildegard of Bingen and Her World (Berkeley, 1998); 'The French Courtly Poet: Marie de France' in Katharina M. Wilson, ed., Medieval Women Writers (Athens, GA, 1984)

FitzGerald, Inspiration and Authority in the Middle Ages: Prophets and Their Critics (Oxford, 2017)

Flori, Jean, La Chevalerie en France au Moyen Âge (Paris, 1995); Richard Coeur de Lion (Paris, 1999), Aliénor d'Aquitaine: La reine insoumise (Paris, 2004); Queen and Rebel (Edinburgh, 2007)

Galignani A. and W., The History of Paris from the Earliest Period to the Present Day (Paris, 1825)

Garland, Lynda, 'Imperial Women and Entertainment at the Middle Byzantine Court', in Byzantine Women: Varieties of Experience, 800–1200 (Aldershot, 2006)

Gaunt, Simon and Sarah Kay, eds, The Troubadours: An Introduction (Cambridge, 1999)

Gaunt, Harvey Paterson, Marcabru: A Critical Edition (Woodbridge, 2007)

Gillingham, John, Richard I (New Haven, 2002); The Angevin Empire (London, 2000)

Gold, Claudia, King of the North Wind (London, 2018)

Gonzalez, El reino de Castilla en la epoca de Alfonso VIII, 3 vols (Madrid, 1960)

Grabois, 'Louis VII Pelerin', Revue d'Histoire de L'Eglise de France, 74 (1988), 5–22

Grant, Lindy, Abbot Suger and St Denis (Harlow, 1998); Blanche of Castile (New Haven, 2016)

Greenhill, Eleanor S., 'Eleanor, Abbot Suger and Saint-Denis', in W. W. Kibler (ed.)

Gaunt and Sarah Kay, eds, The Troubadours: An Introduction (Cambridge, 1999)

Haines, Medieval Song in Romance Languages (Cambridge, 2010)

Hallam, 'Henry II as a Founder of Monasteries', JI Ecclesiastical History, 28 (1977), 18, 124–5

Hanley, Catherine, Matilda: Empress, Queen, Warrior (London, 2019)

Harvey, Ruth E., Eleanor of Aquitaine and the Troubadours; The Poet Marcabru and Love (London, 1989); 'The Two Wives of the "First Troubadour" Duke William IX of Aquitaine', JMH, 19 (1993); 'Eleanor of Aquitaine and the Troubadours' in B&L

Harper-Bill, Christopher and Nicholas Vincent, eds, Henry II: New Interpretations (Woodbridge, 2007)

Hartnell, Jack, Medieval Bodies (London, 2018)

Haskins, Charles H., 'Henry II as a Patron of Literature' in A. G. Little and F. M. Powicke, eds, Essays in Medieval History Presented to Thomas Frederick Tout (Manchester, 1925); Studies in the History of Medieval Science (Cambridge, MA, 1926)

Herlihy, David, Medieval Households (Cambridge, MA, 1985); Women, Family and Society in Medieval Europe: Historical Essays, 1978–1991 (Providence, RI, 1995)

Higounet, Charles, Histoire de Bordeaux, 2, Bordeaux pendant le haut moyen âge (Bordeaux, 1963); Histoire de l'Aquitaine, Documents (Toulouse, 1973)

Hivergneaux, Marie, 'Aliénor d'Aquitaine: le pouvoir d'une femme à la lumière de ses chartes (1152–1204)', in Aurell, La Cour Plantagenêt; 'Queen Eleanor and Aquitaine, 1137–1189', in L&L; 'Aliénor et l'Aquitaine: le pouvoir à l'épreuve des chartes (1137–1204)', in 303; 'Autour d'Aliénor d'Aquitaine: entourage et pouvoir au prisme des chartes (1137–1189)', in P&C

Hodgson, Natasha, Women, Crusading and the Holy Land in Historical Narrative (Woodbridge, 2007)

Holmes, Everyday Living in the Twelfth Century (Madison, 1964)

Holt, Andrew, 'Medieval Masculinity and The Crusades: The Clerical Creation of a New Warrior Identity' (PhD, University of Florida, 2013)

Holt, J. C., 'Aliénor d'Aquitaine, Jean sans terre et la succession de 1199', CCM, 29 (1986)

Hudson, ed., 'The History of English Law: Centenary Essays on "Pollock and Maitland"', Proceedings of the British Academy, 89 (London, 1996)

Bibliography

Hosler, Henry II: A Medieval Soldier at War, 1147–1189 (Leiden, 2007)

Howell, Margaret E., Eleanor of Provence: Queenship in Thirteenth-Century England (Oxford, 1998)

Huneycutt, Lois L., 'Images of Queenship in the High Middle Ages', HSJ, 1 (1989), 65–79; 'Female Succession and the Language of Power in the Writings of Twelfth-Century Churchmen', in Parsons, Medieval Queenship; 'Intercession and the High-Medieval Queen: The Esther Topos', in Jennifer Carpenter and Sally-Beth Maclean, eds, Power of the Weak: Studies on Medieval Women (Champagne-Urbana, 1995); 'Public Lives, Private Ties: Royal Mothers in England and Scotland, 1070–1204' in Parsons and Wheeler, Medieval Mothering; 'Alianora Regina Anglorum', in L&L; Matilda of Scotland: A Study in Medieval Queenship (Woodbridge, 2003)

Johns, Susan M., Noblewomen, Aristocracy and Power in the Twelfth-Century Anglo-Norman Realm (Manchester, 2003)

Johnson, Penelope D., 'Agnes of Burgundy: an eleventh-century woman as monastic patron', Journal of Medieval History, 15 (1989), 93–104

Jolliffe, J. E. A., Angevin Kingship (London, 1963)

Jones, Dan, The Templars (London, 2017)

Jones, Michael and Malcolm Vale, eds, England and Her Neighbours 1066–1453: Essays in Honour of Pierre Chaplais (London, 1989)

Jordan, K., trans. Falla, P. S., Henry the Lion: a Biography (Oxford, 1986)

Kelly, Amy, Eleanor of Aquitaine and the Four Kings (Cambridge, MA, 1956)

Kenaan-Kedar, Nurith, 'Aliénor d'Aquitaine conduite en captivité: les peintures murales commémoratives de Sainte-Radegonde de Chinon', CCM, 41 (1998); 'The Impact of Eleanor of Aquitaine on the Visual Arts in France', in Aurell, Culture politique des Plantagenêts; 'The Wall Painting in the Chapel of Sainte-Radegonde at Chinon in the Historical Context', in Cinquante années d'études médiévales

Kibler, W. W. (ed.), Eleanor of Aquitaine: Patron and Politician (Austin, TX, 1976)

Koopmans, 'Thomas Becket and the Royal Abbey of Reading', EHR 131(548) (2016), 1–30

Kostick, Conor, Eleanor of Aquitaine and the Women of the Second Crusade in Medieval and Early Modern Women: Essays in Honour of Christine Meek (Dublin, 2010)

Kugler, Studienzur Geschichte des Zweiten Keuzzuges (Stuttgart, 1866)

Labande, Edmond-Rene, 'Pour une image veridique d'Alienor d'Aquitaine', Bulletin de la Societe des Antiquaires de l'Ouest, 2 (1952), 174–234; 'Les filles d'Alienor d'Aquitaine: etude comparative', CCM XXIX (1986), 101–12

Laffont, Robert, L'Abbaye De Fontevraud (Paris, 2001)

Landon, Itinerary of Richard I (London, 1935)

Lejeune, Rita, 'Le Rôle littéraire d'Aliénor d'Aquitaine et de sa famille', Cultura Neo-Latin, 14 (1954); 'Le Rôle littéraire de la famille d'Aliénor d'Aquitaine', CCM, 1 (1958); 'La Femme dans les littératures françaises et occitanes du XIe au XIIIe siècles', CCM, 20 (1977)

Lewis, Andrew W., Royal Succession in Capetian France: Studies on Familial Order and the State (Cambridge, MA, 1981); 'The Birth and Childhood of King John: Some Revisions' in L&L

Lindsay, Jack, 'Guilhem of Poitou', in Lindsay, The Troubadours and their World (London, 1976)

London, V. C. M., The Cartulary of Bradenstoke Priory (Wiltshire Record Society, 1979)

LoPrete, Kimberley, 'Adela of Blois as Mother and Countess', in Parsons and Wheeler, Medieval Mothering

Lovatt, Marie, 'Geoffrey (1151?–1212), archbishop of York', in Vincent, ed., Records Administration

Lozinski, Jean Louise, 'Henri II, Aliénor d'Aquitaine et la cathédrale de Poitiers', CCM, 37 (1994) Luchaire, Achille, Études sur les actes de Louis VII (Paris, 1885); 'Louis VI le Gros', Annales de sa vie et de son règne (Paris, 1890); Social France at the Time of Philip Augustus, trans. Edward Benjamin Krehbiel (New York, 1912; reprint 1967)

Luscombe, David and Jonathan Riley-Smith, eds, New CMH, 4, *c.* 1024–*c.* 1198, pt 2

Maalouf, Amin, The Crusades through Arab Eyes (Croydon, 2006)

McCash, June Hall Martin, 'Marie de Champagne and Eleanor of Aquitaine: A relationship re-examined', Speculum 54(4) (1979), 698–711

MacDonald, R. Thomas, 'Ralph de Vermandois (d.1152)', in Medieval France: An Encyclopedia

Magdalino, Paul, The Empire of Manuel Komnenos (Cambridge, 2009)

Mallett, Alex, 'The Battle of Inab', Journal of Medieval History, 39(1) (2013), 48–60

Marenbon, J., The Philosophy of Peter Abelard (Cambridge, 1997); Early Medieval Philosophy (London, 2002)

Maratu Abbe, Girard, évêque d'Angoulême, légat du Saint-Siège (Paris, 1866)

Markale, Jean, Aliénor d'Aquitaine (Paris, 1979; 2nd edn 2000)

Martindale, Jane, Status, Authority and Regional Power (Oxford, 1993); 'Eleanor of Aquitaine: The Last Years' in KJNI

Masson, Geoffroy du Loroux et L'architecture Religieux en Aquitaine (PhD, Bordeaux, 2012)

Meade, Marion, Eleanor of Aquitaine: A Biography (New York, 1977)

Mews, Constant J., 'The Council of Sens (1141): Abelard, Bernard, and the Fear of Social Upheaval', Speculum 77 (2002), 342–82

Morris, Marc, King John (London, 2015)

Nolan, Kathleen, Queens in Stone and Silver (London, 2009)

Norwich, John Julius, The Popes – A History (London, 2011); Kingdom in the Sun (London, 2018)

Orme, Nicholas, Medieval Children (2001)

Ormrod, Mark, England in the Thirteenth Century (Stamford, 1991)

Owen, D. D. R., Eleanor of Aquitaine: Queen and Legend (Oxford, 1993)

Pacaut, Marcel, Louis VII et les élections épiscopales dans le royaume de France (Paris, 1957); Louis VII et son royaume (Paris, 1964)

Painter, Sidney, William Marshal (Baltimore, 1933); 'The Houses of Lusignan and Châtellerault, 1150–1250', in Cazel, Feudalism and Liberty; 'The Lords of Lusignan in the Eleventh and Twelfth Centuries', in Cazel, Feudalism and Liberty; 'To Whom were Dedicated the Fables of Marie de France?', in Cazel, Feudalism and Liberty

Parsons, John Carmi (with Bonnie Wheeler), ed., Eleanor of Aquitaine: Lord and Lady (New York, 2003); Medieval Queenship (New York,

1993); 'Mothers, Daughters, Marriage, Power: Some Plantagenet Evidence, 1150–1500', in Medieval Queenship; Eleanor of Castile: Queen and Society in Thirteenth-Century England (New York, 1995); 'Damned If She Didn't and Damned When She Did: Bodies, Babies, and Bastards in the Lives of Two Queens of France' in L&L; and Bonnie Wheeler, eds, Medieval Mothering (New York, 1996)

Paterson, Linda, The World of the Troubadours (Cambridge, 1993)

Perrot, Françoise, 'Le Portrait d'Aliénor dans le vitrail de la crucifixion à la cathédrale de Poitiers', in 303

Peltzer, Jörge, 'Les Évêques de l'empire Plantagenêt et les rois angevins', in P&C

Pernoud, Régine, Aliénor d'Aquitaine (Paris, new edn, 1965)

Phillips, Jonathan, 'A Note on the Origins of Raymond of Poitiers', EHR, 106 (1991); The Second Crusade: Expanding the Frontiers of Christendom (New Haven, 2007)

Plain, Nancy, Eleanor of Aquitaine and the High Middle Ages (New York, 2005)

Pontfarcy, Yves de, 'Si Marie de France était Marie de Meulan', CCM, 38 (1995)

Power, Daniel, 'The Stripping of a Queen: Eleanor in Thirteenth-Century Norman Tradition', in B&L

Power, Eileen E., Medieval English Nunneries c. 1275 to 1535 (Cambridge, 1922)

Powicke, F. M., The Loss of Normandy (Manchester, 1960); and E. B. Fryde, eds, Handbook of British Chronology (London, 1961)

Prescott, Hilda, 'The Early Use of "Teste Me Ipso"', EHR, 35 (1920)

Rayounard, M., ed., Choix des posies originales des troubadours (Paris, 1816)

Reddy, William, The Making of Romantic Love (Chicago, 2012)

Reilly, Bernard F., The Kingdom of Leon-Castilla under Queen Urraca (New York, 1982)

Reynolds, Gateway to Heaven: Marian Doctrine and Devotion (New York, 2012)

Richard, Alfred, Histoire des comtes de Poitou (Paris, 1903)

Richardson, H. G., 'The Letters and Charters of Eleanor of Aquitaine', EHR, 74 (1959); 'The Coronation in Medieval England', Traditio, 16 (1960)

Riley-Smith, Jonathan, The Crusades: A History (New Haven, 2005)

Rosenthal, Joel T., ed., Medieval Women and the Sources of Medieval History (Athens, GA, 1990)

Runciman, Steven, A History of the Crusades (Cambridge, 1952)

Salter, Elizabeth, 'Courts and Courtly Love' in David Daiches and Anthony Thorlby, eds, Literature and Western Civilization: The Medieval World (London, 1973)

Salzman, L. F., Building in England Down to 1540 (Oxford, 1952)

Sanders, I. J., English Baronies (Oxford, 1960)

Sassier, Ives, Louis VII (Paris, 1991)

Schmolke-Hasselmann, Beate, 'Henry II Plantagenêt, roi d'Angleterre, et la genèse d'Erec et Enide', CCM, 24 (1981)

Seward, Desmond, Eleanor of Aquitaine: The Mother Queen (New York, 1979)

Short, Ian, 'Literary Culture at the Court of Henry II', in HIINI

Smalley, Beryl, Gospels in the Schools (1985)

Soulard-Berger, Isabelle, 'Agnes of Burgundy, Duchess of Aquitaine and Countess of Anjou. Implement political and religious action (1019–c. 1068)', in Bulletin of the Antiquarian Society of the West, VI, 1er quarter (1992)

Southern, R. W., 'Blois, Peter of (1125–1212)', Oxford DNB

Stafford, Pauline, 'The Portrayal of Royal Women in England, Mid-Tenth to Mid-Twelfth Centuries', in Parsons, Medieval Queenship

Stafford, Pauline and Anneke Mulder-Bakker, eds, Gendering the Middle Ages (Oxford, 2000)

Strickland, Agnes, Lives of the Queens of England from the Norman Conquest (London, 1893–99)

Strickland, Matthew, Henry the Young King (New Haven, 2016); 'The Upbringing of Henry, the Young King', in HIINI; 'Longespée [Lungespée], William I', Oxford DNB

Swabey, Fiona, Eleanor of Aquitaine, Courtly Love, and the Troubadours (Greenwood, 2004)

Taruskin, Richard, Music from the Earliest Notations to the Sixteenth Century (Oxford, 2009)

Taylor, Claire, Heresy in Medieval France: Dualism in Aquitaine and the Agenais, 1000–1249 (Woodbridge, 2005)

Thompson, Kathleen, Power and Border Lordship in Medieval France: The County of the Perche (London, 2002)

Tollhurst, Fiona, 'What Ever Happened to Eleanor? Reflections of Eleanor of Aquitaine in Wace's Roman de Brut and Lawman's Brut', in L&L

Topsfield, L. T., Troubadours and Love (Cambridge, 1978)

Tranovich, Margaret, Melisende of Jerusalem: The World of a Forgotten Crusader Queen (London, 2011)

Trindade, Ann, Berengaria: In Search of Richard the Lionheart's Queen (Dublin, 1999)

Turner, Ralph V., Eleanor of Aquitaine: Queen of France, Queen of England (2009); 'Eleanor of Aquitaine and her children: an inquiry into medieval family attachment', Journal of Medieval History 14 (1988), 321–35; The Household of Eleanor of Aquitaine, Henry II's Queen, 1155–1189 (n.d.)

Vacandard, 'Le divorce de Louis le Jeune', Revue des Questions Historiques, 47 (1890), 408–32

Van Houts, 'Elisabeth, Les Femmes dans le Royaume Plantagenet', in P&C

Vann, Theresa, ed., Queens, Regents, Potentates (Sawston, 1993)

Vincent, Nicholas and Christopher Harper-Bill, eds, Henry II: New Interpretations (Woodbridge, 2007) (HIINI); 'The Court of Henry II', in HIINI; Records Administration and Aristocratic Society in the Anglo-Norman Realm (Woodbridge, 2009); 'Politics, Patronage and Piety in the Charters of Eleanor of Aquitaine' (PPP), in P&C; 'Alienor d'Aquitaine, Reine d'Angleterre', in 303; VC (unpublished notes on Eleanor's Charters)

Vones Liebenstein, Ursula, 'Alienor d'Aquitaine Henri le Jeune et la Revolte de 1173', in P&C

Walker, Curtis Howe, 'Eleanor of Aquitaine and the Disaster at Cadmos Mountain on the Second Crusade', AHR, 55 (1949–50); Eleanor of Aquitaine (Chapel Hill, NC, 1950)

Warren, W. L., King John (Berkeley, 1962); Henry II (Berkeley, 1977)

Washington, G., 'King Henry II's mistress, Annabel de Greystoke (née Balliol)', Transactions of the Cumberland and Westmoreland Antiquarian and Archaeological Society (1964), 124–9

Bibliography

Waugh, Scott L., The Lordship of England: Royal Wardships and Marriages in English Society and Politics, 1217–1327 (Princeton, 1988)

Weir, Alison, Eleanor of Aquitaine: By the Wrath of God, Queen of England (London, 2000)

Wertheimer, Laura, 'Adeliza of Louvain and Anglo-Norman Queenship', HSJ, 7 (1995)

West, Francis J., The Justiciarship in England 1066–1232 (Cambridge, 1966)

Wolterbeek, Marc, 'Inventing History, Inventing Her Story: The Case of William of Aquitaine's Marital Affairs', Medieval Association of the Pacific (University of California, Berkeley, March 1995) and International Medieval Congress (Leeds, England, July 1995)

Wood, Charles T., 'Fontevraud, Dynasticism, and Eleanor of Aquitaine', in L&L; 'La Mort et les funérailles d'Henri II', CCM, 38 (1994); 'The Doctor's Dilemma: Sin, Salvation, and the Menstrual Cycle in Medieval Thought', Speculum, 56 (1981), 710–27

Yoshikawa, N. K., Medicine, Religion and Gender in Medieval Culture (Woodbridge, 2015)

List of Illustrations

34. A reconstruction of Old Sarum. Eleanor's main location during her imprisonment, it was also a frequent stay both in her early years as regent for Henry and in her final years in England. (Kurt Kastner)

35. The seal of Geoffrey, Count of Brittany, Eleanor's fourth son by Henry. Like Young Henry, he died during Eleanor's long imprisonment.

36. Eleanor and Rosamund as imagined by Burne Jones. One of many imaginative depictions of Eleanor procuring her supposed rival's death. In fact, at the time of Rosamund's death Eleanor was a prisoner. The suggestion Eleanor was involved dates to centuries after her own death. (Yale Center for British Art, Paul Mellon Fund)

37. The 'Eleanor psalter': some time in around 1186 it appears that Eleanor commissioned this psalter in Fécamp, and had herself depicted on the donor page opposite the 'Beatus' page. (Koninklijke Bibliotheek, Den Haag 76 F 13 (donated in the context of a partnership program), f.28v)

38. Commentators have noted strong stylistic similarities between the psalter depictions and other visual imagery linked to the Plantagenet family. Here the April depiction of a noble shows a vair-lined robe similar to Geoffrey of Anjou's tomb and a flower similar to that carried by Eleanor on her seal. (Koninklijke Bibliotheek, Den Haag 76 F 13 (donated in the context of a partnership program), f.4v)

39. Matilda, Duchess of Saxony, Eleanor's eldest daughter by Henry. She visited England in the early 1180s, bearing her last child in Eleanor's presence. After her return to Germany she commissioned a psalter which depicts her on the donor page. (Walters Art Museum)

40. The famous 'Plantagenet fresco' in the chapel devoted to St Radegonde at Chinon. There is a huge range of theories about who is depicted – and whether Eleanor is the regal figure in the centre. (Chinpat)

41. The mural in context. The chapel adjoins the cell and tomb of St John of Chinon. (Chinpat)

42. By the time of Richard's accession, Eleanor's long residence in England made her a natural authority figure. This church in Barfrestone, Kent, built in the late years of the century, places the queen (inferentially Eleanor) on the right hand of Christ – the position of power. (Author's collection)

43. Eleanor ruled in her own right in Richard's absence. Here, from the archives of Canterbury Cathedral (an institution to which she had close ties), is a letter commanding defences to be raised against an invasion by John supported by Philip Augustus of France. (Courtesy of the Chapter of Canterbury)

44. Eleanor's rule coincided with the foundation of an abbey in honour of St Radegonde (Radegund) on land near Dover which formed part of her granddaughter Mathilde's dowry. (© Ian Capper CC BY-SA 2.0)

45. Eleanor raced to attend Richard's deathbed, and oversaw his burial and remembrance. (AYArktos)

46. The tomb of William Marshal in Temple Church. Eleanor was his first patron, and he would go on to serve Young Henry, Henry II, Richard, John and Henry III. His loyalty to Eleanor never faltered. (Author's collection)

47. John. Eleanor repeatedly demonstrated her own loyalty to and affection for her last child. (Hugh Llewelyn)

Index